# Coalition Agreements as Control Devices

# COMPARATIVE POLITICS

Comparative Politics is a series for researchers, teachers, and students of political science that deals with contemporary government and politics. Global in scope, books in the series are characterized by a stress on comparative analysis and strong methodological rigour. The series is published in association with the European Consortium for Political Research. For more information visit
www.ecprnet.eu

The series is edited by Nicole Bolleyer, Chair of Comparative Political Science, Geschwister Scholl Institute, LMU Munich, and Jonathan Slapin, Professor of Political Institutions and European Politics, University of Zurich.

### OTHER TITLES IN THIS SERIES

Voters Under Pressure
Group-Based Cross-Pressures and Electoral Volatility
*Ruth Dassonneville*

Minority Governments in Comparative Perspective
*Edited by Bonnie N. Field and Shane Martin*

The Government Party
Political Dominance in Democracy
*R. Kenneth Carty*

The New Kremlinology
Understanding Regime Personalization in Russia
*Alexander Baturo and Johan A. Elkink*

Reimagining the Judiciary
Women's Representation on High Courts Worldwide
*Maria C. Escobar-Lemmon, Valerie J. Hoekstra, Alice J. Kang, and Miki Caul Kittilson*

Coalition Governance in Western Europe
*Edited by Torbjörn Bergman, Hanna Back, and Johan Hellström*

Coalition Governance in Central Eastern Europe
*Edited by Torbjörn Bergman, Gabriella Ilonszki, and Wolfgang C. Müller*

Party System Closure
Party Alliances, Government Alternatives, and Democracy in Europe
*Fernando Casal Bértoa and Zsolt Enyed*

# Coalition Agreements as Control Devices

*Coalition Governance in Western and Eastern Europe*

HEIKE KLÜVER
HANNA BÄCK
AND
SVENJA KRAUSS

OXFORD
UNIVERSITY PRESS

# OXFORD
UNIVERSITY PRESS

Great Clarendon Street, Oxford, OX2 6DP,
United Kingdom

Oxford University Press is a department of the University of Oxford.
It furthers the University's objective of excellence in research, scholarship,
and education by publishing worldwide. Oxford is a registered trade mark of
Oxford University Press in the UK and in certain other countries

© Heike Klüver, Hanna Bäck, and Svenja Krauss 2023

The moral rights of the authors have been asserted

All rights reserved. No part of this publication may be reproduced, stored in
a retrieval system, or transmitted, in any form or by any means, without the
prior permission in writing of Oxford University Press, or as expressly permitted
by law, by licence or under terms agreed with the appropriate reprographics
rights organization. Enquiries concerning reproduction outside the scope of the
above should be sent to the Rights Department, Oxford University Press, at the
address above

You must not circulate this work in any other form
and you must impose this same condition on any acquirer

Published in the United States of America by Oxford University Press
198 Madison Avenue, New York, NY 10016, United States of America

British Library Cataloguing in Publication Data

Data available

Library of Congress Control Number: 2022952109

ISBN 978–0–19–289991–0

DOI: 10.1093/oso/9780192899910.001.0001

Printed and bound by
CPI Group (UK) Ltd, Croydon, CR0 4YY

Links to third party websites are provided by Oxford in good faith and
for information only. Oxford disclaims any responsibility for the materials
contained in any third party website referenced in this work.

# Contents

| | |
|---|---|
| *List of figures* | viii |
| *List of tables* | x |
| *Preface* | xii |
| *List of abbreviations* | xiv |

## PART I COALITION AGREEMENTS AND GOVERNING IN COALITIONS

| | |
|---|---|
| 1. Introduction | 3 |
|   1.1 Puzzle and question | 3 |
|   1.2 State of the art | 5 |
|     1.2.1 The literature on coalition governments in parliamentary democracies | 5 |
|     1.2.2 The literature on coalition governance ("control") mechanisms | 9 |
|     1.2.3 The literature on coalition agreements | 11 |
|     1.2.4 The research gap | 14 |
|   1.3 A comparative analysis of coalition agreements | 17 |
|     1.3.1 Theoretical argument | 17 |
|     1.3.2 Empirical strategy | 19 |
|     1.3.3 Overview of the book | 21 |
| 2. Explaining the use of coalition agreements as control devices | 24 |
|   2.1 Central actors | 24 |
|   2.2 Delegation in coalition governments | 25 |
|   2.3 Control instruments | 27 |
|   2.4 Coalition agreements | 30 |
|   2.5 Costs and benefits associated with negotiating coalition agreements | 32 |
|   2.6 Factors explaining the use of coalition agreements as control devices | 35 |
|     2.6.1 Preference configuration | 36 |
|     2.6.2 Ministerial portfolio allocation | 40 |
|   2.7 Conclusion | 44 |

## PART II THE COALITIONAGREE DATASET

| | |
|---|---|
| 3. A new dataset mapping the content of coalition agreements | 49 |
|   3.1 Data collection | 50 |

|   |   |
|---|---|
| 3.2 Data sample | 52 |
| 3.3 Measuring the content of coalition agreements | 58 |
|     3.3.1 Unitization | 59 |
|     3.3.2 Coding | 60 |
| 3.4 Application example | 66 |
| 3.5 Conclusion | 70 |
| **4. The content of coalition agreements** | **72** |
| 4.1 The length of coalition agreements | 72 |
| 4.2 Policies, payoff allocation, or procedural rules? | 79 |
| 4.3 Which policy issues are covered in coalition agreements? | 83 |
| 4.4 Policy positions settled in coalition agreements | 87 |
| 4.5 Conclusion | 95 |

## PART III WHY DO GOVERNMENTS NEGOTIATE COALITION AGREEMENTS?

|   |   |
|---|---|
| **5. Preference configuration and coalition agreements** | **99** |
| 5.1 Introduction | 99 |
| 5.2 Previous research | 101 |
| 5.3 Theoretical argument | 103 |
| 5.4 Research design and data | 108 |
|     5.4.1 Dataset | 108 |
|     5.4.2 Operationalization of the dependent and main independent variables | 108 |
|     5.4.3 Operationalization of control variables | 112 |
| 5.5 Empirical analysis | 113 |
| 5.6 Robustness checks | 118 |
| 5.7 Conclusion | 122 |
| **6. Coalition agreements and ministerial portfolios** | **125** |
| 6.1 Introduction | 125 |
| 6.2 Previous research | 126 |
| 6.3 Theoretical expectations | 127 |
| 6.4 Research design and data | 130 |
|     6.4.1 Empirical strategy | 130 |
|     6.4.2 The dependent variable: Measuring policy payoffs in coalition governments | 132 |
|     6.4.3 Independent variables | 133 |
| 6.5 Empirical analysis | 138 |
| 6.6 Robustness checks | 141 |
| 6.7 Conclusion | 145 |
| **7. Do coalition agreements work?** | **147** |
| 7.1 Introduction | 147 |

| | | |
|---|---|---|
| 7.2 | Previous research | 148 |
| 7.3 | The influence of coalition agreements on stability | 149 |
| 7.4 | Research design | 154 |
| | 7.4.1 Measuring the dependent variable | 154 |
| | 7.4.2 Operationalization of explanatory and control variables | 156 |
| | 7.4.3 Dataset | 160 |
| 7.5 | Conflict in coalition agreements | 160 |
| 7.6 | Data analysis | 162 |
| 7.7 | Robustness check | 168 |
| 7.8 | Conclusion | 170 |

## PART IV COALITION AGREEMENTS, MULTIPARTY GOVERNMENTS, AND DEMOCRACY

| | | |
|---|---|---|
| 8. | Conclusions and implications | 173 |
| | 8.1 The main findings | 173 |
| |     8.1.1 What do coalition agreements in Europe look like? | 175 |
| |     8.1.2 Why do parties negotiate coalition agreements? | 177 |
| |     8.1.3 What is the impact of coalition agreements? | 179 |
| | 8.2 Implications for understanding policy-making | 180 |
| | 8.3 Implications for political representation | 181 |
| | 8.4 Potential avenues for future research | 183 |
| |     8.4.1 Alternative analyses of the impact of coalition agreements | 183 |
| |     8.4.2 Modeling coalition negotiations as a two-dimensional process | 184 |

| | |
|---|---|
| *References* | 186 |
| *Appendix 1 Overview of coalition cabinets* | 197 |
| *Appendix 2 Codebook* | 238 |
| *Appendix 3 Coding instructions* | 273 |
| *Index* | 282 |

# List of figures

2.1. Ministerial shirking and the coalition agreement 42
3.1. Use of coalition agreements between 1945 and 2015 over time and per country 55
3.2. Attention to policy domains in the coalition agreement of the Schröder I cabinet 67
3.3. Attention to External Relations categories in the coalition agreement of the Schröder I cabinet 68
3.4. Frequency of subcategories of category 504 "Welfare State Expansion" in the coalition agreement of the Schröder I cabinet 68
3.5. Frequency of policy categories of domain 5 "Welfare and Quality of Life" in the coalition agreement of the Schröder I cabinet 69
3.6. Frequency of subcategories of category 501 "Environmental Protection: Positive" in the coalition agreement of Schröder I cabinet 69
4.1. Average length of coalition agreements across countries 73
4.2. Length of coalition agreements over time 74
4.3. Length of coalition agreements per country over time 75
4.4. Length of coalition agreements over time by Eastern and Western European countries 76
4.5. Average length of coalition agreements per number of cabinet parties 78
4.6. Length of coalition agreements and left-right range of cabinet parties 79
4.7. Content of coalition agreements across countries 80
4.8. Variation of content over time 81
4.9. Attention to categories of procedural rules across counties 82
4.10. Average attention to categories of procedural rules over time 83
4.11. Average issue attention (in percent) 84
4.12. Issue attention across countries 85
4.13. Variation of policy content over time 86
4.14. Position of coalition agreements on the right-left scale and their distance to the coalition partners' positions 91
4.15. Actual and expected positions of coalitions on the right-left scale 93
4.16. Applying Gameson's law: Expected positions of coalitions on the left-right scale 94

| | | |
|---|---|---|
| 5.1. | The effect of intra-cabinet conflict | 115 |
| 5.2. | The conditioning effect of tangentiality | 116 |
| 5.3. | Three-way interaction between conflict, tangentiality, and joint salience | 117 |
| 6.1. | Policy distance in relation to ministerial portfolio control | 131 |
| 6.2. | Policy distance between coalition parties and their coalition agreements | 133 |
| 6.3. | The effect of ministerial portfolio control | 141 |
| 7.1. | Stages of coalition policy bargaining | 151 |
| 7.2. | Attention to conflictual topics | 161 |
| 7.3. | Conflictual content in coalition agreements | 162 |
| 7.4. | Effect of mean attention on cabinet stability | 166 |
| 7.5. | Effect of median attention on cabinet stability | 168 |

# List of tables

| | | |
|---|---|---|
| 3.1. | Sample of coalition agreements | 53 |
| 3.2. | Explaining the existence of coalition agreements | 57 |
| 3.3. | Overview of policy categories | 62 |
| 3.4. | Illustration of coding scheme development | 63 |
| 3.5. | Categories for procedural rules | 65 |
| 3.6. | Reliability of policy category coding | 66 |
| 4.1. | Frequency of numbers of coalition parties in the sample | 77 |
| 4.2. | Variables used for calculating left-right policy positions | 90 |
| 4.3. | Regression predicting policy position of coalition agreement | 94 |
| 5.1. | Issue areas and codebook categories | 110 |
| 5.2. | Descriptive statistics (Chapter 5) | 113 |
| 5.3. | Results from multilevel regression | 114 |
| 5.4. | Results from multilevel tobit regression | 119 |
| 5.5. | Results from multilevel linear regression with issue fixed effects | 120 |
| 5.6. | Results from multilevel linear regression with policy-related issue attention as the dependent variable | 121 |
| 5.7. | Results from multilevel linear regression with cabinet conflict generated using Chapel Hill Expert survey data | 122 |
| 6.1. | Issue areas and ministerial portfolios | 135 |
| 6.2. | Descriptive statistics (Chapter 6) | 139 |
| 6.3. | Multilevel linear regression explaining issue-specific policy distance | 140 |
| 6.4. | Robustness checks | 142 |
| 6.5. | Robustness check: Aggregate effect of ministerial portfolio control | 143 |
| 6.6. | Results from seemingly unrelated regression | 144 |
| 7.1. | Descriptive statistics (Chapter 7) | 160 |
| 7.2. | The influence of coalition agreements on cabinet stability | 165 |
| 7.3. | Explaining cabinet stability (mean conflict) | 166 |
| 7.4. | Explaining cabinet stability (median conflict) | 167 |
| 7.5. | Explaining cabinet stability (procedural rules) | 169 |
| A.1. | Austrian cabinets included in the sample | 198 |
| A.2. | Belgian cabinets included in the sample | 200 |

| | | |
|---|---|---|
| A.3. | Bulgarian cabinets included in the sample | 203 |
| A.4. | Czech cabinets included in the sample | 204 |
| A.5. | Danish cabinets included in the sample | 206 |
| A.6. | Estonian cabinets included in the sample | 208 |
| A.7. | Finnish cabinets included in the sample | 209 |
| A.8. | German cabinets included in the sample | 212 |
| A.9. | Greek cabinets included in the sample | 214 |
| A.10. | Hungarian cabinets included in the sample | 215 |
| A.11. | Icelandic cabinets included in the sample | 216 |
| A.12. | Irish cabinets included in the sample | 218 |
| A.13. | Latvian cabinets included in the sample | 220 |
| A.14. | Lithuanian cabinets included in the sample | 222 |
| A.15. | Luxembourgian cabinets included in the sample | 223 |
| A.16. | Dutch cabinets included in the sample | 224 |
| A.17. | Norwegian cabinets included in the sample | 226 |
| A.18. | Polish cabinets included in the sample | 227 |
| A.19. | Portuguese cabinets included in the sample | 229 |
| A.20. | Romanian cabinets included in the sample | 230 |
| A.21. | Slovakian cabinets included in the sample | 232 |
| A.22. | Slovenian cabinets included in the sample | 234 |
| A.23. | Swedish cabinets included in the sample | 236 |
| A.24. | British cabinets included in the sample | 237 |

# Preface

Coalition agreements are a fundamental aspect of democratic governance. Before taking over executive offices, political parties negotiate for weeks or months behind closed doors. Negotiating such an agreement not only takes time and resources, but compromises have to be made which may result in intra-party conflicts and electoral costs. Why do coalition parties spend so much time and resources on negotiating coalition agreements even though they are not even legally binding? In this book, we argue that coalition agreements use coalition agreements as control devices, but that their use importantly varies with the preference configuration and the allocation of ministerial portfolios across policy areas. We test our argument based on the newly compiled COALITIONAGREE Dataset, which is based on a systematic collection and content analysis of 229 coalition agreements that have been negotiated by 189 parties between 1945 and 2015 in 24 West and East European countries. This newly compiled COALITIONAGREE Dataset will be made publicly available with this book and opens up entirely new ways to study coalition governments that will be of interest to numerous scholars of coalition cabinets, party competition, legislative politics and political representation. This book is an essential resource for anyone interested in understanding the complex dynamics of coalition politics and the role of coalition agreements in shaping the functioning of democratic governments.

The book would have not been possible without the invaluable support of a number of people that have helped us along the way. First, we are grateful to Christoph Uhl who worked as a doctoral researcher in the project before he unfortunately decided to leave academia. Second, we thank our research assistants and the numerous native coders for assisting us in data collection, coding the agreements and in data analysis, most notably Clara Heinrich, Stefan Papantonatos and Felix Heimburger. Finally, we are grateful to many colleagues and friends who have provided valuable feedback and helped us identifying and compiling the coalition agreements that we analyzed in this book. We would like to thank Torbjörn Bergman, Marc Debus, Theres Matthieß, Patrick Dumont, Johan Hellström, Indridi Indridason, Wolfgang C. Müller and Thomas Saalfeld. We are moreover grateful to Jonathan Slapin,

Dominic Byatt and Nicole Bolleyer for guiding us through the publication process at Oxford University Press. Last but not least, we are grateful to the German Research Foundation which generously funded the research for this book (Grants KL 2692/1-1 and KL 2692/3-1).

Heike Klüver, Hanna Bäck, Svenja Krauss<br>
Berlin, Lund, Vienna, January 2022

# List of abbreviations

| | |
|---|---|
| CA | Coalition agreement |
| CDU/CSU | Christian Democratic Union/Christian Social Union (Christlich Demokratische Union Deutschlands and Christlich-Soziale Union) |
| CIEP | Constitutional inter-election period |
| ERRDA | European Representative Democracy Data Archive |
| EU | European Union |
| FDP | Free Democratic Party (Freie Demokratische Partei) |
| MARPOR | Manifesto Research on Political Representation[1] |
| MP | Member of Parliament |
| ParlGov | Parliaments and governments database: Information on parties, elections and cabinets in modern democracies |
| PM | Prime minister |
| SPD | Social Democratic Party of Germany (Sozialdemokratische Partei Deutschlands) |
| UK | United Kingdom |

[1] Other common abbreviations are MP (Manifesto Project) and CMP (Comparative Manifestos Project).

# PART I
# COALITION AGREEMENTS AND GOVERNING IN COALITIONS

# 1
# Introduction

## 1.1 Puzzle and question

On September 26, 2021, 60.4 million people were invited to vote in Germany's general election for the lower house of parliament, the Bundestag. Even though the fourth wave of the Corona pandemic hit Germany with full force, it took about two months to form a new government. The highly infectious Delta variant spread all over Germany, case numbers had been steadily rising, and the vaccination rate had been far too low to prevent another deadly COVID-19 wave. Virologists, hospitals, and the Robert Koch Institute, Germany's major public health authority, sent warning after warning and called for immediate action by the government. In one of the most dramatic crises the country had ever seen, Germany had however been in a political vacuum. Former chancellor Angela Merkel had been leading a lame-duck administration while the social democratic SPD, the Greens, and the liberal FPD negotiated a 180-pages-long coalition contract for two months instead of taking over executive office immediately. Why was it so important for the incoming coalition parties to negotiate such a lengthy coalition contract instead of swiftly taking office to fight the pandemic and save the lives of their citizens?

When forming a government, many coalition cabinets negotiate lengthy contracts. Instead of swiftly taking over executive offices, most coalition governments opt to invest time and resources into negotiating and writing a coalition agreement, detailing the policies that the government will implement. For instance, Müller and Strøm (2008) show that more than 80 percent of all coalition governments in the 1990s published a coalition contract. Given that negotiating such an agreement takes a lot of time leaving the country without an effective government for weeks and sometimes even for several months, the question is why coalition parties invest so much time, effort, and resources into negotiating a coalition agreement which is not even legally binding. What is more, the design of the agreements varies extensively across coalition governments. Müller and Strøm (2008) show that there is considerable variation regarding the content of coalition agreements. While coalition agreements in Finland and Norway deal for instance exclusively with policies,

Austrian cabinets have only devoted about 50 percent of the content of their coalition agreements to policies. In addition, Klüver and Bäck (2019) show that coalition parties settle some policy issues in great detail while other issues are hardly mentioned in coalition agreements. While economic policy, social policy, civil rights and the environment receive high attention in coalition contracts, other policies such as education policy, agricultural policy, or foreign policy are typically barely mentioned in coalition agreements. This book aims to solve this puzzle by shedding light on why coalition parties negotiate coalition agreements when they enter a multiparty government and by explaining the extensive variation in their design.

Answering these research questions has important implications for our understanding of coalition governance, policy-making, and political representation more generally. First, while parties in single-party governments can autonomously make policy decisions, governing in coalitions requires coordination and compromise as coalition parties typically have diverging policy preferences. If coalition parties would simply pursue their own policy goals without considering the preferences of their partners, severe intra-cabinet conflict would be the result that may ultimately lead to early cabinet breakdown (Lupia and Strøm, 1995; Saalfeld, 2008). Understanding why coalition parties invest so much time and resources into bargaining a coalition agreement and why their design varies so extensively can help us to better understand how cabinet parties manage their conflicts and why some cabinets fail and break down early. Since dysfunctional cabinets and early cabinet breakdowns have important negative consequences for effectively governing a country and political trust, our book makes an important contribution to better understanding coalition governance and its implications for the political system more generally.

Second, while the literature on coalition governments has devoted most attention to studying the formation and termination of multiparty cabinets (see e.g. Riker 1962; De Swaan 1973; Warwick 1994; Lupia and Strøm 1995; Diermeier and Stevenson 1999; Martin and Stevenson 2001; Saalfeld 2008; Schleiter and Morgan-Jones 2009), we have a very limited understanding about how policy-making in coalition governments works during the time of office. For instance, do governments respond to issues that come up during the legislative term or do they simply enact a legislative agenda that was negotiated before taking over executive offices? Given that the performance in government is a major predictor for voters' evaluation of the cabinet (Lewis-Beck and Stegmaier 2000), it is important to understand how policy-making in coalition governments works. Studying why coalition parties negotiate coalition contracts and why their content varies across cabinets can importantly contribute to understanding how coalition governments organize policy-making.

Third, this book also importantly contributes to the literature on political representation. Voters evaluate parties to a large extent on the basis of the policy alternatives they offer to the electorate. It is therefore important for political representation that there is a link between what parties have promised before the election and what they do once they have entered government in order to guarantee congruence between citizens' issue preferences and the policies advocated by their representatives (Miller and Stokes 1963; Powell 2000). While political parties in single-party governments can autonomously decide which policies to promote, coalition governments make the story more complex. Coalition parties cannot simply promote their own policy priorities, but they have to coordinate with their coalition partners in order not to risk breaking the government. As a result, there is no direct connection between election promises and governmental activity, but policies are channeled by internal government negotiations. While scholars of political representation have studied the congruence between the policy views of citizens and political elites (e.g. Powell 2000) or how voters affect government activity (e.g. Soroka and Wlezien 2010), it is unclear how coalition parties translate their election promises into governmental policy. Given that the vast majority of governments in Europe are coalition governments, this book makes an important contribution by, for the first time, shedding light on how parties' policy programs are channeled through coalition agreements.

## 1.2 State of the art

### 1.2.1 The literature on coalition governments in parliamentary democracies

A number of scholars have long stressed the importance of analyzing governments in parliamentary democracies and in understanding why parties act in a certain way when entering a cabinet together with other parties, or when leaving a cabinet. The fact that, in most parliamentary democracies, no party typically gains a majority of the seats in the legislature implies that one single party cannot take control of government without the support of some other parties. As suggested by Müller and Strøm (2000, p. 1), this implies that "coalitions become a necessity," and coalition formation is thus an important phenomenon that follows the elections in most parliamentary democracies.

A lion's share of the work on governments in parliamentary democracies has therefore focused on increasing our understanding of why specific governments form or why some specific parties form coalitions together. Seminal work based on game theoretical reasoning, by von Neumann and Morgenstern (1953) and Riker (1962), assumed that parties are pure office-seekers which only seek the power and prestige that comes with government positions and predicted that minimal winning coalitions will form. Such coalitions are characterized by the fact that if a member leaves the coalition it no longer controls a majority of the seats. Soon after these coalition theories were given their first empirical evaluation, attempts were made to introduce policy-seeking motivations to increase the ability to predict the coalitions that form in the real world. An example of such a theory is Axelrod's (1970) minimal connected winning theory, which predicts that only coalitions between parties that are placed adjacent to each other along some specific ideological dimension should form.

A number of variants of these theoretical predictions have been presented (see e.g. Laver and Schofield 1998 for an overview). Additionally, there is also important work that has shown that institutions matter for which types of governments will form (see e.g. Bergman 1995), and work that relaxes the so-called unitary-actor-assumption, which makes it possible to take into account that intra-party politics matters when political parties form governments (see e.g. Bäck 2008).

A different question which is related to the government formation stage focuses on how political parties distribute payoffs when forming a government.[1] Before coalition parties take over government responsibility, they typically engage in coalition negotiations in which they bargain about the distribution of ministerial offices and about the policy agenda that the coalition will pursue during the time of office. Most of the previous literature that focuses on such payoffs has focused on the distribution of ministerial portfolios, which is not surprising considering that portfolio allocation clearly constitutes a crucial intervening link between party policy and government action through the control of relevant ministries in the government (see e.g. Bäck, Debus, and Dumont 2011).

---

[1] Another more recent literature that is also related to the government formation stage, which we will not describe here, focuses on the question of how long it takes to form a government, on so-called bargaining duration (see e.g. Ecker and Meyer 2017 for an overview of this field).

The literature on portfolio allocation can be divided into two strands, where the first focuses on the quantity of portfolios allocated, asking how many portfolios each party gets. Starting with the early work by Browne and Franklin (1973), who drew on Gamson's (1961) theoretical arguments, a number of studies have analyzed the statistical relationship between party seat shares and ministerial portfolio shares, producing clear-cut empirical findings: coalition parties receive ministerial posts in close proportion to their parliamentary seat contribution to the government. More recent work has also considered that different ministerial posts have different importance, or "weight," but also replicates the strong relationship between seat shares and portfolio shares, a relationship which has been famously dubbed "Gamson's Law" (Warwick and Druckman 2006).

The second strand of the literature on portfolio allocation, which has recently gained more interest, focuses on the quality of ministerial posts, asking in particular which party gets what and why (see e.g. Budge and Keman 1990; Bäck, Debus, and Dumont 2011; Ecker, Meyer, and Müller 2015). Here, early work by Brown and Feste (1975) and Budge and Keman (1990) suggests that parties from different party families prefer different ministerial posts. Bäck, Debus, and Dumont (2011) draw on this work, and argue that the more important a party considers a particular policy area, the more likely it is that this party will try to get the ministerial post controlling this particular policy field. The authors show empirically that parties which stress certain policy issues in their electoral program are indeed more likely to obtain the portfolio controlling these particular policy areas.

The distribution of policy benefits in coalition governments has received little attention in the literature (Budge and Laver 1993; Warwick and Druckman 2006; Däubler and Debus 2009). Budge and Laver (1993) measure the distribution of policy payoffs by comparing the ideal points of coalition parties expressed in their election manifestos and the policy positions reflected in government declarations. Building on this work, Warwick and Druckman (2001), also analyze government declarations and compare the left–right positions adopted by coalition governments in government declarations with the left–right ideal points of its constituent parties. The most important result here is that the seat share of parties positively affects policy payoffs.

All the above-mentioned studies focus on the first stage in the coalition "life cycle," that is the formation of governments. There is also a relatively large literature that focuses on the last stage in this cycle, that is, on the "death" of governments, or on the topic of cabinet survival or duration, asking why some cabinets last longer than others (e.g. Laver 2003; Saalfeld 2008; Schleiter and Morgan-Jones 2009; Hellström and Walther 2019). In this field, some early explanations focused on so-called "structural attributes" and how they influence cabinet duration (e.g. Dodd 1976), for example showing that minimal winning cabinets last longer than minority cabinets and stressing the importance of party system features, such as fragmentation and polarization.

The structural attributes literature was criticized by scholars who instead argued that critical events were more likely to determine how long a cabinet lasts suggesting that most government terminations were driven by unpredictable or random external events, such as deaths or health problems of prime ministers (PM), economic crises, scandals or personal conflict (e.g. Browne, Frendreis, and Gleiber 1984). A key contribution of this literature is the introduction of event history modeling approaches, which have become standard in the literature on cabinet duration (see Saalfeld 2008).

The critical events literature was in turn criticized by scholars who stressed the role of key actors and their strategic behavior. In the theoretical model developed by Lupia and Strøm (1995), decisions to terminate coalitions or call new elections are the result of party leaders' rational responses to the institutional setting, the electoral cycle, and expected vote support. One prediction of their model is for example that "the same external event that causes no dissolution early in a parliament's term could well do so later" (Lupia and Strøm 1995, p. 649), considering that the office benefits left to reap when the end of term is near is lower than they are at the start of the term (see also Kayser 2005; Schleiter and Tavits 2016).

Also, there is a growing literature focusing on the "life" of coalition governments or the so-called coalition governance stage, where most research has been inspired by the work of Strøm (2000) and Strøm, Müller, and Bergman (2003 2008) on delegation in parliamentary democracies.[2] The authors stress the role of delegation and build on the idea that parliamentary democracies can be characterized as an uninterrupted "chain of delegation" that has its origin in the electorate and goes through legislatures delegating power to a prime minister and an executive, which in turn delegates to individual line ministers, who delegate power to the administration.

---

[2] Literature that can be related to this stage, which we will not describe thoroughly here, is work on the policy-making of coalition cabinets (see e.g. Martin and Vanberg 2014 2020a; Bäck, Müller, and Nyblade 2017; Strobl et al. 2019) or on the electoral implications of coalition governments (see e.g. Fortunato and Stevenson 2013; Fortunato and Adams 2015; Meyer and Strobl 2016; Sagarzazu and Klüver 2017; Fortunato 2019; Klüver and Spoon 2020).

When analyzing such relationships, principal–agent theory can be applied, which stresses that certain problems of "agency loss" can occur when a principal, for example, the PM, delegates power to an agent, for example an individual minister in the cabinet. Agency loss constitutes, as described by Müller and Meyer (2010, p. 1068), "the difference between the preferences of the principal and the actual outcome." Agency loss occurs because agents often have incentives and opportunity to do things that are not in line with the interests of the principal. For example, individual ministers belonging to a different party than the PM have incentives to implement a policy reform that is advocated by their own party even though it is not in line with the preferences of the PM. Delegating executive power to ministers inevitably implies granting them some kind of discretion, which may create problems of "agency loss." Drawing on principal–agent theory, several scholars have suggested that such delegation relationships require the principal to employ some "control mechanisms" to mitigate agency loss and hold their agents accountable.

### 1.2.2 The literature on coalition governance ("control") mechanisms

The literature on coalition governance has come up with a number of different mechanisms that political actors can use to control each other when in cabinet. The first distinction that can be made is between control mechanisms that are applied ex ante or ex post delegation. For the delegation relationship within the cabinet, which is most relevant for our study, both *ex ante* and *ex post* mechanisms can be used by the prime minister and the coalition parties to control individual ministers.

Drawing on the work by Kiewiet and McCubbins (1991), Müller and Meyer (2010) argue that there are two main *ex ante* mechanisms that can be used before the minister is appointed as an agent of the PM and the coalition parties. The first one is the one that we will focus on in this book, "contract design." The idea is that the principal can design a contract that establishes what the agent should do when power has been delegated. More specifically, in the context that we analyze here, intra-executive relations, the idea is that the parties in a coalition negotiate and draft an agreement, which details which policies should be implemented when the government is in office, that is, when power has been delegated to individual ministers as heads of departments. We describe this specific control mechanism in more detail in the following section.

The other important *ex ante* mechanism is, according to Müller and Meyer (2010, p. 1068), the screening and selection of candidates to find the best agents. The argument is that principals scan the credentials and past behavior of potential candidates to select the best agents, in order to minimize the risk of agency loss. Usually, the screening of potential cabinet members is assumed to be performed by centralized, cohesive, policy-oriented political parties (see Müller and Strøm 2000; Strøm, Müller, and Bergman 2003). The more recent literature on ministerial selection has focused on this specific control mechanism. For example, Kam et al. (2010, p. 289) argue that "principals must work to ensure that their ministers [...] are behaving as faithful agents behind closed doors of the cabinet office." One way of doing so is to choose ministers who have preferences in line with the principal. What complicates matters here is that ministers do not always have only one principal to which they adhere. There may be competing principals, and in the case of the United Kingdom's (UK) single party cabinets, analyzed by Kam et al. (2010), they suggest that it may be the party leader or the party backbenchers acting as the dominant principal. In coalitions, the problem of multiple potentially competing principals becomes even more complex. Analyzing coalition governments in Germany, Sweden, and Austria, Bäck, Debus, and Müller (2016) argue that there are three potentially dominant principals in ministerial selection in coalitions: the party, the PM, and the coalition as a collective, and which principal becomes dominant, depends on the institutional setting. For example, in countries like Germany, with strong PM powers, politicians who are ideologically close to the Chancellor should be more likely to be appointed to cabinet.

There are also *ex post* mechanisms that can be used by the principal to control her agents. In the general literature on delegation, monitoring is seen as the most obvious way to cope with the fact that the principal has limited information about the agent's behavior when placed in office (see e.g. Müller and Meyer 2010). One such monitoring mechanism in the executive arena is the appointment of "watchdog junior ministers." The idea is that the prime minister or the parties in the coalition may appoint a junior minister in the department where another party is Head of Department, which enables the junior minister to act as a watchdog and monitor the behavior of the main minister. As described by Strøm, Müller, and Smith (2010, p. 524), their "presence helps to reduce information asymmetries between the party holding the portfolio and its coalition partner(s)." Such junior minister appointments are frequently used in some countries, and may be used as an alternative to comprehensive coalition agreements in some systems, mainly in continental Europe (e.g. Thies 2001; Verzichelli 2008).

Lastly, another type of *ex post* mechanism that principals can make use of are so-called institutional checks, which in the executive arena can imply creating some committee or appointing a person that can veto block decisions of the individual ministers as agents. Since it may be difficult for parties to veto policy proposals they have already compromised on in a coalition agreement, even in systems with collective cabinet responsibility, another way of creating some kind of mutual control in the cabinet is to give some ministers responsibilities that cross-cut other ministerial jurisdictions. Here, the Minister of Finance clearly has a special role, and may have strong budgetary oversight (e.g. Hallerberg and Von Hagen 1999), but the prime minister may also have some opportunities to enforce policy coherence in the cabinet (Strøm, Müller, and Smith 2010, p. 524).

Hence, there are a number of control mechanisms that parties can use in the executive arena to control the other members of the coalition when power is delegated to individual ministers. The main control mechanism that we focus on in this book is the use of coalition contracts or agreements, and in the following section we therefore describe previous theoretical and empirical work focusing on coalition agreements.

### 1.2.3 The literature on coalition agreements

Starting with the work by Strøm and Müller (1999*a*), who suggested that coalition agreements were the "keys to togetherness," a number of scholars have recognized that although these agreements are difficult to enforce, they establish what the coalition requires the ministers to do (see also important early work by Timmermans 1996). As argued by Timmermans and Andeweg (2000) when analyzing the Dutch case, some coalition agreements have been characterized as "holy," which should be difficult to deviate from, thereby considerably diminishing ministers' agenda-setting power.

The comparative study of coalition agreements started with the seminal work by Strøm and Müller (1999*a*) who introduced a dataset on such contracts that were negotiated in 13 Western European countries from 1945 until 1996. They showed that three different points are typically settled in coalition treaties: policies, portfolio allocation, and procedural rules. This dataset, which was later extended by Strøm, Müller, and Bergman (2008), records whether a coalition government had drafted a formal or informal agreement, provides data on the length of agreements measured by the number of words they contain, and includes a measure for how comprehensively policies were negotiated.

Analyzing an updated dataset, including 169 coalition agreements in 15 Western European countries, Müller and Strøm (2008) detect some important empirical patterns that should be noted here. First, they make clear that most coalition cabinets, about two-thirds of them, are based on a coalition agreement, and they also show that there has been a clear trend toward using coalition agreements. Second, they show that there is significant variation across and between countries in how long these agreements are. The agreements they analyze vary between 200 words (a Finnish agreement) to 43,000 words (a Belgian agreement). Another important conclusion they draw is that junior watchdog ministers seems to be an alternative to comprehensive agreements. In some countries, mainly in continental Europe, such appointments are more common, whereas comprehensive coalition agreements are more common in the Nordic countries. Much of the later work that has been done on coalition agreements is based on the comparative dataset provided by Strøm and colleagues (2008).

Several authors have analyzed why multiparty cabinets negotiate and publish coalition agreements. Müller and Strøm (2008) show that the likelihood that cabinets negotiate a coalition agreement increases with preference divergence among coalition parties, the uncertainty that cabinet parties face and the level of opportunistic behavior. Moreover, they show that there is a strong historical trend. While only 33 percent of coalition cabinets in the 1940s adopted a coalition agreement, 81 percent of the coalition governments in the 1990s negotiated a contract (Müller and Strøm 2008, 172). Bergman, Ilonszki, and Müller (2019*b*) moreover show that this historical trend toward writing a coalition agreement is not only true in Western Europe, but also in Eastern European countries.

Falcó-Gimeno (2014) makes an important contribution to the literature on coalition agreements by focusing on when parties will employ control mechanisms such as junior watchdog ministers and comprehensive policy agreements. He argues that when coalition partners are satisfied with logrolling policies, or when compromise is self-enforced, then the parties will not implement any control mechanisms. His empirical investigation shows that control mechanisms are less likely to be implemented when partners have "tangential" (non-overlapping) preferences and when they foresee that they will cooperate in the future. However, the empirical evidence is stronger when analyzing watchdog junior ministers than when trying to predict whether coalition partners choose to write comprehensive policy agreements. More precisely, he finds that coalition agreements are less likely to be negotiated when coalition parties have tangential preferences, that is, when they care about different policy issues. At the same time, he finds that the existence of a coalition agreement is more likely when coalitions are likely to form repeatedly over time. This suggests that "precisely those multiparty governments that would observe the compromise anyway are those that generally write their compromises on paper" (Falcó-Gimeno 2014, 349).

Even though coalition agreements generally become more prevalent over time, there is extensive variation in the comprehensiveness and the content of the coalition agreements (Strøm and Müller 1999a; Müller and Strøm 2008), More recent studies have therefore moved beyond merely explaining the existence of coalition agreements, to predicting the overall length of coalition agreements. For example, Indridason and Kristinsson (2013) argue that coalition agreements are a mechanism for avoiding "agency loss." When the risk of such agency loss is severe, we should expect coalition agreements to be negotiated and to be more extensive. Based on an analysis of coalition agreements in Western Europe, Indridason and Kristinsson (2013, p. 840) conclude that the length of agreements increases with factors "likely to exacerbate the moral hazard problem," for example as the ideological diversity between partners increases.

Also focusing on predicting the length of coalition agreements, Bowler et al. (2016) present a formal model aimed at understanding the trade-off between making detailed policy platforms and including details on conflict resolution mechanisms in the agreement. They evaluate predictions drawn from this model using data on coalition agreements in the German Länder, and their results show that when intra-coalition conflict is high, parties write shorter coalition contracts, but are more likely to adopt procedures for conflict resolution.

Eichorst (2014) also focuses on explaining coalition agreements, but instead of analyzing the overall length of agreements, he focuses on the number of words dedicated to policy language in the agreements, following an approach presented by Huber and Shipan (2002). He argues that coalition partners consider both electoral and policy motivations when drafting agreements and that the dominance of one motivation is conditional on the degree of issue saliency and division between partners. Analyzing agreements in 12 Western European countries, he finds that parties include high saliency issues in the agreement on policy dimensions where they are more divided.

Some scholars have focused on analyzing whether coalition agreements seem to have the impact on policy-making that they are assumed to have.

For example, Moury and Timmermans (2013) study coalition agreements in four countries, focusing on whether the agreements include deals over policy issues that the governing parties do not agree on. Moury (2011) analyzes six Western European governments and finds that a majority of cabinet decisions were effectively constrained by the coalition agreement, suggesting that agreements are used to limit agency loss. Bäck, Müller, and Nyblade (2017) take a different approach and focus on the role of coalition agreements in solving so-called "common pool problems," focusing on the budget deficits as a common pool problem. Analyzing government spending in 17 Western European countries, they find support for a conditional hypothesis suggesting that comprehensive coalition agreements significantly reduce the effect of government fragmentation on spending, but only in certain institutional settings, more specifically where prime ministerial power is low.

Another impact that coalition agreements may have on parliamentary governments is that they may influence their longevity or duration, which is something that has been recognized in a smaller number of studies. Saalfeld (2008) puts forward several reasons why coalition agreements can be expected to stabilize coalition cabinets. For example, he suggests that "coalition agreements that include mutually agreed provisions about structured mechanisms for conflict management with regard to unanticipated events in the lifetime of the emergent coalition could be hypothesized to have better survival chances than coalitions where agreement on such institutions do not exist" (Saalfeld 2008, 357). His comparative analysis of coalition governments in Western Europe shows that the presence of a formal coalition agreement reduces the risk of early termination, but only in some models. In a more comprehensive analysis of 23 Western and Eastern European countries, Krauss (2018) evaluates the idea that coalition agreements increase the stability of coalition cabinets since they lower the likelihood of intra-cabinet conflict. In her analysis, the existence of a coalition agreement lowers the risk of early government termination.

### 1.2.4 The research gap

As can be seen above, the previous literature has clearly stressed the importance of coalition agreements. However, there are a number of important open questions that we seek to address in this book. More specifically, we make four major contributions to the literature on coalition governments.

First, we show that the preference configuration among coalition partners importantly explains why coalition parties regulate some policy issues in great detail while others are hardly mentioned in coalition agreements, but that this effect is conditioned by preference tangentiality and the salience of an issue among coalition partners. Some recent studies have focused on explaining their length and how comprehensively policy is covered in the agreements. However, results regarding important predictors are mixed, for example, some scholars show that intra-coalition conflict leads to longer agreements (Indridason and Kristinsson 2013), whereas others show the opposite effect (Bowler et al. 2016). These mixed results may be due to the fact that agreement length may not be the most appropriate dependent variable when we aim to understand how inter-party divisiveness impacts the control mechanisms chosen by parties to limit "agency loss." We therefore suggest that a measure focusing on how much coverage specific issues receive in the agreement, what we call "issue attention," is more suitable to analyze (see also Klüver and Bäck 2019). Merely studying the overall length of an agreement is inappropriate since it is likely to overlook important variation within agreements as some issues may receive high attention whereas others are hardly mentioned in the same coalition contract. Ignoring the variation within agreements may lead to an underestimation of the effect of intra-coalition conflict on the drafting of coalition agreements since the impact of conflict on some issues may be canceled out by a lack of conflict on some other issues. Even though preference configurations between the negotiating parties have been recognized as important predictors of which coalitions form, whether they last, and also whether the parties make use of different coalition governance mechanisms (see e.g. Falcó-Gimeno 2014), no previous study has analyzed the effect of such configurations on the content of coalition agreements. Here, we make both theoretical and empirical contributions to the literature, by elaborating on and empirically analyzing the role of the negotiating parties' preferences in terms of their policy positions and the saliency they place on different policy issues, when explaining why certain policy issues are negotiated in detail in the coalition agreement whereas others are not.

Second, this book makes an important contribution to the literature by showing that portfolio allocation and coalition agreements are importantly linked. Portfolio allocation has, as described above, long been seen as an important topic in the literature on parliamentary government, mainly because ministerial portfolios are seen both as a tangible payoff for the parties entering a coalition government, but also because how portfolios are distributed is likely to influence the policy outputs of a cabinet (see e.g. Bäck,

Debus, and Dumont 2011). A careful distribution of portfolios within the cabinet has also been seen as one way for parties to deal with potential agency loss (see e.g. Kam et al. 2010). However, there are no studies that connect the portfolio allocation to the content of the coalition agreements even though parties are likely to trade off policy and portfolio payoffs (Bäck, Debus, and Dumont 2011). More important for our purposes here, since we are interested in the role of coalition agreements as control mechanisms, no previous study has analyzed whether holding a specific portfolio changes the content of the coalition agreement. Here, we hypothesize that if parties use coalition agreements to control their partners, we should see that the policy distance between a party and the position in a policy area in the agreement is larger when the party controls the ministerial portfolio. Our empirical analyses also find support for this argument, suggesting that it is important to simultaneously analyze the distribution of portfolios and the content of coalition agreements.

Third, we also fill a gap in the literature by showing that coalition agreements are important control instruments that can considerably strengthen cabinet stability, but only if coalition parties regulate conflictual issues in these contracts. We hereby importantly build on previous work that has looked at the impact of the mere presence of coalition agreements on cabinet duration (e.g. Saalfeld 2008; Krauss 2018). We extend this work by arguing and empirically demonstrating that it is not enough to merely negotiate an agreement. If coalition parties only focus on consensual issues and fail to strike a compromise on precisely the issues that divide them, coalition agreements will not have a great effect. However, if coalition parties seriously make an effort to overcome their policy differences and settle divisive issues before they take over governmental offices, coalition agreements will have an important stabilizing effect as intra-cabinet conflict can be contained. By showing that coalition governments last longer if they settle divisive issues in their coalition agreements, this book also makes an important contribution not only to the literature focusing on coalition governance mechanisms, but also to the literature on cabinet duration, which has so far largely overlooked the effect of coalition agreements on cabinet survival.

Fourth, we make an important empirical contribution to the literature on coalition governments, party competition, and political representation by providing a novel, comprehensive dataset on the content of 229 coalition agreements that have been negotiated by 189 parties between 1945 and 2015 in 24 West and East European countries. Our dataset is not only much more comprehensive than previous datasets, but most importantly, we also provide the first content analysis that allows for studying *which policies* are settled in coalition agreements. The dataset is based on a comprehensive content analysis of coalition treaties that draws on human coders to analyze the content of coalition agreements and can be easily linked to existing datasets on the content of election manifestos (e.g. MARPOR, see Volkens et al. 2019*a*) and on parties, elections, and cabinets (e.g. the ParlGov or ERDDA datasets, see Döring and Manow 2010; Bergman, Ilonszki, and Müller 2019*a*). The usefulness of the dataset goes way beyond this particular book and will be without doubt employed by numerous researchers working on coalition governments, legislative politics, party competition, and political representation.

## 1.3 A comparative analysis of coalition agreements

### 1.3.1 Theoretical argument

In this book, we argue that coalition agreements are important control devices that allow coalition parties to keep tabs on their partners (see also Strøm, Müller, and Bergman 2008; Müller and Meyer 2010). However, not all coalition parties decide to write a coalition agreement and even if they do, the design of the agreements varies extensively across coalition governments. Our major argument is that coalition agreements are important control devices, but that their use importantly varies with the preference configuration and the allocation of ministerial portfolios across policy areas. We arrive at this argument by conceiving of the decision whether and how to write a coalition agreement as a careful cost-benefit calculation. Coalition parties compare the benefits of controlling partners and maintaining cabinet stability with the costs that come with negotiating an agreement. Writing detailed coalition contracts takes time and resources, but most importantly, political parties have to make policy compromises. This may be costly in a number of ways, for example, it may come with important electoral costs if a party is seen as having given up too many of the policy promises that it has made in its election manifesto (see e.g. Fortunato 2019; Klüver and Spoon 2020). Thus, political parties entering coalition governments must carefully weigh the costs and benefits of negotiating detailed agreements.

Coalition agreements have the major benefit that they allow coalition parties to effectively constrain their partners during the legislative term. We argue that three mechanisms can explain why coalition parties comply with the coalition agreement even though these contracts are not legally binding. First, coalition parties risk negative electoral repercussions if they do not comply with what they have negotiated. When coalition parties have concluded their coalition talks, they publish their coalition agreement and the media extensively reports about it. The coalition agreement serves as a yardstick against which the performance of the government is evaluated. If a party violates the agreement, its coalition partners will publicly blame the party for not keeping its promises which may result in electoral punishment. Second, coalition parties which violate the negotiated coalition agreement risk the stability of the cabinet. If coalition parties repeatedly deviate from the negotiated policy compromise, intra-cabinet conflicts will arise which may ultimately result in the fall of the government (Saalfeld 2008; Krauss 2018). Third, coalition parties not only endanger the stability of the current government, but they also risk future office opportunities as potential future coalition partners may refrain from forming a government with an unreliable partner (Saalfeld 2008; Tavits 2008).

For example, not complying with the coalition agreement led to the fall of the Ponta II cabinet in Romania in 2014. The three-party coalition consisted of Prime Minister Ponta's Social Democratic Party (PSD), the Conservative Party, and the National Liberal Party (PNL). The PNL left the coalition after the Social Democrat Prime Minister replaced the ministers of interior, finance, health, and economy. He also declined proposals of the PNL for the minister of interior and the deputy Prime Minister. The Liberals took that as a breach of the coalition agreement (dpa 2014). The two parties did not consider entering another shared coalition since. Another violation of the coalition agreement led to a government crisis a few years later. After the 2020 elections, Romania was governed by a three-party coalition of the PNL, an ethnic Hungarian group, and the USR-Plus. Only after a few months, PNL Prime Minister Florin Citu violated the coalition agreement repeatedly by discharging ministers without consulting the coalition partners, even though the coalition agreement was stating that a consultation is mandatory. The Justice Minister was to be replaced with an MP from the Prime Minister's party, despite the coalition agreement assigning that ministry to the USR-Plus party. After unsuccessful crisis talks, the USR left the coalition and withdrew their ministers (Marinas 06.09.2021).

The main idea put forward in this book is that the costs and benefits that come with drafting comprehensive coalition agreements vary depending on the preference configuration of the parties in the coalition and the allocation of ministerial portfolios between coalition partners. First, we argue that parties will only decide to engage in lengthy and resource-intensive negotiation about policy issues when they disagree on an issue that is important to all partners. The benefits of negotiating a compromise on a policy issue in the coalition agreement only outweigh the costs if the issue is divisive and if coalition partners really care about the issue. Second, we moreover theorize that the ministerial portfolio allocation affects the cost-benefit calculation of coalition partners. Since controlling a ministry grants parties with important information advantages and policy-making competences, coalition parties seek to particularly constrain their partners when they control the ministry in charge of a policy area. We therefore suggest that coalition parties will exercise tight control over ministers through the coalition agreement by particularly demanding policy concessions in policy areas that are controlled by hostile ministers.

Finally, we argue that coalition agreements can only stabilize multiparty cabinets if coalition parties settle precisely those policy issues that divide them in their coalition contract. Coalition parties might be tempted to only focus on consensual policy issues in the coalition agreement in order to quickly take over offices and signal efficiency to voters. If coalition parties only focus on uncontroversial issues in their agreement and leave divisive issues open, fights over these issues will sooner or later emerge in the cabinet risking the stability of the cabinet. Thus, we argue that coalition agreements can only stabilize multiparty cabinets if coalition parties settled precisely those policy issues that divide them. We arrive at this argument by conceiving of the bargaining over policies as a two-stage process. Bargaining at the first stage occurs during the coalition formation stage and bargaining during the second stage occurs during the time of office. Coalition parties can freely decide what they settle at the first and what they settle at the second stage. The coalition formation stage importantly differs from the later office stage as bargaining takes place behind closed doors so that the attribution of responsibility is low. In addition, the office-costs of non-agreement are much higher than at later stages while the incentives to differentiate in the light of an upcoming election are low. Given the special context in which coalition negotiations take place, it is much easier to settle divisive issues during the government formation stage than later on when coalition parties are in office. As a result, we conclude that coalition agreements can only contain intra-cabinet conflict and ensure the smooth functioning of the cabinet throughout the legislative term when coalition parties have settled their policy differences.

### 1.3.2 Empirical strategy

Despite the central importance of coalition agreements for coalition governance and policy-making, which has been clearly recognized by a number of scholars (e.g. Strøm and Müller 1999*a*), we know remarkably little about their content, their use and how coalition parties negotiate them. One main reason for this is the lack of a comprehensive comparative dataset that maps the content of coalition agreements. This book is the first that presents such a dataset, which is based on a systematic collection and content analysis of 229 coalition agreements that have been negotiated by 189 parties between 1945 and 2015 in 24 West and East European countries. This newly compiled COALITIONAGREE dataset will be made publicly available with this book and opens up entirely new ways to study coalition governments that will be of interest to numerous scholars of coalition cabinets, party competition, legislative politics, and political representation.

Thereby, this book importantly extends the work by Strøm and Müller (1999*a*), who set the agenda for the empirical study of coalition contracts by compiling a dataset that covers 136 coalition agreements negotiated in 13 Western European countries between 1945 and 1996. This highly valuable dataset, later extended by Strøm, Müller, and Bergman (2008), builds on the analysis of coalition agreements by country experts who coded whether a governing coalition had drafted a formal or informal agreement, also providing information on the overall length of coalition agreements measured by the number of words they contain. The country experts also gauge how comprehensively policies were negotiated in the agreement measured by the share of the content devoted to policies more generally. A drawback of the Strøm, Müller, and Bergman (2008) dataset is that it only captures how much attention is generally devoted to policies in coalition agreements, and does not allow for analyzing the specific content of these policies, which is where our dataset importantly extends their work. Our dataset is not only much more comprehensive in terms of the countries and years covered, but most importantly, we also provide the first dataset that allows for studying *which policies* are settled in coalition agreements.

By hand-coding coalition agreements, we have made our dataset compatible with the comprehensive comparative dataset on the content of election manifestos generated by the Manifesto Research on Political Representation (MARPOR) project (e.g. Budge et al. 2001; Volkens et al. 2017). The MARPOR project developed a classification scheme with 56 categories grouped into seven policy domains. Following their approach, coders with native language skills and country-specific expertise coded the content of the coalition agreements. We followed the coding procedure of the MARPOR Project as closely as possible in order to provide a maximum of comparability between the coalition agreements and the election manifestos. Through using the identifiers employed in the MARPOR, the ERDDA (Andersson, Bergman, and Ersson 2012) and the ParlGov Dataset (Döring and Manow 2019), the COALITIONAGREE dataset can be easily matched with other major datasets. This book therefore also contributes to a growing infrastructure of data on political processes, contributing to ever-expanding databases that can be used by other scholars for a variety of purposes.

### 1.3.3 Overview of the book

This book focuses on the role of coalition agreements as control mechanisms, and we continue the book by presenting our overarching theoretical framework in Chapter 2. We begin this chapter with a discussion of the theoretical assumptions that we make about the central actors and the motivations that drive their behavior. Afterwards, we explain the chain of delegation in coalition governments to understand how multiparty cabinets work and what challenges they are facing. This will be followed by explaining how coalition agreements can be used as control devices to deal with the problems of delegation that occur in coalition cabinets. Most importantly, we will discuss the conditions under which coalition parties use coalition agreements to control their partners. Since writing extensive coalition agreements is costly, coalition governments carefully weigh the costs and benefits of negotiating detailed agreements. Our major argument is that coalition agreements are important control devices, but that their use varies with the preference configuration and the allocation of ministerial portfolios in coalition governments.

Chapter 3 of this book focuses on describing the extensive COALITION-AGREE dataset on the content of coalition agreements that we have newly compiled for this book. Our dataset is not only much more comprehensive than previous datasets on coalition agreements by Müller and Strøm (1999a) and Strøm, Müller, and Bergman (2008) as we cover more cabinets, countries and a longer time period, but most importantly, we also provide the first content analysis that allows for studying *which policies* are settled in coalition agreements. The dataset is based on a comprehensive content analysis of coalition treaties that draws on human coders to identify and measure the content of coalition agreements. The COALITIONAGREE dataset covers 229 coalition agreements that have been negotiated by 189 parties between 1945 and 2015 in 24 West and East European countries. In Chapter 3, we explain in detail how we collected the coalition agreements and how we coded their content.

In the fourth chapter of the book, we use the newly compiled COALITION-AGREE dataset to for the first time provide a detailed and comprehensive analysis of the content of coalition agreements. We start by illustrating how the length of coalition agreements varies across countries and over time. Afterwards, we shed light on what coalition parties regulate in coalition agreements more generally. In other words, we examine whether coalition parties focus on policies, offices, or procedural rules in their coalition agreements. In the following, we for the very first time explore which policy issues are covered in coalition agreements and how the attention to different policy issues varies over time and across countries. Lastly, we also take a look at the policy positions that coalition parties adopt in their coalition agreements, exploring how these positions relate to the policy preferences of coalition partners.

We then move on to the empirical test of our theoretical expectations. Chapter 5 starts with an assessment of how the preference configuration in coalition governments influences the content of coalition agreements. We argue that ideological conflict in coalition cabinets positively affects issue attention as coalition parties have stronger incentives to negotiate a detailed policy agenda that constrains their coalition partners when intra-cabinet conflict is high. However, we expect that this effect is conditioned by preference tangentiality and the overall salience of policy issues among cabinet partners as the incentives to engage in lengthy negotiations about a policy compromise increases with the salience of an issue, but decreases as tangentiality rises. The results presented in this chapter support this argument.

In Chapter 6, we focus on the question of whether ministerial portfolio allocation affects the extent to which coalition agreements are used to limit agency loss. Our main argument in this chapter is that coalition parties exercise control through coalition agreements particularly in those policy areas in which their partners control the ministries. More specifically, we expect that coalition parties demand policy concessions particularly in those areas that are controlled by hostile ministers. By adopting and publicly communicating policy positions that are close to their ideal points, coalition partners leave the minister little room of maneuver. On the basis of our comprehensive content analysis, we measure the dependent variable in this chapter as the absolute distance between the issue-specific ideal points of coalition parties and the issue-specific policy position adopted in the coalition agreement. Our results show that controlling the ministry in charge of a given policy area is associated with a significantly larger distance between the position of the coalition party and the location of the coalition agreement, giving support to the idea that parties try to control each other's ministers through the coalition contract.

Chapter 7 shifts the focus from explaining coalition agreements to examining the effect of coalition agreements on cabinet survival. Thus, instead of treating coalition agreements as the dependent variable as in the preceding chapters, coalition agreements are now treated as the independent variable in order to explain how long coalition governments last. This allows us to say something about the impact of coalition agreements, and whether they in fact "work" as control mechanisms. We argue that cabinets are more stable if parties negotiated compromises not only on uncontested, but more importantly also on conflictual policy issues. More specifically, we hypothesize that cabinets last longer, the more extensive conflictual issues are covered in the coalition agreement. We test our theoretical argument by combining the COALITIONAGREE dataset with data on cabinet survival. The results support our intuition: Coalition governments on average last longer when coalition parties struck a deal on divisive policies in their agreement.

Chapter 8 summarizes the main theoretical arguments and the empirical results of the book. We discuss the implications of our results for our understanding of government formation, coalition governance, and cabinet survival and point out how coalition agreements connect these different stages of the coalition cycle. We also elaborate on what this means for our understanding of parliamentary democracies, and on future work that could be done building on the results found here and the COALITIONAGREE dataset that we provide to the scholarly community with this book. In the light of the findings of this study, we highlight the contribution of this book to the literature on coalition governments, party competition and political representation. Finally, we will illustrate open questions and directions for further research.

# 2
# Explaining the use of coalition agreements as control devices

In this chapter, we illustrate our theoretical framework that guides the subsequent empirical analysis. We first begin with a discussion of the theoretical assumptions that we make about the central actors and the motivations that drive their behavior. Afterward, we explain the chain of delegation in coalition governments to understand how multiparty cabinets work and what challenges they are facing. This will be followed by a discussion of control instruments that coalition parties can use to deal with the problems of delegation that occur in coalition cabinets. Given the focus of this book, we pay particular attention to coalition agreements and explain in detail which role they play for coalition governance. Finally, we will discuss the conditions under which coalition parties use coalition agreements to control their partners. Since writing extensive coalition agreements is costly, coalition parties carefully weigh the costs and benefits of negotiating detailed agreements. Our main argument is that coalition agreements are important control devices, but that their use varies with the preference configuration and the allocation of ministerial portfolios across policy areas.

## 2.1 Central actors

Parties are conceptualized as rational, goal-oriented, and purposeful collective actors. With regard to the preferences of coalition parties, three models of competitive party behavior have emerged from the rational choice tradition: vote-seeking, office-seeking, and policy-seeking parties (Strøm 1990*b*). Following the party behavior model set out by De Swaan (1973), we assume that parties are primarily policy-seeking actors. This means that their behavior will be mainly guided by their wish to influence public policy. We hereby make no assumptions about whether parties intrinsically value policy outcomes or whether they pursue policy goals for strategic electoral reasons. They can either be intrinsically policy-seeking because they really care about a certain policy or they can be instrumentally policy-seeking in order to improve their chances at the next election (Strøm and Müller 1999b). Whatever their underlying motivation may be, what is important for deriving our theoretical argument is that parties strive to shape public policy. In line with the saliency approach of party competition (Budge and Farlie 1983; Petrocik 1996), we furthermore assume that parties value some issues more than others and that they want to maximize their influence on policy-making especially in those areas they care about most. Hence, we assume that political parties value some issues over others and that they at the same time have preferred policy outcomes in different issue areas. Even though we assume that policy goals primarily affect the behavior of coalition parties, Strøm and Müller (1999b) have demonstrated that policy, office, and vote motivations are not necessarily independent of each other and researchers of party competition continue to debate which of these goals better characterizes party behavior (see e.g. Strøm 1990a; Strøm and Müller 1999b). We thus do not claim that policy objectives are the only goals that drive party behavior, but that office and vote considerations also play an important role.

## 2.2 Delegation in coalition governments

Coalition governments are composed of at least two different parties that share executive offices (Müller and Strøm 2008, p. 6). While parties that govern alone in single-party cabinets can independently push through their preferred policies, governing in a coalition is much more complex. Coalition parties are not governing alone, but they have to come to an agreement with their partners which is not always easy. In order to understand how coalition governments work, it is helpful to keep in mind their role in the broader parliamentary setting. Strøm, Müller, and Bergman (2003) have put forward a delegation model according to which the policy process in parliamentary democracies corresponds to a chain of delegation that includes a series of agency relationships. First, delegation from voters to elected representatives (legislators); second, delegation from legislators to the prime minister and his or her cabinet; third, delegation from the cabinet and the prime minister to the line ministers that head the different ministries and fourth, delegation from the ministers to the civil servants within their ministerial department. At each step of the chain of delegation, there is a principal–agent relationship in which a principal delegates powers (temporarily) to an agent. For instance, voters act as principals who delegate policy-making powers through elections to legislators who function as their agents. Similarly, legislators act at the same time as principals who delegate policy-making competences to the prime minister and the cabinet who function as their agents.

At each of the steps of the chain of delegation, *agency problems* may arise. Agency loss occurs if there is a difference between what the principal wants and what the agent delivers (Strøm, Müller, and Bergman 2003, p. 23). Agents may pursue preferences that differ from those of the principal and information asymmetries make it difficult for the principals to ensure compliance as they either may not be able to choose the right agents (adverse selection) or as they may not be able to keep their agents in line once in office (moral hazard). The problem of adverse selection arises when the principal does not have access to relevant information about potential agents (e.g. on their preferences) before power is delegated. Moral hazard problems, on the other hand, arise when agents, once they have been selected, have motives to act in ways that are contrary to the principals interests (Strøm, Müller, and Bergman 2003). As described by Strøm, Müller, and Smith (2010, p. 519), examples of such delegation problems in a representative democracy involve politicians misbehaving through policy drift or rent-seeking activities. For example, representatives may purse policies that differ from those that the citizens prefer, even though they are expected to act in the interests of the voters as the ultimate principal, and representatives may also "use political power to chase personal advantage" (Strøm, Müller, and Smith 2010, p. 519).

We here focus on the third step of the parliamentary chain of delegation, on how power is delegated to individual ministers. The minister is both, the agent of the prime minister and the cabinet as well as the principal of the civil servants working in his ministerial department. While parties that govern alone in single-party cabinets can autonomously make policy choices, governing in coalitions is much more complex. A major problem of multiparty cabinets is preference divergence. Coalition parties join forces for the sake of gaining control over executive offices. In many multiparty democracies, joining a coalition government is often the only way to ever enter the government. Even though ideological proximity is an important factor determining the choice of coalition partners, coalition governments are composed of parties with different policy programs often catering toward different voter groups. Given that coalition parties thus typically pursue different policy objectives, forming a coalition necessarily means that coalition parties cannot unilaterally push through their own agenda, but that they have to find a compromise with their coalition partners.

Due to information asymmetries, coalition parties have the ability to deviate from the coalition compromise in order to attain their own policy goals as shirking may go unnoticed. We assume that ministers are first and foremost agents of their own political parties whom they seek to please by delivering policy proposals in line with the party preferences. We follow Laver and Shepsle (1996) and assume that ministers enjoy a considerable amount of autonomy when it comes to drafting legislative proposals which are subsequently introduced to the cabinet and ultimately to the parliament. Laver and Shepsle (1996, p. 13) posit that ministers are in an advantaged position vis-à-vis the prime minister and the cabinet when it comes to shaping the content of legislative proposals as only the government department with jurisdiction over a particular policy is effectively equipped to develop feasible and implementable policy proposals in that area and present these to the cabinet for decision.

Previous literature has suggested that the prime minister and the coalition leadership face a problem of adverse selection because at the time of appointment, the prime minister does not have complete information about a minister's abilities and preferences to run a department effectively and in accordance with the wishes of the prime minister (see e.g. Kam et al. 2010). Moral hazard problems can arise in this relationship because, as described by Indridason and Kam (2008, p. 624) "all ministers have the motive and opportunity to use their portfolios in a manner that runs against the PM's interests." One reason for this is if ministers become too aligned with their portfolio and the sectoral interests associated with it. Another reason for ministerial drift specific to multiparty systems where coalition governments form is that ministers are likely to adhere to their party leaders and their interests rather than the collective goals of the coalition or the prime minister, since their party is an important principal to them as it decides about a minister's reappointment and future electoral and career prospects (Müller and Meyer 2010; see also Andeweg 2000).

## 2.3 Control instruments

In order to overcome the problems of delegation, principals can rely on a range of *control instruments* (Kiewiet and McCubbins 1991). Principals can rely on "ex ante" instruments that are used before competences are delegated to an agent or they can use "ex post" control mechanisms that are employed once the agent is already working for the principal. The literature typically points to two different ex ante control mechanisms, namely contract design and screening. Principals can design a contract that clearly lays out the duties and responsibilities of an agent leaving as little room of maneuver as possible. Depending on the performance in fulfilling this contract, the agent gets rewarded or punished. Alternatively, principals can rely on screening which describes a careful and comprehensive selection of the agent in order to make sure that the agent behaves in line with the preferences of the principal. Principals screen the past behavior and performance as well as the attitudes of the agent in order to acquire as much information as possible to predict her future behavior. For instance, when selecting a minister, cabinet parties will thoroughly check the candidates' past behavior and voting record in parliament to make sure that they nominate a loyal candidate.

Principals can moreover rely on ex post instruments to control the behavior of incumbent agents. On the one hand, principals can rely on "monitoring" or in the words of McCubbins and Schwartz (1984) "policy patrol oversight" to discover and avoid shirking once power is delegated to an agent. In coalition governments, coalition parties may for instance rely on parliamentary committees or cabinet meetings to acquire information about the behavior of hostile ministers to detect shirking. On the other hand, principals can also rely on so-called "fire alarms" by trusting third parties to oversee the performance of agents. For instance, interest groups may inform coalition partners if a minister has not implemented a promised policy reform.

These general control mechanisms available to principals can also be used by coalitions to hold their ministers accountable (Müller and Meyer 2010), but not all of them are equally effective in coalitions. *Screening* ministerial candidates is an ex ante control instrument that multiparty cabinets could employ. However, screening is much less effective for a coalition than it is for individual parties (Müller and Meyer 2010, p. 1073). Coalition parties carefully investigate the record of potential candidates to identify likely troublemakers. For instance, their voting behavior in parliamentary committees, public statements in the media, and their prior record as ministers is thoroughly vetted. What typically happens is that coalition parties divide the ministerial portfolios between them and that individual coalition parties unilaterally nominate candidates for the ministerial portfolios they obtained (Müller and Strøm 2000, p. 574). Parties are interested in selecting candidates that are loyal to the party line to make sure that the minister does not deviate from the party position when in office. This is turn makes it particularly hard for coalition partners to install a reliable agent as all candidates are biased toward the position of the party that nominated them and have an incentive to shirk from the negotiated coalition compromise.

*Contract design* is an important ex ante control mechanism in coalition governments. Coalition parties can bind their partner through policy commitments written down in the coalition agreement (Müller and Strøm 1999a; Timmermans 2006; Falcó-Gimeno 2014). Coalition partners can prevent ministerial drift through comprehensive coalition agreements, written as "contracts" to control their coalition partner. Given the—often—vast media attention to coalition agreements, political parties can threaten their coalition partners to publicly blame them for not keeping their promises in order to push through their policy priorities. While coalition negotiations are secret, the coalition agreements are made public which enhances the compliance with the negotiated agreement as shirking could lead to public blaming and shaming with negative electoral consequences (see also Timmermans and Breeman 2011, p. 4). Even though these contracts are not legally binding, they define the policy priorities of the coalition government and constrain the behavior of coalition parties in the upcoming term.

For example, the Christian Democrats (CDU/CSU) in Germany publicly blamed their coalition partner, the Social Democratic Party (SPD), for breaching the coalition agreement in 2020. The alleged breach was about the acquisition of armed drones, which was put into the coalition agreement in 2018 after it has been under discussion for two legislative periods (Küstner 2020). In the coalition agreement, the SPD accepted the drone purchase on the condition of in-depth parliamentary discussion of international law, constitutional matters and ethics connected to the purchase of armed drones. When the SPD withdrew their support for the drones, they deemed the discussions insufficient and claimed more comprehensive public debate before making the decision. Still, this was seen as a surprising breach of the coalition agreement (Szymanski 2020).

*Monitoring* is an important ex post control mechanism in multiparty cabinets. Three monitoring instruments are frequently used in coalition governments: Parliamentary committees, cross-partisan junior ministers and intra-coalition management bodies. Martin and Vanberg (2004 2005, 2011a) have shown that coalition parties importantly rely on parliamentary committees to oversee the behavior of other coalition partners. They allow coalition parties to obtain information about the legislative behavior of their partners in a formalized institutional setting and if necessary, coalition parties could also propose amendments to bills prepared by ministries under control of their partners if they are not in line with the negotiated coalition compromise. Another ex post control device consists of junior ministers who serve as "watchdogs" to monitor the behavior of hostile ministers (Thies 2001;

Verzichelli 2008). Junior ministers act as so-called "watchdogs" when they do not belong to the same party as the minister running a portfolio. Their task is to oversee the behavior of the "hostile" minister, to acquire information and to report to their party. As Müller and Meyer (2010, p. 1076) point out, "this mechanism is error-prone as the 'watch-dogs' may become their ministers' lap dogs (which may make life more comfortable for both of them)." It is therefore not surprising that cross-partisan junior ministers are only installed in a few European democracies. Finally, the third monitoring devices are intra-coalition management bodies which are regular meetings with cabinet members and party leaders (Andeweg and Timmermans 2008; Müller and Meyer 2010, p. 1075). Through regular meetings of these bodies, coalition parties obtain information and keep an eye on their coalition partners.

## 2.4 Coalition agreements

In this book, we focus on the role of coalition agreements as control devices that importantly constrain the behavior of coalition partners. As discussed above, coalition agreements are ex ante control mechanisms which are negotiated during government formation. Coalition agreements put limits on ministers in terms of policy-making, since these contracts establish what the ministers should do in office, thereby limiting problems of delegation. Although not every policy detail can be fixed ex ante, coalition agreements establish reference points about future policies, in particular with regard to those issues that are contested between the partners. These reference points are important, as unclearly stated policies tend to produce different expectations among the partners about policy-making during the course of the government. If such expectations are not met, a party which considers that the agreement has not been upheld may choose to retaliate by also breaking the agreement, or may decide to leave the coalition, which may cause the government to fall. As most coalition agreements are public, reputational concerns play a role, and publicity of the deal thus makes it costlier for parties to renege on their concessions and more likely to implement what is specified in the contract.

Coalition agreements are not legal contracts, but they severely constrain coalition policy-making during the legislative term. We posit that there are three mechanisms that explain why coalition parties comply with the coalition agreement. First, if coalition parties do not adhere to what they negotiated in the coalition agreements, they risk severe electoral punishment. While negotiations are typically secret, coalition agreements are public documents whose publication is accompanied by a big press conference and large media coverage. Hence, coalition parties publicly commit to the policies that they settled in the coalition agreement. If coalition parties do not comply with their agreements, coalition partners can publicly blame them for not keeping their promises. Given that the media regularly reports about the extent to which coalition agreements are implemented, voters have a fairly good idea of pledge fulfillment. In addition, coalition partners are quick to publicly invoke the negotiated coalition agreement to pressure their partners to stick to their promises. For instance, the German SPD fought with its coalition partner, the CDU/CSU, in 2019 about an increase of the minimum wage and about revoking the debt brake, but the CDU/CSU opposed these demands by publicly reminding the SPD about the deal they have made in the coalition agreement.[1]

Second, coalition partners risk the breakdown of the cabinet if they do not comply with the coalition agreement. Not complying with the negotiated policy agenda written down in the coalition agreement can have negative consequences for coalition parties because their policy benefits from being part of the government decrease and the risk for intra-cabinet conflict increases. The policy benefits are lower if the joint agreement is broken because, overall, all coalition parties are better off with compromise policies than with pursuing their own preferences in the realm of their portfolios. Regarding the latter, shirking from the coalition agreement increases the risk of intra-cabinet conflict, which can ultimately lead to early government termination. Such a scenario would mean that the coalition parties lose control over executive offices earlier than necessary, thereby also losing influence on public policy (Saalfeld 2008; Krauss 2018).

Third, ignoring the coalition agreement may not only lead to the breakdown of the current cabinet, but coalition parties also jeopardize potential future offices. More specifically, if coalition partners constantly violate the coalition agreement, the probability of being included in future coalition cabinets decreases. Parties that diverge from the compromise policies settled in the coalition agreement will not only be blamed publicly, but will also be less credible in the future (Saalfeld 2008). Possible future coalition partners will not risk cabinet stability by forming a coalition with unreliable parties. Hence, defecting from the coalition agreement can also result in significant future office costs as coalition partners loose their credibility. Tavits (2008) has accordingly shown that if a coalition party brings down a cabinet, this party is likely to be

---

[1] Source: https://www.handelsblatt.com/politik/deutschland/grosse-koalition-cdu-lehnt-spd-kernforderungen-ab/25312694.html?ticket=ST-10930871-eSAUa0WrNCwIUQhyv1gC-ap2

punished and not included by its former coalition partners in future coalition governments.

Thus, even though coalition agreements are not legally binding, they are powerful control devices that allow coalition parties to keep tabs on their partners. Accordingly, empirical research has shown that coalition agreements importantly predetermine the policy agenda of coalition cabinets during the legislative term. Thomson (2001) and Schermann and Ennser-Jedenastik (2014a) for instance show that election pledges to which coalition governments commit themselves in their coalition agreements are significantly more likely to be fulfilled throughout the legislative term. Similarly, Timmermans and Breeman (2011) find that there is correspondence between issue priorities defined in the coalition agreement and the legislative agenda of coalition governments in the Netherlands, in particular in the middle of the electoral cycle. Another study moreover shows that 68 percent of the policy commitments made in coalition agreements negotiated by six cabinets in Belgium, the Netherlands, and in Italy were translated into government decisions (Moury 2011; Moury and Timmermans 2013). In a similar vein, Vehrkamp and Matthieß (2018) show that the Merkel III cabinet has (at least partly) fulfilled about 80 percent of its promises that it made in the 2013 agreement. It is therefore no surprise that De Winter and Dumont (2000, p. 322) refer to coalition agreements as the "coalition bible" since agreements considerably shape and constrain the behavior of coalition parties throughout the legislative term.

## 2.5 Costs and benefits associated with negotiating coalition agreements

Coalition agreements are without doubt an important control device, but there is extensive variation in the use of coalition agreements. Müller and Strøm (2008) have shown that out of the 262 cabinets they studied in 15 West European countries from 1945 until 1999, 65 percent have adopted a coalition agreement. There is moreover a trend toward using coalition agreements as only 33 percent of the cabinets formed in the 1940s negotiated an agreement while 81 percent of the coalition governments in the 1990s published a coalition contract. What is more, coalition agreements vary extensively with regard to their length. The shortest agreement in their sample is just over 200 words long (Finland) while the longest includes more than 43,000 words (Belgium). Thus, writing a coalition agreement is not automatism and even if cabinets write an agreement, their content significantly varies. Indridason and Kristinsson (2013, p. 826) accordingly suggest that writing a coalition agreement involves "two related decisions: whether or not to write an agreement; and how extensive the agreement should be." In order to understand the variation in the use of coalition agreements, it is important to take into account the costs and benefits that coalition parties face when deciding whether and how to write a coalition agreement.

Let us start by discussing the potential costs with writing a coalition agreement. Here, the previous literature has stressed that there are "transaction costs" related to negotiating and drafting a coalition agreement, for example because bargaining takes time, requires extensive resources and leaves the country in a political vacuum. Strøm and Müller (1999a, p. 276) suggest that complex bargaining situations heighten transaction costs, and thus predict that "high transaction costs lead to the adoption of less comprehensive agreements."

A good example for high transaction costs of complex coalition negotiations is the coalition talks in Germany after the elections in September 2017, which turned out to be the lengthiest negotiations that the country had seen. The situation was complicated because there were several possible constellations. First exploratory talks between the CDU/CSU, the FDP and the Greens failed when the Liberals abandoned the conversation after a few weeks. Re-elections and a minority government were discussed afterward before the negotiations between the CDU/CSU and the SPD started and eventually the grand coalition emerged. The process took as long as 171 days leaving Germany without a clear leadership until February 2018 when the coalition agreement was finally published (Siefken 2018).

Another example for high costs constitutes the case of Belgium, when there was no official government after December 2018. The Prime Minister Charles Michel had lost the majority after the New Flemish Alliance party left the coalition as an act of protest against the UN migration pact, which the PM supported. After the elections in May 2019 it took a record high number of 494 days of bargaining to eventually form the seven-party coalition under De Croo. Until this final success, the king had to instruct a record total of 16 politicians to form a government (Gutschker 2020). The particularly long negotiations in Belgium caused concerns about the effectiveness of their political systems in other European countries which wanted to avoid a similar situation. For instance, in the above mentioned coalition formation in Germany, the emergence of the grand coalition was seen as a relief since concerns about "Belgian conditions" were formulated (Siefken 2018, p. 407).

Other potential costs are so-called "audience costs," resulting from the fact that parties have to make compromises with coalition partners when drafting agreements (Müller and Meyer 2010; Martin and Vanberg 2020b). These costs can be associated with the fact that some voters are not likely to appreciate when the party makes too many concessions, and will punish a party in future elections when compromises are perceived as "selling out" the party brand (Fortunato 2019). Accordingly, Martin and Vanberg (2020b, 1138) state that "party elites worry about how the bargain they agree to will be perceived by their supporters." Fortunato (2021, 66) distinguishes two mechanisms that account for the electoral costs of coalition agreements. "First, voters may associate compromise with an inability to win policy concessions from its partners in cabinet; a competence penalty. Second, voters may conclude that a compromising party has changed its policy preferences or perhaps misrepresented its preferences during the previous campaign; a credibility penalty." Audience costs may also be related to the fact that the party members or specific factions within the party do not approve all the concessions the party leadership has made during coalition talks which may put the party leaders at risk of losing their posts (see also Eichorst 2014).

A recent example of audience costs is the coalition agreement that was negotiated between the social democratic SPD, the Green Party and the liberal FDP in Germany after the 2021 Bundestag election. The Green Party was heavily criticized by environmental NGOs and the climate movement Fridays-for-Future for not sticking to its election promises and further escalating the climate crisis with the limited measures they have presented in the coalition agreement.[2] But there was not only external pressure, but also inside the party harsh criticism was voiced. For instance, the Green Party's Youth Organisation publicly stated that this "coalition is not the alliance we wanted. In many areas, such as climate policy and especially social policy, the coalition agreement does not meet society's needs."[3]

What about the benefits of drafting coalition agreements? Why do parties entering a coalition decide to draft an agreement and bear the costs of doing so? We assume that the main benefit of drafting an agreement has to do with their potential to limit "ministerial drift." The underlying argument is that political parties are policy-seeking, either because they intrinsically care about policy, or because they care about pleasing their voters (see e.g. Müller and Strøm 1999b) hence, they should aim to implement their own policy program.

---

[2] Source: https://www.tagesspiegel.de/politik/weitere-eskalation-der-klimakrise-scharfe-kritik-von-gruener-jugend-und-fridays-for-future-am-ampel-vertrag/27831510.html
[3] Source: https://gruene-jugend.de/2021/11/27/unser-blick-auf-den-koalitionsvertrag/

One way for parties in a coalition to structure government policy-making is to establish a sort of "pure ministerial government" model (Laver and Shepsle 1996), where each party is allowed to implement their preferred policy in each departmental jurisdiction, and where no compromises are made between the parties within a policy area. However, as described by Indridason and Kristinsson (2013, p. 824), "pure ministerial government results in Pareto inefficient policy outcomes", i.e. alternative positions that the governing parties prefer to the positions implemented under pure ministerial government are likely to exist. In this sense, "agreements are intended to move issues away from their rightful portfolios to the cabinet level."

Or put in principal-agent terms, when policy-making power is delegated from the Prime minister and the coalition, parties and individuals controlling specific ministerial posts, are expected to implement the policy position preferred by the cabinet or the Prime minister, and not "drift" from this position. However, the problem is that in coalitions, ministers as "agents" may have several competing principals, where the coalition as a whole, the Prime minister and the party leaders may be seen as principals (Bäck, Debus, and Müller 2016). As described by Müller and Meyer (2010, p. 1073), "all ministers have an incentive to shirk (i.e. to pursue party policy goals) in order to appeal to party delegates and leaders who can influence their further careers." This is where "contract design" comes in as a control mechanism, that is, to limit "ministerial drift," and detailed contracts can "help coalitions to keep ministers in line and to prevent deviations in favour of their parties" (Müller and Meyer 2010, p. 1074).

To sum up this discussion, parties clearly have incentives to write coalition agreements and to cover certain policy issues in these "contracts," especially since there may be policy benefits associated with doing so, and there are also costs associated with drafting and presenting an agreement. What features are then likely to influence parties cost-benefit calculus and make it more or less likely that coalition parties use control agreements to control their partners (in a specific policy area)? In the following section, we specify the conditions under which coalition governments make more or less use of coalition agreements as control devices.

## 2.6 Factors explaining the use of coalition agreements as control devices

We have so far established that coalition agreements are important control devices in coalition governance that allow coalition partners to overcome agency problems that occur when delegating powers to ministers. Moreover, we have discussed that the use of coalition agreements in multiparty cabinets varies and that coalition parties have to weigh the costs and benefits of drafting and designing an agreement when negotiating a coalition. We are now turning to explaining why some coalition governments decide to negotiate comprehensive coalition agreements while others only publish very short contracts or even decide not to negotiate an agreement. Since writing extensive coalition agreements is costly, coalition governments carefully weigh the costs and benefits of negotiating detailed agreements. Our main argument is that coalition agreements are important control devices, but that their use varies with the preference configuration, the ministerial portfolio allocation and the availability of other effective control instruments. In what follows, we explain in detail why these three factors crucially affect the use of coalition agreements.

### 2.6.1 Preference configuration

The first factor that importantly affects whether and to what extent coalition parties use coalition agreements to control their partners is the preference configuration in coalition cabinets. If coalition parties would pursue the same policy goals, it would not be necessary to invest time and resources in writing a detailed agreement. However, what is typically the norm in coalition governments is preference divergence or, in other words, that coalition parties pursue different policy objectives. Coalition parties come together for the sake of forming a joint government and taking over executive offices. In many multiparty systems, forming a coalition government is the only way to ever obtain control of political offices. So, political parties in such countries have strong incentives to join a coalition government even though this typically implies that policy concessions have to be made to coalition partners.

Intra-coalition conflict implies a greater risk for ministerial drift when there are large ideological differences in the coalition, ministers coming from specific parties, are more likely to stray from the position of the coalition as a whole or the prime minister simply because they do not agree with it. Hence, when ideological differences are large, ministers left to their own devices in a department are likely to implement their or their preferred party's policy position. This suggests that the potential policy benefits from drafting a coalition agreement are much larger when intra-cabinet conflict is high, and ideologically divided coalitions are thus more likely to write longer coalition agreements Indridason and Kristinsson (2013, p. 828).

Going beyond the previous literature, we argue that it is not only the existence and the overall length of agreements that are affected by the degree of cabinet conflict, but that the attention that is paid to specific policy issues is determined by issue divisiveness. This argument is based on the assumption that the level of detail devoted to a policy issue importantly affects the level of autonomy that ministers have in a policy area. While an agreement that hardly discusses a policy area leaves considerable room of maneuver for the minister, agreements that entail a very detailed discussion of a policy area will determine the legislative agenda in that policy domain in much more detail so that the minister has little autonomy in her jurisdiction. Or, in other words, higher attention to a policy issue in an agreement should constrain the coalition partners by prescribing in detail which policy proposals will be adopted.

The coalition agreement of the FDP and CDU/CSU in Germany after the 2009 elections illustrates the impact of detail in a coalition agreement. As Vorländer (2011) describes, the FDP took, while previously still in the opposition, ownership of the tax policy issue and made it a major point in their program. They were promising tax reduction and simplification. However, the coalition agreement lacked detailed statements on precisely this issue. Furthermore, the Minister of Finance was from the CDU/CSU and could practically veto any proposals due to their sovereignty of interpretation for what is financially feasible (Vorländer 2011). The lack of detailed discussion of the policy areas that are key for the FDP, and as a consequence the freedom of the Finance Minister, led to a sharp decline in popularity for the FDP and eventually to a failure in the consecutive elections in 2013 (Niedermayer 2015, p. 126).

Thus, we argue that important variation within cabinets is overlooked by only looking at the existence and the overall length of an agreement as there may be consensus on some policy issues, but severe conflict over other issues in the cabinet. If there is no disagreement about an issue between cabinet members, coalition parties will not bother to spend a lot of time and effort on prescribing a detailed policy agenda, since coalition parties do not have to fear shirking by their partners. By contrast, if there is severe conflict over an issue between coalition members, parties will devote a lot of attention to the issue in the coalition agreement to settle a detailed policy agenda that leaves little room of maneuver for shirking.

However, to explain the extent of control exercised through coalition agreements, we suggest that it is not only important to specify how divisive specific issues are we should also consider how important, or how salient, various policy issues are for the parties. As argued by Falcó-Gimeno (2014), when coalition parties are satisfied with a pure ministerial government model of policy-making, and with "log-rolling policies," there are weaker incentives to implement control mechanisms. Or differently put, such mechanisms are less necessary when "preference tangentiality" among coalition partners is high, or when issues are of differing saliency to the coalition partners. Hence, when coalition partners do not care about the same policy issues, there is no need to come to a compromise on the issues and coalition parties are happy with abdicating control over policy areas that they do not care about.

The argument is that since it is costly for the parties to negotiate and draft agreements, they may avoid such costs in situations when they do not have strong incentives to come to an agreement. The previous literature on coalition governance has stressed that there are transaction costs related to negotiating and drafting a coalition agreement, for example because bargaining takes time and creates opportunity costs. Strøm and Müller (1999a, p. 276) suggest that complex bargaining situations heighten transaction costs, and thus predict that "high transaction costs lead to the adoption of less comprehensive agreements." Other potential costs are so-called audience costs, resulting from the fact that parties have to make compromises with coalition partners when drafting agreements (Strøm, Müller, and Smith 2010, p. 529).[4]

To clarify, let us give a hypothetical example of a two-party government including party A and B. We here assume that party A has a strong interest in a policy area Z, that is, this policy area is highly salient for party A. We also assume that party B has very little interest in policy area Z, that is party A and party Bs preferences are clearly tangential here. In this situation party B may be satisfied with a pure ministerial government model when it comes to this policy issue, where party A is given complete freedom to do as A pleases, becoming the Head of Department of Ministry Z. Here, party B has no strong incentives to constrain the minister of party A, and seeks to limit transaction costs by not negotiating and drafting text in the coalition agreement on this particular issue. For example, if a Green party, emphasizing environmental issues in its program, coalesces with another party which does not place high saliency on such issues (or issues affected by environmental policy), and is allocated the Ministry of Environment, the Green party is likely to be given free reign in the particular ministry. Hence, since the parties have tangential preferences,

---

[4] An important avenue for future research in this regard is how ideological conflict and transaction as well as audience costs influence coalition negotiations more generally. For instance, are transaction and audience costs particularly high for parties with diverse ideological profiles, and could this explain why some coalition negotiations fail? Thus, when preference tangentiality is high, that is when issues are of differing saliency to the coalition partners, coalition partners do not engage in costly bargaining over the issues.

the coalition parties do not need to engage in extensive negotiations over environmental issues, and thereby limit transaction costs.

The opposite situation arises when parties in a coalition have overlapping preferences, that is, if several partners have strong interests in the same particular policy area, or when tangentiality on an issue is low.[5] Or as Falcó-Gimeno (2014, p. 345) puts it, "when partners preferences overlap (i.e. they care enough about what happens in the jurisdictions controlled by the others in cabinet), the compromise deal is the one they prefer." In such a situation, it becomes worth it for the coalition partners to take on the transaction costs that come with drafting an agreement on this topic since they have strong incentives to limit agency loss in this policy area. Rather than abdicating control, coalition partners engage in managed delegation by constraining their partners through a detailed coalition agreement. Again, using a hypothetical example, assume that party A and B form a coalition, that they both significantly care about policy area Y and that party A is given Ministry Y. In such a situation, party B has strong incentives to try to control party As behavior, and will therefore devote time and energy to draft a very detailed section in the coalition agreement on policy area Y prescribing in detail which policies will be enacted in that policy domain, to avoid that party A shirks from the coalition compromise and implements its own position in Ministry Y.

Finally, we argue that the overall salience of a policy area importantly conditions the effects of intra-cabinet conflict and preference tangentiality. Not all issues are equally important to coalition parties as for instance sports are typically much less important than for example defence. Coalition parties may have diverging preferences on issues that are only of minor importance to them. Since coalition parties typically seek to avoid intra-cabinet conflict in order not to endanger cabinet stability, it is reasonable to expect that coalition parties are less inclined to risk cabinet conflict on an issue that is not important to them. We therefore expect that the negative effect of conflict as well as the conditioning effect of preference tangentiality are conditioned by the overall salience of the issue among coalition partners. Hence, if an issue is not important to any of the coalition parties, conflict and tangentiality should not matter. To clarify, if an issue is not salient to any of the coalition partners, it is reasonable to expect that neither the main effect of conflict, nor the conditioning effect of tangentiality are substantively important.

---

[5] For a thorough description and graphical presentation of the concept of tangentiality, see Falcó-Gimeno (2014, p. 344).

In Chapter 5, we elaborate on this line of argumentation in more detail where we also provide empirical tests of the expectations laid out in this section.

### 2.6.2 Ministerial portfolio allocation

We secondly argue that the extent to which coalition parties use control agreements as control devices depends on the allocation of ministerial portfolios. More specifically, we suggest that the control exercised through coalition agreements is stronger in policy areas where coalition partners control the relevant ministerial portfolio.

During coalition negotiations, coalition partners do not only negotiate a coalition agreement laying out the policy agenda for the upcoming legislative term, but they simultaneously bargain about the allocation of ministerial posts. While the literature on coalition formation has long been studying the distribution of ministerial portfolios (e.g. Browne and Franklin 1973; Warwick and Druckman 2006; Bäck, Debus, and Dumont 2011), the interdependence of bargaining about offices and the coalition agreement at the same time has been ignored in previous research. Coalition parties come together in coalition talks that take place behind closed doors to negotiate about who gets which ministerial portfolio, but also to negotiate the content of the coalition agreement. When coalition parties conclude their talks, they present both, the ministers and the coalition agreement to the public. The negotiated compromise is therefore clearly a package deal that is struck by coalition parties in which policies may be traded for offices and vice versa. Thus, in order to understand the use of coalition agreements as control devices, it is crucial to acknowledge that government formation is a multidimensional bargaining process in which coalition parties simultaneously negotiate policies and offices.

To understand why ministerial portfolios may be related to the design of the coalition agreement, it is important to acknowledge that ministries are an important instrument through which coalition parties can reach their policy goals. Given a certain degree of ministerial autonomy (see e.g. Laver and Shepsle 1996), party control of specific ministries provides an important advantage in implementing preferred policies in the relevant policy area. We do not claim that ministers are "policy dictators" (Laver and Shepsle 1996), but ministers have important advantages over other cabinet members when it comes to designing policies that fall within their jurisdictions. On the one hand, ministers are in charge of policy formulation and implementation. Thus, the coalition agreement may lay down the guidelines for a policy proposal, but the minister in charge can steer the proposal in a certain direction through its policy formulation prerogatives. As it is much more difficult to amend a proposal once a draft is already on the table, ministers can set the agenda in their favor. In addition, policy-making is increasingly complex and legislative proposals are often difficult to comprehend by non-specialists. Since ministers are supported by a large bureaucracy of long-term, specialized civil servants, ministers can also importantly influence policies through information advantages. Given the policy-making competences and the information advantages, ministers are in an advantaged position when it comes to influencing policies.

Even though coalition agreements are not legally binding, they severely constrain coalition policy-making during the legislative term. As we have argued above, there are important office and electoral costs of not complying with the coalition agreement. With regard to political offices, not adhering to the negotiated compromise settled down in the agreement, typically results in intra-cabinet conflict and may ultimately lead to early cabinet breakdown so that coalition parties would lose control over executive offices earlier than necessary. In addition, non-compliance with the coalition agreement may also have detrimental consequences for the future office prospects of coalition parties as possible future coalition partners will not risk cabinet stability by forming a coalition with unreliable parties. Finally, if coalition parties do not stick to the promises made in coalition agreements, coalition partners can publicly blame and shame them which may result in severe electoral repercussions. Empirical research has accordingly shown that coalition parties largely enact what they have promised in the coalition agreement (Thomson 2001; Moury 2011, 2013; Schermann and Ennser-Jedenastik 2014a).

Since coalition partners can prevent ministerial drift through comprehensive coalition agreements, we assume that policy-seeking parties strive to influence the content of the coalition agreement in order to bring the negotiated policy compromise as close as possible to their own ideal point. In an unidimensional policy space, the utility for coalition parties declines with the distance between the position adopted in the coalition agreement and their own policy stance. This utility function is formulated as follows:

$$U_J = -(P_{Party} - P_{CoalitionAgreement})^2 \qquad (2.1)$$

where $U_J$ is the utility for coalition party $J$. $P_{Party}$ is the position of coalition party J on the unidimensional policy scale and $P_{CoalitionAgreement}$ is the location of the coalition agreement in this unidimensional space. Thus, the utility rises as the policy distance between a coalition party and the coalition agreement decreases, and reaches its maximum at zero indicating absolute congruence between the coalition agreement and the preferred position of coalition party J. The closer the coalition agreement to the ideal point of a given coalition party, the smaller the risk of ministerial drift.

One may argue that ministerial drift might still be possible. However, the policy position adopted in the coalition agreement matters a great deal as it determines the extent of overall policy losses a coalition party has to fear from a hostile minister. Figure 2.1 illustrates our intuition. In this hypothetical example, Party A and Party B are bargaining about forming a coalition. The horizontal line presents a specific policy dimension. The policy preferences of Party A and Party B are indicated as well as the positions of two potential coalition agreements (CA 1 and CA 2). In this example, we assume that Party B is granted the ministerial portfolio in charge of the policy dimension in question. We furthermore assume that there is a zone of discretion for ministers to allow some flexibility during policy-making around the position that is adopted in the coalition agreement. The coalition agreement defines not only the policy position of the cabinet (indicated by the solid black circle), but also the zone of discretion around this policy position (the size of the gray circle). Not every single deviation from the position adopted in the coalition agreement is punished or even noticed due to information asymmetries. But the flexibility is not unlimited, there is a red line that ministers should not cross to avoid intra-cabinet conflict. The zone of discretion is illustrated by the gray shaded circle around the two hypothetical positions of the coalition agreement.

During coalition talks, coalition parties bargain about the policy agenda that they seek to enact during the legislative term. Even though they join forces

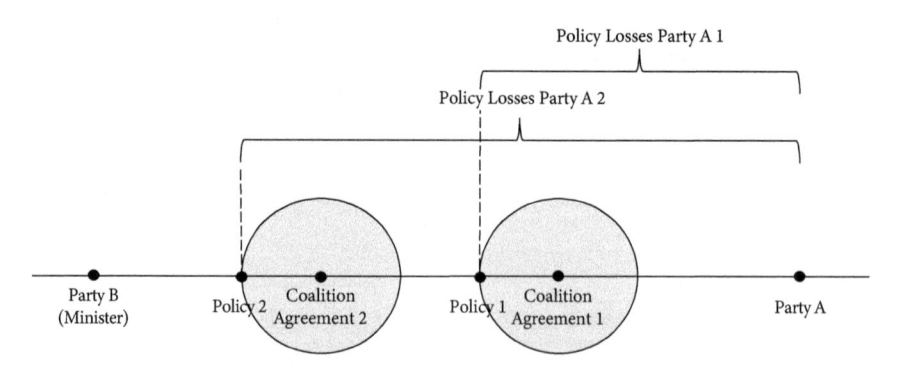

**Figure 2.1** Ministerial shirking and the coalition agreement

to take over the government, coalition parties have diverging policy positions and need to find common ground to effectively govern together. Thus, during coalition negotiations, coalition parties negotiate a joint policy position which is communicated to the public and implemented once they take over governmental responsibility. However, coalition agreements vary extensively in their content and their design as we show in detail in Chapters 3 and 4. While some agreements contain hundreds of pages, others are comparatively short. More importantly, while some policy areas are dealt with in great detail, other policy issues only receive very little attention in the coalition contract. This is an indication that the strength of the control exercised through the coalition agreements (or in other words the zone of discretion) varies across cabinets, but importantly also across issues within a coalition cabinet.

The following examples illustrate our argument:[6] During the election campaign prior to the election of the Bundestag in 2021, the social democratic SPD demanded that the minimum wage should be increased to 12 Euros while the liberal FDP strongly opposed this claim and instead argued that the amount of the minimum wage should be decided by an independent commission composed of employers and trade unions. The coalition agreement that was negotiated between the SPD, the FDP, and the Green party clearly laid out that the cabinet parties will increase the minimum wage to 12 Euros. On this policy issue, the SPD had clearly won and left no discretion to its partners. However, in climate policy, the situation is very different. While the Green party campaigned with the most ambitious position on this issue before the election suggesting numerous concrete measures to fight climate change, the coalition contract contained a clear commitment to the $CO_2$ reduction goals, but the precise instruments through which this policy goal should be achieved were not specified in detail. Thus, while the coalition contract contains policy positions on both issues, there is little to no discretion on the minimum wage issue while the zone of discretion is comparatively large for climate policy.

Assuming that coalition parties seek to maximize the achievement of their own policy preferences, the policy that is finally adopted by the minister corresponds to the most left-leaning position in the zone of discretion (Policy 1 or Policy 2). So ministers would shirk as much as possible without risking intra-cabinet conflict which corresponds to the position in the zone of discretion that comes closest to the position of the minister's party (here Party B). As a result, the policy losses for party A are considerably higher when the coalition agreement is closer to the ideal point of party B which controls the ministry.

---

[6] Source: https://www.deutschlandfunk.de/ampel-koalitionsvertrag-100.html

On this basis, we argue that coalition parties seek to tie the hands of hostile ministers by adopting policy positions that are as close to their own ideal point as possible to avoid overly large policy losses due to ministerial shirking. We therefore expect that coalition parties particularly use coalition agreements to control their partners in policy areas that are controlled by hostile ministers. Since ministers have the strategic incentives and also the means to shirk from the negotiated coalition compromise in order to adopt policies closer to their preferred policy positions, coalition partners want to limit the room of maneuver in that policy area by prescribing a policy position in that policy domain that is as close as possible to their own ideal point. In other words, if a coalition party receives the ministry in a policy area, coalition partners will demand policy concessions in that policy area to limit ministerial drift. Hence, we expect that coalition partners may strike package deals that cut across the division of ministerial posts and the agreement of policy priorities so that ministerial posts might be exchanged for a commitment to a particular policy reform and vice versa.

We further discuss this line of thought in Chapter 6 where we also test this argument empirically.

## 2.7 Conclusion

This chapter laid out the theoretical framework guiding this study. The main argument of this book is that coalition agreements are important control devices, but that their use varies with the preference configuration and with the allocation of ministerial portfolios. Drafting coalition agreements is not for free, but coalition parties have to invest time and resources to negotiate a coalition agreement and they may be severely punished electorally for making policy compromises. As a result, coalition parties carefully weigh the costs and benefits of writing extensive coalition agreements. We firstly suggest that the preference configuration is an important factor that explains the extent to which coalition agreements are used as a control device by coalition partners. More specifically, we argue that intra-cabinet conflict positively affects issue attention as parties have stronger incentives to negotiate a detailed policy agenda that constrains their coalition partners. However, we expect that this effect is conditioned by preference tangentiality and the salience of an issue among coalition partners. Second, we theorize that ministerial portfolio allocation plays an important role in explaining the use of coalition agreements as control devices. Obtaining a ministerial portfolio provides a party with important advantages in implementing preferred policies in the policy area that fall under the jurisdiction of the ministry. Coalition parties will therefore use coalition agreements to tie the hands of their partners in policy areas where they control the ministerial portfolio to limit the potential of ministerial drift. The next chapter turns to the empirical part of the book by illustrating the collection and coding of coalition agreements resulting in the first comprehensive dataset on the content of coalition agreements across 24 West and East European countries from 1945 until 2015.

# PART II
# THE COALITIONAGREE DATASET

# 3
# A new dataset mapping the content of coalition agreements

Coalition agreements are important policy platforms that crucially determine policy-making and coalition governance during the legislative term. Before taking over executive offices, coalition parties engage in lengthy coalition negotiations in which they bargain about who gets what in terms of ministerial portfolios, but also about who gets what in terms of policy payoffs. More specifically, parties bargain over their joint policy agenda that is written down in public coalition agreements (Müller and Strøm 2008). Even though these contracts are not legally binding, they define the policy priorities of the coalition government and importantly constrain the behavior of coalition parties in the upcoming term. Coalition parties can be publicly blamed for not complying with the negotiated coalition compromise which may result in significant credibility loss and electoral costs, and therefore function to keep coalition partners in line (Strøm and Müller 1999a; Müller and Strøm 2008; Müller and Meyer 2010). Thomson (2001) for instance shows that election pledges to which coalition governments commit themselves in their coalition agreements are significantly more likely to be fulfilled throughout the legislative term. Similarly, Timmermans and Breeman (2011) find that there is correspondence between issue priorities defined in the coalition agreement and the legislative agenda of coalition governments in the Netherlands. De Winter and Dumont (2000, p. 322) even refer to coalition agreements as the "coalition bible" since agreements considerably shape and constrain the behavior of coalition parties throughout the legislative term.

However, despite the central importance of coalition agreements for coalition governance and policy-making, we know remarkably little about their content, their use and how coalition parties negotiate them. One major reason why we know so little about coalition agreements is the lack of a comprehensive dataset that maps the content of coalition agreements. This book is the first that presents a comprehensive collection of 229 coalition agreements that have been negotiated by 189 parties between 1945 and 2015 in 24 West and East European countries. Strøm and Müller (1999a) have set the agenda for the

*Coalition Agreements as Control Devices*. Heike Klüver, Hanna Bäck, and Svenja Krauss, Oxford University Press.
© Heike Klüver, Hanna Bäck, and Svenja Krauss (2023). DOI: 10.1093/oso/9780192899910.003.0003

empirical study of coalition contracts by compiling a dataset that covers 136 coalition agreements negotiated in 13 Western European countries between 1945 and 1996. In this highly valuable dataset, which was later extended and presented in the book "Cabinets and Coalition Bargaining" (Strøm, Müller, and Bergman 2008), the authors recorded whether a governing coalition had drafted a formal or informal agreement.

Moreover, they provided data on the length of coalition agreements measured by the number of words they contain, and a measure for how comprehensively policies were negotiated in the agreement measured by the share of the content devoted to policies more generally, without however coding which policy issues the agreements dealt with explicitly. However, a drawback of this dataset is that it only captures how much attention is generally devoted to policies in coalition agreements, and does not allow for analyzing the specific content of these policies. Our dataset is not only much more comprehensive as we cover more cabinets, countries, and a longer time period, but most importantly, we also provide the first content analysis that allows for studying *which policies* are settled in coalition agreements. The dataset is based on a comprehensive content analysis of coalition treaties that draws on human coders to identify and measure the content of coalition agreements. In this chapter, we explain in detail how we collected the coalition agreements and how we coded their content.

## 3.1 Data collection

Following Strøm, Müller and Bergman (2008, p. 170) we define coalition agreements as "the most binding, written statements to which the parties of a coalition commit themselves, that is, the most authoritative document that constrains party behavior." However, we do not analyze all agreements that fall under this rather wide definition. We only include post-electoral and inter-electoral coalition agreements in our dataset as they are negotiated after the bargaining strength, most importantly the share of parliamentary seats parties won in elections, is given. Pre-electoral coalition agreements are excluded as they are drafted before an election in order to increase the electoral prospects of all involved parties without knowledge of the future parliamentary strength. Pre-electoral coalition agreements therefore primarily serve an electoral purpose and are negotiated in an entirely different bargaining context so that the underlying data generating process is fundamentally different from post-electoral and inter-electoral coalition agreements.

Compiling a dataset of coalition agreements negotiated across Europe was far from easy. In particular, we had to overcome two major challenges: identifying which documents are coalition agreements and obtaining access to these documents. To identify coalition agreements in all the countries in our sample, we followed the criteria developed by Bergman (2000, p. 214): First, political parties have to regard a document as the most central and binding text in order to qualify as a coalition agreement. As the document is of high importance for law-making, parties should secondly have invested time and effort in the bargaining process and third, the document needs to be publicly available.

To identify and collect the coalition agreements for all the cabinets in our sample, we used several channels. First, we approached the country experts in the seminal edited volume "Coalition Governments in Western Europe" by Müller and Strøm (2000). Second, we contacted the political parties that were part of a governing coalition and asked them for the coalition agreements that they negotiated. Third, we approached political scientists working on coalition governments and political parties in the countries included in our sample. Fourth, we contacted political archives in the respective countries and fifth, we approached German embassies in the countries where coalition agreements were negotiated, embassies of our target countries in Germany and political foundations which hold offices in all the countries included in our sample to identify and collect coalition agreements.

In some countries (e.g. Germany, the Czech Republic, the Netherlands), identifying coalition agreements was rather straightforward since coalition parties officially publish documents that are literally called "coalition agreements" in their respective languages and the media reports extensively about these agreements. It was therefore comparatively easy to check whether these agreements fulfill our definition of coalition agreements. However, in other countries (e.g. Austria, Sweden, Norway), coalition parties do not present an official "coalition agreement," but they negotiate other documents that fulfill the same function (e.g. government programs in Austria or government declarations in Sweden).

In some Central and Eastern European countries, there is not a single document that falls under our definition of coalition agreements, but cabinet parties negotiate multiple documents. Typically, the documents termed "coalition agreements" are restricted to procedural rules or contain very little policy information and they need to be complemented with other documents in which cabinets laid out their negotiated policy agendas. This was the case in Latvia and Slovakia. In these countries, governments publish coalition agreements that only concern the procedural rules of cooperation without any mentions of the cabinets policy agenda. However, coalition parties in Latvia regard the government program as a binding policy document that contains their negotiated policy agenda (Schmitt et al. 2002-2010, 130-140). In Slovakia, in all coalition agreements negotiated by cabinets since 1990, except for the Fico I cabinet (2006-2010), there is a paragraph that states that the policies of the government are agreed upon in the government program. In Latvia and Slovakia, we therefore combined two documents that jointly constitute the coalition agreement. Here, the documents called "coalition agreement" focus on procedural rules and almost completely ignore policies. These procedural agreements were supplemented by government declarations. This resonates with the strategy Bergman (2000, p. 214) employs in Sweden. In Lithuania on the other hand, the government declaration is not negotiated in detail between the parties as it is not seen as a binding document. Hence, we only coded the procedural coalition agreement.

In Greece, we decided not to use the government declarations by the Tsipras I (2015) and Tsipras II (2015-2019) cabinets because the country experts stated that there is no evidence of programmatic bargaining by these coalition cabinets. Also, our country experts mentioned that a SYRIZA Member of Parliament (MP) indicated in an interview that the SYRIZA manifesto serves as the governments coalition agreement of the Tsipras I cabinet. Thus, we concluded that for Tsipras I and II there was no most central and binding document that qualifies as a coalition agreement. However, for the Samaras II (2013-2015) cabinet prolonged negotiations led to the formulation of a document which outlines what the parties were planning to do in the subsequent legislative term. We therefore treat this document as a coalition agreement and included it in our dataset.

## 3.2 Data sample

Based on our definition of coalition agreements and our identification strategy, we compiled a dataset covering 229 coalition agreements that have been negotiated by 184 parties between 1945 and 2015 in 24 West and East European countries. Table 3.1 provides a summary of all the multiparty cabinets in place during the time period under investigation as well as the sample of coalition agreements included in our sample. Out of the 408 coalition cabinets in power during our time period of investigation, 229 cabinets negotiated public post-electoral coalition agreements. Hence, 56 percent of all coalition governments in place between 1945 and 2015 have negotiated a coalition agreement

Table 3.1 Sample of coalition agreements

| Country | Coalition Governments | Coalition Agreements[a] | Post-electoral | Inter-electoral |
|---|---|---|---|---|
| Austria | 21 | 15 | 15 | 0 |
| Belgium | 38 | 21 | 13 | 8 |
| Denmark | 23 | 8 | 6 | 2 |
| Finland | 44 | 34 | 17 | 17 |
| Germany | 26 | 14 | 12 | 2 |
| Greece | 6 | 2 | 1 | 1 |
| Iceland | 28 | 22 | 17 | 5 |
| Ireland | 15 | 9 | 7 | 2 |
| Luxembourg | 20 | 4 | 4 | 0 |
| Netherlands | 29 | 16 | 15 | 1 |
| Norway | 12 | 4 | 4 | 0 |
| Portugal | 10 | 5 | 4 | 1 |
| Sweden | 10 | 7 | 6 | 1 |
| UK | 1 | 1 | 1 | 0 |
| Bulgaria | 5 | 1 | 1 | 0 |
| Czech Republic | 10 | 6 | 3 | 3 |
| Estonia | 13 | 11 | 6 | 5 |
| Hungary | 9 | 5 | 5 | 0 |
| Latvia | 21 | 17 | 8 | 9 |
| Lithuania | 10 | 5 | 4 | 1 |
| Poland | 15 | 7 | 3 | 4 |
| Romania | 17 | 3 | 1 | 2 |
| Slovakia | 10 | 4 | 4 | 0 |
| Slovenia | 16 | 8 | 5 | 3 |
| **Total** | **408** | **229** | **162** | **67** |

[a] The number refers to the sum of unique agreements. If a coalition agreement has been reused by another cabinet, we do not count it as a new agreement.

before taking over office. 162 of these agreements are post-electoral agreements negotiated right after an election, while 67 agreements are inter-electoral agreements negotiated over the course of the legislative term.

Post-electoral agreements are negotiated by coalition parties that formed a coalition government right after an election. Inter-electoral agreements are by contrast coalition agreements that are negotiated by political parties after an early breakdown of a government throughout the legislative term. One example of such an inter-electoral agreement is the coalition contract that was negotiated by the Kohl I cabinet in 1982. Germany had been governed by a coalition between the social democratic SPD and the liberal FDP which was led by Chancellor Helmut Schmidt since 1974. Due to intra-cabinet conflicts, the four FDP ministers resigned from their posts on September 17, 1982. The FDP entered coalition talks with the CDU/CSU and negotiated an (inter-electoral) coalition agreement. The FDP and the CDU/CSU successfully requested a constructive vote of no confidence on October 1, 1982 which led to the fall of the Schmidt government and the formation of the Kohl I cabinet between the CDU/CSU and the FDP. Tables A.1–A.24 in Appendix 1 provide a detailed overview of all the coalition cabinets that are included in our sample across the 24 West and East European countries.

It is important to note that not all coalition cabinets actually decide to write a coalition agreement. In Germany, for example, there were five coalition cabinets in office between 1966 and 1980, but none of them decided to negotiate a post-electoral coalition agreement. Additionally, cabinets sometimes write a coalition agreement, but do not release it to the general public. In Luxembourg, for example, it is known that all coalition cabinets since 1945 negotiated coalition agreements, but these agreements were only publicly released since 1999 (Dumont, Kies and Poirier 2015, p. 27). Similarly, the first coalition agreement negotiated in Austria in 1949 (Müller and Strøm 2000, p. 101), and the Danish coalition agreements written by cabinets between 1968 and 1978, were also not published (Christiansen and Pedersen 2014, 368). Coalition agreements that are not publicly released serve a different purpose than publicly released agreements. Coalition agreements that are kept secret cannot be used as a device to discipline their partners by blaming and shaming them publicly for breaking their promises as their commitments have never been made public. In addition, coalition parties can also not control their partners through secret coalition agreements by building on future office costs of non-compliance with the agreement. The idea of exercising control through coalition agreement by imposing future office costs in case of non-compliance rests on the idea that other political parties can monitor to what extent a coalition party sticks to the commitments made in the coalition contract. If the coalition agreement is never made public, other parties cannot hold coalition parties accountable for shirking. As a result, we do not include these agreements in our sample (see also our definition of coalition agreements above). Finally, a very frequent phenomenon that we encounter is that coalition cabinets not always negotiate a new coalition agreement, but instead rely on the agreement that was negotiated by the previous cabinet. For instance, the coalition agreement of the Gorbach II (1963–1964) cabinet in Austria was kept as the official agreement after a new chancellor took over power. The same phenomenon took place in Belgium in 1981, when the government remained unchanged and Mark Eyskens took over power from Wilfried Martens.

Has the use of coalition agreements changed over time? Figure 3.1 displays the frequency of coalition agreements over time and across countries. While coalition agreements have not been the rule in the 1940s, things were different in the following decades. While only 38 percent of all coalition cabinets in power in the 1940s have negotiated a coalition agreement, over 55 percent of all cabinets in the following decades have negotiated coalition agreements. Peaking in the 1970s with 78 percent, the share of coalition cabinets releasing a coalition agreement before taking over governmental offices is stabilizing at 70 percent since the 2000s. Thus, even though there is some variation across

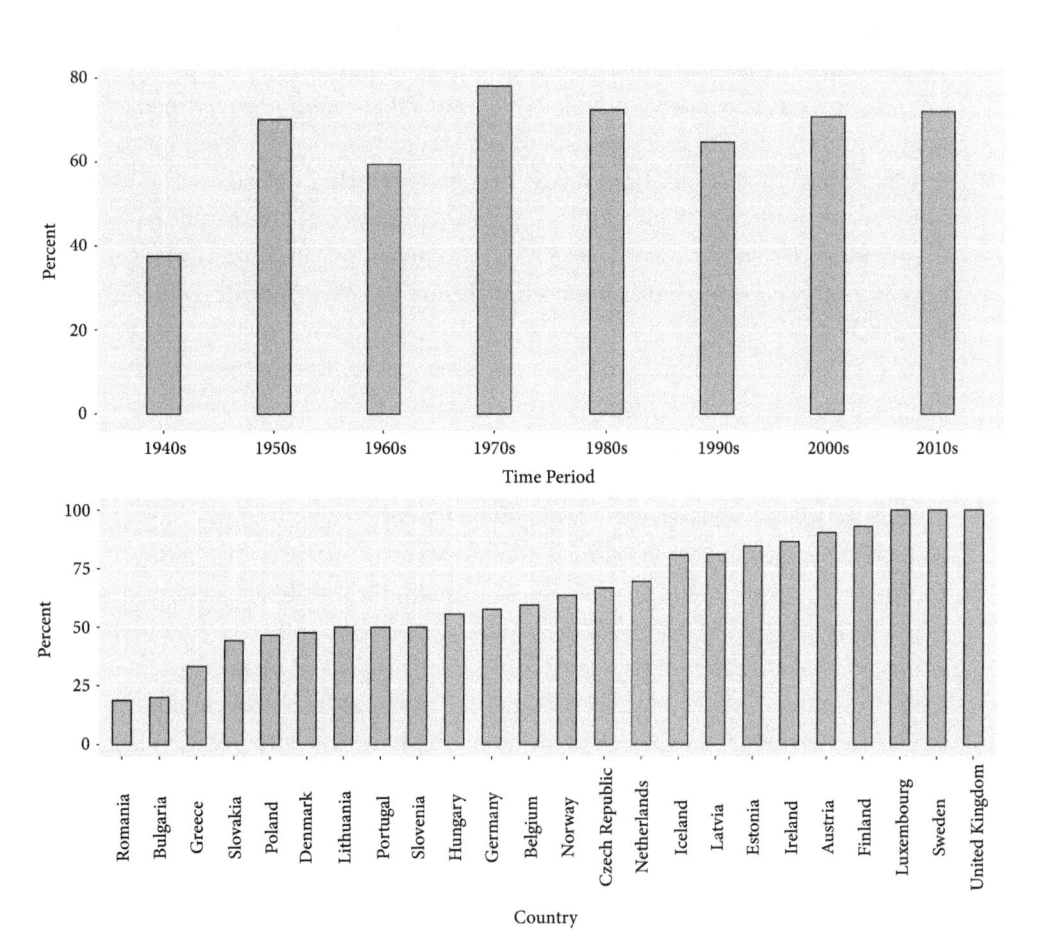

**Figure 3.1** Use of coalition agreements between 1945 and 2015 over time and per country

decades, one can indeed speak of a historical trend toward writing more coalition agreements. Further, the use of coalition agreements varies on the country level. While in Luxembourg and Sweden all of the coalition cabinets in power since 1945 negotiated a coalition agreement, in Romania, this is the case for only 18 percent of the cabinets.

We find further support for the notion that time plays an important role with regard to coalition agreements in Table 3.2. Here, we analyze the existence of coalition agreement and find that it is mainly time that explains the existence of coalition agreements. Data was taken from Andersson, Bergman, and Ersson (2014) and extended with data from Krauss (2018) and the COALITIONAGREE project. In contrast to the 1940s, coalition governments are way more likely to write joint agreements in later decades, particularly in the 2000s and 2010s. Additionally, our results also show that time matters in another dimension as well. The maximum possible cabinet duration has a strong and positive influence on our dependent variable. This means that coalition governments are more likely to write joint agreements, the more time they have left in the legislative term. Especially from a cost-benefit approach, this makes a lot of sense. Aside from this, we only find a significant influence of bicameralism on the existence of coalition agreement. Odds ratios below one indicate a decreasing effect. This means that bicameral countries are less likely to write coalition agreements.

As previously mentioned, coalition agreements are not the only control mechanisms that are at the disposal of coalition parties. Previous research has already shown that individual control mechanisms are not independent from but dependent on each other. There are two different logics here that are of interest for this book. First, the interdependence between ex ante and ex post control mechanisms and second the interdependence between two ex post control mechanisms.In the former case, Müller and Meyer (2010) have argued that ex ante and ex post control mechanisms reinforce each other. Or, in other words, that ex ante and ex post control mechanisms are complements rather than substitutes. Their analysis shows that the use of coalition committees is more likely if there is a coalition agreement. Similarly, Kim and Loewenberg (2005) find a relationship between committee chairs and coalition agreements: coalition partners use committee chairs to monitor the behavior of their partners more often if there is a coalition agreement. More recently, Höhmann and Krauss (2021) have shown that a higher comprehensiveness of coalition agreements increases the use of parliamentary questions as a tool to keep tabs on the coalition partners. In the latter case, the few studies that have analyzed the interdependence between ex post mechanisms point toward a substitute logic: the presence of cross-partisan junior ministers decreases

Table 3.2 Explaining the existence of coalition agreements

| DV: Existence of a coalition agreement | Model 3.1 | Model 3.2 | Model 3.3 |
|---|---|---|---|
| 1950s | 4.051** | 3.713** | 2.952* |
|  | (2.715) | (2.376) | (1.688) |
| 1960s | 2.092 | 1.924 | 5.579 |
|  | (2.265) | (2.043) | (5.878) |
| 1970s | 5.599* | 5.105* | 9.847* |
|  | (5.404) | (4.895) | (12.326) |
| 1980s | 4.456 | 4.082 | 7.813 |
|  | (5.111) | (4.747) | (10.745) |
| 1990s | 3.695 | 4.065 | 49.988*** |
|  | (3.564) | (4.093) | (54.461) |
| 2000s | 5.458* | 5.781* | 18.016*** |
|  | (5.270) | (5.777) | (16.650) |
| 2010s | 7.329* | 6.717* | 14.549** |
|  | (7.835) | (7.564) | (18.750) |
| Max. poss. cab. duration | 1.001*** | 1.001*** | 1.001*** |
|  | (0.000) | (0.000) | (0.000) |
| Length of CIEP | 1.695 | 1.570 | 0.762 |
|  | (0.898) | (0.781) | (0.243) |
| Minimal winning status | 1.812 | 1.458 | 2.049 |
|  | (0.782) | (0.626) | (1.276) |
| Minority status | 0.593 | 0.510 | 0.977 |
|  | (0.286) | (0.267) | (0.972) |
| No. of cab. parties | 0.947 | 0.937 | 0.712 |
|  | (0.192) | (0.194) | (0.242) |
| Ideological divisiveness | 1.014 | 1.011 | 1.021 |
|  | (0.010) | (0.010) | (0.020) |
| Bicameralism | 0.445* | 0.453* | 0.566 |
|  | (0.189) | (0.196) | (0.630) |
| Strength of committees |  | 2.667 |  |
|  |  | (6.610) |  |
| Existence of junior ministers |  |  | 1.407 |
|  |  |  | (0.966) |
| N | 396 | 377 | 177 |
| Log likelihood | −217.198 | −203.209 | −87.738 |

*** $p \leq 0.01$, ** $p \leq 0.05$, * $p \leq 0.10$; Cluster standard errors in parentheses; 1940s is the reference category

the use of mutual control in parliament (Martin and Vanberg 2005, 2011b) and the use of junior ministers is less likely if there is a strong committee system (Lipsmeyer and Pierce 2011). In order to control for potential synergies between coalition agreements and other control mechanisms, we included the strength of committees as well as the existence of junior ministers in our analysis. Data for the committee strength comes from André, Depauw, and Martin (2016) while data for the junior ministers has been taken from Strøm, Müller, and Bergman (2008). We do not find any significant effects for both of these other, potential control mechanisms. The results therefore add to existing research that shows that coalition agreements seem to be the decisive factor for questions about which other control mechanisms to use but that it is not the other way around.

## 3.3 Measuring the content of coalition agreements

A major goal of this book is to map the content of coalition agreements to better understand how coalition cabinets work. In order to measure the content of coalition agreements, we conducted a comprehensive hand-coded content analysis of all the coalition agreements that we collected. While fully automated or semi-automated quantitative text analysis techniques have the advantage to be 100 percent reliable and replicable, human coding is generally considered to be superior with regard to the validity of the measurement (see e.g. Klüver 2009). In addition, statistical content analysis treats words as data and is therefore language-sensitive. Given that we aim to perform an analysis of coalition agreements in 24 West and East European countries, human coding is also more promising as the technique can be applied to texts in any language. Another important advantage of human coding is the compatibility with data on the content of election manifestos generated by the Manifesto Research on Political Representation (MARPOR) project (Budge et al. 2001; Klingemann et al. 2006b; Volkens et al. 2017).

The MARPOR project developed a classification scheme with fifty-six categories grouped into seven policy domains. Where possible, directly opposing pro and contra categories were specified (e.g. Welfare state expansion vs. Welfare state limitation). Human coders divided the election manifestos into units of analysis and then allocated each unit to one of the specified categories. Following the MARPOR approach, coders with native language skills and country-specific expert knowledge were employed to code the content of the coalition agreements on the basis of our codebook. All our coders underwent intensive coder training and were closely supervised by our research team. We followed the coding procedure of the MARPOR project as closely as possible in order to provide a maximum of comparability between the coded coalition agreements and the coded election manifestos. The coding process is divided in two analytical steps: Our coders have first of all divided the coalition agreements into units of analysis (Unitization) and then secondly allocated each unit to one of the categories specified in our codebook (Coding).

### 3.3.1 Unitization

In order to divide coalition agreements into units of analysis that can be coded by our country experts, we follow the MARPOR project and rely on so-called "quasi-sentences" as the units of analysis. A quasi-sentence is defined as "an argument or phrase which is the verbal expression of one idea or meaning" (Klingemann et al. 2006a, p. xxiii). Even though criticism has been raised against using quasi-sentences as the units of analysis (Däubler 2012), we have decided to stick to quasi-sentences as the unit of analysis in order to ensure maximum comparability to the election manifestos coded by the MARPOR project.

To identify quasi-sentences, we followed the rules provided by the MARPOR coding instructions (Werner, Lacewell, and Volkens 2014). The basic rule for identifying quasi-sentences is that one natural sentence is at least one quasi-sentence. However, it is possible that one natural sentence contains more than one quasi-sentence. Werner, Lacewell, and Volkens (2014, p. 6) explain two typical scenarios in which a natural sentence must be split: First, one natural sentence contains two statements that are not related or second, a natural sentence comprises "two statements that are related (e.g. they come from the same policy field), but address different aspects of a larger policy" (Werner, Lacewell, and Volkens 2014, p. 6).

The paragraph below which is taken from the coalition agreement of the Irish Kenny I cabinet (2011–2016) illustrates an example of a natural sentence that contains three unrelated statements.

> We have a secure and stable mandate and we will use it to build a secure and stable Government. A Government that will restore our country's finances, / / will radically reform an outdated system of administration / / and will rebuild Ireland's reputation on the international stage.
> (Department of the Taoiseach, Ireland 2011, p. 1).

The second sentence has to be divided into three quasi-sentences. Here, three different policy sectors are addressed in one natural sentence. While the first part of the sentence is concerned with the country's finances, the second part refers to administrative reforms and the third part speaks about international politics.

The other scenario in which a natural sentence must be split refers to statements that are related, but address different aspects of a policy. The example below from the coalition agreement of the Kenny I cabinet illustrates such a unitization:

> Exchequer funding for hospital care will go into a Hospital Insurance Fund which will subsidize or pay insurance premia for those who qualify for subsidy. The Hospital Insurance Fund will oversee a strong and reformed system of community rating and risk equalisation; // provide direct payments to hospitals for services that are not covered by insurance such as Emergency Departments and ambulances; // and provide matching payment to hospitals for treatments delivered.
> (Department of the Taoiseach, Ireland 2011, p. 33).

The second natural sentence in this text passage has to be broken down into three different quasi-sentences. Even though the entire second sentence refers to health care, each of the three parts of the sentence presents a distinctive policy proposal in the health care domain. The first part addresses the administrative system of the Hospital Insurance Fund, the second part promises direct payments to hospitals for services that are not covered by insurances and the third part proposes financial compensation of hospitals for treatments they have provided to patients.

### 3.3.2 Coding

In order to allocate the identified quasi-sentences to thematic categories to measure the content of the coalition agreements, we have developed a codebook that constitutes an extended version of the latest MARPOR coding scheme (Werner, Lacewell, and Volkens 2014). We aimed for a codebook that allowed for a more fine-grained analysis of specific issues discussed in the coalition agreements as some policy issues such as migration or health care cannot be coded unambiguously using the original MARPOR codebook. We therefore created additional subcategories for the policy categories of the MARPOR codebook that allow for a mapping of specific policy issues in the coalition agreements. More specifically, we kept the hierarchical MARPOR structure of major domains, policy categories and subcategories and extended the codebook by adding additional subcategories to ensure compatibility with the MARPOR election manifesto data. Our extended codebook includes the seven major MARPOR policy domains, 58 policy categories, and 215 subcategories. Table 3.3 provides an overview of the domains and the categories included in our codebook and in Appendix 2 you can find the complete codebook including a list of all the 215 subcategories. For some categories, we decided not to include any subcategories either because they are already specific enough or because the underlying concepts are not tangible. We used the category descriptions in the MARPOR coding scheme as a first starting point to create the additional subcategories to make sure that the content of our subcategories is consistent with the content of the policy categories coded by the MARPOR project.

The main challenge in designing this codebook consisted of developing subcategories that capture all major policy issues discussed in coalition agreements, but that were at the same time mutually exclusive, so that any given quasi-sentence could be clearly assigned to one single subcategory. Following the procedure adopted by the Policy Agendas Project (Baumgartner and Jones 1993), we moreover included a "General" subcategory in addition to the substantial subcategories for each MARPOR policy category to capture quasi-sentences that clearly refer to the MARPOR category (e.g. social welfare), but which refer to a policy issue for which we decided not to include a specific substantial subcategory since it occurs only very infrequently (e.g. statutory accident insurance). We also classified statements into these "general" categories that would have applied to more than one subcategory in a policy domain (and were not separated into two quasi-sentences), or that were too general to fit into a meaningful subcategory. To illustrate how our codebook differs from the MARPOR coding scheme, Table 3.4 displays the subcategories that we created for the MARPOR social welfare categories. By adding subcategories to the social welfare categories, we are able to distinguish whether a coalition agreements talks about health care, child/youth care, elderly care or social housing instead of just measuring whether a quasi-sentence refers to social welfare which is a very broad policy area.

Additionally, we code each quasi-sentence according to the polity level it pertains to in order to distinguish between policy statements referring to the national or the European level (see also Wüst and Volkens 2003). Given that policy-making in the member states of the European Union (EU) takes place on multiple levels of government, it is important to make this distinction in order to capture whether coalition parties refer to policy-making at the national or the European level when they talk about a specific policy issue. The

Table 3.3 Overview of policy categories

**Domain 1: External Relations**
101 Foreign Special Relationships: Positive
102 Foreign Special Relationships: Negative
103 Anti-Imperialism: Positive
104 Military: Positive
105 Military: Negative
106 Peace: Positive
107 Internationalism: Positive
108 European Integration: Positive
109 Internationalism: Negative
110 European Integration: Negative
**Domain 2: Freedom and Democracy**
201 Freedom and Human Rights: Positive
202 Democracy
203 Constitutionalism: Positive
204 Constitutionalism: Negative
**Domain 3: Political System**
301 Decentralization: Positive
302 Centralization: Positive
303 Governmental and Administrative Efficiency: Positive
304 Political Corruption: Negative
305 Political Authority: Positive
**Domain 4: Economy**
401 Free Enterprise:Positive
402 Incentives: Positive
403 Market Regulation: Positive
404 Economic Planning: Positive
405 Corporatism: Positive
406 Protectionism: Positive
407 Protectionism: Negative
408 Economic Goals
409 Keynesian Demand Management: Positive
410 Economic Growth: Positive
411 Technology and Infrastructure: Positive
412 Controlled Economy: Positive
413 Nationalization: Positive
414 Economic Orthodoxy: Positive
415 Marxist Analysis: Positive
416 Anti-Growth Economy: Positive
**Domain 5: Welfare and Quality of Life**
501 Environmental Protection: Positive
502 Culture: Positive
503 Equality: Positive
504 Welfare State Expansion
505 Welfare State Limitation
506 Education Expansion
507 Education Limitation
**Domain 6: Fabric of Society**
601 National Way of Life: Positive
602 National Way of Life: Negative
603 Traditional Morality: Positive
604 Traditional Morality: Negative
605.1 Law and Order: Positive
605.2 Law and Order: Negative
606 Civic Mindedness: Positive
607 Multiculturalism: Positive
608 Multiculturalism: Negative
**Domain 7: Social Groups**
701 Labour Groups: Positive
702 Labour Groups: Negative
703.1 Agriculture and Farmers: Positive
703.2 Agriculture and Farmers: Negative
704 Middle Class and Professional Groups: Positive
705 Minority Groups: Positive
706 Non-Economic Demographic Groups: Positive

MARPOR categories 108 "European Integration: Positive" and 110 "European Integration: Negative" by contrast cover only structural aspects of vertical and horizontal integration of the European Union referring to a general transfer of competences from the national to the European level or the functioning of the institutional architecture of the EU.

Table 3.4 Illustration of coding scheme development

| 504 Welfare State Expansion (MARPOR) | 505 Welfare State Limitation (MARPOR) |
|---|---|
| 504.01 General: Expansion | 505.01 General: Limitation |
| 504.02 Health Care: Expansion | 505.02 Health Care: Limitation |
| 504.03 Child/Youth Care: Expansion | 505.03 Child/Youth Care: Limitation |
| 504.04 Elderly Care: Expansion | 505.04 Elderly Care: Limitation |
| 504.05 Social Housing: Expansion | 505.05 Social Housing: Limitation |
| (…) | (…) |

Categories 504 and 505 are obtained from MARPOR, subcategories listed below the main categories were additionally created for the COALITIONAGREE dataset.

By splitting the original MARPOR categories into more fine-grained subcategories, we are furthermore able to use subcategories from different policy domains to construct new measures for topics that are scattered across the original MARPOR categories. For instance, in the MARPOR codebook, gender equality is coded under 503 "Equality: Positive" and general assistance to women is classified under 706 "Non-Economic Demographic Groups: Positive." However, since category 706 is not exclusively devoted to women issues, but also covers mentions of other non-economic groups such as old people or students, we cannot unambiguously create a measure for the attention to women's issues based on the MARPOR codebook. We therefore added subcategories for women, both to the "Equality: Positive" and to the "Non-Economic Demographic Groups: Positive" category. This enables us to combine the subcategories into an unambiguous aggregated measure of attention to women in politics.

In order to allow for estimating the policy positions of coalition cabinets on specific policy issues, we created positional categories wherever possible to get a more nuanced picture of the issue-specific policy stances of coalition cabinets. The MARPOR coding scheme contains 56 policy categories. We transformed two MARPOR categories into positional ones by splitting them into positive and negative categories. First, we split the MARPOR category 605 "Law and Order" into the positional categories 605.1 "Law and Order: Positive"and 605.2 "Law and Order: Negative." Second, we created two different categories for agriculture, namely category 703.1 "Agriculture and Farmers: Positive" and 703.2 "Agriculture and Farmers: Negative." In order to make sure that not only the categories, but also the additional subcategories capture positional views, all the subcategories also mirror the directionality of the categories.

For other categories, there are however no meaningful positional distinctions. On so-called valence issues such as environmental protection or peace, no party would openly take a contrasting position. For our coalition agreement codebook, we therefore decided not to add positional subcategories to such policy categories. For these policy areas, policy positions could be computed by contrasting existing categories (see also Veen 2011; Lowe et al. 2011). For instance, to compute a position on environmental protection, the categories 416 "Anti-growth economy: Positive" and 501 "Environmental protection: Positive" which both reflect an environmental friendly position can be opposed to category 410 "Economic Growth: Positive" which reflects a skeptic position on the environmental policy dimension. Overall, we then arrive at 58 policy categories.

The coding IDs of our subcategories always have five digits. Following the MARPOR logic, the first digit of the code indicates the domain. The first three digits identify the policy category while the additional fourth and fifth category unambiguously identify the subcategories. Whenever we divided the original MARPOR categories into positional ones, the fourth digit is a "1" or a "2" to identify whether the newly created positional category is a left or right mention of the issue in question (e.g. 605.1 "Law and order: Positive" [right] and 605.2 Law and order: Negative [left]). In case the MARPOR codebook has already included positional categories for the same policy issue (e.g. 603 "Traditional Morality: Positive" and 604 "Traditional Morality: Negative"), we simply kept those first three digits and added a "0" as a fourth digit to denote the subcategories (e.g. 604.04 "Abortion and Birth Control: Positive" and 604.02 "Family: Progressive").

Another novel and important element in the codebook is the mapping of procedural rules included in coalition agreements. Coalition governments frequently include a section on procedural rules in coalition agreements. Procedural rules are not concerned with policies, but with the internal functioning of coalition cabinets during the time of office. Since these procedural rules are important to understand coalition governance during the legislative term, we extended the MARPOR codebook by including a category for procedural rules in the codebook which distinguishes six different procedural aspects that coalition parties frequently settle in coalition agreements. Table 3.5 illustrates the categories created for mapping procedural rules in coalition agreements. Category 900.02 covers mentions of the distribution of ministerial portfolios between coalition partners as well as discussions of the allocation of competences between different ministries. Category 900.03 applies to text passages

Table 3.5 Categories for procedural rules

| Category | Description |
| --- | --- |
| 900.01 | General |
| 900.02 | Portfolio allocation |
| 900.03 | Cabinet meetings |
| 900.04 | Junior ministers |
| 900.05 | Legislative discipline |
| 900.06 | Conflict-solving mechanisms |
| 900.07 | Decision-making mechanism |

in which coalition parties talk about the type and frequency of cabinet meetings that they plan to hold during the time of office. Category 900.04 covers all discussions of (cross-partisan) junior ministers which fulfill an important monitoring function in coalition cabinets (e.g. Thies 2001), for instance their competences and their assignment to ministerial portfolios. Category 900.05 captures all mentions of legislative discipline. It is for instance often discussed in coalition agreements that all members of the cabinet parties' party groups have to vote in line with the negotiated coalition compromise. Category 900.06 refers to conflict resolution mechanisms that coalition parties install to manage conflicts between coalition parties and between different ministries. Finally, category 900.07 includes mentions of decision-making procedures within the coalition cabinet. For instance, coalition parties frequently lay out the internal decision-making process for developing and coordinating a legislative proposal before it is introduced to parliament. Additionally, we added a general category for procedural matters (900.01) which covers all mentions of procedural aspects that could not be allocated to a more specific procedural rules category. For instance, many coalition cabinets state that the coalition agreement is the basis for the policy-making activities of the cabinet.

One of the major challenges in a hand-coded content analysis is the reliability of the coding (Mikhaylov, Laver, and Benoit 2012). In order to ensure inter-coder reliability, we have taken various measures. First, all our coders are native speakers with country-specific expertise so that they share a common cultural, historical and political background. Second, all our coders underwent extensive coder training in which we have discussed coalition agreements as a text source and provided a thorough introduction to the coding rules and all the categories covered in our codebook. We have provided examples from our coalition agreement corpus for all categories covered in our codebook and discussed potential ambiguities in depth. In addition, all our coders have conducted various test codings that have been checked and discussed

Table 3.6 Reliability of policy category coding

| Country | Krippendorf's $\alpha$ | Percentage agreement |
| --- | --- | --- |
| Austria | 0.96 | 0.97 |
| Belgium | 0.81 | 0.83 |
| Bulgaria | 0.86 | 0.88 |
| Czech Republic | 0.85 | 0.86 |
| Denmark | 0.91 | 0.92 |
| Estonia | 0.73 | 0.79 |
| Finland | 0.79 | 0.83 |
| Germany | 0.97 | 0.97 |
| Greece | 0.80 | 0.82 |
| Hungary | 0.84 | 0.89 |
| Iceland | 0.89 | 0.90 |
| Latvia | 0.90 | 0.90 |
| Luxembourg | 0.85 | 0.88 |
| Netherlands | 0.86 | 0.87 |
| Norway | 0.91 | 0.92 |
| Poland | 0.96 | 0.97 |
| Portugal | 0.83 | 0.86 |
| Slovakia | 0.95 | 0.96 |
| Slovenia | 0.87 | 0.88 |
| Sweden | 0.86 | 0.88 |
| **Average** | 0.87 | 0.89 |

with our research team. If the results of the coding tests were satisfactory, the coders started coding the coalition agreements negotiated in their home country. During the coding process, all our coders were closely supervised by our research team and regular meetings were held in which questions were discussed. Finally, we conducted regular reliability tests to maximize inter-coder reliability and monitor the coding. Table 3.6 provides information about the intercoderreliability across countries. The average inter-coder reliability based on the percent agreement amounts to 89 percent while the average Krippendorffs alpha amounts to 0.87.

## 3.4 Application example

In order to demonstrate the coding of coalition agreements, we illustrate the content of the coalition agreement negotiated by the Schröder I cabinet in Germany (1998–2002) between the Social Democratic Party (SPD) and the

Green Party. The general election took place on September 27, 1998 and the coalition negotiations were finished on October 20, 1998 with the adoption of the common coalition agreement. The agreement includes 16,536 words and is divided into 12 sections.

Figure 3.2 sheds light on the attention to the major policy domains in the coalition agreement negotiated by the Schröder I cabinet. Most of the quasi-sentences were classified into the major policy domain 5 "Welfare and Quality of Life," followed by domain 4 "Economy" and domain 1 "External Relations." While the high emphasis on welfare-related and economic issues is little surprising for a coalition cabinet led by a social democratic party, the considerable attention to domain 1 "External Relations" is somewhat puzzling for a left government. An inspection of the subcategories of domain 1 reveals that the attention for external relations is driven by issues related to the European Union and international cooperation. As Figure 3.3 shows, over 50 percent of the quasi-sentences coded into domain 1 "External Relations" were coded into the policy categories 107 Internationalism: Positive and 108 European Integration: Positive. Overall, 117 of the 233 (sub-)categories of our codebook were used to code the content of this single coalition agreement.

With our extended coalition agreement codebook, we have a more fine-grained insight into the composition of the relatively broad MARPOR categories. To demonstrate how our refined codebook allows for a much more issue-specific analysis of the content of coalition agreements, we use the 504 "Welfare State Expansion" category as an illustrative example. While MARPOR classified all mentions of an expansive welfare state policy into category

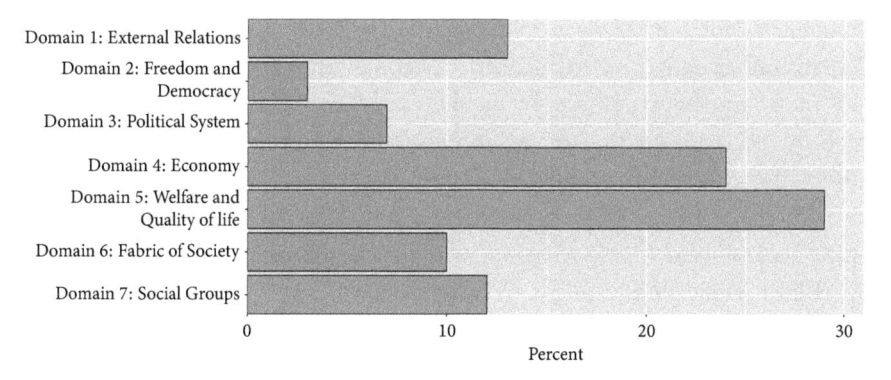

**Figure 3.2** Attention to policy domains in the coalition agreement of the Schröder I cabinet

## 68 A NEW DATASET MAPPING THE CONTENT OF COALITION AGREEMENTS

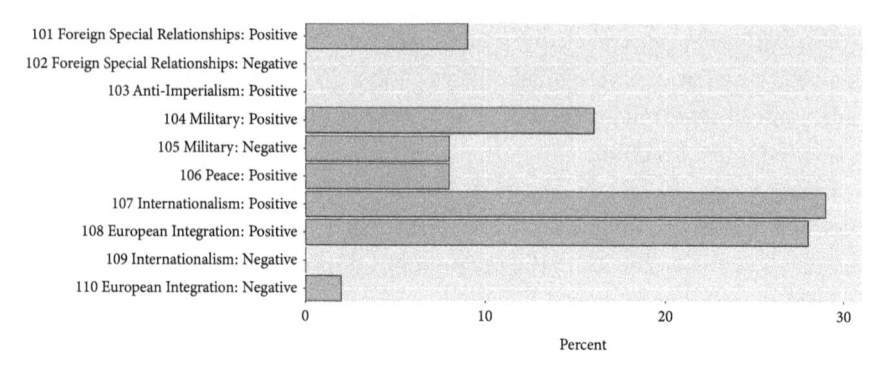

**Figure 3.3** Attention to External Relations categories in the coalition agreement of the Schröder I cabinet

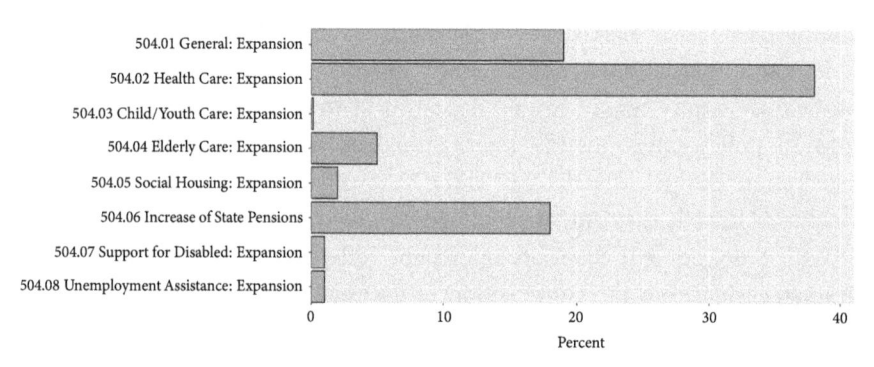

**Figure 3.4** Frequency of subcategories of category 504 "Welfare State Expansion" in the coalition agreement of the Schröder I cabinet

504, our codebook allows for a much more fine-grained analysis of the specific welfare state policies a government favors. In Figure 3.4, we present the frequencies for our newly devised subcategories of the 504 "Welfare State Expansion" category. For the Schröder I cabinet, the expansion of health care was most important, followed by the increase of state pensions and the expansion of child and youth care. By contrast, the expansion of support for the disabled, the unemployed, and social housing were only of minor importance for this government. Relying on the additional subcategories enables us to more accurately identify governments issue priorities even within the original MARPOR categories.

Given that the Green party entered the Schröder I government as a junior party, it can be expected that environmental policy should play a major role in the coalition negotiations. An inspection of major policy domain 5 "Welfare and Quality of Life" confirms this expectation. As shown in Figure 3.5, which

APPLICATION EXAMPLE 69

- 501 Environmental Protection: Positive
- 502 Culture: Positive
- 503 Equality: Positive
- 504 Welfare State Expansion
- 505 Welfare State Limitation
- 506 Education Expansion
- 507 Education Limitation

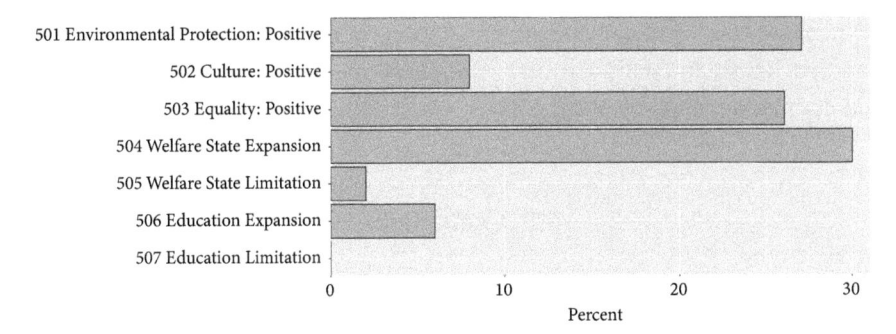

(Percent, 0 to 30)

**Figure 3.5** Frequency of policy categories of domain 5 "Welfare and Quality of Life" in the coalition agreement of the Schröder I cabinet

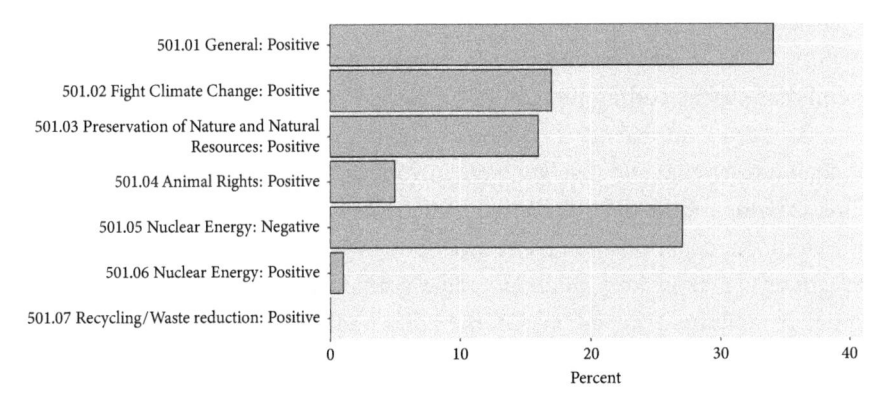

- 501.01 General: Positive
- 501.02 Fight Climate Change: Positive
- 501.03 Preservation of Nature and Natural Resources: Positive
- 501.04 Animal Rights: Positive
- 501.05 Nuclear Energy: Negative
- 501.06 Nuclear Energy: Positive
- 501.07 Recycling/Waste reduction: Positive

(Percent, 0 to 40)

**Figure 3.6** Frequency of subcategories of category 501 "Environmental Protection: Positive" in the coalition agreement of Schröder I cabinet

shows the frequency of the policy categories of domain 5 "Welfare and Quality of Life" in the coalition agreement negotiated by the SPD and the Green party, over 26 percent of all quasi-sentences coded under this major policy domain are devoted to environmental issues. All in all, this is equivalent to nearly 8 percent of all quasi-sentences in the coalition agreement. This result squares well with our intuition that a green party in government dedicates more attention to "green topics." Prioritizing green issues in the coalition agreement thus provides preliminary evidence that the Greens were able to push through some of their issue priorities during the coalition negotiations.

The refined codebook moreover enables us to identify which were the most important issues in the environmental policy domain for the SPD and the Green Party. Figure 3.6 displays the attention to different policy issues in the environmental policy domain. Upon closer inspection of the environmental subcategories, we can see that the Schröder I cabinet was mostly concerned with promoting the nuclear phase-out, fighting climate change and the preservation of nature and natural resources while animal rights and waste reduction did not play a major role for the government at the time.

## 3.5 Conclusion

In this chapter, we have described the construction of the new COALITIONAGREE dataset which is a novel and unprecedented dataset on the content of coalition agreements. More precisely, we conducted a comprehensive analysis of coalition agreements that draws on human coders to analyze the content of 229 coalition agreements that have been negotiated by 184 parties between 1945 and 2015 in 24 West and East European countries.

Building on the coding procedure developed by the MARPOR project, we have developed an extended codebook for the hand-coded content analysis of coalition agreements that we have introduced in this chapter. The codebook extends the MARPOR coding scheme in two important ways. On the one hand, our coalition agreement codebook includes considerably more subcategories that allow for a much more fine-grained analysis of the policy issues settled in coalition agreements. On the other hand, we have added positional categories to nearly all policy domains and subcategories in order to be able to shed light on the issue-specific policy positions that coalition parties adopt in their coalition agreement. We have demonstrated how our dataset can be used to shed light on the policy content of coalition agreements based on an illustrative case study analyzing the coalition agreement negotiated by the first red-green cabinet in Germany governing between 1998 and 2002.

The COALITIONAGREE dataset for the first time allows for systematically studying the policy content of coalition agreements across cabinets, countries and over time. In the next chapter, we will shed light on what coalition parties talk about in their coalition agreements more generally and how the content of coalition agreements varies across countries and over time. On the basis of this dataset, Chapters 5, 6, and 7 will test our theoretical expectations regarding the role of coalition agreements as control devices. While the COALITIONAGREE dataset was primarily created in order to empirically examine our theoretical argument, the dataset is made publicly available to other scholars and can be used for answering a wide variety of different research questions. We thereby make a fruitful and lasting contribution to the research on coalition governments in European countries, enabling scholars to link data on election manifestos (e.g. MARPOR, see Volkens et al. 2019*a*) and on parties, elections, and cabinets (e.g. the ParlGov or ERDDA datasets, see Döring and Manow 2010; Bergman, Ilonszki, and Müller 2019a) to detailed information on coalition agreements (COALITIONAGREE) in order to address questions referring to aspects such as coalition building, legislative policy-making and government performance.

# 4
# The content of coalition agreements

The vast majority of coalition governments that have been formed in Western and Eastern Europe have drafted a coalition agreement. Coalition parties spend several weeks if not months on negotiating and formulating a coalition treaty that importantly determines their behavior in office. A recent study which investigated the enactment of more than 5,000 policy pledges made in coalition agreements by 87 coalition governments in 20 Western and Eastern European countries from 2000 to 2015 has shown that the majority of policy pledges made in coalition agreements are enacted by coalition governments during the legislative term (Klüver, Alberto, and Ellger 2021). Thus, coalition agreements have important consequences for policy-making during the time of office. However, we hardly know anything about the content of these agreements.

In this book, we therefore seek to open this black box by providing a novel and comprehensive content analysis of coalition agreements published by multiparty cabinets across 24 West and East European countries from 1945 until 2015. On the basis of this newly compiled dataset which we described in the previous chapter, we are now turning to uncover the content of the agreements.

## 4.1 The length of coalition agreements

At first, we are looking at the overall length of coalition agreements. A number of recent studies have suggested that the length of coalition agreements is an important indicator of the extent to which an agreement is used as a control device (e.g. Indridason and Kristinsson 2013; Eichorst 2014; Bowler et al. 2016; Klüver and Bäck 2019). It is argued that the length of a coalition agreement signals the strength of the control mechanism. Long coalition agreements are typically much more detailed when it comes to prescribing what policies will be enacted during the legislative term. If a coalition agreement only entails one or two pages, it is obvious that coalition parties cannot say much about specific policy proposals that will be enacted throughout the legislative term. By contrast, if coalition parties adopt a coalition agreement that includes for instance a hundred pages, they can be much more precise in laying out a detailed list of policy reforms. Accordingly, Indridason and Kristinsson (2013, p. 830) argue that longer coalition agreements should at least have a "greater potential to impose constraints than shorter ones." The coalition agreement negotiated by the CDU/CSU and the SPD after the 2013 Bundestag election is for instance over 130 pages long. It includes detailed policy reforms on a large number of topics like employment policy, health care, finance, culture, and many more. It is therefore no surprise that many of the specific policy proposals mentioned in the coalition agreement such as the minimum wage or higher pensions for mothers have been enacted shortly after the election. The coalition agreement written by the German Christian Democratic CDU/CSU and the Liberal FDP in 1983 on the other hand is only 10 pages in length. While it covers a range of different topics, there are no specific policy reforms discussed so that the agreement left considerable room of maneuver for the coalition parties and their individual ministers.

Figure 4.1 illustrates how the length of the 229 coalition agreements in our sample varies across countries. On average, coalition agreements in our sample contain 11,339 words (635 quasi-sentences). The shortest agreement is only 86

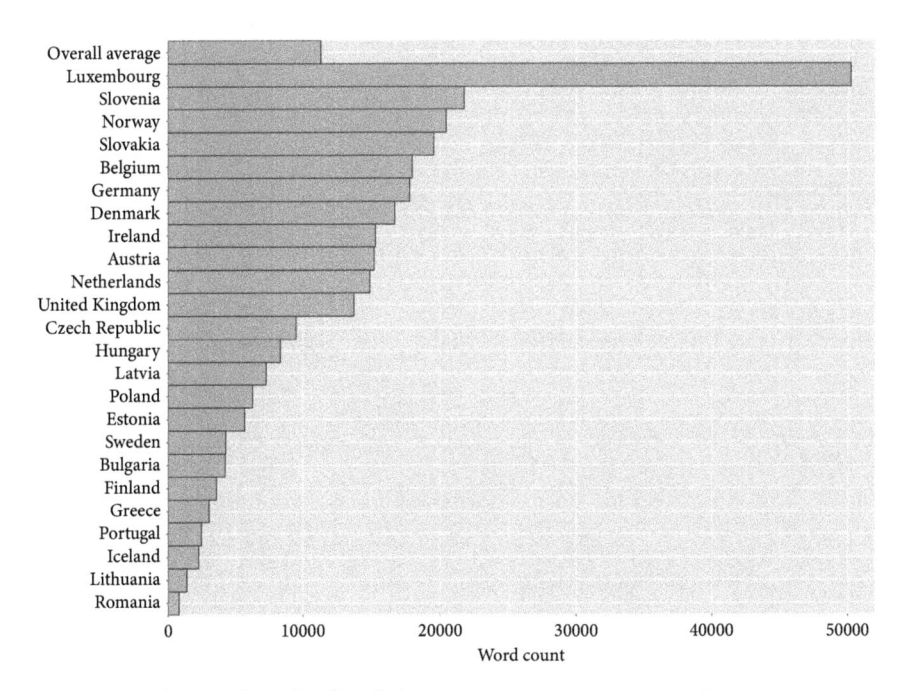

**Figure 4.1** Average length of coalition agreements across countries

words (seven quasi-sentences) long and was drafted by the Finnish Kekkonen V cabinet composed of the Social Democratic and the Centre Party and in power from October 1954 until March 1956. The longest coalition agreement contains 67,066 words (2,964 quasi-sentences) and was published by the Bettel I cabinet that was formed by the Democratic Party, the Socialist Workers' Party and the Greens in Luxembourg in 2013 and lasted until the next regular election in 2018.

Previous research by Indridason and Kristinsson (2013) shows that the length of coalition agreements has on average increased over time. Based on an analysis of 118 coalition agreements drafted from 1944 until 2000 in 13 Western European countries that were largely compiled by Strøm, Müller, and Bergman (2008), they demonstrated that coalition agreements have grown longer which they interpret as "a greater effort to contain ministerial drift" (Indridason and Kristinsson 2013, p. 835). How does the length of coalition agreements vary in our much larger and more recent sample? Have coalition agreements increased further in length in the post-2000 period? What about coalition agreements drafted in Eastern European cabinets? Have they similarly increased over time?

As can be seen in Figure 4.2, the length of coalition agreements included in the sample has similarly increased over time. While in the 1940s, the average word count of a coalition agreement was 1,131 words (61 quasi-sentences),

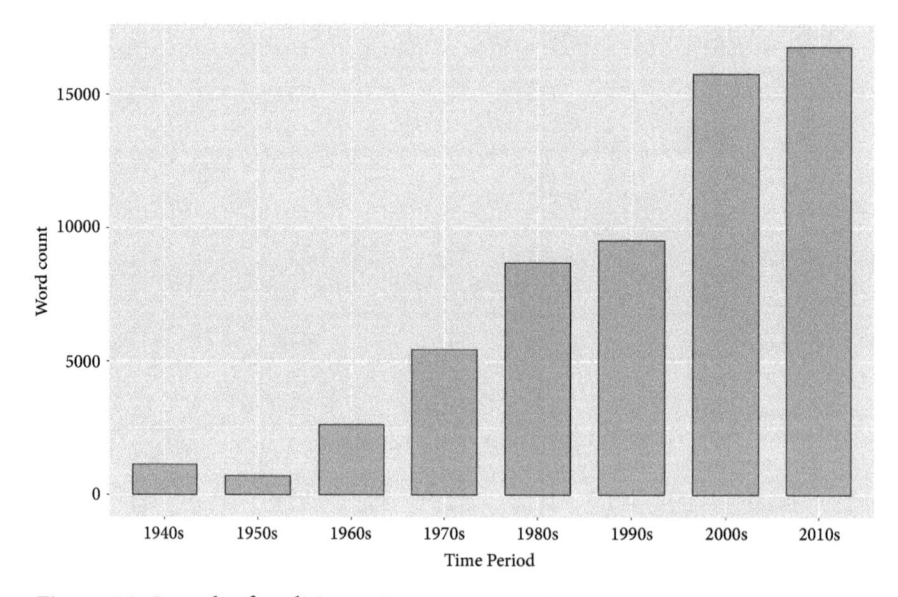

Figure 4.2 Length of coalition agreements over time

THE LENGTH OF COALITION AGREEMENTS 75

it increased step by step since the 1950s, reaching an average of 5,436 words (305 quasi-sentences) in the 1970s and an average of 16,166 words (956 quasi-sentences) in the post-2000 period. On average, there is thus a very clear trend toward writing ever longer coalition agreements over time. The rising length of coalition treaties provides suggestive evidence that coalition agreements have become increasingly important control devices for coalition parties. However, to what extent is this overall historical trend reflected on the country level? Is this a general trend or is it driven by just a few countries?

Figure 4.3 illustrates the variation in the length of coalition agreements over time, based on the country level. The solid circles indicate the average length of coalition agreements measured as the number of words. Longer agreements are represented by bigger circles. While in most Northern and Western European countries, there is a steady increase in the word count of coalition agreements, this trend is less strong for cabinets from Eastern European countries. The word count, while strongly varying across these countries, is quite constant over time in each country. For example, the 17 coalition agreements negotiated by Latvian cabinets from 1993 until 2014 have an average length of 7,297 words (618 quasi-sentences) with a standard deviation of 2,520 words

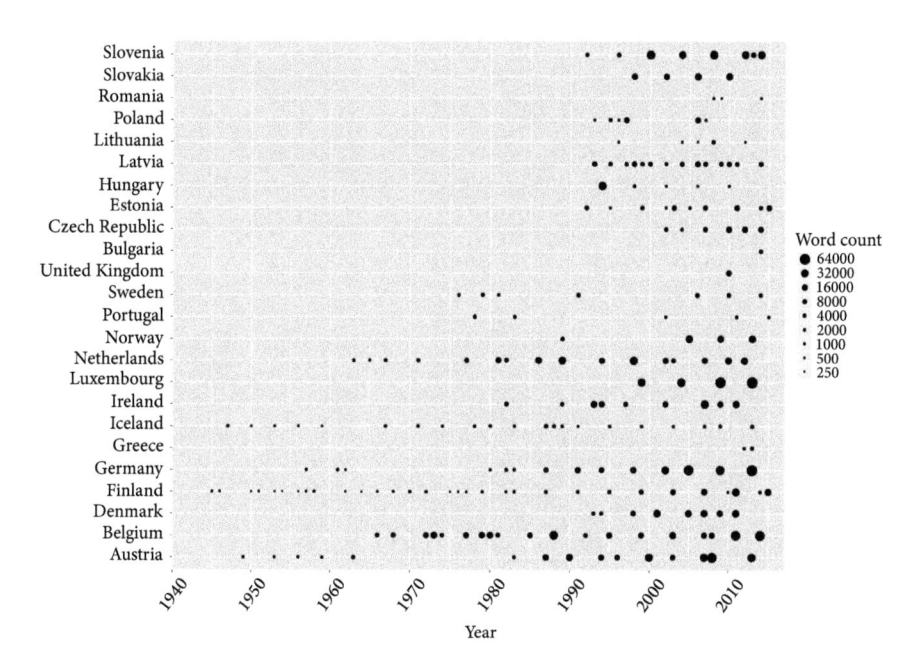

**Figure 4.3** Length of coalition agreements per country over time

76  THE CONTENT OF COALITION AGREEMENTS

(231 quasi-sentences). This variation is not as clearly reflected in a historical trend as it is in Western European countries: The coalition agreement drafted by the Birkavs I cabinet in 1993 has a length of 9,141 words (714 quasi-sentences) and the latest coalition agreement drafted by the Straujuma II cabinet in 2014 has a length of 7,021 words (429 quasi-sentences). The shortest (3,630 words) and the longest (12,476 words) coalition agreement negotiated by Latvian cabinets have been drafted within a four-year period from 2002 until 2006. This provides suggestive evidence for a diffusion process as Eastern European cabinets may have adopted procedures they have seen in Western European cabinets by writing similarly long coalition agreements. But, as illustrated in Figure 4.4, the trend of increasing length of coalition agreements is not entirely absent in Eastern European countries. From 1990 until 2010, the average length of a coalition agreement drafted by Eastern European cabinets increased by 3,493 words. In the same period, the average length of coalition agreements drafted by Western European cabinets increased by 10,928 words.

Another question that arises is why the overall length of coalition agreements varies so extensively not only over time, but also across countries.

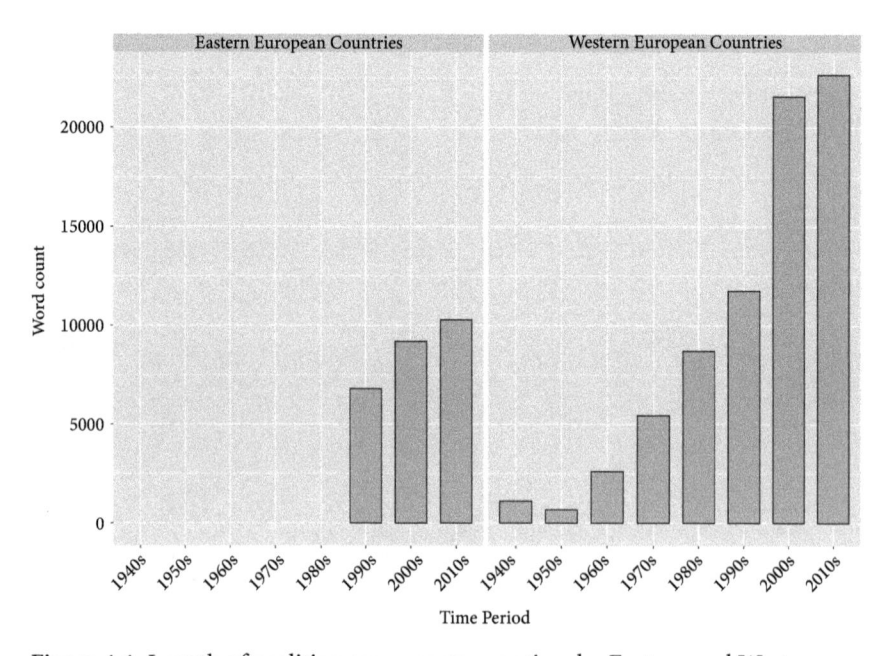

**Figure 4.4** Length of coalition agreements over time by Eastern and Western European countries

Table 4.1 Frequency of numbers of coalition parties in the sample

| Number of coalition parties | Frequency | Percentage |
|---|---|---|
| 2 | 96 | 41.9 |
| 3 | 60 | 26.2 |
| 4 | 46 | 20.1 |
| 5 | 22 | 9.6 |
| 6 | 5 | 2.2 |

Previous findings in the literature are contradicting: One prominent argument is that the degree of intra-cabinet conflict is positively related to the overall length of coalition agreements (e.g. Indridason and Kristinsson 2013; Eichorst 2014; Klüver and Bäck 2019). However, Bowler et al. (2016) show that when intra-coalition conflict is high, parties write shorter agreements, but are more likely to adopt procedures for conflict resolution. We are therefore investigating how the number of cabinet parties and the ideological range in coalition governments is related to the overall length of coalition agreements.

Taking the number of coalition parties as an indicator of the degree of intra-cabinet conflict, one could assume that the number of coalition parties is positively correlated with the length of coalition agreements. As Table 4.1 shows, over 40 percent of the coalition agreements included in the sample have been negotiated by two parties, nearly 50 percent by three or four coalition partners and no more than 12 percent have been negotiated by cabinets of five or more parties. Therefore, generalizing from the results illustrated in Figure 4.5 would be a mistake. The small difference between the average length of coalition agreements negotiated by two parties (11,615 words) and four parties (9,195 words) might indicate that there is no clear trend toward longer or shorter coalition agreements with a rising number of coalition partners.

Given that three of the five cabinets consisting of six coalition parties have been formed in Belgium, a country with two different main cultural communities and an average length of coalition agreements above the overall average of the sample (see Figure 4.1), it is reasonable to expect that the ideological range is related to the length of coalition agreements. We therefore also shed light on how the length of coalition agreements varies as the ideological diversity in coalition governments changes. We operationalize ideological diversity as the range of the left-right policy positions held by all cabinet parties, which corresponds to the absolute distance between the policy position of the most left-winged and the policy position of the most right-winged

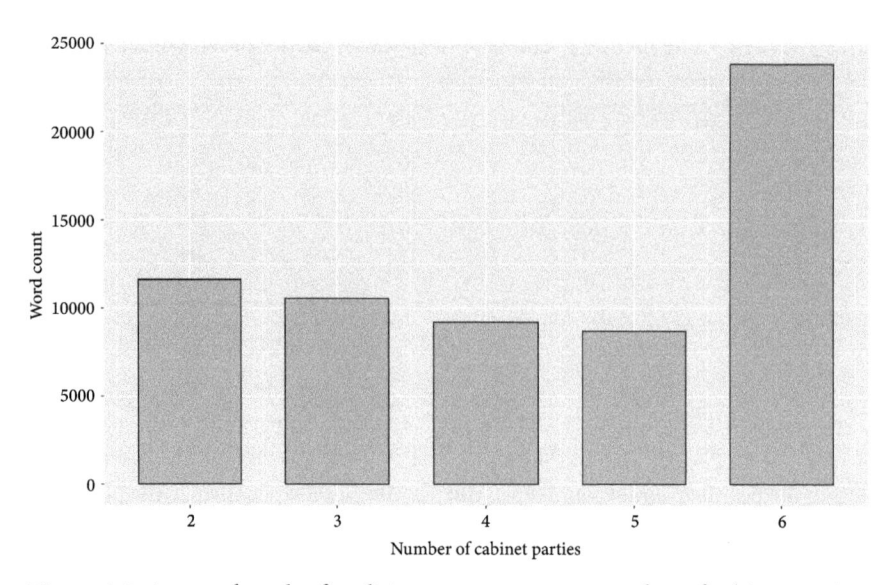

**Figure 4.5** Average length of coalition agreements per number of cabinet parties

member of the cabinet (see Tsebelis 2002). The left-right policy positions of the coalition parties were estimated on the basis of the MARPOR project data (Volkens et al. 2017) using the widely used additive percentage scores advocated by (Budge 1999). First, the percentages of left and right quasi-sentences of the total number of coded quasi-sentences are computed. Then the percentage of left sentences is subtracted from the percentage of right sentences. Positive scores indicate right positions and negative scores indicate left positions.

Figure 4.6 plots the length of coalition agreements against the ideological diversity of coalition governments measured as the range on the left-right dimension. Leaving cabinets with a maximal distance of policy positions of more than 30 points on the left-right scale aside because of the small amount of data in this segment, we can see that coalition agreements indeed tend to be longer as the ideological diversity between coalition parties increases. Thus, the descriptive data suggests that policy conflict plays an important role when negotiating coalition agreements. However, so far we have only investigated the bivariate relationship which may be confounded by other alternative explanatory factors. We will come back to the relationship between policy conflict and the content of coalition agreements in Chapter 5 in which we explore this relationship in much more depth.

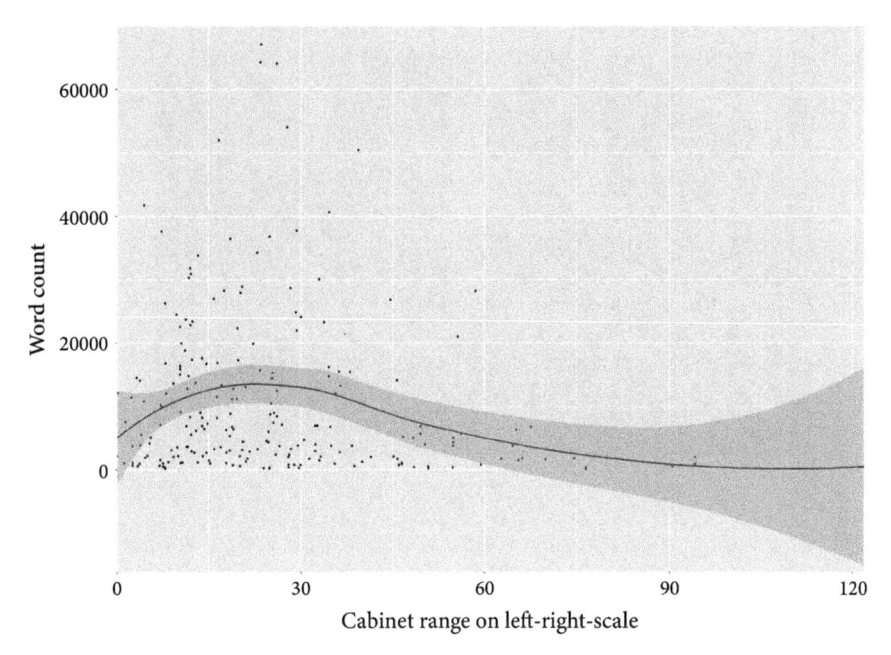

Figure 4.6 Length of coalition agreements and left-right range of cabinet parties

## 4.2 Policies, payoff allocation, or procedural rules?

Strøm and Müller (1999*a*) show, based on a sample of coalition agreements drafted in 13 West European coalition cabinets from 1945 until 1996, that three different points are typically settled in coalition treaties: policy agreements, portfolio allocation, and procedural rules. In this section, we want to shed further light on the relative importance of these issues in coalition agreements in our sample which not only covers more recent coalition governments, but which most importantly also comprises East European coalition governments.

Figure 4.7 sheds light on whether coalition parties primarily talk about policies, about the distribution of ministerial offices or about procedural rules for coalition management in their coalition agreements. The figure clearly shows that coalition agreements are first and foremost policy agreements. More precisely, coalition governments devote on average as much as 92 percent of their agreements to policies. This supports the view that coalition agreements are important policy documents that crucially determine the policy-making activities of coalition cabinets during the time of office. By contrast, procedural rules receive very little attention with on average only 5.9 percent of quasi-sentences devoted to these rules in coalition agreements. Finally, the allocation of ministerial offices receives least attention in coalition agreements as on average only

80   THE CONTENT OF COALITION AGREEMENTS

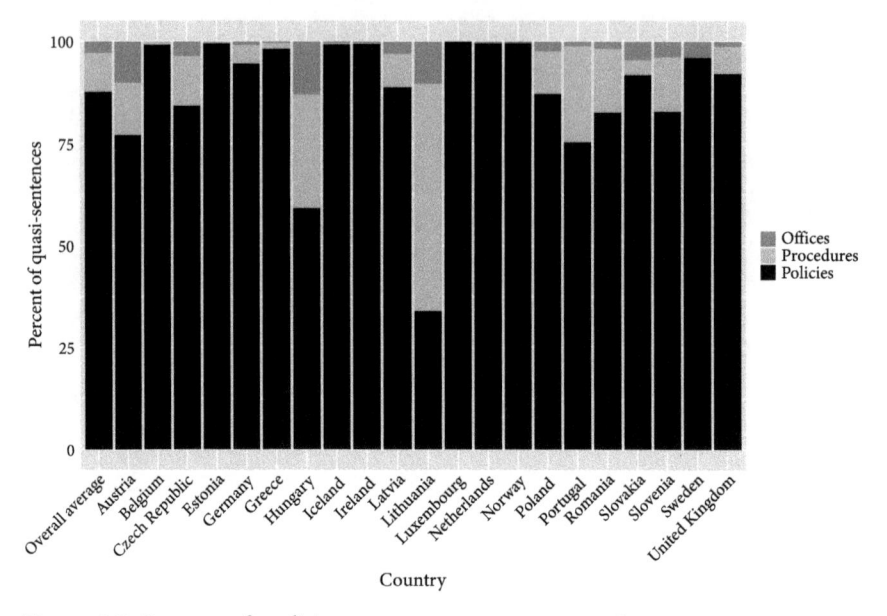

Figure 4.7 Content of coalition agreements across countries

2.1 percent of the quasi-sentences are devoted to the question who gets which ministerial portfolios.

However, there is some country-specific variation. While countries like Denmark and Estonia almost exclusively talk about policies in their coalition agreements, Lithuanian coalition agreements mostly consist of procedural rules. 56 percent of the quasi-sentences in Lithuanian coalition agreements are devoted to procedural rules while policies are only discussed in 34 percent of the quasi-sentences. Lithuania therefore constitutes a puzzling outlier that would be an interesting case for a future in-depth case study.

Has the role of coalition agreements changed over time? Given the less extensive use and length of coalition agreements in the first decades after World War II, it is reasonable to expect that policies were only marginally touched upon during the first decades after the war while they have gained in importance during recent decades. Figure 4.8 plots the attention that coalition agreements have paid to policies, payoff allocation, and procedural rules over time.

Figure 4.8 clearly shows that coalition agreements have always been primarily about policies. Policies have always dominated the content of coalition agreements even during the early decades after the war. There is some slight variation with policies being most important in the 1970s and 1980s, but overall, policies have always been much more prominent in coalition agreements

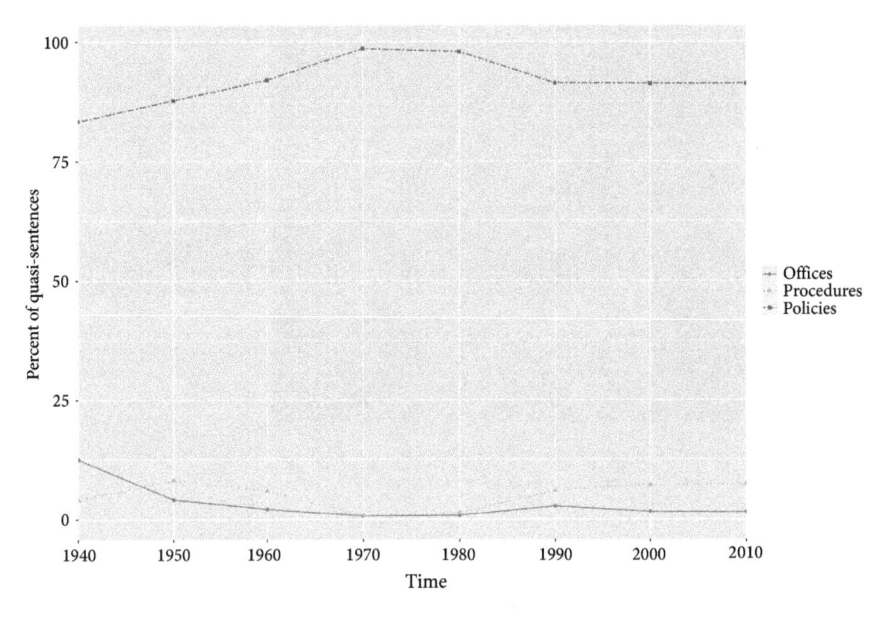

**Figure 4.8** Variation of content over time

than procedural rules or the allocation of ministerial offices. The fact that policies have somewhat lost in prominence while procedural rules have become slightly more important after 1990 can be explained by the entry of the Eastern European countries which, as Figure 4.3 shows, have devoted comparatively more attention to procedural rules.

So far, we have treated procedural rules as one big block without further differentiating between different types of procedural rules. As discussed in the previous chapter, we have created a category for procedural rules in our content analysis codebook that includes seven specific subcategories, namely: Portfolio allocation, Cabinet meetings, Junior ministers, Legislative discipline, Conflict-solving mechanisms, Decision-making mechanisms, and a General procedural rules category that applies to all mentions of procedural aspects that could not be allocated to a more specific procedural rules category. Cabinet meetings are meetings of the cabinet that take place during the time of office. Cross-partisan junior ministers are frequently appointed to monitor the behavior of a "hostile" minister. Legislative discipline refers to agreements regarding the voting behavior of Members of Parliament that belong to the cabinet's party groups. Conflict resolution mechanisms refer to instruments that coalition parties install to manage conflicts between coalition parties and between different ministries. Finally, decision-making

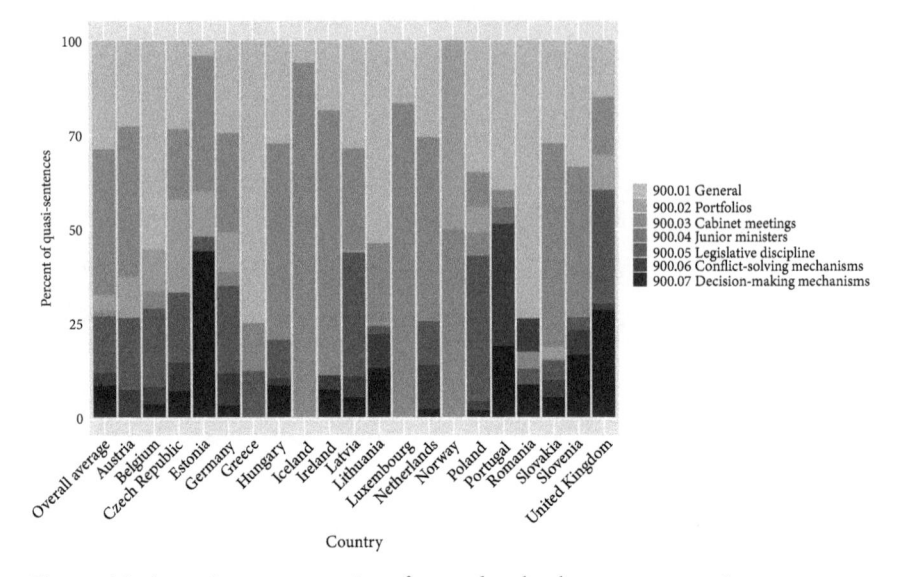

**Figure 4.9** Attention to categories of procedural rules across counties

*Note:* The coalition agreements negotiated by Bulgarian, Danish, Finish, and Swedish cabinets did not contain any quasi-sentences referring to procedural rules (see Figure 4.7). Therefore, these countries have been excluded from this figure.

procedures within the coalition cabinet describe for instance processes for developing and coordinating a legislative proposal before it is introduced to parliament.

Figure 4.9 illustrates how much coalition parties talk about the different procedural rules in their coalition agreements across countries and Figure 4.10 shows how the use varies over time. On average, coalition parties devote more than one third (39 percent) of all quasi-sentences referring procedural rules to portfolio allocation, 28 percent to general procedural rules, 15 percent to issues referring to legislative discipline, 8 percent to decision-making mechanisms and less than 5 percent to each cabinet meetings, conflict-solving mechanisms and junior ministers.

Figure 4.10 shows how the use of procedural rules in coalition agreements has changed over time. There are two general trends over time that immediately catch the attention. On the one hand, coalition agreements devoted much more attention to procedural rules during the 1940s and 1950s. On the other hand, there is a clear spike in the attention to procedural rules in coalition agreements around 1990. This suggests that the nature of the control exercised through coalition agreements has changed over time. Even though policies have always been most important in coalition agreements, the

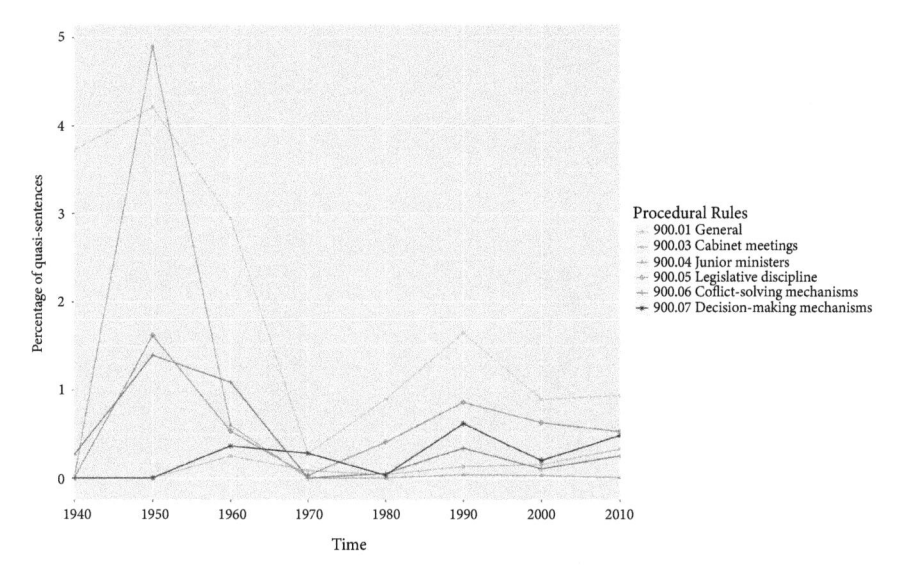

**Figure 4.10** Average attention to categories of procedural rules over time

decreasing attention to procedural rules suggests that using coalition agreements as a basis for ex post monitoring through installing conflict resolution has importantly decreased over time. Thus, control exercised through coalition agreements happens primarily through ex ante contract design. In other words, coalition parties negotiate the policy agenda for the upcoming term during government formation and write it down in the coalition agreement to bind their partners to the negotiated policy compromise. This historical trend was only interrupted by the inclusion of East European coalition governments after 1990. Since East European countries have however followed a similar pattern by devoting ever more attention to policies instead of procedural rules since their democratization, coalition governments generally prioritize contract ex ante contract design rather than provisions for ex post monitoring in their coalition agreements.

## 4.3 Which policy issues are covered in coalition agreements?

While we have so far looked at the length of coalition agreements and the relative importance of policies, offices, and procedural rules in these contracts, we are now turning to probably the most interesting question for many scholars: Which policy issues are covered by coalition agreements? The policy content

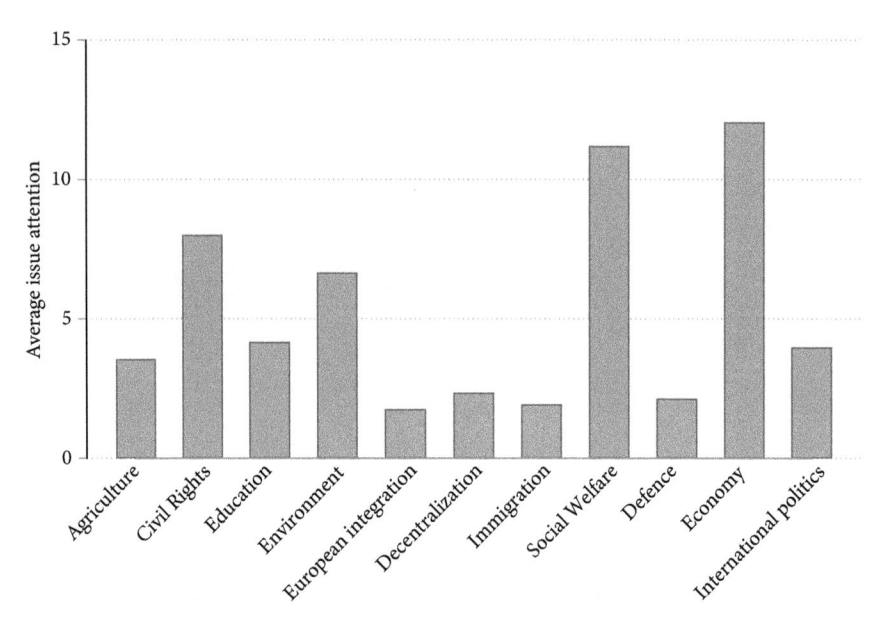

**Figure 4.11** Average issue attention (in percent)

of coalition agreements is a completely unknown territory in the coalition literature. Since the COALITIONAGREE dataset systematically identifies and maps the policy content of coalition agreements across cabinets, countries, and over time, we can for the first time shed light on what coalition parties talk about in their contracts.

Figure 4.11 plots the average attention that coalition governments pay to different policy issues in their agreements across countries and over time. The policy issues that receive most attention in coalition contracts are Economy (12.05 percent), Social Welfare (11.20 percent), Civil Rights (8.00 percent), and Environment (6.66 percent). Economic policy, social welfare, and civil rights are clear positional issues on which political parties have very distinct policy positions, suggesting that coalition parties devote a lot of attention to potentially divisive policy issues. The environment is by contrast a valence issue, but given that the emergence of green parties challenging established mainstream parties is strongly associated with the rise of the environmental issue (Spoon, Hobolt, and de Vries 2014; De Vries and Hobolt 2020), it is not surprising that this issue also triggers a lot of attention.

By contrast, policy issues that are only moderately covered in the coalition agreements are Agriculture (3.55 percent), Education (4.16 percent) and International Politics (3.98 percent), which are issues that are typically not

WHICH POLICY ISSUES ARE COVERED IN COALITION AGREEMENTS? 85

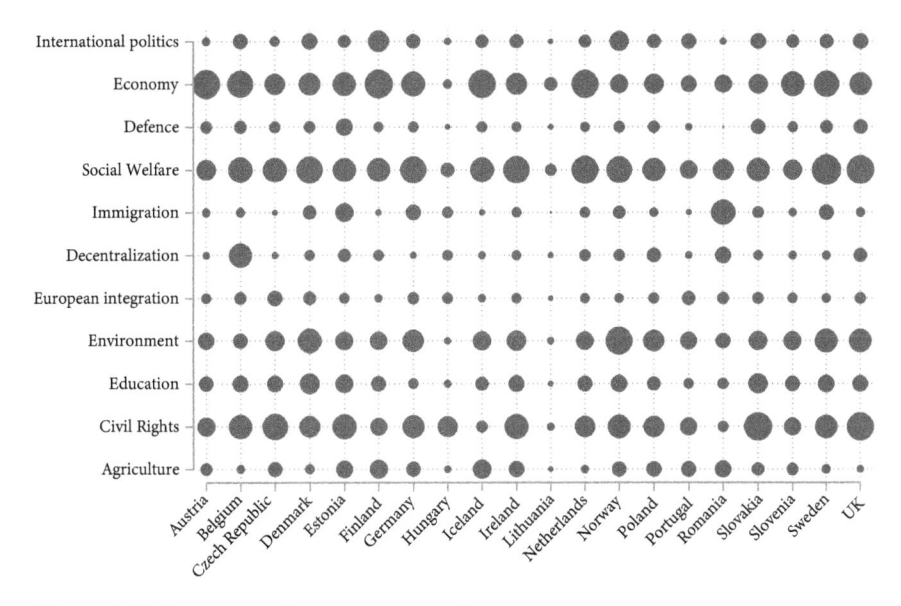

Figure 4.12 Issue attention across countries

"owned" by any particular party,[1] and are issues on which government parties are typically not particularly polarized. Least attention receive European integration (1.75 percent), Decentralization (2.34 percent), Defence (2.14 percent) and Immigration (1.94 percent). While European integration, Defence, and Decentralization are policy issues that are usually not very divisive among government parties in most European democracies, at least until recently, the comparatively low level of attention to immigration is surprising and may be due to some overlap with the civil rights issue area.

To gain some understanding as to how issue attention varies across countries, Figure 4.12 plots the average attention that coalition parties in the different countries in our sample pay to various policy issues in their coalition agreements. The larger the circle, the higher the attention to the specific policy issue. Overall, this figure confirms the aggregated picture as the Economy, Social Welfare, Civil Rights, and the Environment are policy issues that generally receive a lot of attention across countries, while other issues, such as European integration, Defence, or Decentralization generally receive very little coverage in the coalition agreements. However, there is some variation across countries, for example the issue attention in Lithuania is generally very

---

[1] An exception may be the case of "agricultural," or farmers' parties in Scandinavian countries.

86　THE CONTENT OF COALITION AGREEMENTS

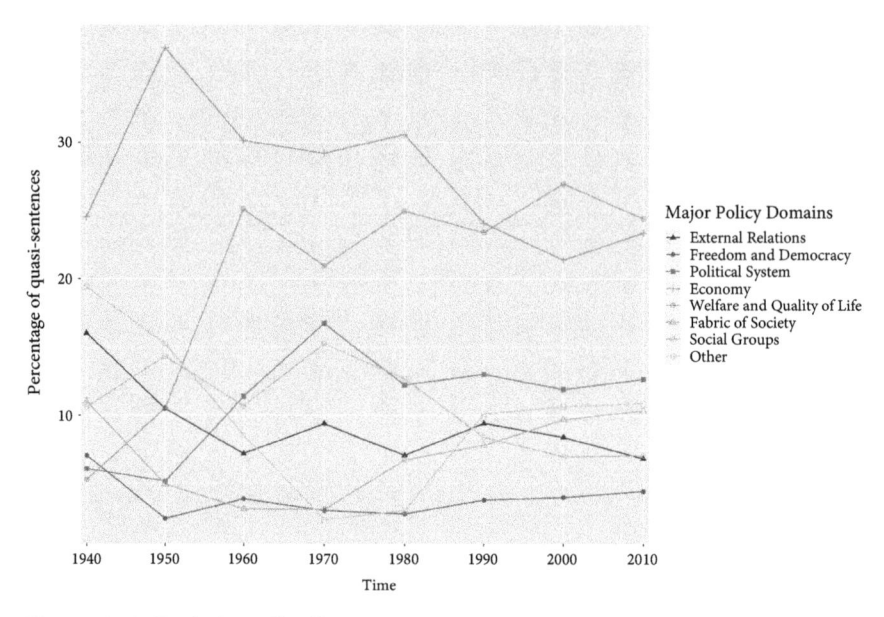

**Figure 4.13** Variation of policy content over time

low compared to the other countries. This is explained by the fact that Lithuanian coalition cabinets primarily focus on conflict resolution mechanisms in their coalition agreements, while hardly including any policy commitments in their coalition treaty (see Figure 4.7).

Finally, to further investigate how issue coverage changes over time, Figure 4.13 plots the attention to policy domains over time. Similar to the previous two figures, Figure 4.13 shows that, even over time, Economy and Welfare and Quality of Life are the most important domains. Interestingly, Welfare and Quality of Life gets more important over the years and receives even more attention than the Economy in coalition agreements since the mid-1990s. Figure 4.13 also demonstrates that the attention devoted to certain policy domains varies a lot over time. The salience for the Economy, for example, varies between 20 percent in the year 2000 and 45 percent during the 1950s. Similarly, the attention devoted to Welfare and Quality of Life is also highly volatile. It ranges between 5.3 percent and 29.7 percent with a mean salience of 23.1 percent. Such a high volatility of the two most important policy domains might partly be due to the government composition. While left-wing governments care more about welfare policies, right-wing governments are more concerned with the way the economy works. Another factor to explain this variance could be time. Right after the Second World War, governments had to mainly concentrate on the economy and could only put more emphasis on the welfare state after they rebuilt their economy.

## 4.4 Policy positions settled in coalition agreements

We have so far shown which policy issues coalition parties talk about in their coalition agreements. It is important to examine which policies are mentioned and how the attention to these policy issues varies in coalition agreements. However, understanding the policy content of coalition agreements not only concerns the *attention* to different policy issues in coalition agreements, but also the *positions* that coalition parties adopt on these issues. When coalition partners negotiate about policies, coalition parties naturally try to push through their own policy objectives in order to enact favored policies and to please their voters. It is therefore a crucial question which coalition partners were successful in shifting the coalition agreement towards their own preferred policy position.

The question which policies positions are adopted in coalition agreements has hardly received any attention in the literature. In fact there is only one study that we are aware of which systematically measures the policy positions of coalition contracts. Däubler and Debus (2009) present an analysis of government formation after state-level elections in Germany. Drawing on state-level coalition agreements and election manifestos, they compare the policy positions of coalition governments and their constituent parties on the economic and the social policy dimension. Their findings most importantly confirm that seat share has a positive effect on policy benefits on both, the economic and the social policy dimension. While this study is an important contribution to the literature as it directly compares what coalition parties aimed for and what they got out of coalition negotiations in terms of policies, the analysis is limited to the subnational level in Germany which makes the generalizability of the findings difficult. In addition, Däubler and Debus (2009) solely analyze policy positions on two policy dimensions. As political parties may struck package deals across different policy dimensions, it is important to have a more fine-grained picture of the policies settled in coalition agreements.

The following example illustrates the adoption of policy positions in the coalition agreement. During the time Austria's second Kurz cabinet was in office, the chancellor's Austrian People's Party (ÖVP) pushed for a restrictive approach to asylum, migration and Islam and enshrined this in the coalition agreement. The issue gained public attention a year after the coalition formed, when three children, including a girl who was born in Austria, were deported to Georgia and Armenia in January 2021 (Pausackl 2021). The Greens as the junior coalition partner publicly criticized the procedure carried out by the ÖVP-run ministry of the interior, calling it inhumane and irresponsible (Trübswasser 2021). This statement made not merely by the opposition, but a governing party, shows the heavy concessions the Greens made to the ÖVP. The Greens had to vote against their own positions because of the coalition discipline agreement. In general, the Greens' positions did not play a big role in the coalition agreement, except in the environmental policy space (Pausackl 2021).

The COALITIONAGREE dataset for the first time allows to systematically measure the policy positions adopted in coalition agreements across multiple policy dimensions for 229 coalition cabinets that have been in office between 1945 and 2015 in 24 West and East European countries. Since the coalition agreements have been coded on the basis of the MARPOR project, which provides a rich database on the policy content of election manifestos, it is possible to directly compare the policy objectives that coalition parties have advocated in their election manifestos with the outcome of coalition negotiations to shed light on how policy payoffs have been allocated. In this section, we make us of this rich new data source and shed light on how the policy positions adopted in coalition agreements relate to the policy stances that coalition parties have advocated in their election manifestos.

We display the policy positions of coalition agreements on the left-right dimension in relation to the parties' positions based on their election manifestos. We chose the left-right scale as this is the primary dimension of political conflict in most Western democracies (Marks and Steenbergen 2002). We estimated the policy positions using the widely used additive percentage scores advocated by Budge (1999). The central idea is that parties compete with each other by emphasizing different policy priorities rather than by directly opposing each other on the same issues. The left-right scale was constructed in the following way: First, the percentages of left and right categories of the total number of coded quasi-sentences were calculated. Then, the percentage of left sentences was subtracted from the percentage of right sentences (see Equation 4.1). Negative scores represent left positions and positive scores represent right positions. The policy positions of individual coalition parties were, based on the MARPOR project dataset (Volkens et al. 2019*a*), extracted from their election manifestos released before the election that preceded the formation of the coalition.

$$PolicyPosition_i = R_i - L_i \qquad (4.1)$$

The parameters $R_i$ and $L_i$ relate to the percentage of quasi-sentences of the parties' manifestos devoted to categories associated with right ($R_i$) and left ($L_i$) positions as coded in the Manifesto project (Volkens et al. 2019b). Table 4.2 gives an overview of the categories that are used to estimate the left-right positions. For example, per601 indicates the percentage of quasi-sentences devoted to the category "National Way of Life: Positive" (*right*) and per107 reflects the percentage of quasi-sentences devoted to the category "Internationalism: Positive" (*left*).

The policy position of the coalition government as adopted in the coalition agreements are measured on the basis of our newly compiled COALITION-AGREE dataset. Given that we closely followed the coding procedure of the MARPOR project dataset, the coded coalition agreements and the coded election manifestos can be easily compared. Table 4.2 displays how the codebook categories for estimating the left-right scale in the MARPOR project dataset relate to the codebook categories employed for our COALITIONAGREE dataset. Equation (4.2) follows a similar logic as Equation (4.1). Positive measures reflect a right position of the cabinet, negative measures reflect a left position of the cabinet.

$$CabinetPosition_j = R_j - L_j \qquad (4.2)$$

Figure 4.14 presents the left-right positions adopted in coalition agreements in comparison to the policy positions that coalition partners have published in their preceding election manifestos. The black dots indicate the policy positions settled in the coalition agreements, whereas the gray symbols indicate the policy positions of the coalition partners. Gray triangles indicate the junior partners' positions and gray dots the position of the parties holding the prime minister position. As we would expect, coalition agreements are typically a compromise between coalition partners and fall in between the positions held by individual coalition partners.

Surprisingly, the policy positions settled in coalition agreement are however not always in between those of the coalition partners, but sometimes exceed either the leftist or rightist position of one of the partners. More specifically, 50.45 percent of the coalition agreements fall in between the positions

Table 4.2 Variables used for calculating left-right policy positions

| Variable MARPOR (Party positions) | Variable COALITIONAGREE (Coalition positions) | Category |
|---|---|---|
| *Variables devoted to right positions* | | |
| per104 | cat_104_pr | Military: Positive |
| per201 | cat_201_pr | Freedom and Human Rights: Positive |
| per203 | cat_203_pr | Constitutionalism: Positive |
| per305 | cat_305_pr | Political Authority: Positive |
| per401 | cat_401_pr | Free Enterprise: Positive |
| per402 | cat_402_pr | Incentives: Positive |
| per407 | cat_407_pr | Protectionism: Negative |
| per414 | cat_414_pr | Economic Orthodoxy: Positive |
| per505 | cat_505_pr | Welfare State Limitation |
| per601 | cat_601_pr | National Way of Life: Positive |
| per603 | cat_603_pr | Traditional Morality: Positive |
| per605 | subcat_60511_pr + subcat_60512_pr + subcat_60513_pr + subcat_60514_pr + subcat_60515_pr | Law and Order: Positive |
| per606 | cat_606_pr | Civic Mindedness: Positive |
| *Variables devoted to left positions* | | |
| per103 | cat_103_pr | Anti-Imperialism: Positive |
| per105 | cat_105_pr | Military: Negative |
| per106 | cat_106_pr | Peace: Positive |
| per107 | cat_107_pr | Internationalism: Positive |
| per202 | cat_202_pr | Democracy: Positive |
| per403 | cat_403_pr | Market Regulation: Positive |
| per404 | cat_404_pr | Economic Planning: Positive |
| per406 | cat_406_pr | Protectionism: Positive |
| per412 | cat_412_pr | Controlled Economy: Positive |
| per413 | cat_413_pr | Nationalism: Positive |
| per504 | cat_504_pr | Welfare State Expansion |
| per506 | cat_506_pr | Education: Expansion |
| per701 | cat_701_pr | Labour Groups: Positive |

Scales are obtained from Budge (1999).

expressed by coalition parties before the election. This finding is puzzling and unexpected from the standpoint of coalition research which only focuses on the interaction among coalition parties to explain bargaining outcomes. In order to understand why coalition parties may sometimes adopt a policy position that does not fall within the winset, it is necessary to look at the external constraints that coalition parties are facing. Ellger and Klüver (2019) have for

POLICY POSITIONS SETTLED IN COALITION AGREEMENTS    91

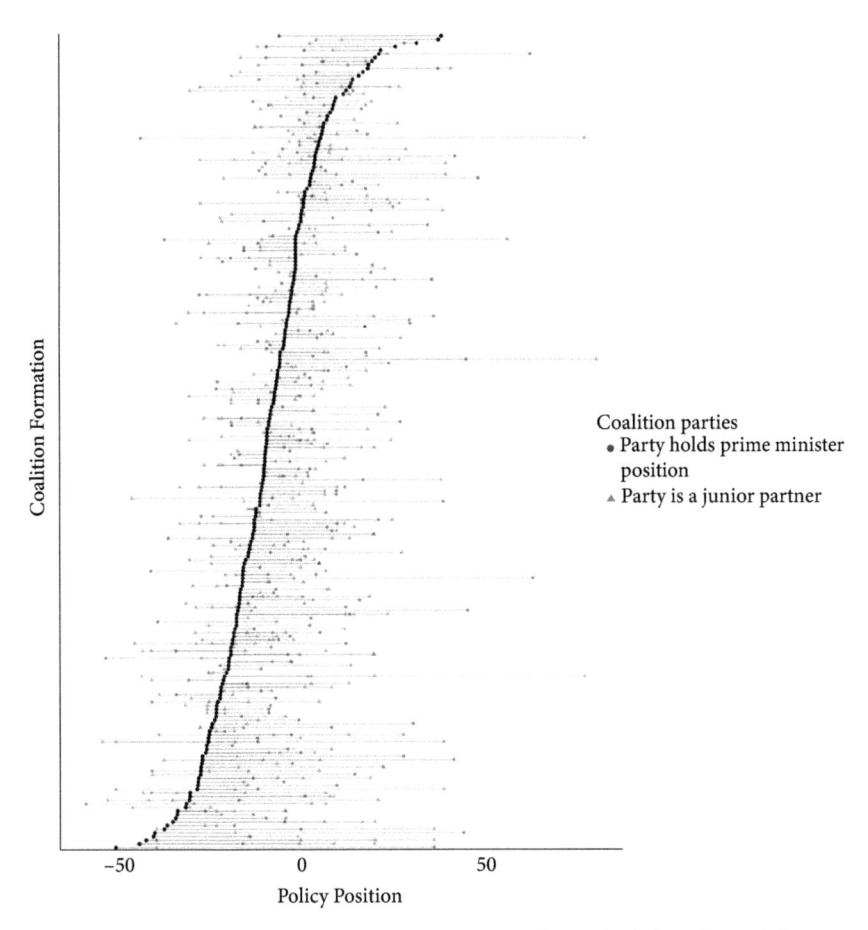

**Figure 4.14** Position of coalition agreements on the right-left scale and their distance to the coalition partners' positions

*Note:* Black dots indicate the policy positions settled in the coalition agreements; gray triangles indicate the junior partners' positions; gray dots the position of the parties holding the prime minister position.

instance shown that coalition parties adopt more immigration-skeptical positions than one would expect given their own position on the issue if they face a strong radical right challenger party.

We have so far only compared the position of the coalition agreement with the policy stances advocated by coalition parties in the preceding election campaign. However, building on decades of research on the allocation of ministerial portfolios, we can move beyond such a naive comparison by investigating the expected position of coalition agreements. In the early 1960s, Gamson (1961, p. 376) has argued that coalition parties should receive ministerial posts in close proportion to the parliamentary seats they contribute to the coalition. This proposition has received strong empirical support as dozens of studies of ministerial portfolio allocation have produced clear-cut empirical findings in favor of the proportionality of ministerial portfolio and legislative seat share (see e.g. Browne and Franklin 1973; Browne and Frendreis 1980; Schofield and Laver 1985; Warwick and Druckman 2006). As Laver and Schofield (1998, p. 7) notes, Gamson's proposition has produced "one of the highest non-trivial R squared figures in political science (0.93)." It is therefore no surprise that it turned into one of the very few uncontested social science regularities that was famously termed "Gamson's law."

Building on this work, we shed light on whether Gamson is not only able to predict the distribution of ministerial offices, but whether Gamson's law can also be applied to predict the policy output of coalition negotiations. Figure 4.15 plots the actual left-right policy positions of coalition agreements in comparison to the expected policy positions of the coalition agreements. Actual policy positions are marked with black dots, expected positions with gray dots. The expected policy positions were estimated by weighting the policy positions of coalition parties obtained from election manifestos by the share of legislative seats they contribute to the coalition (see Equation 4.3). The expected policy position of a coalition $j$ corresponds to the sum of all coalition parties' $i$ positions, weighted by the seat share of each party $i$.

$$ExpectedPosition_j = \sum_{i=1}^{N} PolicyPosition_i * SeatShare_i \qquad (4.3)$$

Comparing Figures 4.14 and 4.15 shows that the distance between a cabinet's actual policy position and the position expected by weighting the coalition partners' positions according to their seat share is in fact smaller than that of the positions settled in coalition agreements and the raw pre-electoral positions of the coalition parties. Thus, the descriptive graphical illustration provides initial support for Gamson's law. To shed further light on the predictive power of Gamson's law for explaining policy outcomes of coalition negotiations, we estimate a multivariate regression model in which we predict the left-right policy position of the coalition agreement with its expected left-right position that we obtain from weighting the policy position of coalition parties by their cabinet seat share. Table 4.3 presents the results of the regression analysis.

The regression analysis confirms our intuition. The expected position of coalition governments that was estimated based on weighting the policy positions of individual coalition parties by their cabinet seat share is a strong predictor of the left-right position of the coalition agreement. A one unit move to the right of the expected position on the left-right scale is associated with a shift of 0.616 units to the right of the coalition agreement. Thus, Gamson's law cannot only explain the allocation of ministerial portfolios in multiparty cabinets, but it also importantly contributes to predicting the policy output of the bargaining process during coalition formation.

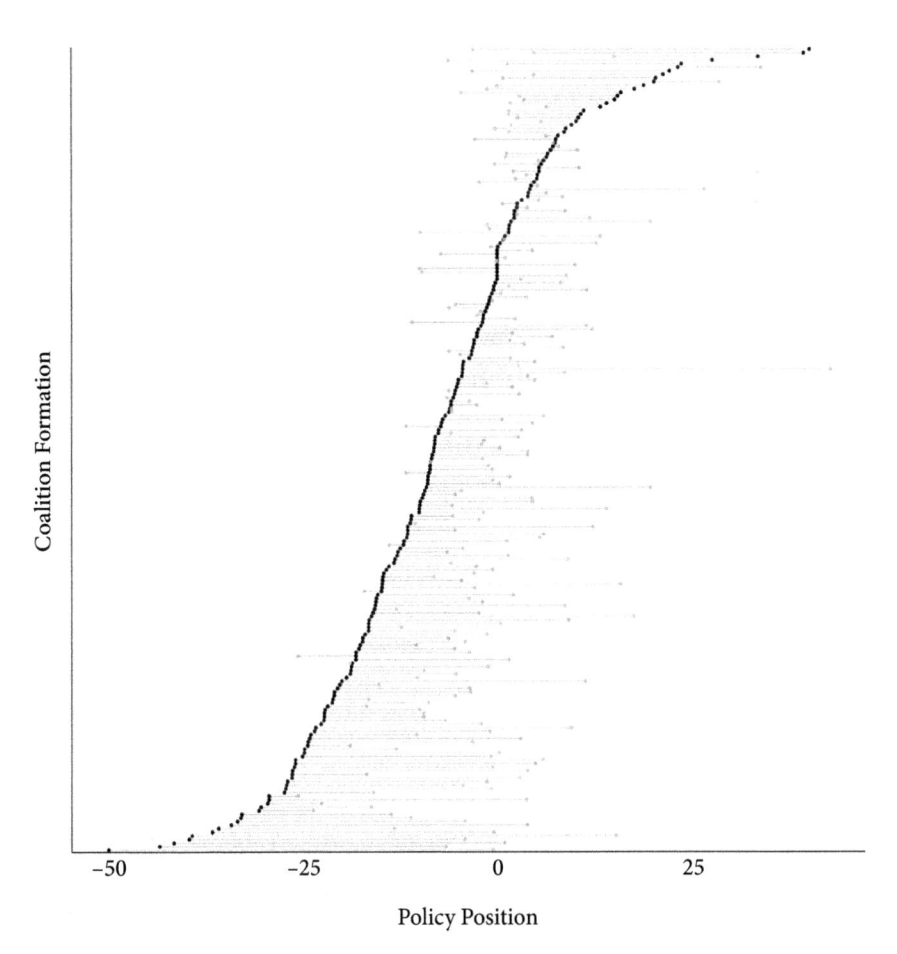

**Figure 4.15** Actual and expected positions of coalitions on the right-left scale

*Note:* Black dots indicate the actual policy positions of the coalition agreements; gray dots indicate the expected positions.

**Table 4.3** Regression predicting policy position of coalition agreement

|  | Model 4.1<br>Dependent Variable:<br>Left-right position of coalition agreement |
|---|---|
| Expected position | 0.616*** |
|  | (0.101) |
| Constant | −7.744*** |
|  | (2.147) |
| Observations | 229 |
| $R^2$ | 0.142 |

*** $p \leq 0.01$, ** $p \leq 0.05$, * $p \leq 0.10$; Standard errors clustered by countries in parentheses

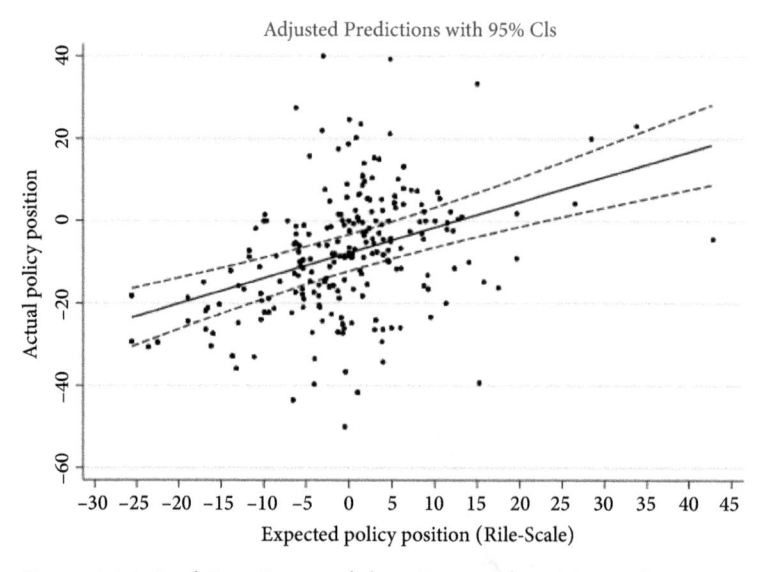

**Figure 4.16** Applying Gameson's law: Expected positions of coalitions on the left-right scale

However, as Figure 4.16 illustrates, the relationship is not as strong as the relationship between the share of ministerial offices and the share of legislative seats a coalition party contributes to the coalition as the $R^2$ amounts to 0.14 which is considerably smaller than in previous analyses of portfolio allocation where the $R^2$ amounts to 0.93 (see Laver and Schofield 1998: 7). Thus, Gamson can help us to understand both, the allocation of ministerial offices and the distribution of policy payoffs, but it is a stronger predictor of portfolio allocation. The deviation from the expected position is an indication that coalition parties do not only adopt a policy position based on a simple assessment of how many seats a party brings to the negotiation table, but that more complex bargaining processes are at play. In fact, given the theoretical argument that we make in Chapter 2, we are not surprised to see deviations from the expected positions as we suggest that coalition parties will demand policy concessions in return for granting a ministerial portfolio to a partner.

A case illustrating such complex bargaining processes are the coalition negotiations between the Christian Democratic CDU/CSU and the Liberal FDP following the 2009 Bundestag election in Germany.[2] Chancellor Angela Merkel made considerable concessions in the distribution of ministerial portfolios securing key policy objectives in the coalition agreement. Contrary to major policy demands of the FDP, the coalition agreement did not entail changes to the protection against dismissal and to co-determination in companies. The chancellor and prominent CDU leaders wanted to avoid conflicts with trade unions and therefore strongly opposed these policy demands of the FDP. In return for the policy concessions made by the FDP on these two issues, the FDP obtained five out of 15 ministerial portfolios which was more than what we would expect given Gamson's law. We empirically evaluate this argument in much more detail in Chapter 6.

## 4.5 Conclusion

In this chapter, we have used the newly compiled COALTIONAGREE dataset to provide a detailed and comprehensive analysis of the content of coalition agreements. We have started by illustrating how the length of coalition agreements varies across countries and over time. We have shown that the length of coalition agreements has on average increased over time, a trend that we do not only observe in Western European countries, but also in Eastern European countries.

We have afterward shed light on what type of issues are settled in coalition governments. We find that on average as much as 92 percent of the agreements are devoted to policies. By contrast, procedural rules and the allocation of ministerial offices receive very little attention. Thus, our analysis supports the view

---

[2] Source: https://www.sueddeutsche.de/politik/kabinett-merkel-schaeuble-guttenberg-und-ein-paar-neue-1.27523

that coalition agreements are important policy documents that set the stage for the policy-making activities of coalition cabinets during the time of office.

As our COALTIONAGREE dataset for the first time allows for measuring the attention to different policy issues, we analyzed which policy issues are covered in coalition agreements and how the attention to different policy issues varies over time and across countries. We find that policy issues that receive most attention in coalition contracts are Economy, Social Welfare, Civil Rights, and Environment. Economic policy, social welfare, and civil rights are clear positional issues on which political parties have very distinct policy positions, suggesting that coalition parties devote a lot of attention to potentially divisive policy issues. Environmental issues are by contrast valence issues, but given that the emergence of green parties challenging established mainstream parties is strongly associated with the rise of the environmental issue (Spoon, Hobolt, and de Vries 2014; De Vries and Hobolt 2020), it is not surprising that this issue also triggers a lot of attention. Hence, the analysis of issue coverage suggests that coalition parties particularly deal with divisive policy issues in coalition agreements. This finding provides support for the argument that coalition parties use coalition agreements as control devices to contain intra-cabinet conflict, a point to which we come back in Chapters 5 and 7.

Finally, we also shed light on the policy positions that coalition parties adopt in their coalition agreements. We find that Gamson's law cannot only explain the allocation of ministerial portfolios in multiparty cabinets, but that it also importantly contributes to predicting the policy positions adopted in coalition agreements. However, even though Gamson can help us to understand both, the allocation of ministerial offices and the distribution of policy payoffs, it is a stronger predictor of portfolio allocation. The fact that Gamson can only explain part of the story is actually not surprising for us. Since we argue in Chapter 2 that coalition parties demand policy concessions in return for granting a ministerial portfolio to a partner, we are not surprised to see deviations from the expected positions. Chapter 6 will return to this point and provide evidence for a multidimensional bargaining process in which ministerial offices are exchanged for policy concessions.

# PART III
# WHY DO GOVERNMENTS NEGOTIATE COALITION AGREEMENTS?

# 5
# Preference configuration and coalition agreements

## 5.1 Introduction

Why do coalition parties settle some policy issues in great detail while other issues are hardly mentioned in coalition agreements?[1] Coalition agreements are important policy platforms that crucially determine policy-making and coalition governance during the legislative term. Before taking over executive offices, coalition parties engage in lengthy coalition negotiations, bargaining over their joint policy agenda that is written down in public coalition agreements (Müller and Strøm 2008). Even though these "contracts" are not legally binding, previous research has shown that they significantly constrain the behavior of coalition partners (see e.g. Bäck, Müller, and Nyblade 2017). Schermann and Ennser-Jedenastik (2014b) for instance show that election pledges to which coalition governments commit themselves in their coalition agreements are significantly more likely to be fulfilled throughout the legislative term. Similarly, Timmermans and Breeman (2011) find that there is correspondence between issue priorities defined in the coalition agreement and the legislative agenda of coalition governments in the Netherlands. However, despite the central importance of coalition agreements for coalition governance and policy-making, we know remarkably little about what determines their content. Importantly, while coalition partners settle some policy issues in great detail, prescribing a detailed policy agenda, other issues are hardly mentioned in the agreement. In this chapter, we seek to explain this important puzzle by shedding light on why the attention that coalition parties devote to policy issues in coalition agreements varies so extensively.

Most previous empirical research on coalition agreements has focused on explaining either the presence of coalition agreements or their overall length,

---

[1] This chapter constitutes a revised and extended version of Klüver and Bäck "Coalition Agreements, Issue Attention and Cabinet Governance," which was published in *Comparative Political Studies* 52(13–14):1–37 (2019), DOI: 10.1177/0010414019830726.

or on explaining the variation in how comprehensively policies are generally covered (e.g. Strøm and Müller 1999a; Strøm, Müller, and Bergman 2008; Moury 2011; Indridason and Kristinsson 2013; Moury and Timmermans 2013; Eichorst 2014; Bowler et al. 2016). However, empirical results in this literature are characterized by contradictory findings as some scholars for example show that intra-coalition conflict leads to longer agreements (Indridason and Kristinsson 2013), whereas others show the opposite effect (Bowler et al. 2016). We suggest that these mixed results may be the result of focusing on the overall length of coalition agreements so that important variation across different policy issues is overlooked.

We know from previous literature on issue competition that political parties importantly differentiate between different policies (e.g. Budge and Farlie 1983; Petrocik 1996; Green-Pedersen 2007; van de Wardt, de Vries and Hobolt 2014; Spoon, Hobolt, and de Vries 2014; Klüver and Spoon 2016). For instance, imagine a coalition government in which there is severe conflict between coalition partners on economic policy while they largely agree on civil rights. We argue that such a cabinet would devote a lot of attention to economic policy in its coalition agreement prescribing a detailed policy agenda in order to leave little room of maneuver for their partners to prevent shirking in this contested domain. However, we expect that civil rights issues should hardly be mentioned in the agreement, as there is no need to engage in lengthy bargaining since the partners have similar views on the issue. At the aggregate level, the differences between these issues would cancel each other out so that merely looking at the overall length of coalition agreements as done by previous research overlooks important variation within cabinets.

The 2018 coalition agreement between the far-right League and the 5Star Movement in Italy, for example, is a case where the overlaps and conflicts between the two parties became clear. Pereira and Moury (2018) found that the parties had congruent views on European treaties and immigration, and the issue of foreign policy was only mentioned in considerably vaguer terms in the coalition agreement than institutional and public administration reform. The latter, in contrast, was remarkably specific in the coalition agreement, since the coalition parties differed on the issues of direct democracy and the "cost of politics."

We accordingly posit that just focusing on the length of coalition agreements is not sufficient to understand how features like divisiveness within the cabinet impacts coalition agreements. Instead, we suggest that a dependent variable focusing on how much coverage specific issues receive in the coalition agreement, what we here call issue attention, is much more appropriate.

On the basis of the theoretical framework presented in Chapter 2, we argue that ideological conflict in coalition cabinets positively affects issue attention as coalition parties have stronger incentives to negotiate a detailed policy agenda that constrains their coalition partners when intra-cabinet conflict is high (Indridason and Kristinsson 2013). However, we expect that this effect is conditioned by preference tangentiality among coalition partners the higher the tangentiality of a policy issue, the smaller the positive effect of cabinet conflict on issue attention. Our theoretical expectations are tested drawing on the newly compiled COALITIONAGREE dataset which we have presented in Chapters 3 and 4 in this book. This dataset is based on a comprehensive quantitative content analysis of agreements in 24 West and East European countries from 1945 until 2015. Using this novel dataset, we test our theoretical argument studying 224 coalition agreements negotiated by 189 political parties.

The results show support for our theoretical expectations, suggesting that both ideological conflict and preference tangentiality matter for how much attention is given to specific policy issues in the coalition agreement. Parties are clearly more likely to spend a lot of effort on negotiating and agreeing on issues that are divisive within the coalition, especially if they have overlapping preferences, that is, when similar issues are salient to several coalition partners. Our results suggest that parties draft coalition agreements to limit "ministerial drift" and have important implications for our understanding of coalition governance in parliamentary democracies.

## 5.2 Previous research

Strøm and Müller (1999*a*) set the agenda for the empirical study of coalition contracts, introducing a comparative dataset on coalition agreements in 13 Western European countries (1945–1996), showing that three different points are typically settled in coalition treaties: policy agreements, portfolio allocation, and procedural rules. This dataset, which was later extended by Strøm, Müller, and Bergman (2008), records whether a coalition had drafted a formal or informal agreement, provides data on the length of agreements measured by the number of words they contain, and includes a measure for how comprehensively policies were negotiated, measured by the share of the content devoted to policies more generally.

Several studies have focused on the impact of coalition agreements. For example, Moury and Timmermans (2013) study coalition agreements in Germany, Belgium, Italy, and the Netherlands, focusing on whether the agreements include deals over policy issues that the governing parties do not agree on. Moury (2011) analyzes how coalition agreements constrain the impact of ministers on policy decisions. Bäck, Müller, and Nyblade (2017) focus on the role of coalition agreements in solving so-called "common pool problems." Analyzing spending behavior in 17 Western European countries, they find that coalition agreements significantly reduce the negative effect of government fragmentation on spending in institutional contexts where prime ministerial power is low. Timmermans (2006, p. 265) focuses on the role of agreements in managing coalition conflicts, and suggests that written coalition agreements are drafted in order to "reduce mistrust and uncertainty" among party leaders. He suggests that a point of departure for assessing the impact of coalition agreements is the issues that were divisive during government formation. He argues that parties should focus on points that divide them, and that the agreement enables the party leaders to publicly "establish a policy equilibrium"(Timmermans 2006, p. 265).

Some recent scholarly work focuses on explaining the existence and the overall length of coalition agreements, thereby drawing primarily on the dataset provided by Strøm, Müller, and Bergman (2008). For example, Indridason and Kristinsson (2013) argue that coalition agreements are a mechanism for "taming moral hazard" and for avoiding "ministerial drift." They suggest that in cases where the moral hazard problem is serious, we should expect coalition agreements to be negotiated and to be more extensive. Empirically, they focus on 227 cabinets in 13 Western European countries, and the dependent variables in their analysis describe whether an agreement was negotiated at all, and how long the agreement was. Indridason and Kristinsson (2013, p. 840) conclude that the length of coalition agreements increases with factors "likely to exacerbate the moral hazard problem," for example as the ideological diversity between partners increases.

Also focusing on predicting the length of coalition agreements, Bowler et al. (2016) present a formal model aimed at understanding the trade-off between making detailed policy platforms and including details on conflict resolution mechanisms in the agreement. They evaluate predictions drawn from this model using data on coalition agreements in the German Länder, and show that when intra-coalition conflict is high, parties write shorter agreements, but are more likely to adopt procedures for conflict resolution.

Eichorst (2014) focuses on the number of words dedicated to policy language in the agreements (see also Huber and Shipan 2000). Analyzing agreements in 12 Western European countries, he finds that parties include high saliency issues in the agreement on policy dimensions where they are more divided.

Finally, Falcó-Gimeno (2014) presents an important explanation to why coalitions employ control mechanisms, such as, coalition agreements, focusing on the role of "preference tangentiality" as a predictor. "Preference tangentiality" among coalition partners is high when parties in a coalition have preferences that are not overlapping, or when issues are of differing saliency to the coalition partners. He suggests that when coalition parties are satisfied with a pure ministerial government model of policy-making, and with log-rolling policies, there are weaker incentives to implement control mechanisms. Looking at the existence of comprehensive coalition agreements, he finds support for this hypothesis.

To sum up, the previous literature has made important contributions by showing that coalition agreements affect policy-making and conflict resolution. Moreover, some studies have focused on explaining the overall length of coalition agreements, drawing primarily on the dataset by Strøm and colleagues (2008). However, the results are characterized by contradictory findings as some scholars show that intra-coalition conflict leads to longer agreements (Indridason and Kristinsson 2013), whereas others show the opposite (Bowler et al. 2016). As mentioned above, these mixed results may be due to the fact that important variation across different policy issues is overlooked when looking at the overall length of agreements. We instead suggest focusing on explaining "issue attention" across agreements. In the next section, we present our theoretical expectations predicting issue attention.

## 5.3 Theoretical argument

In Chapter 2, we have presented our theoretical framework explaining the use of coalition agreements as control devices in great detail. Our major argument is that coalition agreements are important control devices, but that their use varies with the preference configuration and the ministerial portfolio allocation. In this chapter, we focus on how the preference configuration among coalition partners affects the use of coalition agreements as control devices. In what follows, we first summarize our general theoretical argument and then discuss our expectations how the preference configuration affects the design of coalition contracts.

While parties that govern alone in single-party cabinets can autonomously make policy choices, governing in coalitions is much more complex. A major problem of multiparty cabinets is preference divergence. Coalition parties have important incentives to deviate from the coalition compromise in order to attain their own policy goals which is facilitated by information asymmetries as shirking may go unnoticed. However, pushing through favored policies without consulting coalition partners typically leads to intra-cabinet conflict and may ultimately result in early cabinet breakdown (Lupia and Strøm 1995; Saalfeld 2008). Since coalition parties want to avoid losing executive offices early due to disagreements with their partners, they frequently make use of control instruments to keep their partners in line (Thies 2001; Martin and Vanberg 2011a; Müller and Meyer 2010; Falcó-Gimeno 2014).

An important instrument through which coalition parties can control their partners are coalition agreements that are negotiated during the government formation stage before taking over executive offices. Even though these coalition agreements are not legally binding, they define the policy priorities of the coalition government and constrain the behavior of coalition parties in the upcoming term. While coalition negotiations are secret, coalition agreements are publicly released which enhances the compliance with the negotiated agreement as shirking could lead to public blaming and shaming. Accordingly, Thomson (2001), Moury (2011), and Schermann and Ennser-Jedenastik (2014b) show that election pledges to which coalition governments commit themselves in their coalition agreements are significantly more likely to be fulfilled throughout the legislative term than pledges not mentioned in the agreement.

We furthermore argue that the extent of control exercised through coalition agreements varies across issues. If policy issues are only briefly mentioned in a coalition agreement, the coalition agreement has little potential to constrain policy-making activity in this policy area. If coalition parties however spend dozens of pages on laying out their negotiated compromise in a specific policy area, ministers face a clearly prescribed legislative agenda that severely constrains their policy-making activity. Thus, while little attention to a given policy domain in the coalition agreement leaves considerable room of maneuver, devoting a lot of attention to a policy domains allows for laying out in much more detail what policies will be launched throughout the legislative term. In other words, coalition agreements are more capable of constraining the coalition partners by prescribing in detail which policy proposals will be adopted when the attention to a given policy issue is high.

While coalition agreements clearly have important benefits as they allow for controlling coalition partners, drafting coalition contracts also involves important costs. On the one hand, negotiating a coalition agreement involves important transaction costs as bargaining takes time, resources and creates opportunity costs. On the other hand, coalition agreements involve so-called "audience costs" as coalition parties typically have to make policy concessions to their partners (Müller and Meyer 2010, p. 529; Martin and Vanberg 2020*b*). Voters may not appreciate when the party makes too many concessions, and are likely to punish a party in future elections when compromises are perceived as "selling out" the party brand (Fortunato 2019).

For instance, the government formation in the Netherlands following the elections in March 2021 showed both types of costs, as well as preference divergence. The third Rutte cabinet resigned in January 2021 as they took responsibility for a scandal revolving wrongly labeling families fraudsters who were claiming child welfare benefits. The previous coalition consisted of the PM's People's Party for Freedom and Democracy (VVD), the centre-left D66, Christian Union (CU), and the Christian Democrats (CDA). The following elections brought 17 parties into parliament, the most fragmented Dutch parliament since World War II (Dimitrova and Steunenberg 2021). The coalition talks were particularly difficult because of divisive preferences over medical-ethical issues. The D66 initiated a draft bill for making euthanasia more accessible, which was backed by the VVD (Schleim 2021). The Christian Union was subsequently ruled out as a coalition partner, as their fundamentalist views strongly oppose that proposal. Only six months after the elections, the D66 leader announced they would consider joining a coalition with the CU again, and stressed the importance of drafting a coalition agreement (Corder 30.09.2021). For both the D66 and the CU this meant to risk compromising on an issue that is important to both of them, in order to limit the cost of even longer negotiations.

Specified as a simple cost-benefit calculus, the expected utility of giving "attention" to a policy issue in an agreement can be described as such: $U(attention) = PBC$, where P describes the probability that the coalition agreement will be adhered to, B describes the benefits associated with negotiating a deal, for example including policy benefits being the result of reduced "ministerial drift," and C describes the costs associated with making such a deal. Parties should thus give attention to a policy issue in the agreement when $PB > C$. What features are then likely to influence parties cost-benefit calculus and make it more or less likely that an issue is covered in the coalition agreement?

In this chapter, we focus on how the preference configuration of coalition parties affects the use of coalition agreements as control devices, or more specifically, the attention that coalition parties devote to different policy issues in the contract. Even though coalition parties join forces for the sake of taking over government, they have their own policy agenda. Despite the fact that coalitions are more likely to form between ideologically proximate partners (De Swaan 1973), coalition parties have typically different policy priorities and are more divided on some policy issues than on others. For instance, coalition parties may be united on fighting climate change, but they may be divided on the question whether to postpone the retirement age.

The incentive to shirk from the negotiated coalition agreement are much higher on highly divisive issues as coalition parties seek to enact their own preferred policies. Thus, the need for strong control is higher on issues that divide the cabinet as coalition parties seek to limit ministerial draft in these policy domains. We therefore argue that coalition parties are more willing to bear the costs associated with negotiating a detailed policy compromise in divisive policy areas. By contrast, if coalition parties share the same policy views on an issue, there is no need to invest time and resources in writing down dozens of pages about an issue. Thus, we expect that coalition parties focus primarily on divisive issues in coalition agreements to effectively control their partners throughout the legislative term and to avoid intra-cabinet conflict during the time of office.

**Hypothesis 1:** *The higher the intra-cabinet conflict over a policy issue, the higher the attention to the issue in the coalition agreement.*

However, the costs and benefits of drafting coalition agreements are not only affected by the conflict between coalition partners. The preference configuration in coalition governments is also importantly shaped by the tangentiality of the preferences of government parties (Luebbert 1986; Falcó-Gimeno 2014). Coalition parties may have opposing views on an issue, but that does not necessarily imply that coalition parties would have a fight over the issue. For instance, imagine a hypothetical coalition government consisting of party A and party B. Party A strongly cares about agricultural policy while party B places very little emphasis on this issue. At the same time, family policy is a major issue for party B while party A pays very little attention to this issue. Even though these parties have different policy positions in these two issue areas, the likelihood for intra-cabinet conflict is low since they do not care about the same issues or, in other words, since they do not have overlapping preferences.

Thus, when coalition partners do not care about the same policy issues, there is no need to come to a compromise on the issues, even though they may be highly divisive. For example, if a Green party, which emphasizes environmental issues in its program, coalesces with another party which does not care much about environmental policy (or issues affected by environmental policy), the Green party is likely to be given "free reign" in the Ministry of Environment, and the parties do not need to negotiate which policy objectives to realize in this policy area within the process of coalition bargaining. Hence, there will be little attention paid to environmental issues in the coalition agreement. Following this line of argument, we suggest this conditional hypothesis:

**Hypothesis 2:** *The positive effect of intra-cabinet conflict on the control exercised through coalition agreements decreases with the tangentiality among coalition parties.*

Finally, it is not only the policy conflict or the tangentiality of government preferences that is decisive for the cost-benefit calculation of whether to regulate a policy area in much detail in the coalition agreement, but also the overall salience of a policy area is important. If an issue is not important to any of the coalition partners, it should not matter much in coalition negotiations irrespective of potential differences that coalition parties might have on the issue. For instance, sport policy is typically an issue that is of much less relevance to government parties than other high-salience issues such as defense, the economy, or social welfare. As coalition partners seek to avoid intra-cabinet conflict in order not to risk a breakdown of the cabinet, it is very unlikely that a low salience issue will create any major disagreements during the legislative term. Thus, coalition parties have little incentive to invest time and resources into preparing lengthy sections on this for the coalition agreement.

We therefore expect that the negative effect of conflict as well as the conditioning effect of preference tangentiality are conditioned by the overall salience of the issue among coalition partners. Hence, if an issue is not important to any of the coalition parties, conflict and tangentiality should not matter. To clarify; if an issue is not salient to any of the coalition partners, it is reasonable to expect that neither the main effect of conflict, nor the conditioning effect of tangentiality are substantively important. We therefore expect that there is a three-way interaction affect at play.

**Hypothesis 3:** *The lower the joint salience of an issue, the smaller the effect of intra-cabinet conflict and the smaller the conditioning effect of preference tangentiality.*

## 5.4 Research design and data

In the following, we will explain how we test our theoretical argument regarding the effect of preference configuration among cabinet members. More specifically, we begin by explaining the operationalization of the dependent variable before we turn to the measurement of the independent variables. At the end of this section, descriptive statistics for all variables will be reported.

### 5.4.1 Dataset

To evaluate our theoretical expectations explaining the issue attention in coalition agreements, we will make use of the newly compiled COALITION-AGREE dataset on the policy content of coalition agreements that we have illustrated and presented in Chapters 3 and 4. In this particular chapter, the analysis is based on 224 coalition agreements negotiated by 181 political parties in 24 West and East European countries from 1945 until 2015.[2] These countries include Austria, Belgium, Bulgaria, the Czech Republic, Denmark, Estonia, Finland, Germany, Greece, Hungary, Iceland, Ireland, Latvia, Lithuania, Luxembourg, the Netherlands, Norway, Poland, Portugal, Romania, Slovakia, Slovenia, Sweden, and the United Kingdom. The selection of countries follows the established standard in coalition research and only includes European democracies that were governed by coalition cabinets that have publicly released a coalition agreement at least once in the time period under investigation (see e.g. Andersson, Bergman, and Ersson 2014). This country sample is characterized by variation in several institutional features, which strengthens the external validity of our findings.

### 5.4.2 Operationalization of the dependent and main independent variables

On the basis of the content analysis of coalition agreements laid out in Chapters 3 and 4, we measure issue attention in coalition agreements by the

---

[2] As matching the coalition agreement dataset with data from the Manifestos Project (Volkens et al. 2017) is necessary for the analysis conducted in this chapter the number of coalition agreements reduced from 229 agreements included in our original dataset to 224 agreements as the Manifestos Project has not (yet) coded the coalition partners' respective election manifestos for five cabinets in our sample.

percentage of quasi-sentences (positive and negative) in the coalition agreement devoted to a policy issue (see also Bäck, Debus, and Dumont 2011; Klüver and Spoon 2016; Spoon and Klüver 2014, 2015). The underlying rationale for using this approach is the following: A coalition agreement has a finite number of words that parties can use to express their stance on different policy issues. When drafting their coalition agreement, parties therefore have to decide how much attention they place on different issues, that is, how many words they will allocate to different policy domains. Devoting more attention to a policy issue necessarily includes a longer bargaining process about this issue as coalition parties typically settle on a much more detailed policy agenda in this issue area (Strøm, Müller, and Bergman 2008).

In order to test the effect of issue-specific cabinet conflict on the attention that is devoted to different policy issues in the coalition agreement, we rely on the election manifesto data provided by the above-mentioned Manifestos Project, computing issue-specific policy positions using the widely used additive percentage scores advocated by Budge (1999). The positions are estimated by calculating the percentages of positive and negative mentions of a policy issue, and then subtracting the percentage of negative mentions from the percentage of positive mentions of that issue. We identified 11 issue areas based on the Manifestos Project for which the codebook includes positional categories so that we can estimate not only the attention to the issue, but also the issue-specific policy positions of the parties (see table 5.1 for an overview of the issue areas and the associated codebook categories). Second, following Tsebelis (2002), we then generated the range of the policy positions held by cabinet parties in the 11 issue areas to operationalize issue-specific cabinet conflict.

Our second hypothesis suggests that preference tangentiality decreases the positive effect of intra-cabinet conflict on issue attention in coalition agreements. Tangentiality refers to the relative salience of policy issues for coalition parties. Preferences of coalition parties are highly tangential if a policy issue is highly salient to one coalition party, but not salient to the coalition partners. We operationalize the tangentiality of coalition parties preferences over a policy issue as follows. First, we measure the salience of a policy issue for all coalition parties by the relative number of quasi-sentences devoted to the issue in their respective election manifestos. Second, we compute the standard deviation of the issue-specific salience scores of all coalition parties. Thus, as a measure for preference tangentiality, the standard deviation expresses

Table 5.1 Issue areas and codebook categories

| Issue Area | MARPOR policy categories | COALITIONAGREE policy categories Left position | COALITIONAGREE policy categories Right position |
|---|---|---|---|
| Agriculture | 406: Protectionism (positive)<br>407: Protectionism (negative)<br>703: Agriculture and farmers (positive) | 406 Protectionism: Positive<br>703.1 Agriculture and Farmers: Positive | 407 Protectionism: Negative<br>703.1 Agriculture and Farmers: Negative |
| Civil rights | 201: Freedom and human rights<br>202: Democracy<br>603: Traditional Morality (positive)<br>604: Traditional Morality (negative)<br>605: Law and order<br>705: Underprivileged minority groups<br>706: Noneconomic demographic groups | 201 Freedom and Human Rights: Positive<br>202 Democracy<br>604 Traditional Morality: Negative<br>605.2 Law and Order: Negative<br>705 Minority Groups: Positive<br>706 Noneconomic Demographic Groups: Positive | 603 Traditional Morality: Positive<br>605.1 Law and Order: Positive |
| Education | 506: Education expansion<br>507: Education limitation | 506 Education Expansion | 507 Education Limitation |
| Environment | 416: Antigrowth economy (positive)<br>501: Environmental protection<br>410: Economic growth (positive) | 416 Antigrowth Economy: Positive<br>501 Environmental Protection: Positive | 410 Economic Growth: Positive |
| European integration | 108: EC/EU (positive)<br>110: EC/EU (negative) | 108 European Integration: Positive | 110 European Integration: Negative |
| Decentralization | 301: Decentralization<br>302: Centralization | 301 Decentralization: Positive | 302 Centralization: Positive |

| | | |
|---|---|---|
| Immigration | 601: National way of life (positive) | 601 National Way of Life: Positive |
| | 602: National way of life (negative) | 602 National Way of Life: Negative |
| | 607: Multiculturalism (positive) | 607 Multiculturalism: Positive |
| | 608: Multiculturalism (negative) | 608 Multiculturalism: Negative |
| Social welfare | 503: Equality (positive) | 503 Equality: Positive |
| | 504: Welfare state expansion | 504 Welfare State Expansion |
| | 505: Welfare state limitation | 505 Welfare State Limitation |
| Defense | 104: Military (positive) | 104 Military: Positive |
| | 105: Military (negative) | 105 Military: Negative |
| Economy | 401: Free market economy | 401 Free Enterprise: Positive |
| | 402: Incentives | 402 Incentives: Positive |
| | 403: Market regulation | 403 Market Regulation: Positive |
| | 404: Economic planning | 404 Economic Planning: Positive |
| | 409: Keynesian demand management | 409 Keynesian Demand Management: Positive |
| | 412: Controlled economy | 412 Controlled Economy: Positive |
| | 413: Nationalization | 413 Nationalization: Positive |
| | 414: Economic orthodoxy | 414 Economic Orthodoxy: Positive |
| International politics | 101: Foreign and special relations (positive) | 101 Foreign Special Relationships: Positive |
| | 102: Foreign and special relations (negative) | 102 Foreign Special Relationships: Negative |
| | 103: Anti-imperialism (positive) | 103 Anti-Imperialism: Positive |
| | 106: Peace (positive) | 106 Peace: Positive |
| | 107: Internationalism (positive) | 107 Internationalism: Positive |
| | 109: Internationalism (negative) | 109 Internationalism: Negative |

the varying salience of a policy issue for the different coalition parties (see Falcó-Gimeno 2014). The smaller the standard deviation, the larger the overlap of coalition parties preferences as a policy issue is equally salient to all partners.

Our third hypothesis stresses the importance of the joint salience of the issue among coalition partners, which is expected to condition the impact of tangentiality and issue-specific cabinet conflict. We measure the joint salience of an issue by computing the salience of an issue to each coalition partner drawing on the relative number of quasi-sentences devoted to the issue in the coalition parties election manifestos, and then computing the average of the salience of the issue across all cabinet parties.

### 5.4.3 Operationalization of control variables

To analyze the impact of intra-cabinet conflict, preference tangentiality, and joint issue saliency, we control for several variables which might potentially confound the hypothesized effects. First, we control for the effective number of parliamentary parties as more parties in parliament potentially provide more alternative coalition options for cabinet parties and uncertainty increases with the number of parties in parliament. Tighter control mechanisms, like detailed coalition agreements, are therefore more likely to prevent an early breakdown of the cabinet when coalition parties have potentially more alternative partners in a situation of greater uncertainty. Second, we control for the number of cabinet parties (Müller and Strøm 2008) since the number of parties involved in a multiparty cabinet may increase preference heterogeneity so that coalition parties negotiate longer, more detailed agreements. Third, we also include a variable measuring the minority status of a coalition in the empirical analysis as Indridason and Kristinsson (2013) show that minority status importantly affects the likelihood and the length of coalition agreements. Fourth, we also control for the minimal winning status of a cabinet as the incentives for comprehensive coalition agreements are higher in minimal winning coalitions because each party's contribution is necessary for the coalition's functioning (Müller and Strøm 2008).

The data for measuring the effective number of parliamentary parties, the number of cabinet parties and minority status are obtained from the Parliaments and Governments Database (ParlGov) (Döring 2013; Döring and Manow 2016), while the minimal winning status was measured by relying

Table 5.2 Descriptive statistics (Chapter 5)

| Variable | N | Mean | Std. Dev. | Min | Max |
| --- | --- | --- | --- | --- | --- |
| Issue attention | 2,464 | 5.251 | 5.755 | 0.000 | 56.944 |
| Issue-specific cabinet conflict | 2,464 | 5.765 | 6.753 | 0.000 | 54.756 |
| Preference tangentiality | 2,464 | 2.911 | 3.224 | 0.000 | 28.930 |
| Joint salience | 2,464 | 6.268 | 5.941 | 0.000 | 34.964 |
| Effective number of parliamentary parties | 2,464 | 4.579 | 1.337 | 2.195 | 9.051 |
| No of cabinet parties | 2,464 | 3.018 | 1.086 | 2.000 | 6.000 |
| Minority status | 2,464 | 0.156 | 0.361 | 0.000 | 1.000 |
| Minimal winning status | 2,464 | 0.571 | 0.495 | 0.000 | 1.000 |

on data gathered from the European Representative Democracy Data Archive (ERRDA) (Andersson and Ersson 2012). Descriptive statistics for all variables are presented in Table 5.2.

## 5.5 Empirical analysis

In this section, we will test our theoretical expectations based on the new COALITIONAGREE dataset we compiled. We present the results of multilevel regression analyses evaluating the impact of issue-specific cabinet conflict, preference tangentiality, and joint issue salience on issue attention in coalition agreements.

Our data is hierarchically structured as the coalition agreements in our sample are negotiated by cabinet parties in 24 different countries. Given that these countries vary extensively with regard to their electoral system, the structure of the party system and their experience with coalition governance, coalition cabinets in the same country face the same contextual characteristics that are different from those in other countries. Estimating an ordinary linear regression model on the basis of such a data structure may result in deflated standard errors and inflated type I error rates so the significance of estimated effects may be overrated (Steenbergen and Jones 2002, pp. 219–220). To model this particular data structure, we rely on a multilevel linear regression model that takes the clustering of cabinets in countries into account by allowing for residual components at the country level.

Table 5.3 presents the results of the multilevel linear regression analysis. Model 5.1 includes all main effects as well as the interaction effect between

Table 5.3 Results from multilevel regression

| DV: Issue attention in coalition agreements | Model 5.1 | Model 5.2 |
|---|---|---|
| *Fixed effects* | | |
| Issue-specific cabinet conflict | 0.281*** | 0.283*** |
|  | (0.032) | (0.067) |
| Preference tangentiality | −0.006 | −0.120 |
|  | (0.061) | (0.127) |
| Joint salience | 0.488*** | 0.566*** |
|  | (0.022) | (0.033) |
| Effective no of parliamentary parties | 0.207* | 0.209* |
|  | (0.126) | (0.125) |
| No of cabinet parties | −0.298* | −0.292* |
|  | (0.163) | (0.164) |
| Minority status | 0.294 | 0.281 |
|  | (0.397) | (0.396) |
| Minimal winning status | 0.461 | 0.478 |
|  | (0.299) | (0.298) |
| Issue-specific cabinet conflict * Preference tangentiality | −0.017*** | −0.001 |
|  | (0.002) | (0.006) |
| Issue-specific cabinet conflict * Joint salience |  | −0.007 |
|  |  | (0.004) |
| Preference tangentiality * Joint salience |  | −0.002 |
|  |  | (0.008) |
| Conflict* Preference tangentiality * Joint salience |  | −0.000 |
|  |  | (0.000) |
| Constant | 0.734 | 0.565 |
|  | (0.662) | (0.678) |
| *Random effects* | | |
| Country-level variance | 0.967 | 0.983 |
|  | (0.401) | (0.403) |
| Cabinet-level variance | 20.704 | 20.569 |
|  | (0.593) | (0.589) |
| N | 2464 | 2464 |
| Log likelihood | −7248 | −7240 |
| AIC | 14518 | 14509 |

*** $p \leq 0.01$, ** $p \leq 0.05$, * $p \leq 0.10$; Standard errors in parentheses

conflict and preference tangentiality while Model 5.2 additionally includes a three-way interaction effect between conflict, preference tangentiality and joint salience. In line with hypothesis 1, the regression analysis shows that issue-specific cabinet conflict has a statistically significant positive effect on the attention that coalition parties pay to policy issues in their agreements. Hence, coalition parties talk more extensively in their treaty about the issues that divide them. If coalition partners have strongly diverging preferences on an issue, they choose to spell out the policy agenda in this issue area in great detail to leave as little room of maneuver as possible to their partners. The more detailed the description of the policy proposals that will be enacted, the smaller the potential for shirking or "ministerial drift."

To further illustrate the effect of issue-specific cabinet conflict on the attention that coalition parties pay to different policy issues in their coalition agreement, we have simulated predicted values as suggested by King, Tomz, and Wittenberg (2000). Figure 5.1 plots the simulated predicted issue attention (y-axis) and as intra-cabinet conflict over policy issue varies (x-axis) while holding all control variables constant at their mean (continuous variables) and median (categorical variables) values. The solid line represents the predicted values and the dashed lines indicate the 95 percent confidence interval. The tick marks along the x-axis indicate the distribution of the conflict variable. Figure 5.1 clearly shows that the attention that is devoted to policy issues in the coalition agreement increases substantially with the ideological conflict among coalition partners. The larger the conflict over an issue among coalition parties, the more attention they devote to this issue in their coalition agreements.

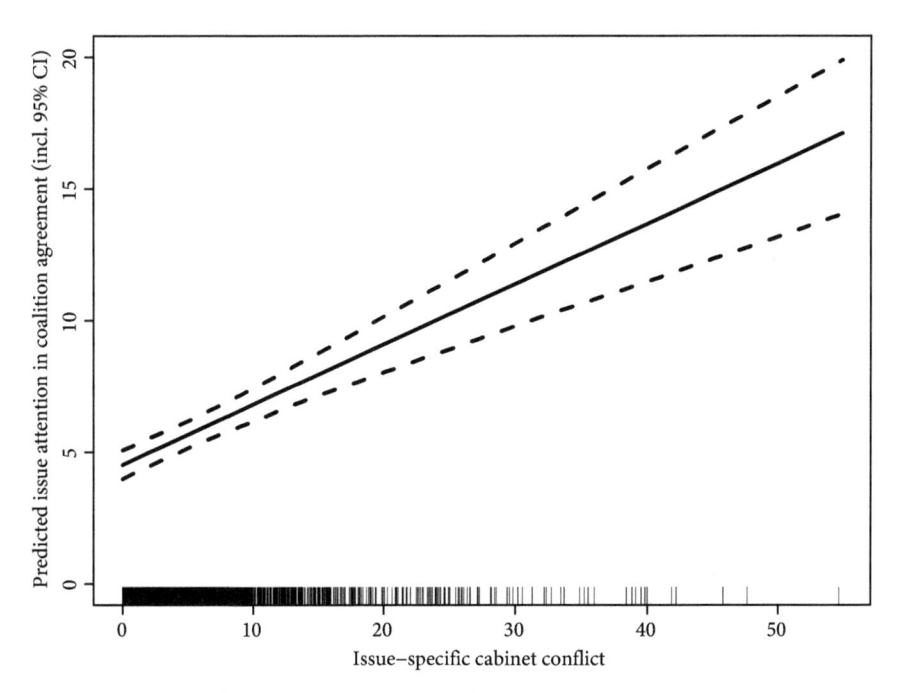

**Figure 5.1** The effect of intra-cabinet conflict
*Note:* The figure is based on Model 5.1.

Turning to evaluate our second hypothesis, we ask if the effect of intra-cabinet conflict varies depending on the tangentiality of different issues. In line with hypothesis 2, the empirical analysis indicates that preference tangentiality conditions the effect of intra-cabinet conflict. More specifically, Model 5.1 shows that there is a statistically significant negative interaction effect, suggesting that the positive effect of conflict decreases as preference tangentiality increases. In other words, intra-coalition conflict seems to matter a great deal when preference tangentiality is low, that is when all coalition partners equally care about a policy issue. If that is the case, all coalition partners have strong incentives to bind their coalition partners by spelling out the policy agenda in great detail, to make sure there is no room of maneuver left for their partners to defect from the compromise. By contrast, if preference tangentiality is high, that is, if one coalition party cares a lot about an issue while its partners are largely indifferent to the issue, parties talk less about the issue. To further illustrate the conditioning effect of preference tangentiality, we have computed a marginal effects plot (see Brambour, Clark, and Golder 2006). Figure 5.2 shows the marginal effect of issue-specific intra-cabinet conflict on issue attention in coalition agreements as preference tangentiality varies. The

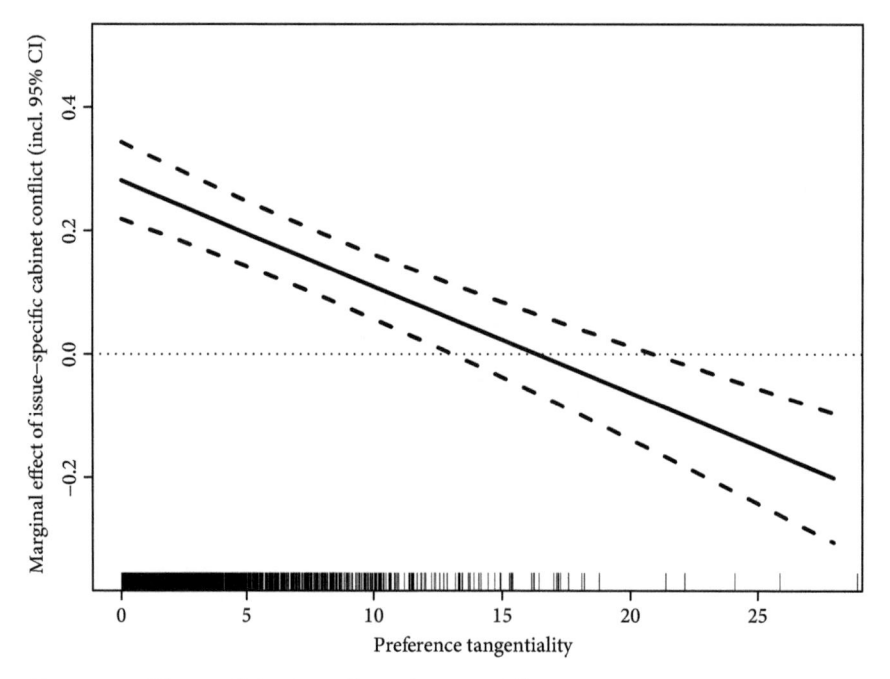

**Figure 5.2** The conditioning effect of tangentiality
*Note:* The figure is based on Model 5.2.

solid line indicates the point estimates of the marginal effect, while the dashed lines indicate the 95 percent confidence interval. The figure clearly demonstrates that the positive effect of intra-cabinet conflict over policy issues on the attention paid to these issues in the coalition agreement declines as preference tangentiality rises.

Finally, in order to empirically assess whether the joint salience of a policy issue has an effect on the attention to the issue in the coalition agreement, we have estimated a second model that includes a three-way interaction effect between intra-cabinet conflict, tangentiality and joint salience (see Model 5.2 in Table 5.3). Even though the coefficient of the three-way interaction term is statistically insignificant in Model 5.2, it is possible that the marginal effect of conflict is significant for substantively relevant values of the modifying variables (Brambour, Clark, and Golder 2006, p. 74). We have therefore computed a marginal effects plot on the basis of Model 5.2 to investigate how the effect of intra-cabinet conflict varies with tangentiality and the joint salience of an issue among cabinet parties as recommended by Brambor et al. (2006).

Figure 5.3 shows the marginal effect of cabinet conflict on issue attention in the coalition agreement as tangentiality varies from its minimum

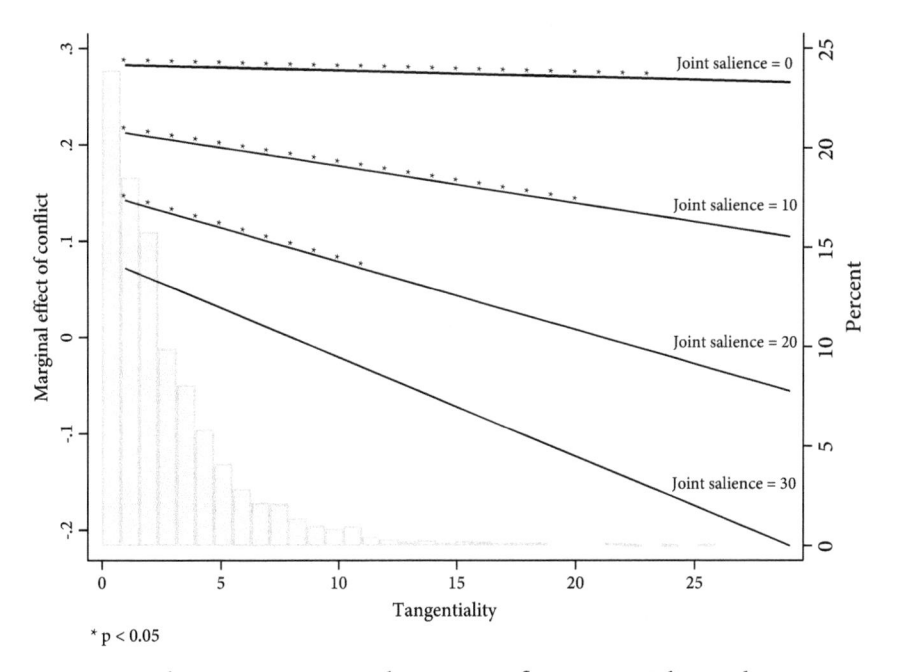

**Figure 5.3** Three-way interaction between conflict, tangentiality, and joint salience

*Note:* The figure is based on Model 5.2.

to maximum value for different values of joint salience. The solid lines indicate the point estimates of the marginal effects while the stars indicate the statistical significance of the marginal effects. The figure demonstrates that the marginal effect of conflict declines with tangentiality while it increases with the joint salience of an issue among coalition partners.

To sum up our results, analyzing the variation of policy issue attention across coalition agreements, our hypotheses are supported. We find that the higher the intra-cabinet conflict over a policy issue, the higher the attention to the issue in the coalition agreement. However, the effect of cabinet conflict is clearly conditional on preference tangentiality and the overall salience of the issue within the cabinet as the effect of conflict declines with tangentiality, while it increases with the joint salience of an issue among coalition partners.

## 5.6 Robustness checks

In order to test the robustness of the findings, we have estimated a number of additional model specifications in order to make sure that our results are not driven by a specific modeling decision. First, the dependent variable issue attention is a percentage, not a continuous variable which suggests that a linear regression model may not be appropriate. In addition, about 15 percent of the observations are zeros which is not an overly excessive share of zeros, but something to keep in mind. We therefore also estimated a multilevel tobit regression to take into account that the dependent variable can only take on values between 0 and 100. Since tobit models allow for estimating the probability of observing a zero as well as for estimating the magnitude of the dependent variable in case of a non-zero outcome when calculating the regression coefficients, tobit models are also frequently estimated when a dataset is zero-inflated (McDonald and Moffitt 1980). Table 5.4 presents the results of the multilevel tobit model. The results are essentially the same as the findings we obtain using the linear multilevel model.

Second, given that the dependent variable measures the attention that parties pay to 11 different policy issues in their agreements, we have also estimated an alternative model specification that additionally includes issue-specific fixed effects to account for any issue-specific variance in our data (see Table 5.5). The results similarly confirm our main findings.

Third, since coalition agreements not only contain policy-related content, but also talk about procedural rules and payoff allocation (see Figure 4.7), we

**Table 5.4** Results from multilevel tobit regression

| DV: Issue attention in coalition agreements | Model 5.3 | Model 5.4 |
|---|---|---|
| *Fixed effects* | | |
| Issue-specific cabinet conflict | 0.281*** | 0.283*** |
| | (0.032) | (0.067) |
| Preference tangentiality | −0.006 | −0.120 |
| | (0.061) | (0.127) |
| Joint salience | 0.488*** | 0.566*** |
| | (0.022) | (0.033) |
| Effective no. of parliamentary parties | 0.207* | 0.209* |
| | (0.126) | (0.126) |
| No. of cabinet parties | −0.298* | −0.292* |
| | (0.163) | (0.164) |
| Minority status | 0.294 | 0.281 |
| | (0.400) | (0.399) |
| Minimal winning status | 0.461 | 0.478 |
| | (0.300) | (0.300) |
| Issue-specific cabinet conflict * Preference tangentiality | −0.017*** | −0.001 |
| | (0.002) | (0.006) |
| Issue-specific cabinet conflict * Joint salience | | −0.007 |
| | | (0.004) |
| Preference tangentiality * Joint salience | | −0.002 |
| | | (0.008) |
| Conflict * Preference tangentiality * Joint salience | | −0.000 |
| | | (0.000) |
| Constant | 0.734 | 0.565 |
| | (0.667) | (0.683) |
| *Random effects* | | |
| Country-level variance | 0.967** | 0.982** |
| | (0.401) | (0.403) |
| Cabinet-level variance | 20.704*** | 20.569*** |
| | (0.593) | (0.589) |
| N | 2,464 | 2,464 |
| Log likelihood | −7248 | −7240 |
| AIC | 14518 | 14509 |

*** $p \leq 0.01$, ** $p \leq 0.05$, * $p \leq 0.10$; Standard errors in parentheses

have also conducted a robustness check in which we created the dependent variable issue attention only on the basis of the policy-related quasi-sentences included in coalition agreements. The multilevel analysis confirms the results of our main model specification (see Table 5.6).

**Table 5.5** Results from multilevel linear regression with issue fixed effects

| DV: Issue attention in coalition agreements | Model 5.5 | Model 5.6 |
|---|---|---|
| *Fixed effects* | | |
| Issue-specific cabinet conflict | 0.204*** | 0.213*** |
| | (0.030) | (0.063) |
| Preference tangentiality | −0.026 | −0.225* |
| | (0.057) | (0.120) |
| Joint salience | 0.255*** | 0.280*** |
| | (0.027) | (0.038) |
| Effective no. of parliamentary parties | 0.196* | 0.195 |
| | (0.119) | (0.118) |
| No. of cabinet parties | −0.259* | −0.264* |
| | (0.153) | (0.154) |
| Minority status | 0.273 | 0.262 |
| | (0.373) | (0.373) |
| Minimal winning status | 0.430 | 0.433 |
| | (0.280) | (0.279) |
| Issue-specific cabinet conflict * Preference tangentiality | −0.010*** | 0.005 |
| | (0.002) | (0.006) |
| Issue-specific cabinet conflict * Joint salience | | −0.004 |
| | | (0.004) |
| Preference tangentiality * Joint salience | | 0.010 |
| | | (0.008) |
| Conflict * Preference tangentiality * Joint salience | | −0.001** |
| | | (0.000) |
| Constant | 1.321* | 1.407** |
| | (0.694) | (0.712) |
| *Random effects* | | |
| Country-level variance | 1.186 | 1.180 |
| | (0.449) | (0.446) |
| Cabinet-level variance | 17.924 | 17.858 |
| | (0.513) | (0.511) |
| N | 2,464 | 2,464 |
| Log likelihood | −7074 | −7069 |
| AIC | 14190 | 14186 |

*** $p \leq 0.01$, ** $p \leq 0.05$, * $p \leq 0.10$; Standard errors in parentheses

Fourth, in order to check whether our results hold when using an alternative data source for measuring intra-cabinet conflict, we have looked into expert survey data from the Chapel Hill expert survey which is the most comprehensive expert survey that is available for policy positions of political parties

**Table 5.6** Results from multilevel linear regression with policy-related issue attention as the dependent variable

| DV: Issue attention in coalition agreements | Model 5.7 | Model 5.8 |
|---|---|---|
| *Fixed effects* | | |
| Issue-specific cabinet conflict | 0.299*** | 0.299*** |
|  | (0.035) | (0.074) |
| Preference tangentiality | 0.004 | −0.132 |
|  | (0.067) | (0.139) |
| Joint salience | 0.534*** | 0.628*** |
|  | (0.024) | (0.037) |
| Effective no. of parliamentary parties | 0.213 | 0.216 |
|  | (0.137) | (0.137) |
| No. of cabinet parties | −0.294 | −0.284 |
|  | (0.179) | (0.180) |
| Minority status | 0.409 | 0.394 |
|  | (0.435) | (0.433) |
| Minimal winning status | 0.499 | 0.521 |
|  | (0.328) | (0.327) |
| Issue-specific cabinet conflict * Preference tangentiality | −0.019*** | 0.002 |
|  | (0.003) | (0.007) |
| Issue-specific cabinet conflict * Joint salience |  | −0.008* |
|  |  | (0.005) |
| Preference tangentiality * Joint salience |  | −0.002 |
|  |  | (0.009) |
| Conflict * Preference tangentiality * Joint salience |  | −0.000 |
|  |  | (0.000) |
| Constant | 0.785 | 0.577 |
|  | (0.718) | (0.735) |
| *Random effects* | | |
| Country-level variance | 0.986 | 1.004 |
|  | (0.423) | (0.426) |
| Cabinet-level variance | 25.171 | 24.968 |
|  | (0.721) | (0.715) |
| N | 2,464 | 2,464 |
| Log likelihood | −7487 | −7478 |
| AIC | 14997 | 14983 |

*** $p \leq 0.01$, ** $p \leq 0.05$, * $p \leq 0.10$; Standard errors in parentheses

(Bakker et al. 2015; Polk et al. 2017). Unfortunately, this dataset only contains position data for 605 observations out of our 2,464 included in the entire dataset. Thus, we can only conduct a robustness check for about 25 percent of our data. The results are presented in Table 5.7. The findings essentially correspond to our main analysis.

**Table 5.7** Results from multilevel linear regression with cabinet conflict generated using Chapel Hill Expert survey data

| DV: Issue attention in coalition agreements | Model 5.9 | Model 5.10 |
|---|---|---|
| **Fixed effects** | | |
| Issue-specific cabinet conflict | 0.144 | −0.167 |
|  | (0.154) | (0.210) |
| Preference tangentiality | 0.179* | 0.707*** |
|  | (0.107) | (0.195) |
| Joint salience | 0.573*** | 0.519*** |
|  | (0.034) | (0.059) |
| Effective no. of parliamentary parties | 0.140 | 0.202 |
|  | (0.231) | (0.229) |
| No. of cabinet parties | 0.104 | 0.074 |
|  | (0.279) | (0.275) |
| Minority status | 0.707 | 0.451 |
|  | (0.698) | (0.689) |
| Minimal winning status | 0.372 | 0.339 |
|  | (0.576) | (0.567) |
| Issue-specific cabinet conflict * Preference tangentiality | −0.068* | −0.144* |
|  | (0.040) | (0.082) |
| Issue-specific cabinet conflict * Joint salience |  | 0.079*** |
|  |  | (0.026) |
| Preference tangentiality * Joint salience |  | −0.031** |
|  |  | (0.013) |
| Conflict * Preference tangentiality * Joint salience |  | −0.001 |
|  |  | (0.006) |
| Constant | 0.029 | −0.227 |
|  | (1.271) | (1.301) |
| **Random effects** | | |
| Country-level variance | 1.323 | 1.416 |
|  | (0.605) | (0.619) |
| Cabinet-level variance | 14.106 | 13.390 |
|  | (0.827) | (0.785) |
| N | 605 | 605 |
| Log likelihood | −1672 | −1658 |
| AIC | 3367 | 3343 |

***$p \leq 0.01$, **$p \leq 0.05$, *$p \leq 0.10$; Standard errors in parentheses

## 5.7 Conclusion

Why do coalition parties settle some policy issues in great detail, thus prescribing a detailed policy agenda, while other issues are hardly mentioned in coalition agreements? This chapter has focused on answering this question by explaining variation in the content of coalition agreements presented in parliamentary democracies. Our theoretical starting point was that parties have clear incentives in bearing the costs of negotiating an agreement on specific policy issues, especially when ideological divisiveness among coalition partners on issues is high. In such situations, we theorized, coalition partners will draft coalition agreements covering divisive issues at length in order to avoid that coalition partners deviate from the coalition position when given power over a specific department. In other words, to limit "ministerial drift." However, we also theorized that they should only do so when all included coalition partners care about the specific policy issue, that is, when preference tangentiality is low and joint salience is high.

Using the newly compiled COALITIONAGREE dataset on the content of 224 coalition agreements in 24 West and East European countries drafted by coalition governments formed during the post-war period, we find support for our expectations. We find that political parties are clearly more likely to focus extensively on a specific policy issue in the coalition agreement when the coalition partners cannot agree on it. Hence, this supports the idea that coalition partners negotiate agreements to limit potential "agency loss" when delegating power to individual ministers in specific departments. We also find that the impact of intra-cabinet conflict on the attention given to an issue in the coalition agreement is weaker when joint salience is low and when preference tangentiality is high, that is, when the parties in government do not place equal salience on an issue. In such cases, it seems that ministers from different parties are allowed a high degree of "autonomy" or freedom to implement their preferred policy, as the coalition partners do not particularly care about the specific policy issue. Hence, our results show clear support for a coalition governance model suggesting that parties draft agreements to limit delegation problems.

While this chapter has provided important insights for our understanding of cabinet formation and coalition governance, much remains to be done. One of the potential problems of our approach, and the approach by most other scholars focusing on coalition agreements, is that coalition partners not only bargain about the policy priorities that guide legislative activity in the upcoming term, but they simultaneously negotiate the division of ministerial posts. This means that coalition partners may strike package deals that cut across the division of ministerial posts and the agreement of policy priorities so that ministerial posts might be exchanged for a commitment to a particular policy reform and vice versa. Thus, it may be argued that payoff allocation in coalition negotiations should be conceptualized as a two-dimensional process in which the allocation of ministerial portfolios cannot be treated independently from policy compromises settled in the coalition agreement (Linhart and Pappi

2009; Shikano and Linhart 2010). For simplicity, we have not taken the distribution of portfolios into account here, but the next chapter systematically analyzes the relationship between ministerial portfolio allocation and control exercised through coalition agreements.

# 6
# Coalition agreements and ministerial portfolios

## 6.1 Introduction

An important part of coalition negotiations is the allocation of ministerial portfolios. Coalition parties not only bargain about policies when drafting a coalition agreement, but they also have to decide the distribution of ministerial offices during coalition talks. Political parties pursue different policy objectives, and are typically forced to compromise on these objectives when forming a coalition with other parties for the purpose of entering government. At the beginning of the legislative term, coalition parties therefore engage in intense bargaining and negotiate over the allocation of ministerial posts as well as over the coalition agreement that sets out the policy priorities for the upcoming term.

We argue that coalition bargaining is a two-dimensional process in which coalition parties simultaneously negotiate the policy compromise settled in the coalition agreement and who gets which offices in government. The two-dimensionality of coalition talks cannot be ignored when explaining how coalition governance is organized during the legislative term. Since ministerial portfolios grant coalition parties important policy competences and information advantages vis-à-vis their partners (Laver and Shepsle 1996), coalition partners have strong incentives to tie the hands of hostile ministers through prescribing policies in the coalition agreement.

We test our theoretical argument on the basis of the newly compiled COALITIONAGREE dataset which we have presented in Chapters 3 and 4 in this book. This dataset is based on a comprehensive quantitative content analysis of agreements in 24 West and East European countries from 1945 until 2015. Using this novel dataset, we test the relationship between ministerial portfolio distribution and control exercised through coalition agreements studying 224 coalition contracts negotiated by 189 political parties.

The results show support for our theoretical expectations as obtaining control over a ministerial portfolio comes at the expense of policy losses vis-à-vis

*Coalition Agreements as Control Devices.* Heike Klüver, Hanna Bäck, and Svenja Krauss, Oxford University Press.
© Heike Klüver, Hanna Bäck, and Svenja Krauss (2023). DOI: 10.1093/oso/9780192899910.003.0006

coalition partners who leave ministers with little room of maneuver. Our empirical analyses show that policy and office payoffs in coalition governments cannot be analyzed independently, but the allocation of ministerial offices has to be taken into account when explaining coalition governance. Coalition parties exercise stronger control in policy areas that are regulated by hostile ministers. Our findings suggest that parties draft coalition agreements to limit ministerial drift and have important implications for our understanding of coalition governance in parliamentary democracies.

In this chapter, we first discuss previous research on portfolio allocation and payoffs in coalition agreements before we lay out our theoretical argument. Then, we proceed by illustrating the empirical strategy used in order to test the hypothesis and discuss the results of our analysis.

## 6.2 Previous research

Previous research studying the outcome of coalition negotiations has primarily focused on who gets what in coalition talks. Portfolio allocation is the most straightforward indicator of the payoffs parties bargain for when entering a coalition government, as this is the part of the formation process which is just as important for policy-pursuing as for office-seeking political actors. Analyses of "quantitative" portfolio allocation have produced clear-cut empirical findings: coalition parties receive ministerial posts in close proportion to their parliamentary seat contribution (see e.g. Browne and Franklin 1973; Warwick and Druckman 2006).

The qualitative aspect of portfolio allocation, or the question of "who gets what and why," has received less attention. Early work by Budge and Keman (1990) predicted portfolio allocation on the basis of the expected preferences of different party families, and Laver and Shepsle (1996) predicted that a ministerial post should go to the party holding the median position on the policy dimension controlled by the post. More recently, Bäck, Debus, and Dumont (2011) provided one of the first extensive multivariate analyses of qualitative portfolio allocation and suggested that the higher the salience of a given policy area to a coalition party, the higher the likelihood that this party will obtain control over the ministerial post controlling this particular policy field.

While the literature on coalition governments in parliamentary democracies has devoted considerable attention to explaining the allocation of portfolios, the policy outcomes of coalition negotiations have largely been neglected (for exceptions, see Budge and Laver 1993; Warwick 2001; Däubler and Debus 2009). Budge and Laver (1993) measure the distribution of policy payoffs by comparing the ideal points of coalition parties expressed in their election manifestos and the policy positions reflected in government declarations. Building on this work, Warwick (2001) uses the same data and shows that the seat share of parties positively affects policy payoffs and that this effect is more pronounced once controlling for other factors such as formateur status. Däubler and Debus (2009) present an analysis of government formation after state-level elections in Germany. Drawing on state-level coalition agreements and election manifestos, they compare the policy positions of coalition governments and their constituent parties on the economic and the social policy dimension. Their findings confirm that seat share has a positive effect on policy benefits on both, the economic and the social policy dimension.

While previous literature focused on the allocation of primarily office payoffs in coalition talks, the relationship between ministerial portfolio distribution and control exercised through coalition agreements has been overlooked. The main contribution of this chapter is that we consider coalition bargaining as a two-dimensional process in which coalition parties simultaneously negotiate the allocation of ministerial posts and the content of the coalition agreement. More specifically, as will be explained in the next section, we hypothesize that there is an important trade-off between policies and offices—controlling the ministerial portfolio in charge of a specific policy area may come with the cost of tighter policy control in that policy domain exercised through coalition agreements.

## 6.3 Theoretical expectations

In this section, we summarize our theoretical argument about the effect of ministerial portfolio allocation on the use of coalition agreements as control devices that we have laid out in detail in Chapter 2.

In order to understand the use of coalition agreements as control instruments, it is important to acknowledge that coalition agreements function in several ways as control devices. As the outcome of coalition negotiations, they codify both policy positions and an agenda for the legislative term as well as the distribution of ministerial posts. Coalition parties join forces to take over government, but they have distinct policy preferences. During coalition talks, coalition parties therefore negotiate the policy agenda that shall be enacted during the legislative term and spell out these negotiated policies in the coalition agreement. However, during coalition negotiations, coalition parties not only have to find a deal when it comes to policies that are settled in coalition agreements, but they also have to decide which party gets which ministry and which individuals become ministers. Thus, in order to understand the use of coalition agreements as control devices, it is crucial to acknowledge the interdependence of simultaneously negotiating policies and offices during government formation.

Ministerial portfolio allocation is not only simultaneously negotiated alongside policies in coalition talks, but ministerial portfolios also have an important impact on policy-making during the legislative term. Laver and Shepsle (1996) have argued that ministers can act as "policy dictators" in their jurisdiction as coalition parties engage in log-rolling and each minister can essentially autonomously decide policies in her policy domain without interference from coalition partners. This is admittedly a very strong assumption and we do not go as far as Laver and Shepsle (1996) by conceiving of ministers as "dictators" of policies in their realm. However, what has to be acknowledged, is that ministers certainly enjoy important advantages vis-à-vis coalition partners that allow them to importantly influence policies in their favor.

First, ministers are typically in charge of drafting legislative proposals that fall in their jurisdiction. Since it is much more difficult to change policy initiatives once a proposal has been drafted, ministers have important agenda-setting power as they decide what goes into the proposal. Second, ministers enjoy important informational advantages over coalition partners as they are supported by the ministerial bureaucracy in their policy domain. The bureaucracy of one ministry is typically composed of hundreds and sometimes thousands of highly qualified civil servants who have life-time positions and therefore develop long-term policy expertise and specialized knowledge. Coalition partners have no chance to compete with the information advantages that come with the bureaucratic support of a minister. Hence, even though we do not consider ministers as "policy dictators", it is reasonable to expect that ministers have a considerable impact on policies in their jurisdiction.

When negotiating the distribution of ministerial portfolios, we assume that coalition parties are aware of the institutional and informational advantages that ministers enjoy. Coalition governments have been the norm in most European democracies (Anderson, Mendes, and Tverdova 2004; Strøm, Müller, and Bergman 2008; Bergman, Ilonszki, and Müller 2019*b*) and it is thus reasonable to expect that political parties are aware of the policy implications of controlling a ministerial portfolio. We therefore expect that coalition parties seek to counteract potential ministerial shirking by constraining the room of maneuver for ministers.

An important instrument through which coalition parties can control their partners is contract design. In the terminology of principal–agent theory, principals can design a contract that clearly lays out the duties and responsibilities of an agent leaving as little room of maneuver as possible. Depending on the performance in fulfilling this contract, the agent gets rewarded or punished. We argue that coalition agreements precisely serve this purpose and are used to limit "ministerial drift"—to avoid that coalition partners deviate from the coalition position when given power over a specific department. Detailed contracts can "help coalitions to keep ministers in line and to prevent deviations in favor of their parties" (Müller and Meyer 2010, p. 1074). Consequently, the extent to which coalition parties use coalition agreements as control devices depends on the allocation of ministerial portfolios.

The negotiations following the 2017 federal elections in Germany illustrate the use of contract design to limit ministerial drift. Angela Merkel (CDU), who had been chancellor for the three previous terms, had to make strong concessions to the SPD to make a coalition work and this way win another term as German chancellor. She said it was painful to let their coalition partner have the ministry of finance, which previously was taken by the CDU, however the coalition agreement enabled the Union to retain some control: "I want to say that we (the conservatives) have also approved the policies (in the agreement) and the finance minister cannot simply do as he likes." Thereby, the control of the finance minister through the coalition agreement made this deal acceptable for the CDU (Nasr 2018).

Thus, coalition parties have particularly strong incentives to exercise control through the coalition agreement in the policy areas that fall into the jurisdiction of ministers that belong to other coalition parties. Coalition parties which are confronted with a hostile minister seek to tie the hands of the minister by contract design. In other words, coalition parties will exercise tight control over ministers through the coalition agreement by demanding policy concessions in their favor. By adopting and publicly communicating policy positions that are close to their ideal points, coalition partners leave the minister little room of maneuver. Even if the minister attempts to deviate from the negotiated policy position, coalition partners can publicly blame and shame the minister for not sticking to the commitments made in the coalition agreement.

**Hypothesis 4:** *The policy distance between a coalition party and the coalition agreement is larger in policy areas where the party controls the relevant ministerial portfolio.*

## 6.4 Research design and data

In the following, we will explain how we test our theoretical expectations regarding the interdependence of ministerial portfolio allocation and the use of coalition agreements as control devices. We first explain the empirical strategy before we illustrate the operationalization of the dependent and independent variables.

### 6.4.1 Empirical strategy

In order to test the argument that coalition parties exercise control through coalition agreements particularly in those policy areas in which their partners control the ministries, we have to overcome the following challenge: Ministerial portfolio allocation is effectively a zero-sum game in which one party wins a portfolio that another necessarily loses. Given limited resources and also constitutional restrictions, the number of ministerial portfolios cannot freely be increased, but coalition parties have to divide the ministries among themselves. This in turn implies that every time a coalition party obtains control over a ministerial department, it is confronted with at least one other coalition partner who seeks to control the minister. As a result, operationalizing the use of coalition agreements as control device with the attention to an issue does not make sense as every minister is confronted with a coalition partner who seeks to control her. To circumvent this problem, we rely on the policy position rather than on issue attention as a measure of control exercised through coalition partners.

The underlying idea is the following: Imagine a coalition between two hypothetical parties A and B which both consider environmental policy as an important policy domain and have diverging preferences on the issue. Party A obtains control of the environmental ministry. Party B in turn seeks to make sure that the environmental minister belonging to party A does not single-handedly push through the policies preferred by party A. We argue that the negotiations over the ministerial portfolio in charge of environmental issues and over the environmental policy position adopted in the

```
                              b
                      — — — — — — —
                          a
              — — — — — — — — — — —

|Anti environmental regulation|              |              |              Pro environmental regulation|
            Party B         Coalition       Coalition       Party A
                            Agreement       Agreement
                         (if A controls the (if B controls the
                              ministry)        ministry)
```

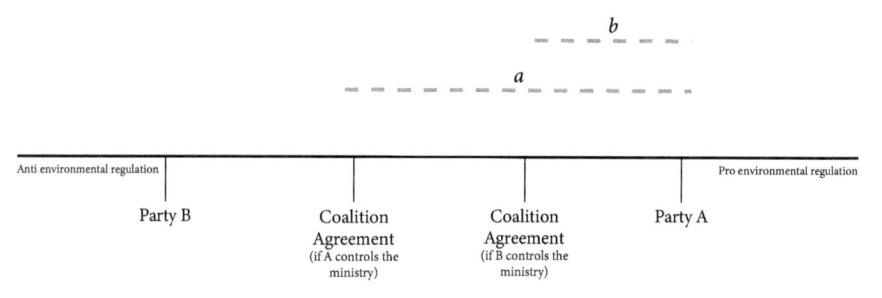

**Figure 6.1** Policy distance in relation to ministerial portfolio control

*Note:* The dashed lines represent distances between the two hypothetical coalition agreements and Party A.

coalition agreement are not independent of each other. Instead, we argue that party B demands important policy concession in exchange for granting the environmental ministry to party A.

Figure 6.1 illustrates our argument. If party A controls the environmental ministry, party B demands more policy concessions by insisting on a policy position in the coalition agreement that is closer to its ideal point. Thus, in terms of policies, the party controlling the ministerial department has to live with policy losses in exchange for obtaining the executive office. Vice versa, if party B controls the ministry in charge of environmental policy, we expect that the policy position of the coalition agreement with regard to the environment is much closer to party A.

More generally, policy and office payoffs cannot be analyzed independently of each other (Sened 1995; Linhart and Pappi 2009; Shikano and Linhart 2010). As policy-seeking coalition parties value both direct policy commitments as well as ministerial portfolios to achieve their policy goals, we expect that coalition parties strike package deals across the two dimensions. If a coalition party manages to get all its favored policy commitments into the coalition agreement, it will be more willing to grant its coalition partner a disproportionately high number of ministerial portfolios. Vice versa, a coalition party will be more willing to settle on policy commitments demanded by its coalition partners if it in exchange gains control over the ministerial portfolios in charge of these policy areas. Hence, coalition parties are likely to trade policy commitments for ministerial portfolios and vice versa, and we therefore hypothesize that a party will get a smaller amount of policy payoffs, in terms of the negotiated policy agreement, in a policy area where the party obtains the ministerial post.

During the coalition negotiations in Germany 2009, for example, the allocation of ministerial posts became an important part of the coalition agreement.

The Liberal Democratic Party (FDP) made concessions to the Christian Democratic Union parties (CDU/CSU), as some of their policy demands like changes in employee participation or protection against dismissal were refused by the CDU/CSU. To balance these concessions, the Union had to grant the FDP five ministries: the foreign affairs ministry, ministries of economics and technology, justice, economic cooperation, and the ministry of health (Braun, Blechschmidt, and Hulverscheidt 2009).

The case of the government formation in the Czech Republic 2018 is another example for a clear policy and office payoff. Debiec (2018) describes how the Czech Social Democrats, who won 15 out of 200 seats at the 2017 elections, were granted five ministries, including the interior ministry. Their coalition partner ANO on the other hand, who won nearly a third of all votes and 78 seats in parliament, only secured nine ministries, even though their vote share was about four times as high as the Social Democrats' share. The strong concessions to the Social Democrats were necessary to form a coalition government at all: The ANO had previously tried to rule as a single-party minority government, and lost the vote of confidence in parliament a few months after the elections. After coalition talks with other parties failed, the ANO had to give their junior partner the ministries in order to stay in government (Debiec 2018).

### 6.4.2 The dependent variable: Measuring policy payoffs in coalition governments

On the basis of our comprehensive content analysis, we measure the dependent variable policy distance as the absolute distance between the ideal points of coalition parties and the policy position adopted in the coalition agreement. The policy positions of the coalition agreements were obtained by relying on the content analysis of the agreements that we have conducted. The policy positions of the coalition parties were extracted from their election manifestos which have been coded by the MARPOR project. We identified eleven issue areas based on the MARPOR project for which the codebook includes positional categories so that we can estimate not only the attention to the issue, but also the issue-specific policy positions of the parties (see the first columns in Table 6.1 for an overview of the issue areas and the associated MARPOR categories).

The issue-specific policy positions were generated using the widely-used additive percentage scores advocated by Budge (1999). First, the percentages of left and right issue-specific quasi-sentences of the total number of coded

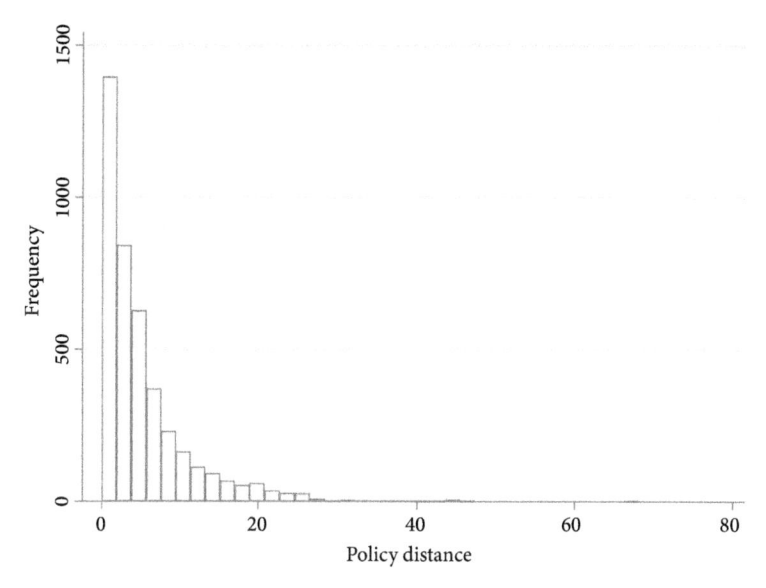

**Figure 6.2** Policy distance between coalition parties and their coalition agreements

quasi-sentences are computed. Then the percentage of issue-specific left sentences is subtracted from the percentage of issue-specific right sentences. Positive scores indicate issue-specific right positions and negative scores indicate issue-specific left positions. For example, if a coalition agreement—or election manifesto—would include 1000 quasi-sentences on social welfare policies, of which 500 (50 percent) are classified into the left social welfare category and 300 (30 percent) are allocated to the right social welfare category, it would obtain a score of -20 on the social welfare dimension (that is, 30-50). Figure 6.2 illustrates the policy distance between coalition parties and the respective coalition agreements across issue areas.

### 6.4.3 Independent variables

In order to measure ministerial portfolio control we rely on a variable that is coded "1" if a coalition party controls the ministry that is in charge of a given policy area while it is coded "0" if another coalition partner controls the responsible ministerial office. We rely on data about the partisan control over ministerial portfolios that was compiled by Taglarsson.[1]

---

[1] Source: http://www.kolumbus.fi/taglarsson/

To examine the expected link between ministerial portfolio allocation and policy payoffs, we have to assign the policy issues settled in coalition agreements to ministerial portfolios. To match the ministerial portfolios and the issue areas according to which the coalition agreements and the manifestos were coded, we use a matching procedure that only relies on unambiguous matches of issue areas and ministerial portfolios (see Table 6.1). For instance, the issue area "Civil rights" cannot clearly be matched to any ministerial portfolio across countries as sometimes the Internal Affairs and sometimes the Justice Ministry is responsible for civil rights issues. Higher measurement validity can thus be achieved by solely relying on unambiguous matches and excluding issue areas and ministries respectively which cannot be unambiguously matched.

In order to test our theoretical expectations, we have furthermore controlled for several variables that may otherwise confound the hypothesized relationships. First, we control for the party's share of legislative seats the cabinet controls. Political parties that won a large number of parliamentary seats therefore provide their partners with considerable legislative resources that are necessary to achieve the common policy objective. Numerous empirical studies have accordingly shown that the coalition party's contribution to the legislative seats controlled by the government parties is proportionally related to the number of ministerial posts coalition parties obtain during government formation (e.g. Browne and Franklin 1973; Warwick and Druckman 2006). This relationship was first suggested by Gamson (1961) and has therefore been termed "Gamson's law". Däubler and Debus (2009) have demonstrated that party's share of legislative seats the cabinet controls is also an important predictor for policy payoff allocation among coalition parties and we therefore expect that parties that bring a large number of legislative seats are particularly able to pull the coalition agreement toward their ideal point. In order to measure the party's share of legislative seats the cabinet controls, we rely on data from the Parliaments and governments database (ParlGov) (Döring 2013; Döring and Manow 2016).

Second, we control for cabinet conflict which has been shown to importantly affect government formation and the content of coalition agreements more specifically (e.g. Indridason and Kristinsson 2013; Klüver and Bäck 2019). In order to measure intra-cabinet conflict, we rely on left-right policy positions extracted from the election manifesto data provided by the MARPOR project (see the discussion above). Following Tsebelis (2002), we generated the range of the left-right policy positions held by cabinet parties in order to operationalize intra-cabinet policy conflict.

Table 6.1 Issue areas and ministerial portfolios

| Issue Area | MARPOR policy categories | COALITIONAGREE policy categories | | Ministerial Portfolio |
|---|---|---|---|---|
| | | Left position | Right position | |
| Agriculture | 406: Protectionism (positive)<br>407: Protectionism (negative)<br>703: Agriculture and farmers (positive) | 406 Protectionism: Positive<br><br>703.1 Agriculture and Farmers: Positive | 407 Protectionism: Negative<br>703.2 Agriculture and Farmers: Negative | Agriculture |
| Civil rights | 201: Freedom and human rights<br>202: Democracy<br>603: Traditional Morality (positive)<br>604: Traditional Morality (negative)<br>605: Law and order<br>705: Underprivileged minority groups<br>706: Noneconomic demographic groups | 201 Freedom and Human Rights: Positive<br>202 Democracy<br><br>604 Traditional Morality: Negative<br>605.2 Law and Order: Negative<br>705 Minority Groups: Positive<br>706 Noneconomic Demographic Groups: Positive | <br><br>603 Traditional Morality: Positive<br><br>605.1 Law and Order: Positive | No clear match |
| Education | 506: Education expansion<br>507: Education limitation | 506 Education Expansion | 507 Education Limitation | Education |

*Continued*

Table 6.1 Continued

| Issue Area | MARPOR policy categories | COALITIONAGREE policy categories Left position | COALITIONAGREE policy categories Right position | Ministerial Portfolio |
|---|---|---|---|---|
| Environment | 416: Antigrowth economy (positive)<br>501: Environmental protection | 416 Antigrowth Economy: Positive<br>501 Environmental Protection: Positive | | Environment |
| European integration | 410: Economic growth (positive)<br>108: EC/EU (positive)<br>110: EC/EU (negative) | 108 European Integration: Positive | 410 Economic Growth: Positive<br>110 European Integration: Negative | No clear match |
| Decentralization | 301: Decentralization<br>302: Centralization | 301 Decentralization: Positive | 302 Centralization: Positive | No clear match |
| Immigration | 601: National way of life (positive)<br>602: National way of life (negative)<br>607: Multiculturalism (positive)<br>608: Multiculturalism (negative) | 602 National Way of Life: Negative<br>607 Multiculturalism: Positive | 601 National Way of Life: Positive<br>608 Multiculturalism: Negative | No clear match |
| Social welfare | 503: Equality (positive)<br>504: Welfare state expansion<br>505: Welfare state limitation | 503 Equality: Positive<br>504 Welfare State Expansion | 505 Welfare State Limitation | Social welfare |

| Defense | 104: Military (positive) | | 104 Military: Positive | Defense |
| | 105: Military (negative) | 105 Military: Negative | | |
| Economy | 401: Free market economy | | 401 Free Enterprise: Positive | Economy |
| | 402: Incentives | | 402 Incentives: Positive | |
| | 403: Market regulation | 403 Market Regulation: Positive | | |
| | 404: Economic planning | 404 Economic Planning: Positive | | |
| | 409: Keynesian demand management | 409 Keynesian Demand Management: Positive | | |
| | 412: Controlled economy | 412 Controlled Economy: Positive | | |
| | 413: Nationalization | 413 Nationalization: Positive | | |
| | 414: Economic orthodoxy | | 414 Economic Orthodoxy: Positive | |
| International politics | 101: Foreign and special relations (positive) | 101 Foreign Special Relationships: Positive | | Foreign policy |
| | 102: Foreign and special relations (negative) | | 102 Foreign Special Relationships: Negative | |
| | 103: Anti-imperialism (positive) | 103 Anti-Imperialism: Positive | | |
| | 106: Peace (positive) | 106 Peace: Positive | | |
| | 107: Internationalism (positive) | 107 Internationalism: Positive | | |
| | 109: Internationalism (negative) | | 109 Internationalism: Negative | |

Third, we control for the joint salience of the issue among coalition partners as issues that are important to all coalition partners should receive more attention in the coalition agreement. Accordingly, previous research has shown that the salience of issues to cabinet parties importantly affects their legislative behavior while they are in government as cabinets for instance prioritize bills in issue areas that are salient to all partners (e.g. Martin 2004; Zubek and Klüver 2015). We measure the joint salience of an issue by computing the salience of an issue to each coalition partner by taking the relative number of quasi-sentences devoted to the issue in the coalition parties election manifestos, and then computing the average of the salience of the issue across all cabinet parties.

Fourth, we control for preference tangentiality in coalition agreements as previous research has shown that it affects cabinet governance and influences which issues are mentioned in coalition agreements (e.g. Falcó-Gimeno 2014; Klüver and Bäck 2019). Tangentiality refers to the relative salience of policy issues for coalition parties. Preferences of coalition parties are highly tangential if a policy issue is highly salient to one coalition party, but not salient to the coalition partners. In order to measure preference tangentiality, it was first of all necessary to measure the salience of policy issues for the different coalition parties. We operationalize issue salience based on the relative number of quasi-sentences devoted to the issue in the respective election manifestos using data from the MARPOR project. Afterward, we compute the standard deviation of the issue-specific salience scores of all coalition parties. Thus, the standard deviation expresses the varying salience of a policy issue for the different coalition parties, and can be used as a measure of tangentiality (see Falcó-Gimeno 2014). The smaller the standard deviation, the larger the overlap of coalition parties preferences as a policy issue is equally salient to all partners. Descriptive statistics for all variables included in the analysis are presented in Table 6.2.

## 6.5 Empirical analysis

In this section, we evaluate our theoretical expectations. Before presenting the empirical results, it is important to acknowledge the hierarchical structure of our data. Our data is clustered into coalition cabinets as coalition agreements are negotiated by coalition parties belonging to the same multiparty cabinet. Political parties that form a coalition cabinet strive to shape the content of the same coalition agreement. It is therefore important to take the clustering into

Table 6.2 Descriptive statistics (Chapter 6)

| Variable | N | Mean | Std. Dev. | Min | Max |
| --- | --- | --- | --- | --- | --- |
| Issue-specific policy distance | 4,154 | 5.266 | 6.150 | 0 | 68.183 |
| Issue-specific cabinet conflict | 4,154 | 6.355 | 6.935 | 0 | 54.756 |
| Joint salience | 4,154 | 6.480 | 5.602 | 0 | 34.682 |
| Preference tangentiality | 4,154 | 3.051 | 3.150 | 0 | 28.930 |
| Ministerial portfolio control over issue area | 4,154 | 0.319 | 0.466 | 0 | 1.000 |
| Party's share of cabinet seats | 4,154 | 33.000 | 21.453 | 0 | 95.062 |

coalition cabinets into account. Estimating an ordinary least squares regression model on the basis of such a data structure may result in deflated standard errors and inflated type I error rates so the significance of estimated effects may be overrated (Steenbergen and Jones 2002, pp. 219–220). Thus, to model this particular data structure, we rely on a multilevel linear regression model that acknowledges the clustering into multiparty cabinets. As the ministerial offices and the policy concessions that coalition parties in the same cabinet receive are furthermore not independent of each other, we follow Carroll and Cox (2007) and estimated a multilevel regression analysis in which we randomly drop one coalition party per cabinet.

Table 6.3 presents the results of the multilevel regression analysis. The reported results show that there is indeed a statistically significant effect of ministerial portfolio control on the policy distance between the coalition agreement and the policy position of coalition parties not controlling the ministerial portfolio in a given policy area. More specifically, controlling the ministry in charge of a given policy area is associated with a significantly larger distance between the position of the coalition party and the location of the coalition agreement in the policy space. If a coalition party controls the ministry in a given policy area, the distance between the coalition agreement and the party's policy preference in that policy domain is on average 1.091 units larger. Thus, controlling the ministry is associated with larger policy concessions in that policy area.

Figure 6.3 illustrates the effect of ministerial portfolio control on the predicted issue-specific policy distance between a coalition party and the coalition agreement while holding all other variables at their mean values. The circles indicate the point estimates while the surrounding markers reflect the 95 percent confidence interval. Figure 6.3 clearly shows that ministerial portfolio control has a statistically significant positive effect on the policy distance to

**Table 6.3** Multilevel linear regression explaining issue-specific policy distance

| DV: Issue-specific policy distance | Model 6.1 |
|---|---|
| *Fixed effects* | |
| Ministerial portfolio control over issue area | 1.091*** |
| | (0.181) |
| Party's share of cabinet seats | −0.011*** |
| | (0.004) |
| Issue-specific cabinet conflict | 0.012 |
| | (0.024) |
| Joint salience | 0.775*** |
| | (0.019) |
| Preference tangentiality | 0.153*** |
| | (0.055) |
| Constant | −0.219 |
| | (0.176) |
| *Random effects* | |
| Cabinet-level variance | 0.000 |
| | (0.000) |
| Residual variance | 17.338 |
| | (0.465) |
| N | 2,783 |
| Log likelihood | −7919 |

*** $p \leq 0.01$, ** $p \leq 0.05$

the coalition agreement. Coalition parties that obtained the ministerial portfolio in charge of a policy area are significantly less successful in pushing the coalition agreement in that policy domain toward their ideal point.

With regard to the control variables, we find that parliamentary seat share has a statistically significant effect on the policy distance between the coalition agreement and the coalition party's ideal point. Thus, the larger a party's seat share, the closer the coalition agreement to the preferred policy position of the coalition party. More specifically, as the seat share of a coalition party increases by one percentage point, the distance between the coalition treaty and the coalition party decreases by 0.011 units. As a result, coalition parties that bring a lot of parliamentary seats to the negotiation table are in a much better position to influence the policy agenda settled in the coalition agreement than small parties.

We moreover find that the joint salience of an issue area also decreases the policy payoffs. The larger the salience of an issue among all coalition parties,

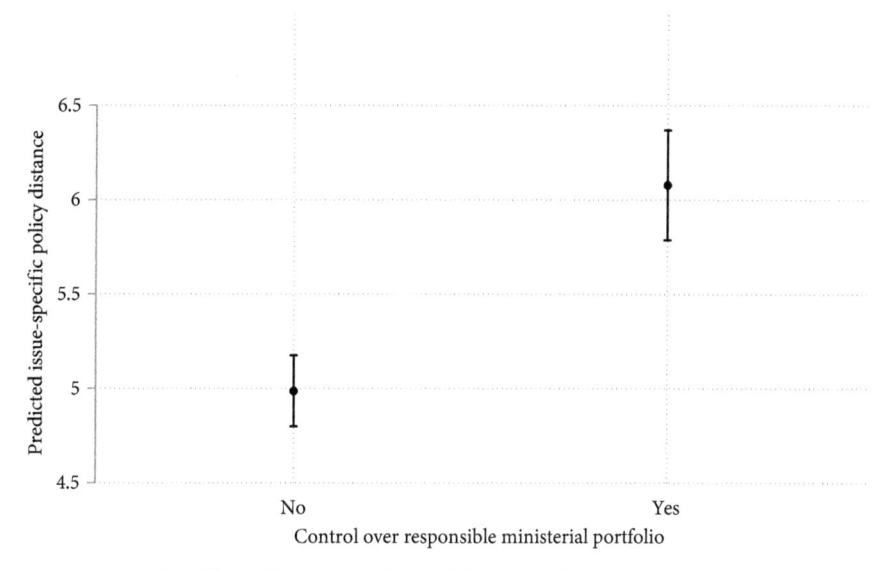

**Figure 6.3** The effect of ministerial portfolio control

the smaller the policy payoffs a coalition party can obtain in the policy domain. This indicates that it is more difficult for a coalition party to obtain policy benefits when its partners also care about the issue while it is easier to pull the coalition agreement toward the preferred position when coalition partners are largely indifferent to an issue.

## 6.6 Robustness checks

In order to test the robustness of our findings, we have estimated a number of additional model specifications to make sure that the detected effect of ministerial portfolio control was not caused by our modeling strategy.

First, Table 6.4 reports the findings of a multilevel regression analysis that includes all cabinets parties in the sample without randomly dropping any observations (Model 6.2). The results are substantially the same as in the main model. Since the dependent variable is empirically limited to values between 0 and approximately 68, we have estimated another model in which we rely on multilevel tobit specification (Model 6.3). The results similarly support the findings of our main model.

So far, we have relied on a model specification in which we rely on ministerial portfolio control on the level of specific policy areas. For instance, we investigate with such a specification if controlling the environmental ministry comes at the cost of tighter policy control in this policy domain. Another way to

Table 6.4 Robustness checks

| DV: Issue-specific policy distance | Model 6.2 | Model 6.3 |
|---|---|---|
| | Complete sample | Multilevel Tobit |
| *Fixed effects* | | |
| Ministerial portfolio control over issue area | 1.044*** | 1.091*** |
| | (0.142) | (0.181) |
| Party's share of cabinet seats | −0.010*** | −0.011*** |
| | (0.003) | (0.004) |
| Issue-specific cabinet conflict | 0.054*** | 0.012 |
| | (0.020) | (0.024) |
| Joint salience | 0.780*** | 0.775*** |
| | (0.015) | (0.019) |
| Preference tangentiality | 0.001 | 0.153*** |
| | (0.042) | (0.055) |
| Constant | −0.142 | −0.219 |
| | (0.141) | (0.176) |
| *Random effects* | | |
| Cabinet-level variance | 0.000 | 0.000 |
| | (0.000) | (0.000) |
| Residual variance | 16.370 | 17.338 |
| | (0.359) | (0.465) |
| N | 4,154 | 2,783 |
| Log likelihood | −11701 | −7919 |
| AIC | 23417 | 15851 |

*** $p \leq 0.01$, ** $p \leq 0.05$

think about the interrelationship of ministerial portfolio allocation and control exercised through coalition agreements is an aggregate effect across all policy areas. In other words, does obtaining a large share of ministerial portfolios in a coalition cabinet come with more extensive policy control exercised by coalition partners across policy areas?

In order to examine whether our argument not only holds for specific policy issues, we have estimated another model specification in which we operationalize ministerial portfolio control as the share of ministerial portfolios held by a coalition party of all the portfolios in a cabinet. The dependent variable in this analysis is the overall distance of coalition parties on the left-right dimension measured on RILE scale as suggested by Budge (1999). First, the percentages of left and right quasi-sentences of the total number of coded quasi-sentences are computed. Then the percentage of left sentences is subtracted from the percentage of right sentences. Positive scores indicate

**Table 6.5** Robustness check: Aggregate effect of ministerial portfolio control

| DV: Left-right distance between coalition agreement and manifesto | Model 6.4 | Model 6.5 |
|---|---|---|
| | Complete sample | One party per cabinet randomly dropped |
| *Fixed effects* | | |
| Share of ministerial portfolios | 10.351*** | 13.922*** |
| | (2.850) | (3.579) |
| Cabinet conflict on left-right scale | 0.244*** | 0.280*** |
| | (0.253) | (0.315) |
| Preference tangentiality | 0.551** | 0.560** |
| | (0.179) | 0.206 |
| Constant | 4.572** | 2.412 |
| | (1.448) | (1.808) |
| *Random effects* | | |
| Cabinet-level variance | 8.297 | 13.031 |
| | (7.354) | (12.512) |
| Residual variance | 173.571 | 179.872 |
| | (11.543) | (16.456) |
| N | 672 | 449 |
| Log likelihood | −2701 | −1818 |
| AIC | 5414 | 3647 |

*** $p \leq 0.01$, ** $p \leq 0.05$

right positions and negative scores indicate left positions. The results are presented in Table 6.5. The aggregate level analysis supports our main findings. The larger the share of ministerial portfolios a coalition party receives in the cabinet, the larger the policy constraints it has to face.

We have argued that coalition parties particularly use coalition agreements to exercise control in policy areas that fall under the jurisdiction of ministries that are controlled by their partners. Empirically, we have found evidence for this argument as controlling the ministry in charge of a policy area is associated with significantly larger policy distances between the coalition agreement and the policy position of the party that the minister belongs to. However, there are two sides to this story. Not only does obtaining control over a ministerial portfolio increase the policy distance to the coalition agreement in that area, the policy distance between a coalition party and the coalition agreement in a policy domain should in turn also be positively linked to the probability to obtain that ministry.

Table 6.6 Results from seemingly unrelated regression

|  | Model 6.7 |
|---|---|
| **DV: Issue-specific policy distance** | |
| Ministerial portfolio control over issue area | 2.060*** |
|  | (0.141) |
| Party's share of cabinet seats | −0.017*** |
|  | (0.003) |
| Issue-specific cabinet conflict | 0.058*** |
|  | (0.019) |
| Joint salience | 0.778*** |
|  | (0.015) |
| Preference tangentiality | −0.003 |
|  | (0.042) |
| Constant | −0.246* |
|  | (0.141) |
| **DV: Ministerial portfolio control over issue area** | |
| Policy distance | 0.024*** |
|  | (0.002) |
| Party's share of cabinet seats | 0.007*** |
|  | (0.000) |
| Issue-specific cabinet conflict | −0.005** |
|  | (0.002) |
| Joint salience | −0.018*** |
|  | (0.002) |
| Preference tangentiality | 0.004 |
|  | (0.005) |
| Constant | 0.104*** |
|  | (0.015) |
| N | 4,154 |

***$p \leq 0.01$, **$p \leq 0.05$; Cluster robust standard errors in parentheses

In order to acknowledge the interdependence of policy and office payoffs, we perform another robustness check by fitting a seemingly unrelated regression analysis. Since coalition parties simultaneously negotiate policies and office during government formation, estimating the design of the coalition agreement and predicting the allocation of ministerial portfolios is interdependent. It is therefore unrealistic to expect that predicting the bargaining outcomes with regard to policies and offices in coalition negotiations can be estimated independently as the error terms will most likely be correlated. Seemingly unrelated regression is a technique that allows for taking into account the interdependence of bargaining over policies and offices by estimating a system of linear equations with correlated error terms (Zellner 1962).

Table 6.6 presents the results of the seemingly unrelated regression. The seemingly unrelated regression analysis supports our main findings. When coalition parties receive the ministerial portfolio in charge of a policy area, they face policy losses in that policy domain. Similarly, the probability of obtaining a ministerial portfolio in a given policy area increases with the policy distance between the party's ideal point and the policy position settled in the coalition agreement.

## 6.7 Conclusion

In this chapter, we have focused on the question if ministerial portfolio allocation affects the extent to which coalition agreements are used to limit agency loss. Our main argument is that coalition parties exercise control through coalition agreements particularly in those policy areas in which their partners control the ministries. We tested our theoretical argument on the basis of the newly compiled COALITIONAGREE dataset which we have presented in Chapters 3 and 4 in this book. Using this novel dataset, we tested the relationship between ministerial portfolio distribution and control exercised through coalition agreements studying 224 coalition contracts negotiated by 189 political parties.

The results show support for our theoretical expectations as obtaining control over a ministerial portfolio comes at the expense of policy losses vis-à-vis coalition partners who leave ministers with little room of maneuver. Our empirical analyses show that policy and office payoffs in coalition governments cannot be analyzed independently, but the allocation of ministerial offices has to be taken into account when explaining coalition governance. Coalition parties exercise stronger control in policy areas that are regulated by hostile ministers. Ministerial portfolio allocation does therefore not result in simple log-rolling of policies. Ministers cannot autonomously decide which policies to enact in their jurisdiction, but they receive very clear policy instructions in the coalition agreement.

Our findings thus suggest that parties particularly use coalition agreements to limit ministerial drift and have important implications for our understanding of coalition governance in parliamentary democracies. This chapter therefore makes an important contribution to the literature on coalition governments as it has been shown for the first time that coalition governance and payoff allocation are not independent of one another. It matters a great deal who wins and who loses in ministerial portfolio allocation for the design of control instruments in coalition cabinets. Ministerial portfolios grant coalition parties with important policy-making advantages due to information asymmetries and policy-making powers of the minister. Coalition parties therefore seek to tie the hands of hostile ministers through contract design. In other words, coalition partners leave ministers with little room of maneuver by demanding policy concessions and nailing down a policy compromise that is close to their ideal point. A recent study by Klüver, Alberto, and Ellger (2021) which analyzed the enactment of more than 5,000 policy pledges by 87 coalition governments in 20 Western and Eastern European countries from 2000 to 2015 has accordingly shown that the majority of policy pledges made in coalition agreements are enacted by coalition governments. Thus, obtaining policy concessions in coalition agreements have important implications as most of the policy commitments are implemented once in office.

In conclusion, this chapter has two important lessons for future coalition research. First, it is important to take into account the interdependence of ministerial portfolio allocation and the design of control instruments in multiparty cabinets. The level of control exercised through coalition agreements not only varies with the preference configuration, that is the conflict, the salience and the tangentiality of preferences among cabinet parties, but also with the allocation of ministerial positions to coalition partners. Second, while this book focuses on the control function of coalition agreements, future research on payoff allocation should also take into account the interdependence of office and policy payoffs in coalition negotiations. Coalition parties simultaneously negotiate offices and policies and the exclusive focus of previous research on ministerial portfolios (e.g. Browne and Franklin 1973; Warwick and Druckman 2006; Bäck, Debus, and Dumont 2011) or on policies (Budge and Laver 1993; Warwick 2001; Däubler and Debus 2009) is too simplistic. Payoff allocation has to be modeled as a multidimensional bargaining process.

# 7
# Do coalition agreements work?

## 7.1 Introduction

Do coalition agreements influence the stability of coalition governments? In this book, we have argued that coalition agreements are important control instruments which coalition parties use to keep tabs on their partners. The preceding chapters were devoted to showing that coalition parties indeed use coalition agreements as control devices by examining how the preference configuration among coalition partners and the distribution of ministerial portfolios affects the use of coalition contracts. However, little is known about whether coalition agreements actually work. Can coalition agreements really help coalition parties to overcome their differences and settle disputes in government? Do coalition governments that rely on extensive coalition agreements really last longer than multiparty cabinets that have not negotiated an agreement or that have only written a few pages? In this chapter, we take a look at precisely these questions by investigating the effect of coalition agreements on cabinet stability.

An important implication of our argument presented in Chapter 2 is that coalition agreements influence cabinet stability. Coalition parties do not spend time and resources on negotiating a coalition agreement without a reason. Coalition agreements can help coalition parties to settle their differences and to focus on a joint policy agenda for the legislative term. Accordingly, Krauss (2018) has shown that the existence and the overall length of coalition agreements positively affect cabinet survival. However, coalition agreements vary extensively as we have seen in the preceding chapters. In particular, coalition parties might be tempted to only include policy issues in the coalition agreement that they can easily agree on while excluding conflictual issues to quickly take over offices and signal efficiency to voters. In such a case, a coalition agreement might not necessarily have a positive influence on the stability of the cabinet as unsettled divisive issues can lead to serious conflicts between coalition partners throughout the legislative term.

In this chapter, we accordingly argue that cabinets are more stable if parties negotiated compromises not only on uncontested, but more importantly also on conflictual policy issues. More specifically, we hypothesize that cabinets last longer, the more extensive conflictual issues are covered in the coalition agreement. We extend previous work by arguing and empirically demonstrating that it is not enough to merely negotiate an agreement. If coalition parties only focus on consensual issues and fail to struck a compromise on precisely the issues that divide them, coalition agreements will not have a great effect. However, if coalition parties seriously make an effort to overcome their policy differences and settle divisive issues before they take over governmental offices, coalition agreements have an important stabilizing effect as intra-cabinet conflict can be contained.

The chapter proceeds as follows. In the next section, we first of all discuss previous research on cabinet stability before we explain our theoretical expectations in more detail. Afterward, we illustrate the research design of this chapter before we present the results of the empirical analysis. We conclude this chapter with a summary of our results and a discussion of the broader implications for coalition governance and cabinet survival.

## 7.2 Previous research

Understanding why some coalition governments last longer than others has been one of the central questions for coalition scholars. The literature can be divided into three different approaches.

First, the so-called "attributes approach" argues that structural properties of multiparty cabinets can explain cabinet duration. For instance, previous research has found that the majority status of a cabinet (see e.g. Sanders and Herman 1977; Saalfeld 2008), the minimal winning status (see e.g. Laver 1974; Saalfeld 2008) and the ideological compactness of coalition cabinets (see e.g. Warwick 1979) are positively related to cabinet survival. In addition, the attributes approach has also identified a number of institutional rules that affect how long a coalition government lasts. For instance, the parliamentary dissolution powers of the head of state (see e.g. Strøm and Swindle 2002) and of the prime minister (see e.g. Schleiter and Morgan-Jones 2009) have been shown to influence coalition survival.

The second so-called "critical events approach" has argued that critical events like deaths or health problems of prime ministers, economic crises, scandals, or international conflicts best explain why coalition governments fall (see e.g. Browne, Frendreis, and Gleiber 1984; Frendreis, Gleiber, and Browne 1986). In this vein, Saalfeld (2008) has for instance found that the unemployment rate and high levels of inflation have a negative influence on cabinet duration.

According to the third "game theoretic approach" cabinet survival is importantly affected by strategic decisions of government actors. According to this view, coalition parties have three different choices: elections, non-electoral reorganization, or the status quo (Lupia and Strøm 1995). Parties decide which option to choose by carefully comparing the costs and benefits of these options. Building on this work, Diermeier and Stevenson (1999) distinguish between cabinet dissolution and cabinet replacement and show that dissolution hazards rise toward the end of the legislative term while replacement hazards stay flat (Diermeier and Stevenson 1999, p. 636).

Even though the large number of studies on coalition governance have shown that coalition parties extensively use control mechanisms such as cross-partisan junior ministers (e.g. Thies 2001; Verzichelli 2008), parliamentary committees (e.g. Martin and Vanberg 2004 2005 2011a), screening of ministerial candidates (e.g. Müller and Meyer 2010) or coalition agreements (e.g. Klüver and Bäck 2019) to settle intra-party conflicts, we have hardly any knowledge about the effectiveness of these control instruments with regard to cabinet stability (for an exception, see Krauss 2018). In this chapter, we address this important gap by studying how coalition agreements affect the survival of coalition governments.

## 7.3 The influence of coalition agreements on stability

In the previous chapters, we have argued that coalition agreements are important control devices that allow coalition parties to keep tabs on their partners. The underlying idea is that coalition agreements are contracts that bind the behavior of coalition parties during the legislative term. We have argued that three mechanisms can explain why coalition parties comply with the coalition agreement even though these contracts are not legally binding. First, coalition parties risk negative electoral repercussions if they do not comply with what they have negotiated. When coalition parties have concluded their coalition talks, they publish their coalition agreement and the media extensively reports about it. The coalition agreement serves as a yardstick against which the performance of the government is evaluated. If a party violates the agreement, its coalition partners will publicly blame the party for not keeping its promises which may result in electoral punishment. Second, coalition parties which violate the negotiated coalition agreement risk the stability of the cabinet. If coalition parties repeatedly deviate from the negotiated policy compromise, intra-cabinet conflicts will arise which may ultimately result in the fall of the government (Saalfeld 2008; Krauss 2018). Third, coalition parties not only endanger the stability of the current government, but they also risk future office opportunities as potential future coalition partners may refrain from forming a government with an unreliable partner (Saalfeld 2008; Tavits 2008).

However, coalition agreements vary extensively as we have shown in Chapter 4. For instance, when it comes to length, they range from only 86 words to over 67,000 words. But not only the length varies, also the attention to different policy issues varies considerably across coalition governments. Some issues are covered in great detail while others are hardly mentioned. Hence, coalition agreements are not the same in every coalition government, but their use differs extensively. In terms of understanding how coalition agreements can increase cabinet stability, it is important that coalition agreements can only make governments more durable if coalition parties have settled *divisive* policy issues. Coalition parties might be tempted to only focus on consensual policy issues in the coalition agreement in order to quickly take over offices and signal efficiency to voters. In such a case, a coalition agreement might not necessarily have a positive influence on the stability of the cabinet as unsettled divisive issues can lead to serious conflicts between coalition partners throughout the legislative term. Thus, we argue that coalition agreements can only stabilize multiparty cabinets if coalition parties settled precisely those policy issues that divide them.

In order to understand why settling divisive issues in coalition agreements can increase cabinet stability, we conceive of the bargaining over policies in coalition agreements as a two-stage process. Bargaining at the first stage occurs during the coalition formation stage and bargaining during the second stage occurs during the time of office (which we denote coalition governance here). Coalition parties can freely decide what they settle at the first and what they settle at the second stage. So, coalition parties may decide to quickly finalize coalition talks by only focusing on policy issues in the coalition agreement they can easily agree on while postponing bargaining about conflictual issues to the coalition governance stage. Or coalition parties may decide to take more time for policy bargaining during the first coalition formation stage in order to achieve a compromise on all policy issues to avoid intra-party conflicts during the time of office.

It is crucial to recognize how these two stages differ in order to understand the implications of these decisions for cabinet survival. Figure 7.1 illustrates how the coalition formation stages differs from the coalition governance stage.

| First Stage | | Second stage |
|---|---|---|
| **Coalition Formation** | ➡ | **Coalition Governance** |

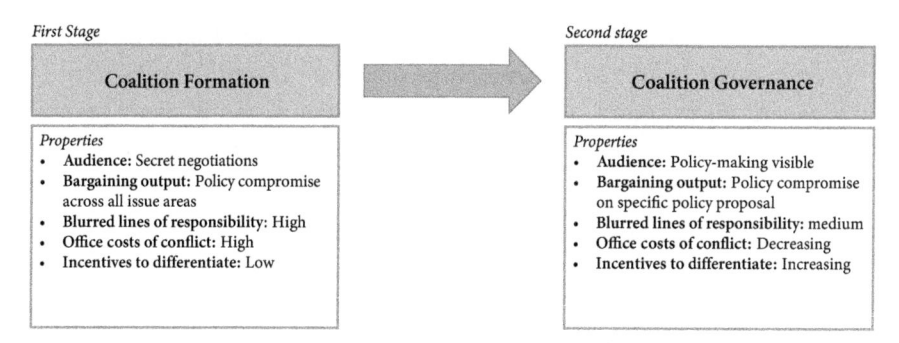

*Properties*
- Audience: Secret negotiations
- Bargaining output: Policy compromise across all issue areas
- Blurred lines of responsibility: High
- Office costs of conflict: High
- Incentives to differentiate: Low

*Properties*
- Audience: Policy-making visible
- Bargaining output: Policy compromise on specific policy proposal
- Blurred lines of responsibility: medium
- Office costs of conflict: Decreasing
- Incentives to differentiate: Increasing

**Figure 7.1** Stages of coalition policy bargaining

During the coalition formation stage, coalition parties bargain about policy behind closed doors. Coalition parties only go public once they have reached an agreement with regard to the policy agenda for the upcoming term and the distribution of ministerial portfolios. The bargaining results are typically published at a press conference during which the coalition agreement is presented to the general public.

The secrecy of coalition negotiations has important advantages for coalition parties. Coalition parties can freely bargain and fight about policies without having to fear immediate electoral repercussions. In order to form a coalition government, policy concessions are unavoidable. Coalition parties have diverging policy preferences and seek to satisfy their specific supporters. However, in a coalition government, political parties cannot single-handedly pursue their own policy objectives as this would lead to intra-cabinet conflict and may ultimately result in an early breakdown of the cabinet (Warwick 1994; Lupia and Strøm 1995; Saalfeld 2008). Hence, coalition parties are forced to come to an agreement with regard to the policy agenda for the joint time in office. The secrecy of coalition negotiations allows coalition parties to offer policy concessions to their partners without having to suffer from the negative electoral consequences such a cooperative behavior may have. As Fortunato (2019) has for instance shown, voters punish coalition parties for making policy compromises and coalition parties therefore do not want to be seen as "selling out" their policy agenda.

The secrecy becomes clear whenever some information leaks to the media before the results of the negotiations are officially published and the parties have to respond to the involuntary release of information. For example, during the coalition negotiations between Italy's populist 5Star Movement and the far-right League in 2018, an early coalition agreement draft was leaked to the Italian press. It was outlining plans to renegotiate EU-treaties and introduce an "opt-out" mechanism from the Euro currency. After the leak had caused turmoil amongst foreign creditors and the financial market, the two parties subsequently dismissed the document as "outdated" and claimed there was no plan to leave the eurozone (Politi 2018). To give another example, the 2021 coalition negotiations in the Netherlands were interrupted following the resignation of the leading negotiators due to a document leak. The politicians leading the talks from the liberal-left D66 party and the Prime Minister's liberal People's Party for Freedom and Democracy (VVD) quit, after the former was photographed while leaving the talks due to a positive coronavirus test. On that photo, secret notes she carried were visible and revealed information about the position of a senior lawmaker of the Christian Democrats (CDA) and possible cabinet constellations (*Coalition scouts quit after Ollongren accidentally reveals explosive notes* 2021). The two scouts released a statement admitting that "[...] they can no longer continue their work in an unfettered and unbiased manner" (Schaart and Adkins 2021).

Since coalition negotiations take place behind closed doors, bargaining during this stage has the important advantage that voters cannot identify who was responsible for a policy compromise. As the coalition agreement is collectively presented and coalition parties take collective responsibility for the negotiated policy agenda, it is unknown to the general public which party came forward in making policy concessions. Coalition parties can exploit the blurred lines of responsibility by justifying deviations from their proclaimed policy stances by publicly blaming their partners for the compromise that was unavoidable to form a government. Thus, coalition parties can openly cooperate in coalition negotiations exploiting the veil of secrecy while they can shift responsibility for policy concessions to their partners upon publication of the coalition agreement.

In addition, coalition negotiations have the advantage that coalition parties can negotiate about the entire policy agenda covering all policy areas. Such a multidimensional bargaining environment has the important advantage that policy deals can be struck across different policy dimensions opening up multiple opportunities for policy compromise. For instance, policy concessions on environmental policy by party A to party B can be compensated by policy concessions by party B to party A on labor market policy. In addition, since also the distribution of ministerial portfolios is negotiated during the government formation stage, there are widespread opportunities for policy compromises as for instance a policy reform that is of crucial importance to party A can be compensated by granting party B a specific ministerial portfolio that party B desires (see Chapter 6).

If coalition parties decide not to settle divisive policy issues during the government formation stage, the situation is much more difficult. Reaching a policy compromise during the time of office is much harder. Even though coalition parties can of course still bargain about a policy reform behind closed doors, it is much easier for voters to assign responsibility when only a single or just a handful of policy issues are touched upon. Unlike during the government formation stage when the entire policy agenda across multiple issues can be negotiated all at once, policy-making during the legislative term typically revolves around specific policy issues which are only loosely connected. Surely, coalition parties can always strike a bargain across two issues, but since the legislative machinery works very slowly, coalition parties can only deal with a limited number of proposals at a time. So losing out on one issue cannot be easily compensated by winning on another. Thus, given the secrecy, the multidimensionality and the blurred lines of responsibility of coalition negotiations, it is much easier to resolve policy conflicts at this stage before officially entering government.

Last but not least, coalition negotiations take place at the beginning of the legislative term when the next election is still four or five years away. Negotiating a policy compromise at this stage has a number of important advantages. First, at the beginning of the term, coalition parties have a full legislative term ahead of them during which they can enjoy the perks of office and enact preferred policies. Coalition parties therefore have strong incentives not to risk the stability of the cabinet as the breakdown of the cabinet would involve tremendous costs. However, as the legislative term progresses, the benefits of staying in the current government declines with every month in office. Thus, the potential for policy compromises decrease over the course of the legislative term as the benefits of office no longer outweigh the electoral costs of making policy concessions. Second, as it is important for coalition parties that voters identify their distinct policy profiles (Klüver and Spoon 2020), coalition parties have strong incentives to differentiate from their partners in the light of upcoming elections (Sagarzazu and Klüver 2017). Toward the end of the term, it is therefore much harder to resolve policy conflicts as coalition parties seek to distance themselves from their partners. Finally, voters typically have a short-term memory when it comes to assessing party performance. What happened four or five years ago, has typically faded away in the memory of voters when the next election approaches. So, the electoral costs of policy compromises increase over the electoral cycle as voters particularly take into account the performance of parties shortly before the next election. Given the changing cost-benefit calculation for coalition parties over the electoral cycle, it is much easier to make policy compromises during the government formation stage than during the time in office.

In conclusion, coalition agreements are important control devices that coalition parties can use to control their partners. Given the special context in which coalition negotiations take place, it is much easier to settle divisive issues during the government formation stage than later on when coalition parties are in office. Coalition agreements can only contain intra-cabinet conflict and ensure the smooth functioning of the cabinet throughout the legislative term when coalition parties have settled their policy differences. If coalition parties instead only focus on consensual issues in their coalition agreements and leave divisive issues open, fights over these issues will sooner or later emerge in the cabinet which may lead to conflict among the coalition partners, eventually resulting in a collapse of the coalition.

**H5:** *The more conflictual issues are settled in the coalition agreement, the lower the risk of early government termination.*

## 7.4 Research design

In this section we present our research design. We start by describing the operationalization of our dependent variable, cabinet duration, followed by the operationalization of the main explanatory variable, settled conflict in the coalition agreement, and the control variables. Afterward, we introduce the dataset that we rely on in order to test our theoretical expectation.

### 7.4.1 Measuring the dependent variable

In order to test our theoretical argument that coalition agreements can increase cabinet stability, we rely on cabinet duration as the dependent variable in this chapter.[1] Cabinet duration can be measured in two different ways. One the one hand, cabinet duration can be measured by relying on the absolute number of days a cabinet was in office. On the other hand, the stability of a cabinet could be operationalized by the relative duration which takes into account the constitutionally defined term limit of a government.

---

[1] Throughout this chapter, we use the terms "cabinet stability" and "cabinet duration" interchangeably. For a discussion about the differences between these two concepts, see Laver (2003).

Following most scholars in the literature (e.g. Saalfeld 2008; Schleiter and Morgan-Jones 2009), we measure cabinet duration as the actual duration in days. Nevertheless, we control for the length of the constitutional inter-election period as well as the maximum possible cabinet duration in our analysis in order to account for the fact that the constitutionally defined length of the legislative terms varies between countries. Cabinet duration is then calculated by subtracting the start date from the end date of the coalition cabinet. The data for the start and end dates of the cabinets were taken from the ERDDA dataset for coalition governments before 2012 (Andersson and Ersson 2012) and from the ParlGov dataset (Döring 2013; Döring and Manow 2019) for later cabinets.

To measure the duration of a cabinet, it is necessary to first define rules about how to decide when a cabinet started and when it ended. In this chapter, we follow the definition given by Andersson, Bergman, and Ersson (2014). A new cabinet is formed if any of the following statements are true: there was a general election, there was a change in the set of parties holding cabinet portfolios or there was a change of the head of cabinet (Andersson, Bergman, and Ersson 2014). The start date of a cabinet is defined as the "date that the PM/cabinet was inaugurated by the head of state alternatively the date of the investiture" (Andersson, Bergman, and Ersson 2014, 1). The definition of the end date of a cabinet is the date of the formal resignation of the cabinet or the date of the general election (Andersson and Ersson 2012).

We further included information on *how* the cabinets were terminated in our analysis. Müller, Bergman, and Strøm (2008) distinguish between technical terminations, conflictual terminations as well as voluntary early elections. Technical terminations are those that are not at the discretion of the cabinet such as the end of the legislative term. Most cabinets in Germany, for example, run until the end of the legislative term and have to be terminated because the next regularly scheduled election is taking place. Conflictual terminations take place whenever a conflict between the coalition parties, between the cabinet and the parliament or even within parties leads to an early demise of the cabinet. For instance, the Czech governments in our sample were almost always terminated due to internal conflicts. Lastly, some cabinets are terminated due to voluntary early elections. Some governments in Denmark, for example, call voluntary early elections to get the popular support for major policy reforms. Data on the way cabinets were terminated originate from Müller, Bergman, and Strøm (2008) for Western European countries until 1999. The data for cabinets after 1999 and for the Eastern coalitions was taken from Krauss (2018).

### 7.4.2 Operationalization of explanatory and control variables

We constructed two main explanatory variables that measure the level of settled conflict in the coalition agreement. We decided to not look at the overall level of conflict, but to measure conflict in 11 different issue areas. Only investigating for instance the general left-right dimension does not allow for mapping policy compromises and concessions that have been made in specific policy areas which is important for understanding the outcomes of coalition negotiations. The issue areas are the following: agriculture, civil rights, education, environment, European integration, decentralization, immigration, social welfare, defense, economy, and international politics. Table 5.1 in Chapter 5 provides an overview of the issue areas and how they were constructed based on our content analysis codebook.

To measure the policy conflict between potential coalition partners, we rely on the following measure: We use the range of the issue-specific policy positions held by all cabinet parties, which corresponds to the absolute distance between the policy position of the most left-winged and the policy position of the most right-winged member of the cabinet on a given issue (see Tsebelis 2002). We operationalize the policy positions of political parties on the basis of the Manifestos Project (MARPOR) (Volkens et al. 2018). The MARPOR has generated the most comprehensive and most widely used dataset on parties policy positions by applying a manual content analysis to election manifestos. Human coders have divided election manifestos into so-called "quasi-sentences" defined as "an argument or phrase which is the verbal expression of one idea or meaning" (Klingemann et al. 2006*b*, xxiii) and have allocated these quasi-sentences to policy categories specified a priori in a coding scheme. Where possible, directly opposing categories were specified (e.g. Military: Positive vs. Military: Negative) so that not only the attention to different policy issues, but also the ideal points of political parties can be estimated on the basis of the MARPOR data. The issue-specific policy positions were generated using the widely used additive percentage scores advocated by Budge (1999). First, the percentages of issue-specific left and right quasi-sentences of the total number of issue-specific coded quasi-sentences are computed. Then the percentage of left sentences is subtracted from the percentage of right sentences. Positive scores indicate right positions on an issue and negative scores indicate left positions on an issue.

Our main explanatory variable is the attention to conflictual topics in a coalition agreement. In order to arrive at this measure, we make use of the ideological distance between the cabinet members and compute the mean and the median conflict for each government in the next step. By doing so, we can determine those issues on which the coalition parties mostly agree on and, more importantly, those issues that are most divisive among coalition parties. We decided to use the mean and the median level of conflict as a government-specific benchmark for determining conflictual content because the level of conflict within governments varies substantially, which importantly influences the way the government handles conflict. For example, for a coalition government that consists of parties that are ideologically close, even a rather low level of conflict might be disruptive for their work. By contrast, coalitions formed between ideologically different parties might be more suited to deal with conflict since they are at least more prepared to face and solve conflict during the legislative term. We decided to use two different measures of settled conflict in the coalition agreements. The first one relies on the mean level of conflict as a benchmark for identifying conflictual content in coalition agreements. The second one is operationalized based on the median level of conflict between the coalition parties.

After computing the mean and median level of conflict in a coalition agreement, we basically divide the joint agreement into two parts: the first one covers those topics that are below the mean and median level of conflict. The second one includes those issues on which the coalition parties have conflicting views (i.e. the ideological distance is above the mean or median level of the coalition agreement respectively). For our analysis, the second part is the crucial one. In order to arrive at our measure of attention to conflictual topics in a coalition agreement, we therefore add up all quasi-sentences allocated to those issues that are above the mean and median conflict level respectively. This leaves us with the number of quasi-sentences devoted to conflictual issues in a coalition agreement as our main explanatory variables.

We decided to rely on the absolute number of quasi-sentences instead of a relative measure because we know from previous research that the length of coalition agreements actually matters for cabinet stability (Krauss 2018). Imagine a coalition agreement that includes a lot of conflictual topics, but is rather short. Even though the coalition parties concentrated on conflictual topics during coalition negotiations, a short coalition agreement is not able to sustainably settle policy conflict because laying out a policy compromise requires a lot of space. Hence, a short agreement would still leave considerable room of maneuver for the ministers to shirk from the compromise policies. A long coalition agreement, which includes a lot of quasi-sentences devoted to conflictual topics, is better able to constrain the ministers in the long run. Finally, we end up with a measure of settled conflict in coalition agreements that ranges between 0 and 1,420 for the mean level of conflict and 0 and 2,070 for the median level of conflict respectively.

In order to test our theoretical argument, we additionally control for a number of variables that may otherwise confound the expected relationship, namely the ideological divisiveness of the coalition cabinet, the status of a minimum winning coalition, the status of a minority government, the effective number of parliamentary parties as well as the length of the constitutional inter-election period (CIEP) and the maximum possible cabinet duration. First, we control for three different structural attributes of multiparty cabinets. We start with the overall ideological divisiveness of a coalition cabinet. Previous research has shown that a high level of ideological divisiveness in the cabinet substantially increases the risk of early government termination (see e.g. Sanders and Herman 1977; Saalfeld 2008; Schleiter and Morgan-Jones 2009). Ideological divisiveness is operationalized as the difference between the most extreme parties of the coalition based on the overall left-right positions held by cabinet parties. We measure ideological divisiveness on the left-right scale as this is the primary dimension of political conflict in most Western democracies (Marks, Haesly, and Mbaye 2002). We operationalize the policy positions of political parties on the basis of the Manifestos project (MARPOR) discussed above (Volkens et al. 2017). The left-right policy positions were estimated on the basis of the Manifesto project data using the widely used additive percentage scores advocated by (Budge 1999). First, the percentages of left and right quasi-sentences of the total number of coded quasi-sentences are computed. Then the percentage of left sentences is subtracted from the percentage of right sentences. Positive scores indicate right positions and negative scores indicate left positions.

We additionally control for the status of a minimal winning coalition. Minimal winning coalitions are those coalitions that do not include more parties than necessary in order to have a majority in the parliament. It is assumed that the distribution of policy and office spoils are ideal in the case of a minimal winning coalition which increases the benefits from being part of the coalition, thereby decreasing the motivation to terminate the cabinet early (see e.g. Laver 1974; Saalfeld 2008). We relied on data provided by the ParlGov database to operationalize this variable (Döring 2013; Döring and Manow 2019). Lastly, we also control for whether the coalition is a minority cabinet or not. Minority cabinets are said to be less durable because they have a higher vulnerability toward a defeat in parliament and votes of no confidence (Strøm and Swindle 2002; Saalfeld 2008). The risk of early government termination should therefore be higher if the cabinet is a minority coalition. The variable originates from the ParlGov database (Döring 2013; Döring and Manow 2019).

Aside from cabinet attributes, we also control for the effective number of parliamentary parties. On the one hand, this variable is a proxy for the intricacy of the bargaining environment in which the coalition governs. On the other hand, there are more potential outside options for the coalition parties to form alternative governments, the more parties are in parliament (Saalfeld 2008). The risk of early government termination should therefore increase with a higher effective number of parliamentary parties. The effective number of parliamentary parties was measured on the basis of the ParlGov database (Döring 2013; Döring and Manow 2019).

Lastly, we also control for temporal aspects. As has previously been mentioned, cabinet duration is dependent not only on the length of the constitutional inter-election period, but also on the maximum possible cabinet duration at the time the government is formed. We control for both variables in our analyses. The length of the constitutional inter-election period is measured in years and was coded by going through government records on- and offline. The maximum possible cabinet duration is defined as the time that is left until the next regularly scheduled election (Saalfeld 2008). While most governments have the full legislative term at their disposal when they get into office, some governments are formed after lengthy coalition negotiations or during the legislative term if another government terminated early without calling new elections. Especially for those governments, the benefits of being in office are smaller which is why the opportunity costs of calling new elections decrease (Lupia and Strøm 1995; Saalfeld 2008; Schleiter and Morgan-Jones 2009). We rely on data provided by ERDDA (Andersson, Bergman, and Ersson 2014) for the governments before 2012 and calculate the maximum possible cabinet duration ourselves for the coalitions after 2012 by adding the constitutional inter-election period to the past election date and subtracting the cabinet formation date. Both variables, the length of the constitutional inter-election period as well as the maximum possible cabinet duration, are hypothesized to have a risk-reducing influence on cabinet stability. Descriptive statistics for all variables can be found in Table 7.1.

**Table 7.1** Descriptive statistics (Chapter 7)

| Variable | Min. | Max. | Mean | Std. Dev. | N |
|---|---|---|---|---|---|
| Cabinet duration | 46 | 1861 | 826.58 | 489.65 | 224 |
| Settled conflict (mean) | 0 | 1420 | 224.98 | 271.27 | 224 |
| Settled conflict (median) | 0 | 2070 | 325.21 | 367.67 | 224 |
| Ideological divisiveness | 0 | 121.87 | 26.60 | 21.16 | 224 |
| Effective number of parties | 2.20 | 9.05 | 4.58 | 1.34 | 224 |
| Length of CIEP | 4 | 5 | 4.07 | 0.25 | 224 |
| Max. poss. cabinet duration | 284 | 1821 | 1269.94 | 324.58 | 224 |

| Variable | Value | Percentage | Frequency | N = 224 |
|---|---|---|---|---|
| Minimal winning coalition | Yes | 57.14 | 128 | |
| | No | 42.86 | 96 | |
| Minority status | Yes | 15.63 | 35 | |
| | No | 84.38 | 189 | |

### 7.4.3 Dataset

In order to test our theoretical argument that dealing with divisive issues in the coalition agreement lowers the risk of early government termination, we rely on the newly compiled COALITIONAGREE dataset on the content of coalition agreements that we have illustrated and presented in Chapters 3 and 4 of this book. In this particular chapter, the analysis is based on 224 coalition agreements negotiated by 181 political parties in 24 West and East European countries from 1945 until 2015. These countries include Austria, Belgium, Bulgaria, the Czech Republic, Denmark, Estonia, Finland, Germany, Greece, Hungary, Iceland, Ireland, Latvia, Lithuania, Luxembourg, the Netherlands, Norway, Poland, Portugal, Romania, Slovakia, Slovenia, Sweden, and the United Kingdom. The selection of countries follows the established standard in coalition research and only includes European democracies that were governed by coalition cabinets that have publicly released a coalition agreement at least once in the time period under investigation (see e.g. Andersson, Bergman, and Ersson 2014). This country sample is characterized by variation in several institutional features, which strengthens the external validity of our findings.

## 7.5 Conflict in coalition agreements

Before we empirically test our hypothesis, we take a closer look at our explanatory variable, conflict in coalition agreements. The distribution of our two

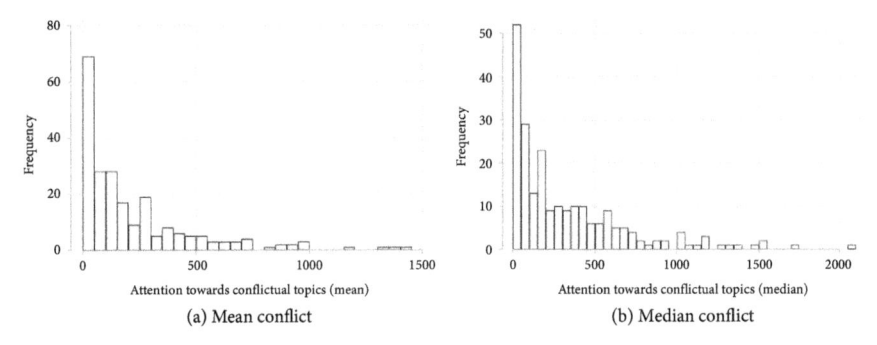

**Figure 7.2** Attention to conflictual topics

main explanatory variables can be found in Figure 7.2. The graphs are clearly skewed to the right and most of the coalition agreements allocate 250 quasi-sentences or less to conflictual topics (or less than 500 quasi-sentences for the median level of conflict). Accordingly, the mean value of the mean attention toward conflictual topics is at around 225 quasi-sentences (with a standard deviation of around 271) while the mean value of the median attention toward conflictual topics amounts to 325 quasi-sentences (with a standard deviation of around 368).

One question we may ask ourselves is whether coalition agreements are just cheap talk or not. While our explanatory variables allow for assessing the extent to which coalition agreements deal with divisive issues, it would be interesting to see how conflictual topics relate to the overall content of coalition contracts. In order to do this, we have divided the number of quasi-sentences devoted to conflictual issues by the total number of quasi-sentences in a coalition agreement. By doing so, we end up with the share of conflictual quasi-sentences in the coalition agreements. Low levels of conflict would lend support to the expectation that coalition agreements are just cheap talk whereas higher scores would indicate that the coalition partners are actually trying to solve their ideological differences during the negotiations and, by including them in the coalition agreement, making an effort to stick to these compromise policies during the legislative term. The distribution of these shares can be found in Graph 7.3.

In general, the attention toward conflictual issues varies between different coalition agreements and is comparatively high. The shares for the measure of mean conflict levels ranges between 0 and 0.79 with a mean value of 0.37 whereas the median measure varies between 0 and 0.83 with a mean of 0.54. Figure 7.3a is additionally fairly normally distributed whereas Figure 7.3b is

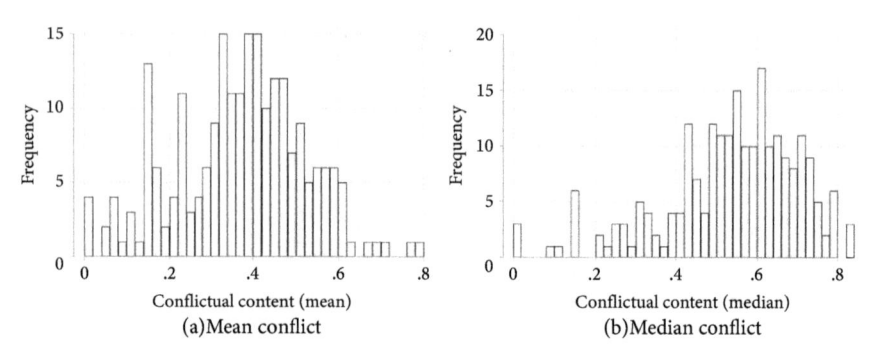

**Figure 7.3** Conflictual content in coalition agreements

slightly skewed to the left. Overall, these graphs show that coalition agreements in general are attentive toward conflictual topics. The coalition partners do not only include consensual topics in the coalition agreement, but they actually invest time and effort into finding a compromise on divisive issues. Hence, coalition agreements are not just cheap talk. Since they do include a substantial amount of conflictual topics, they can be used by the coalition partners to constrain the ministers if they are trying to shirk and they can actually help to solve or even prevent conflict between the coalition parties. This suggests that coalition agreements are an important tool for coalition parties to manage coalition governance and to prevent early government termination. In the next part of this chapter, we will analyze if the risk of early government termination indeed decreases with the attention that coalition parties pay to divisive issues in their coalition contract.

## 7.6 Data analysis

In this section, we present the results of our empirical analysis. We begin by discussing the data structure and the model specification we employ in order to test our theoretical argument on the basis of the compiled data. Afterward we present the results of the empirical analysis before we illustrate the detected effects.

As we are interested in analyzing the effect of dealing with divisive policy issues in coalition agreements on cabinet survival, our dependent variable is the duration of a cabinet. As discussed in the research design section, the duration of a cabinet is measured as the number of days a cabinet stays in office. The phenomenon of interest is therefore the duration until a coalition government is terminated so that we are dealing with duration data. Event history models are designed to model such duration data where the phenomenon of interest is duration until a certain event occurs (Box-Steffensmeier and Zorn 2001; Box-Steffensmeier and Jones 2004). One of the great advantages of event history analysis over ordinary regression analysis is the ability to handle censored data. Duration datasets typically include a number of cases that are still in progress. While ordinary regression would simply exclude these observations from the dataset or would assign a duration value that underestimates their likelihood to survive, event history models can handle censoring and allow for making use of all the information that is conveyed by cases that are still pending.

Censoring is a major issue in studying cabinet stability. Governments that last until the end of the legislative term are usually censored because they would have lasted longer if they had been unconstrained by the constitutionally defined term limits. While King et al. (1990) argued that all governments that lasted until 12 months before the next election should be censored because of the proximity to the election, Diermeier and Stevenson (1999) developed the competing risks approach building on the work by Lupia and Strøm (1995). They argued that there were two different ways of termination: dissolution and replacement. Dissolution means that the cabinet and parliament are dissolved and new elections are held (Diermeier and Stevenson 1999, p. 1502). Replacement on the other hand means that the current cabinet is directly replaced by a new one without new elections (Diermeier and Stevenson 1999, p. 1502). Only the cabinets that reach the end of the constitutional inter-election period or are terminated due to technical reasons were randomly censored (Diermeier and Stevenson 1999, p. 1060).

In this chapter, we follow Diermeier and Stevenson (1999) and analyze the survival of coalition cabinets using the competing risks approach. When analyzing the hazards of cabinet dissolution, we will censor all coalitions governments that terminated due to technical reasons such as the end of the constitutionally defined inter-election period or the death of the prime minister and all cabinets that were terminated due to replacement. Accordingly, we will censor all coalition governments that were terminated by early elections and all cabinets that terminated due to technical reasons when analyzing the risks of cabinet replacement. We additionally estimate another risk that is of particular interest in this chapter: conflictual termination. Since our theoretical argument is that coalition agreements can increase cabinet stability by containing intra-cabinet conflict throughout the legislative term, we expect the effect should be strongest for conflictual terminations.

We run four different models: conflictual terminations, replacements, dissolutions as well as a pooled sample. Since our theoretical argument suggests that the level of settled conflict should decrease the risk of potential conflict in the coalition, our main model concentrates on conflictual terminations (Model 7.1 and Model 7.5 respectively). Models 7.2 and 7.3 (and Models 7.6 and 7.7 respectively) account for the competing risks approach brought forward by Diermeier and Stevenson (1999). Replacements are those terminations that do not end with new elections but with a new government being formed whereas dissolutions end with new elections (Diermeier and Stevenson 1999). These two ways of termination follow different logics since dissolutions, in contrast to replacements, effectively reset the clock, especially with regard to seat allocation. Accordingly, Diermeier and Stevenson (1999, pp. 636–638) have shown that dissolution hazards increase toward the end of the legislative term whereas the hazards for replacements remain flat. The last model (7.4, 7.8 respectively) includes the pooled sample where voluntary early elections are no longer censored.

Before we run our main analysis, we first run four models in which we check if the existence of a coalition agreement as such decreases the risk of early government termination as previous research has suggested (Saalfeld 2008; Krauss 2018). The results can be found in Table 7.2. In part contrary to previous research, we only find a significant and risk-decreasing influence of coalition agreements on early elections and not on conflictual or pooled terminations (even though it just so fails to reach conventional levels of statistical significance for pooled terminations). One potential explanation for this difference could be the different samples. These findings further strengthen the need to take a closer look at the content of coalition agreement since a purely dichotomous measure does not do justice to the enormous variance with regard to the design and the content of coalition agreements.

The results for the mean conflict attention measure can be found in Table 7.3. The coefficient displayed here are hazard ratios. A hazard ratio above 1 indicates a risk-increasing effect whereas a hazard ratio below one reduces the risk of early government termination (Box-Steffensmeier and Jones 2004). In three of the four models, the hazard ratio for mean attention is below one and statistically significant at least at the 5 percent level. Hence, the results of these three models support our hypothesis: the more conflictual topics are covered in the coalition agreement, the lower the risk of early government termination. The hazard ratio of mean attention for dissolution hazards, however, is above one and not significant. Hence, there is no influence of the attention toward conflictual topics on dissolutions. One reason for this might be that early elections reset the clock and even a coalition agreement that pays

**Table 7.2** The influence of coalition agreements on cabinet stability

| DV: Cabinet duration | Model 7.1 | Model 7.2 | Model 7.3 | Model 7.4 |
|---|---|---|---|---|
|  | Conflict | Replacement | Dissolution | Pooled |
| **Explanatory variable** |  |  |  |  |
| Existence of coalition agreement | 0.857 | 1.204 | 0.503*** | 0.795 |
|  | (0.149) | (0.254) | (0.130) | (0.127) |
|  | (0.0004) | (0.001) | (0.001) | (0.000) |
| **Control variables** |  |  |  |  |
| Ideological divisiveness | 1.003 | 1.000 | 1.008 | 1.003 |
|  | (0.004) | (0.004) | (0.006) | (0.004) |
| Minimal Winning Coalition | 0.748 | 0.540*** | 2.129* | 0.762 |
|  | (0.147) | (0.113) | (0.942) | (0.143) |
| Minority Cabinet | 0.918 | 0.721 | 2.554** | 1.136 |
|  | (0.213) | (0.188) | (1.143) | (0.239) |
| Effective Number of Parties | 1.113* | 1.112* | 0.970 | 1.100* |
|  | (0.064) | (0.062) | (0.140) | (0.060) |
| Length of CIEP | 0.922 | 0.520** | 2.580*** | 1.008 |
|  | (0.273) | (0.157) | (0.869) | (0.277) |
| Max. poss. cabinet duration | 0.999*** | 1.000 | 0.999*** | 0.999*** |
|  | (0.000) | (0.000) | (0.000) | (0.000) |
| Observations | 396 | 396 | 396 | 396 |
| Failures | 173 | 132 | 67 | 199 |
| Log likelihood | −902.905 | −714.933 | −354.752 | −1029.003 |

*** $p \leq 0.01$, ** $p \leq 0.05$, * $p \leq 0.10$; Coefficients displayed are hazard ratios

attention to conflictual topics is not able to prevent the wish for a dissolution of parliament.

With regard to control variables, we find that the effective number of parliamentary parties coherently increases the risk of early government termination (except for dissolutions hazards) whereas the maximum possible cabinet duration has a risk-reducing influence (except for dissolution hazards). Both of these variables are in line with the conventional expectations in the coalition literature.

In order to further illustrate the effect of settling divisive issues in the coalition agreement on cabinet stability, Figure 7.4 shows the survival hazards of the coalition cabinets in our sample and is based on Model 7.1. The x-axis displays the number of days since the formation of the coalition while the y-axis shows the percentage of governments that have not yet been terminated. We make a distinction between cabinets with the minimum value of settled conflict (solid line), the mean value (dashed line) and the maximum value (dotted line). This figure clearly shows that the level of settled conflict in coalition agreements has

## 166 DO COALITION AGREEMENTS WORK?

Table 7.3 Explaining cabinet stability (mean conflict)

| DV: Cabinet duration | Model 7.1 | Model 7.2 | Model 7.3 | Model 7.4 |
|---|---|---|---|---|
|  | Conflict | Replacement | Dissolution | Pooled |
| **Explanatory variable** |  |  |  |  |
| Salience (mean conflict) | 0.999** | 0.998*** | 1.001 | 0.999** |
|  | (0.0004) | (0.001) | (0.001) | (0.000) |
| **Control variables** |  |  |  |  |
| Ideological divisiveness | 0.999 | 0.996 | 1.015 | 0.999 |
|  | (0.005) | (0.005) | (0.012) | (0.005) |
| Minimal Winning Coalition | 0.853 | 0.646* | 2.843 | 0.861 |
|  | (0.201) | (0.159) | (2.082) | (0.195) |
| Minority Cabinet | 0.873 | 0.891 | 2.586 | 1.001 |
|  | (0.290) | (0.318) | (2.006) | (0.308) |
| Effective Number of Parties | 1.133* | 1.243*** | 0.810 | 1.128* |
|  | (0.085) | (0.097) | (0.180) | (0.081) |
| Length of CIEP | 1.044 | 1.310 | 0.819 | 1.169 |
|  | (0.503) | (0.692) | (0.518) | (0.520) |
| Max. poss. cabinet duration | 0.999*** | 0.999*** | 0.999 | 0.998*** |
|  | (0.0004) | (0.0004) | (0.001) | (0.0003) |
| Observations | 224 | 224 | 224 | 224 |
| Failures | 110 | 90 | 30 | 120 |
| Log likelihood | −519.000 | −433.646 | −145.134 | −560.424 |

*** $p \leq 0.01$, ** $p \leq 0.05$, * $p \leq 0.10$; Coefficients displayed are hazard ratios

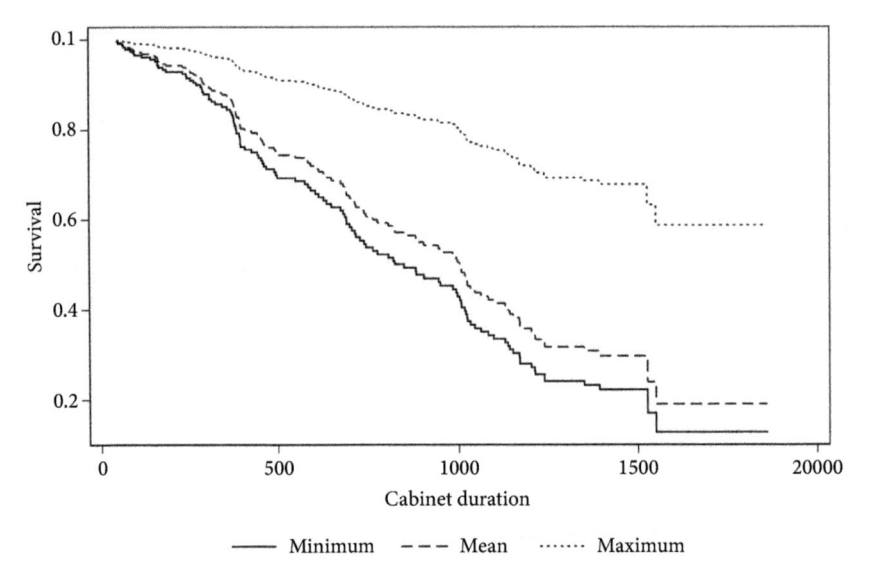

Figure 7.4 Effect of mean attention on cabinet stability

Table 7.4 Explaining cabinet stability (median conflict)

| DV: Cabinet duration | Model 7.5 | Model 7.6 | Model 7.7 | Model 7.8 |
|---|---|---|---|---|
|  | Conflict | Replacement | Dissolution | Pooled |
| **Explanatory variable** |  |  |  |  |
| Salience (median conflict) | 0.999** | 0.999*** | 1.000 | 0.999** |
|  | (0.0003) | (0.0004) | (0.0004) | (0.0003) |
| **Control variables** |  |  |  |  |
| Ideological divisiveness | 0.999 | 0.995 | 1.015 | 0.999 |
|  | (0.005) | (0.005) | (0.012) | (0.005) |
| Minimal Winning Coalition | 0.832 | 0.612** | 2.890 | 0.841 |
|  | (0.195) | (0.148) | (2.117) | (0.190) |
| Minority Cabinet | 0.822 | 0.798 | 2.679 | 0.944 |
|  | (0.272) | (0.281) | (2.093) | (0.290) |
| Effective Number of Parties | 1.140* | 1.255*** | 0.815 | 1.136* |
|  | (0.086) | (0.098) | (0.178) | (0.082) |
| Length of CIEP | 1.037 | 1.313 | 0.871 | 1.166 |
|  | (0.498) | (0.693) | (0.536) | (0.518) |
| Max. poss. cabinet duration | 0.999*** | 0.999*** | 0.999 | 0.998*** |
|  | (0.0004) | (0.0004) | (0.001) | (0.0003) |
| Observations | 224 | 224 | 224 | 224 |
| Failures | 110 | 90 | 30 | 120 |
| Log likelihood | −518.885 | −433.456 | −145.330 | −560.216 |

***$p \leq 0.01$, **$p \leq 0.05$, *$p \leq 0.10$; Coefficients displayed are hazard ratios

a substantial influence on cabinet stability. The higher the attention to divisive issues in coalition contracts, the longer the cabinet lasts.

Table 7.4 includes the results for the attention to conflictual issues above the median conflict level. Similarly to the first analysis, the hazard ratio of our main explanatory variable is below one and statistically significant for conflictual terminations, replacements as well as the pooled sample. These results lend further support for our hypothesis. The more conflictual issues are covered in the coalition agreement, the lower the risk of early government termination. With regard to control variables, we again find that the effective number of parliamentary parties has a risk-increasing effect while the maximum possible cabinet duration decreases the risk of early government termination.

Figure 7.5 shows the survival hazards for the minimum (solid line), mean (dashed line) and maximum value (dotted line) of settled conflict in the coalition agreement and is based on Model 7.5. It again demonstrates the substantial influence of the level of settled conflict in a coalition agreement on the risk of early government termination.

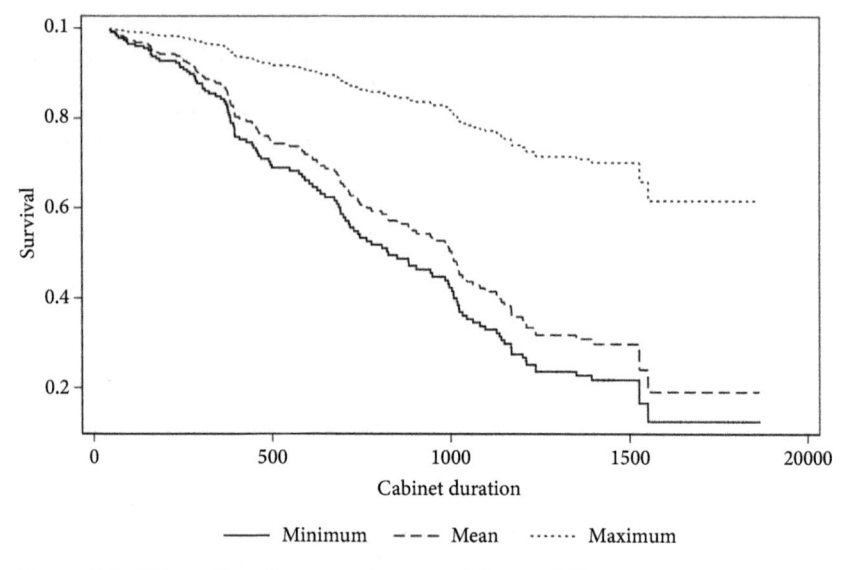

**Figure 7.5** Effect of median attention on cabinet stability

In conclusion, our analysis has shown that the attention to conflictual issues in coalition agreements importantly matters for cabinet stability. Overall, our hypothesis is broadly supported by our empirical results: The higher the attention to conflictual issues in the coalition agreement, the lower the risk of early government termination. The content of coalition agreements thus matters a great deal which contradicts the notion of coalition agreements being cheap talk.

## 7.7 Robustness check

According to Müller and Strøm (2008), coalition agreements include policies, office allocation, and procedural rules. They found that coalition agreements are mostly concerned with policies, but that procedural rules are important as well (see also Chapter 4). Saalfeld (2008) argues that, amongst other things, coalition agreements have a positive influence on cabinet stability because they make it easier for coalition parties to deal with conflicts that arise during the legislative term. Accordingly, an alternative explanation about why coalition agreements have an influence on cabinet stability would be that the procedural rules included in coalition contracts are responsible for the stabilizing effect. By relying on the newly compiled COALITIONAGREE dataset, we can now

Table 7.5 Explaining cabinet stability (procedural rules)

| DV: Cabinet duration | Model 7.9 | Model 7.10 | Model 7.11 | Model 7.12 |
|---|---|---|---|---|
| | Conflict | Replacement | Dissolution | Pooled |
| **Explanatory variable** | | | | |
| Procedural rules | 1.000 | 1.000 | 0.993 | 0.999 |
| | (0.002) | (0.002) | (0.006) | (0.002) |
| **Control variables** | | | | |
| Ideological divisiveness | 1.001 | 0.998 | 1.012 | 1.000 |
| | (0.005) | (0.005) | (0.011) | (0.005) |
| Minimal Winning Coalition | 0.825 | 0.608** | 2.897 | 0.824 |
| | (0.200) | (0.152) | (2.099) | (0.192) |
| Minority Cabinet | 0.830 | 0.805 | 2.497 | 0.943 |
| | (0.277) | (0.288) | (1.980) | (0.292) |
| Effective Number of Parties | 1.072 | 1.144* | 0.835 | 1.066 |
| | (0.079) | (0.089) | (0.174) | (0.076) |
| Length of CIEP | 0.839 | 0.938 | 0.924 | 0.942 |
| | (0.395) | (0.491) | (0.562) | (0.410) |
| Max. poss. cabinet duration | 0.998*** | 0.999*** | 0.999 | 0.998*** |
| | (0.0004) | (0.0004) | (0.001) | (0.0003) |
| Observations | 224 | 224 | 224 | 224 |
| Failures | 110 | 90 | 30 | 120 |
| Log likelihood | −521.832 | −438.918 | −145.286 | −563.391 |

***$p \leq 0.01$, **$p \leq 0.05$, *$p \leq 0.10$; Coefficients displayed are hazard ratios

test if this alternative mechanism can account for the positive effect of coalition agreements on cabinet duration.

The results of this analysis can be found in Table 7.5. The independent variable, procedural rules, is operationalized as the number of quasi-sentences devoted to procedural rules in the coalition agreement.[2] The event history analysis shows that procedural rules do not have any systematic influence on the risk of early government termination. Or, in other words, the risk of early government termination does not decrease with the attention to procedural rules in the coalition agreement. Thus, the stabilizing effect of coalition agreements is not due to procedural rules settled in the coalition treaty. What matters is that coalition parties seriously make an effort of overcoming their differences and codify a policy compromise in the coalition agreement.

---

[2] For more details regarding procedural rules, please see the coding scheme in Chapter 3.

## 7.8 Conclusion

Do coalition agreements work? In this chapter we have analyzed if coalition agreements have an influence on cabinet stability. More specifically, we have argued that it is important to take into account the content of coalition agreements with regard to cabinet stability. Coalition agreements should only be able to properly serve as a control mechanism if the parties were successful in finding compromise policies for conflictual issues. If the parties only include those issues on which they can agree on easily, there is a considerable risk that fights over conflictual issues will emerge during their term in office. Hence, we hypothesized that the risk of early government termination is lower, the more conflictual topics the coalition parties settle in their coalition agreements. We tested our theoretical argument by relying on the newly compiled COALITIONAGREE dataset.

The results support our theoretical expectations: Coalition governments on average last longer when coalition parties struck a deal on divisive policies in their agreement. Coalition agreements have an important potential to contain cabinet conflict and increase cabinet stability. However, it is important that coalition parties actually sit down and seriously make an effort to overcome their policy differences. Just talking about consensual issues does not help much. What counts is that coalition parties find and codify a compromise on policy issues that divide them. Or, in other words, if coalition governments are able to compromise on conflictual topics and if they include these compromise policies in the coalition agreement, then these governments are less likely to terminate early.

Our results therefore suggest that yes, coalition agreements do indeed work, at least with regard to cabinet duration and that it is important to take into account the actual content of coalition agreements. Hence, this chapter makes an important contribution to the literature on coalition governments and cabinet stability by showing that not only the existence and length, but also the content of coalition agreements is crucial for the stability of coalition cabinets. Future research should therefore take into account the content of coalition agreements for analyses of payoff allocation, coalition governance, and also cabinet survival. As the new COALITIONAGREE dataset presented in this book is made publicly available with this monograph, future coalition studies can easily take the content of coalition agreements into account when studying coalition governments.

PART IV

COALITION AGREEMENTS,
MULTIPARTY GOVERNMENTS,
AND DEMOCRACY

# 8
# Conclusions and implications

## 8.1 The main findings

Coalition agreements are important policy platforms that play a crucial role for policy-making and coalition governance in parliamentary democracies. Before taking over office, parties entering a multiparty government typically engage in lengthy coalition negotiations in which they bargain about who gets what in terms of policy payoffs. In most situations when a coalition government forms, parties bargain over a joint policy agenda that is written down in public coalition agreements. Even though these contracts are not legally binding, they define the policy priorities of governments taking over office.

Why do political parties in parliamentary democracies go through the ordeal of negotiating lengthy agreements with their coalition partners when forming a government? Parties which form governments together clearly have different policy priorities, which should make it difficult to reach compromises and to draft detailed coalition agreements. So why do coalition parties negotiate coalition agreements? This was the question we set out to answer at the start of this book.

We have argued that the decision of coalition parties whether to draft comprehensive coalition agreements is based on a careful cost-benefit calculation. Coalition agreements are important control devices that coalition parties can employ to keep their partners in line. However, writing detailed coalition contracts takes time and resources, but most importantly, political parties have to make policy compromises for which parties may be punished at the next election (see e.g. Fortunato 2019; Klüver and Spoon 2020). The main idea put forward in this book is that the decision whether to negotiate a comprehensive coalition agreement depends on the preference configuration among coalition parties and the allocation of ministerial portfolios.

In Chapter 2, we have argued that parties will only decide to engage in lengthy and resource-intensive negotiations about policy issues when they disagree on an issue that is important to all partners (see also Chapter 5).

Second, we have moreover theorized that the ministerial portfolio allocation affects the cost-benefit calculation of coalition partners (see also Chapter 6). Since controlling a ministry grants parties with important information advantages and policy-making competences, coalition parties seek to particularly constrain their partners when they control the ministry in charge of a policy area. Finally, changing the perspective by looking at the effect of coalition agreements on cabinet stability, we have argued that coalition agreements can only serve as effective control devices stabilizing multiparty cabinets if coalition parties settled precisely those policy issues that divide them (see also Chapter 7). Coalition parties might be tempted to only focus on consensual policy issues in the coalition agreement in order to quickly take over offices and signal efficiency to voters. In such a case, a coalition agreement might not necessarily have a positive influence on the stability of the cabinet as unsettled divisive issues can lead to serious conflicts between coalition partners throughout the legislative term.

Despite the central importance of coalition agreements for coalition governance and policy-making, there has been remarkably little research on this topic. The main reason for this is the lack of a comprehensive dataset that maps their content. We have addressed this problem by presenting the comprehensive COALITIONAGREE dataset that covers over 200 coalition agreements that have been negotiated by coalition parties between 1945 and 2015 in 24 West and East European countries in Chapter 3. This dataset is based on a comprehensive content analysis of coalition agreements performed by human coders with country-specific expertise and native language skills. They classified the content of the agreements into a large number of policy categories that can be easily linked to existing datasets on the content of election manifestos (Budge et al. 2001; Klingemann et al. 2006*b*; Volkens et al. 2013) and on parties, elections, and cabinets (e.g. the ParlGov or ERDDA datasets, see Döring and Manow 2019; Bergman, Ilonszki, and Müller 2019*a*). The usefulness of the dataset goes way beyond this particular book and will be without doubt employed by numerous researchers working on coalition governments, legislative politics, party competition, and political representation.

Based on the novel COALITIONAGREE dataset, we have presented important new evidence on the design and content of coalition agreements and how this varies across cabinets, countries, and over time. In the following, we will briefly summarize our main findings. We start out by summarizing our main descriptive findings about the use and content of coalition agreements and how the patterns have changed over time. We then turn to answering our main research question by summarizing our findings as to why parties draft coalition agreements. Lastly, we discuss the conclusions we can draw about the impact of coalition agreements on cabinet stability on the basis of our empirical analyses.

### 8.1.1 What do coalition agreements in Europe look like?

Analyzing over 400 coalition cabinets formed over the postwar period (1945–2015) in Western and Eastern Europe, we show that nearly 60 percent have negotiated an agreement that is publicly announced before taking office. Hence, not all coalition cabinets actually decide to write an agreement, and in some cases parties draft a contract, but do not release it to the general public. It should also be noted that coalition cabinets do not always negotiate a new coalition agreement, but instead sometimes rely on the agreement that was negotiated by the incumbent government. We moreover detected significant variation across countries, for example, in Luxembourg and Finland, all or almost all coalition governments negotiated and announced coalition agreements, whereas in Romania and Bulgaria, this is the case for 20 percent or less of the coalition cabinets that have formed.

Has the use of coalition agreements changed over time? While coalition agreements were not that common in the 1940s, things have clearly changed over the following decades. While only about 40 percent of all coalition cabinets in the 1940s were based on a coalition agreement, over 55 percent of all cabinets in the 1950s and 1960s did negotiate such contracts. The increasing trend peaks in the 1970s with almost 80 (78) percent of the governments being based on coalition agreements, and then the trend stabilizes at around 70 percent since the 2000s. Thus, there does seem to be a historical trend toward more coalition governments presenting a written contract to the public.

A number of recent studies have suggested that the length of coalition agreements is an important indicator of the extent to which an agreement is used as a control device (e.g. Indridason and Kristinsson 2013). How long are the coalition agreements in post-war Western and Eastern Europe that we have assembled for the COALITIONAGREE dataset? On average, coalition agreements in our sample contain about 11,000 words. However, the length varies substantially both across and within countries, with the shortest agreement only being 86 words long (the Kekkonen V cabinet in Finland), and the longest coalition agreement containing over 67,000 words (the Bettel I cabinet in Luxembourg).

Previous research by Indridason and Kristinsson (2013) shows that the length of coalition agreements has on average increased over time in Western Europe. How does the length of coalition agreements vary in our larger sample covering a more recent time period and also comprising Eastern European countries? We show in Chapter 4 that while in the 1940s, the average word count of a coalition agreement was around 1,000 words, it increased continuously since the 1950s, reaching an average of over 5,000 words in the 1970s, and an average of over 16,000 words in the post-2000 period. Thus, there is a very clear trend toward writing ever longer coalition agreements over time.

Müller and Strøm (1999a) show based on a sample of coalition agreements drafted in 13 West European countries that three different points are typically settled in coalition treaties: policy agreements, portfolio allocation, and procedural rules. Covering a more recent time period, and also East European countries, we can now update their analysis. We show in Chapter 4 that coalition agreements are first and foremost policy agreements. More precisely, coalition governments devote on average over 90 percent of their agreements to policies. By contrast, procedural rules receive very little attention and the allocation of ministerial offices are typically only very briefly mentioned in coalition agreements. Our results show that there is some country-specific variation here. While countries like Denmark and Estonia almost exclusively talk about policies in their coalition agreements, Lithuanian coalition agreements mostly consist of procedural rules.

Having established that most coalition agreements are policy documents, which policy issues are generally covered in these agreements? In Chapter 4 we present the average attention that coalition governments pay to different policy issues in their agreements across countries and over time. We show that the policy issues that receive most attention in coalition contracts are the Economy, Social Welfare, Civil rights, and the Environment. By contrast, policy issues that are only moderately covered in the coalition agreements are Agriculture, Education, and International Politics.

Using our dataset, it is also possible to analyze how issue coverage changes over time. In Chapter 4 we show that, across the entire time period, Economy and Welfare and Quality of Life are the most important policy domains covered in the coalition agreements in the European countries. There are some common patterns over time. For instance, Welfare and Quality of Life have become more and more important over the years, receiving even more attention than the Economy in coalition agreements since the mid-1990s.

There are also some policy areas that show high volatility over time, with some governments clearly focusing on them, whereas others are not doing so. For example, the salience for the Economy varies between 20 percent in the year 2000 and 45 percent during the 1950s. Similarly, the attention devoted to Welfare and Quality of Life is also highly volatile, ranging between 5 and 30 percent. Clearly such variation may be related to both over-time contextual changes and to changes in government composition.

### 8.1.2 Why do parties negotiate coalition agreements?

The main puzzle that we have aimed to resolve in this book is why political parties in parliamentary democracies negotiate lengthy and detailed agreements with their coalition partners when forming a government. There are a number of important costs involved in reaching coalition agreements. Coalition parties typically have to make policy concessions and compromise on policies they have promised to their voters during the preceding election campaign which may come with both a risk of intra-party conflict and electoral costs. Why do coalition parties risk intra-party conflict and electoral punishment? Why don't they simply distribute ministerial posts and let each party have their way in the department that they control?

To resolve this puzzle, we have started out in Chapter 2 by presenting our theoretical argument. Our major argument is that coalition agreements are important control devices that coalition parties use to keep tabs on their partners, but that their use importantly varies with the preference configuration and the allocation of ministerial portfolios across policy areas. First, we have argued that parties will only decide to engage in lengthy and resource-intensive negotiations about policy issues when they disagree on an issue that is important to all partners. Second, since controlling a ministry grants parties with important information advantages and policy-making competences, we have suggested that coalition parties seek to particularly constrain their partners when they control the ministry in charge of a policy area.

In Chapter 5 we set out to empirically evaluate part of this theoretical argument, asking the question, "Why do coalition parties settle some policy issues in great detail while other issues are hardly mentioned in coalition agreements?" Drawing on the more general argument about the costs and benefits of establishing coalition agreements as control mechanisms, we for example predict that political parties will focus on specific policy issues in a coalition agreement when they disagree with their coalition partner over the issue, and when the issue is highly salient to their own party.

We argue, and show using our comparative dataset on the content of coalition agreements, that ideological conflict over an issue in a coalition positively affects issue attention as coalition parties have stronger incentives to negotiate a detailed policy agenda that constrains their coalition partners when intra-cabinet conflict is high. However, we argued that this effect is conditioned by preference tangentiality among coalition partners. We find support for this argument in our empirical analysis, showing that it is only if the parties actually care about the same policy issues and have opposing views, that they negotiate a lengthy agreement about the issue. In other cases, when coalition parties do not care much about a policy domain, they are more likely to grant the coalition partner discretion to pursue their preferred policies, even if they hold an opposing view on how the issue should be dealt with.

Chapter 5 thus presents strong evidence in favor of the idea that coalition agreements are used as control mechanisms by the parties when they enter a government. If they did not consider that such contracts could constrain the behavior of individual ministers, or at least publicly give them a reason to do so, they should not negotiate issues where they deviate from their coalition partners in such detail. Reaching an agreement with your coalition partners on policy issues where you deviate from each other should be especially costly, as it is likely to involve some policy compromises that are publicly presented in the coalition agreements. Such policy concessions come with important electoral costs as voters are likely to punish parties which compromise too much and do not keep the promises that they have made during the electoral campaign.

In Chapter 6, we continue with evaluating the general theoretical argument that parties use coalition agreements as control mechanisms, but now focus on the question if ministerial portfolio allocation affects the extent to which coalition agreements are used to limit agency loss. The idea is that detailed policy contracts can "help coalitions to keep ministers in line and to prevent deviations in favor of their parties" (Müller and Meyer 2010, p. 1074). Consequently, coalition parties have particularly strong incentives to exercise control through the coalition agreement in the policy areas that fall into the jurisdiction of ministers that belong to other coalition parties. Coalition parties which are confronted with a "hostile" minister seek to tie the hands of the minister by contract design. In other words, coalition parties will exercise tight control over ministers through the coalition agreement by demanding policy concessions in their favor. By adopting and publicly communicating policy positions that are close to their ideal points in the coalition agreement, coalition partners leave the minister little room of maneuver.

On the basis of our comprehensive content analysis, we measure the dependent variable in this chapter as the absolute distance between the ideal points of coalition parties and the policy position adopted in the coalition agreement. Our results show that controlling the ministry in charge of a given policy area is associated with a significantly larger distance between the position of the coalition party and the location of the coalition agreement, providing support to the idea that parties try to control each other's ministers through the coalition contract. Hence, again, we find strong support for the idea that parties draft coalition agreements in order to deal with problems of coalition governance, and delegation of power within cabinets. Thus, our answer to the overarching question is clear: Coalition parties draft coalition agreements, and carry the costs of doing so, because they believe that they can help them reach their goals, by constraining and controlling their coalition partners in cabinet.

### 8.1.3 What is the impact of coalition agreements?

The overarching puzzle of the book focuses on explaining why parties draft costly coalition agreements, and the empirical analyses presented in Chapters 5 and 6 were dedicated to showing that coalition parties indeed use coalition agreements as control devices by examining how the preference configuration among coalition partners and the distribution of ministerial portfolios affects the use of coalition contracts.

However, relatively little is known about whether coalition agreements actually work and what their impact is on coalition governance. Can coalition agreements really help coalition parties to overcome their differences and settle disputes in government? In Chapter 7, we turn to this question, focusing on one of the implications of our main argument. If negotiating a coalition agreement allows coalition parties to control their partners in a satisfactory manner, we should also observe an effect on cabinet stability. Coalition governments that draft coalition agreements should survive longer since they have settled their differences at the start of the term. Chapter 7 therefore investigates whether coalition agreements influence the survival of cabinets.

More specifically, we hypothesize that cabinets last longer, the more extensive conflictual issues are covered in the coalition agreement. We extend previous work by arguing that it is not enough to merely negotiate a coalition agreement, but specific issues have to be settled. If coalition parties only focus on consensual issues and fail to compromise on the policy issues that divide them, coalition agreements will not have much of an impact on the survival of cabinets. However, if coalition parties seriously make an effort to overcome their policy differences and settle divisive issues before they take over governmental offices, coalition agreements should have an important stabilizing effect as intra-cabinet conflict can be contained.

The comprehensive COALITIONAGREE dataset that we have collected on the content of coalition agreements allows us to evaluate this argument, and we find clear empirical support for the idea that the higher the attention toward conflictual topics in the coalition agreement, the lower the risk of early government termination. Our results therefore suggest that yes, coalition agreements do indeed work, at least with regard to cabinet duration and that it is important to take into account the actual content of coalition agreements. Hence, Chapter 7 makes an important contribution to the literature on coalition governments and cabinet stability by showing that not only the existence and length, but also the content of coalition agreements is crucial for the stability of coalition cabinets.

## 8.2 Implications for understanding policy-making

Our findings have moreover important implications for our understanding of how policy-making works in multiparty democracies. Even though coalition governments are the norm in most European democracies, we have a very limited understanding about how policy-making in coalition governments actually works. We have shown that election promises of political parties do not directly translate into governmental policy, but that coalition governments invest a lot of resources and time into negotiating a coalition contract that predetermines their legislative activity during the time of office. Coalition parties settle many policy disputes already at the government formation stage codifying their policy compromise in the coalition agreement. Given that most policy commitments made in coalition agreements are actually implemented during the time of office (Klüver, Alberto, and Ellger 2021), coalition agreements have to be taken into account systematically by any study trying to explain policy-making in multiparty cabinets.

Beyond generally showing that coalition agreements substantially determine the policy-making activity of coalition governments during the legislative term, the COALITIONAGREE dataset offers manifold opportunities for scholars analyzing policy-making in specific policy fields. For example, scholars focusing on various aspects of environmental policy have increasingly focused on domestic politics, and the question of how political parties and governments make policy reforms (see e.g. Duit 2014; Duit, Feindt, and Meadowcroft 2016). For example, Knill, Debus, and Heichel (2010) provide a systematic comparative analysis of the extent to which political parties affect national environmental policy outputs, analyzing the impact of the environmental policy positions of governments. Relying on constructed measures drawing on coalition parties' policy positions, which assumes that parties have a policy impact that is relative to their parliamentary size, this type of research could benefit from using our dataset which allows scholars to include more specific measures of governments' stances on environmental policy and other related policy issues. By making use of our dataset, scholars should thus be able to increase our understanding of why important environmental policy reforms are implemented by governments in some countries, but not in others.

Another field of study that should for example benefit from making use of the COALITIONAGREE dataset is the literature on foreign policy making and conflict. Scholars in these fields have long assumed that foreign policy outcomes are the result of human decision-making, and much work in this field focuses on the decision-making of political leaders (Hudson 2005). Several scholars have gathered and analyzed comparative systematic data on the personal features of individual leaders with the goal of explaining various foreign policy outcomes (see e.g. Goemans, Gleditsch, and Chiozza 2009; Horowitz, Stam, and Ellis 2015). However, some scholars have recognized that we need a more in-depth understanding of the inner workings of multiparty governments in order to fully understand why certain foreign policy strategies are pursued by a country. For example, Oppermann, Kaarbo, and Brummer (2017), argue, in a symposium introduction, that since multi-party governments "are the locus of national foreign-policy-making, the dynamics of coalition government have significant implications for International Relations." In line with this, Oppermann, Brummer, and Van Willigen (2017, p.490) suggest that foreign policy research should open up the "black box" of coalition governance in foreign affairs as this would promise "more fine-grained insights into the drivers and characteristic of coalition foreign policy." By making use of our COALITIONAGREE dataset, which allows for the measurement of policy positions of coalition governments on foreign policy related issues, scholars within this field should be able to make considerable progress in such endeavors.

## 8.3 Implications for political representation

Understanding how policies and offices are distributed in coalition negotiations also has crucial implications for political representation and the responsiveness of policy-makers to citizens. At elections, voters evaluate parties to a large extent on the basis of the policy alternatives they offer to the electorate. It is therefore important for political representation that there is a link between what parties have promised before the election (e.g. in their manifestos and campaigns), and what they do once they enter government, in order to guarantee congruence between citizens' issue preferences and the policies advocated by their representatives (Miller and Stokes 1963; Powell 2000).

While political parties in single-party governments can autonomously decide which policies to promote, coalition governments make the story more complex. Coalition parties cannot simply promote their own policy priorities, but they have to coordinate with their coalition partners in order not to risk breaking the government. As a result, there is no direct connection between election promises and governmental activity, but policies are channeled by internal government negotiations. How do these coalition negotiations work and which parties are successful in such negotiations? In order to assess the quality of political representation, it is important to understand how coalition agreements are negotiated as they crucially determine the policies that are enacted during the time of office.

In this book, we have found strong empirical support for the idea that parties in coalition governments take the policy commitments they have made before the election seriously. Even though they cannot directly enact their policy agenda as they share government responsibility with at least one other partner, the design of coalition agreements signals clear commitment of coalition parties to the policies that they promised during the preceding election campaign. The empirical evidence presented in this book shows that coalition agreements serve the purpose to nail down a policy compromise and bind coalition partners to implement the negotiated policies during the time of office. They constitute an important ex ante control mechanism that allows coalition partners to ensure the implementation of preferred policies even in policy areas that fall into the hands of a hostile minister. Our findings demonstrate that parties make strong efforts to implement the policies they have advocated for during the election campaign and structure coalition governance in order to maximize the fulfillment of promised policies.

This is good news for representative democracy in multiparty democracies. By voting for a party that has presented a policy program that is proximate to the preferences of voters, voters are most likely to get at least some policy priorities enacted when this party enters government. Of course, parties entering coalition governments have to negotiate over which ministerial portfolios they will get and the policy compromises that have to be done, but coalition parties still aim for implementing large parts of their policy programs. Even when they had to give up a ministerial portfolio controlling an important policy area to another party, coalition parties use the opportunity to draft detailed coalition contracts to influence policies that fall under the jurisdiction of hostile ministers. Thus, coalition agreements are clearly an important part of the democratic chain of delegation in parliamentary democracies.

## 8.4 Potential avenues for future research

### 8.4.1 Alternative analyses of the impact of coalition agreements

We have in this book analyzed one of the potential impacts that coalition agreements may have, focusing on how the content of coalition agreements influences cabinet survival. However, coalition agreements may also influence other features in the so called "life cycle" of coalition governments (Strøm, Müller, and Bergman 2008). Importantly, coalition agreements should not only influence the "death" of governments, but also the so called coalition governance stage, the stage when the parties in a coalition government actually govern together and engage in policy-making.

So far relatively few studies have focused on evaluating the impact of coalition agreements on policy-making (see e.g. Moury and Timmermans 2013). Moury (2013) has for example demonstrated that coalition agreements importantly constrain ministers as most of the policy reforms suggested in coalition agreements are enacted once the cabinet is in office. Thomson (2001) and Schermann and Ennser-Jedenastik (2014a) furthermore show, in country case studies, that election pledges to which coalition governments commit themselves in their coalition agreements are significantly more likely to be fulfilled throughout the legislative term than pledges not mentioned in the agreement. However, here more systematic comparative work needs to be done, analyzing whether the negotiated content of coalition agreements is actually followed through in the policy-making of individual cabinets, and under what circumstances these agreements are not enacted.

Another venue for future research is to focus on the role of coalition agreements when it comes to solving potential problems that may arise in multiparty governments. Bäck, Müller, and Nyblade (2017) examine the role of coalition agreements in solving so-called "common pool problems." They draw on the economic literature which has suggested that coalition governments may end up with high budget deficits and higher spending because they face more severe common pool problems since parties use their control over specific ministries to advance their specific spending priorities rather than practice budgetary discipline (e.g. Hallerberg and Von Hagen 1999). Bäck et al. 2017 draw on the literature on coalition governance, which suggests that certain control mechanisms, such as the drafting of comprehensive policy agreements determine the ability of coalition governments to limit the policy discretion of individual parties in their ministerial jurisdictions, which has the potential to solve the sort of "common pool" problems described in the economic literature. This type of argument is also in line with the work by fiscal institutionalists who suggest that negotiated spending targets for each ministry can lead to smaller deficits (see, e.g. Von Hagen and Harden 1995). Analyzing spending behavior in 17 Western European countries, Bäck and colleagues 2017 find support for a conditional hypothesis suggesting that comprehensive coalition agreements significantly reduce the negative effect of government fragmentation on spending in certain institutional contexts.

Our COALITIONAGREE dataset allows scholars to extend this line of research by analyzing how the content of coalition agreements may influence and potentially solve common pool problems in coalition governments, reducing the risk that multiparty governments result in high budget deficits and other economic distortions. By analyzing which particular issues have been covered in the coalition agreements, we should be better able to say whether the parties have aimed for constraining individual ministers held by other parties in the coalition. In addition, our data contains information on specific budget rules included in the coalition agreements which allows scholars to directly evaluate an argument that spending targets and budgetary discipline included in such contracts influences the level of spending or the deficits that governments run.

### 8.4.2 Modeling coalition negotiations as a two-dimensional process

While this study has provided important insights for our understanding of cabinet formation and coalition governance, much remains to be done. The fact that coalition partners not only bargain about the policy priorities that guide legislative activity in the upcoming term, but they simultaneously negotiate the division of ministerial posts is something that we have considered in this book. We did so by taking portfolio allocation into account when analyzing payoff allocation in terms of policy (see Chapter 6). Hence, we have here considered that coalition partners may strike package deals that cut across the division of ministerial posts and the agreement of policy priorities so that ministerial posts might be exchanged for a commitment to a particular policy reform and vice versa. However, more work should be done explicitly taking into account that payoff allocation in coalition negotiations should be conceptualized as a two-dimensional process in which the allocation of ministerial portfolios cannot be treated independently from direct policy payoff allocation (Linhart and Pappi 2009; Shikano and Linhart 2010).

Viewing coalition negotiations as a two-dimensional process should also influence the way we analyze portfolio allocation. The literature on portfolio allocation can be divided into two strands, where the first focuses on the quantity of portfolios allocated, asking how many portfolios each party gets. Comparative analyses of portfolio allocation have produced clear-cut empirical findings: Coalition parties receive ministerial posts in close proportion to their parliamentary seats contribution (e.g. Warwick and Druckman 2006). The second strand of the literature focuses on the quality of ministerial posts, asking in particular "which party gets what and why?" For example, Bäck, Debus, and Dumont (2011) suggest that the more salient a policy area is to the party, the more likely it is that this party will try to get the ministerial post controlling this particular policy field. Their empirical analysis shows that parties who stress certain policy issues in their electoral program are indeed more likely to obtain the portfolio controlling these policy areas (see also Ecker, Meyer, and Müller 2015). These two strands of the literature have until recently not been connected to each other, mainly for methodological reasons, since it is difficult to model both the quantitative and qualitative dimension of portfolio allocation simultaneously (see however Martin 2016).

Hence, the literature on portfolio allocation seems to have a long way to go until policy payoffs as indicated in the coalition agreements can be fully taken into account. Bäck and colleagues 2011 made a first attempt to consider the role of coalition agreements when analyzing portfolio allocation. They argued that the fact that the drafting of comprehensive coalition agreements is aimed at constraining the actions of cabinet ministers, the qualitative allocation of portfolios according to party preferences should be less important for policy-seeking partners that "sought to have at least some of their priorities written down in each minister's marching orders than if no such comprehensive coalition agreement exists." Thus, Bäck et al. 2011 hypothesize that if there is a comprehensive formal policy agreement, the effect of saliency should be weaker at the portfolio allocation stage. However, they do not find strong support for this hypothesis in their comparative analysis of 12 Western European countries. Ideally, we would also like to analyze portfolio allocation in a multidimensional way by considering what policy deals have been simultaneously struck between the coalition partners during government formation talks. It is reasonable to expect that parties which have been successful in influencing the policies that coalition parties committed to in the coalition agreement may have been less successful in terms of obtaining their preferred portfolios. Hence, there may be significant trade-offs between the office and policy payoffs, which should be considered when explaining both outcomes.

# References

Anderson, Christopher J., Silvia M. Mendes, and Yuliya V. Tverdova. 2004. "Endogenous economic voting: evidence from the 1997 British election." *Electoral Studies* 23(4): 683–708.

Andersson, Staffan, Torbjörn Bergman, and Svante Ersson. 2012. *The European Representative Democracy Data Archive, Release 3*. URL (consulted September 2014): www.erdda.se.

Andersson, Staffan, Torbjörn Bergman, and Svante Ersson, eds. 2014. *European Representative Democracy Codebook*. URL (consulted September 2014): www.erdda.se.

Andeweg, Rudy B. 2000. "Ministers as double agents? The delegation process between cabinet and ministers." *European Journal of Political Research* 37(3):377–395.

Andeweg, Rudy B. and Arco Timmermans. 2008. Conflict management in coalition governments. In *Cabinets and Coalition Bargaining: The Democratic Life Cycle in Western Europe*, ed. Kaare Strøm, Wolfgang C. Müller, and Torbjörn Bergman. Oxford: Oxford University Press. pp. 269–300.

André, Audrey, Sam Depauw, and Shane Martin. 2016. "'Trust is good, control is better': Multiparty government and legislative organization." *Political Research Quarterly* 69(1):108–120.

Axelrod, Robert. 1970. *Conflict of Interest*. Chicago: Markham.

Bäck, Hanna. 2008. "Intra-party politics and coalition formation: Evidence from Swedish local government." *Party Politics* 14(1):71–89.

Bäck, Hanna, Marc Debus, and Patrick Dumont. 2011. "Who gets what in coalition governments? Predictors of portfolio allocation in parliamentary democracies." *European Journal of Political Research* 50(4):441–478.

Bäck, Hanna, Marc Debus, and Wolfgang C. Müller. 2016. "Intra-party diversity and ministerial selection in coalition governments." *Public Choice* 166(3-4):355–378.

Bäck, Hanna, Wolfgang C. Müller, and Benjamin Nyblade. 2017. "Multiparty government and economic policy-making. Coalition agreements, prime ministerial power and spending in Western European cabinets." *Public Choice* 170(1–2):33–62.

Bakker, Ryan, Catherine de Vries, Erica Edwards, Liesbet Hooghe, Seth Jolly, Gary Marks, Jonathan Polk, Jan Rovny, Marco Steenbergen, and Milada Anna Vachudova. 2015. "Measuring party positions in Europe: The Chapel Hill expert survey trend file, 1999–2010." *Party Politics* 21(1):143–152.

Baumgartner, Frank R. and Bryan D. Jones. 1993. *Agendas and Instability in American Politics*. Chicago: University of Chicago Press.

Bergman, Torbjörn. 1995. *Constitutional rules and party goals in coalition formation: an analysis of winning minority governments in Sweden*. PhD thesis: Umeå universitet.

Bergman, Torbjörn. 2000. Sweden: When minority cabinets are the rule and majority coalitions the exception. In *Coalition Governments in Western Europe*, ed. Wolfgang C. Müller and Kaare Strøm. Oxford: Oxford University Press. pp. 192–230.

# REFERENCES

Bergman, Torbjörn, Gabriella Ilonszki, and Wolfgang C. Müller. 2019a. *The European Representative Democracy Data Archive.* URL (consulted December 2019): http://www.erdda.org.

Bergman, Torbjörn, Gabriella Ilonszki, and Wolfgang C. Müller, eds. 2019b. *Coalition Governance in Central Eastern Europe.* Oxford: Oxford University Press.

Bowler, Shaun, Thomas Bräuninger, Marc Debus, and Indridi H. Indridason. 2016. "Let's just agree to disagree: Dispute resolution mechanisms in coalition agreements." *Journal of Politics* 78(4):1264–1278.

Box-Steffensmeier, Janet M. and Bradford S. Jones. 2004. *Event History Modeling: A Guide for Social Scientists.* Cambridge: Cambridge University Press.

Box-Steffensmeier, Janet M. and Christopher J. W. Zorn. 2001. "Duration models and proportional hazards in political science." *Americal Journal of Political Science* 45(4):972–988.

Brambour, Thomas, William Roberts Clark, and Matt Golder. 2006. "Understanding interaction models: Improving empirical analysis." *Political Analysis* 14(1):63–82.

Braun, S., C. Blechschmidt, and C. Hulverscheidt. 2009. "Schäuble, Guttenberg und ein paar Neue: Das schwarz-gelbe Kabinett: Schäuble kümmert sich um Finanzen, um die Wirtschaft der Liberale Brüderle, Guttenbergwird Verteidigungsminister. Weitere Überraschungen folgen." *Süddeutsche Zeitung.* URL: https://www.sueddeutsche.de/politik/kabinett-merkel-schaeuble-guttenberg-und-ein-paar-neue-1.27523

Browne, Eric C. and John P. Frendreis. 1980. "Allocating coalition payoffs by conventional norm: An assessment of the evidence from cabinet coalition situations." *American Journal of Political Science* 24(4):753–768.

Browne, Eric C, John P, Frendreis, and Dennis W Gleiber. 1984. "An 'events' approach to the problem of cabinet stability." *Comparative Political Studies* 17(2):167–197.

Browne, Eric C. and Karen Ann Feste. 1975. "Qualitative dimensions of coalition payoffs." *American Behavioral Scientist* 18(4):530–556.

Browne, Eric C. and Mark N. Franklin. 1973. "Aspects of coalition payoffs in European parliamentary democracies." *American Political Science Review* 67(2):453–469.

Budge, Ian. 1999. *Estimating Party Policy Preferences: From Ad Hoc Measures to Theoretically Validated Standards.* Essex Papers in Politics and Government, 139: University of Essex and Department of Government.

Budge, Ian and Dennis J. Farlie. 1983. *Explaining and Predicting Elections: Issue Effects and Party Strategies in Twenty-three Democracies.* London: George Allen and Unwin.

Budge, Ian, Hans-Dieter Klingemann, Andrea Volkens, Judith Bara, and Eric Tanenbaum. 2001. *Mapping Policy Preferences I: Estimates for Parties, Electors, and Governments 1945-1998.* Oxford: Oxford University Press.

Budge, Ian and Hans E. Keman. 1990. *Parties and Democracy: Coalition Formation and Government Functioning in Twenty States.* Oxford: Oxford University Press.

Budge, Ian and Michael Laver. 1993. "The policy basis of government coalitions: A comparative investigation." *British Journal of Political Science* 23(4):499–519.

Carroll, Royce and Gary W. Cox. 2007. "The logic of Gamson's Law: Pre-election coalitions and portfolio allocations." *American Journal of Political Science* 51(2):300–313.

Christiansen, Flemming Juul and Helene Helboe Pedersen. 2014. "Regeringsgrundlag I Danmark. Hvordan benytter regeringen dem, og hvordan reagerer oppositionen?" *Politica* 46(3):362–385.

Coalition scouts quit after Ollongren accidentally reveals explosive notes. 2021. *DutchNews.* URL: https://www.dutchnews.nl/news/2021/03/coalition-scouts-quit-after-ollongren-accidentally-reveals-explosive-notes/

Corder, Mike. 30.09.2021. "Leaders of 4 Dutch parties open to renewing coalition." *The Washington Post.* URL: https://www.washingtonpost.com/politics/centrist-dutch-party-opens-door-to-4-party-coalition-talks/2021/09/30/23601824-21e0-11ec-a8d9-0827a2a4b915_story.html

Däubler, Thomas. 2012. "The preparation and use of election manifestos: Learning from the Irish case." *Irish Political Studies* 27(1):51–70.

Däubler, Thomas and Marc Debus. 2009. "Government formation and policy formulation in the German states." *Regional & Federal Studies* 19(1):73–95.

De Swaan, Abram. 1973. *Coalition Theories and Cabinet Formation.* Amsterdam: Elsevier.

De Vries, Catherine E. and Sara B. Hobolt. 2020. *Political Entrepreneurs: The Rise of Challenger Parties in Europe.* Princeton: Princeton University Press.

De Winter, Lieven, Arco Timmermans and Patrick Dumont. 2000. Belgium: On government agreements, evangelists, followers and heretics. In *Coalition Governments in Western Europe*, ed. Wolfgang C. Müller and Kaare Strøm. Oxford University Press. pp. 300–355.

Debiec, Krzysztof. 2018. "Czech Republic: The government of Babiš and the left." URL: https://www.osw.waw.pl/en/publikacje/analyses/2018-07-12/czech-republic-government-babis-and-left-0

Department of the Taoiseach, Ireland. 2011. *Statement of Common Purpose.Coalition Agreement of the Irish Kenny I Cabinet.*

Diermeier, Daniel and Randolph T. Stevenson. 1999. "Cabinet survival and competing risks." *American Journal of Political Science* 43(4):1051–1068.

Dimitrova, Antoaneta and Bernard Steunenberg. 2021. "What lessons can be learned from the failure to form a government in Bulgaria and the Netherlands?" URL: https://blogs.lse.ac.uk/europpblog/2021/09/29/what-lessons-can-be-learned-from-the-failure-to-form-a-government-in-bulgaria-and-the-netherlands/

Dodd, Lawrence. 1976. *Coalitions in Parliamentary Government.* Princeton: Princeton University Press.

Döring, Holger. 2013. "The collective action of data collection: A data infrastructure on parties, elections and cabinets." *European Union Politics* 14(1):161–178.

Döring, Holger and Philip Manow. 2010. *Parliaments and governments database (ParlGov): Information on parties, elections and cabinets in modern democracies. Version 10/02.* URL (last accessed December 2010): http://www.parlgov.org/.

Döring, Holger and Philip Manow. 2016. *Parliaments and governments database (ParlGov): Information on parties, elections and cabinets in modern democracies. Development version.* URL (last accessed September 2017): http://www.parlgov.org/.

Döring, Holger and Philip Manow. 2019. *Parliaments and governments database (ParlGov): Information on parties, elections and cabinets in modern democracies.* URL (last accessed Decemmber 2019): http://www.parlgov.org/.

dpa. 2014. "Liberale verlassen rumänische Regierung: Rumäniens Premier Victor Ponta muss sich einen neuen Koalitionspartner suchen: Die Liberalen werfen ihm Vertragsbruch vor und wollen nicht mehr mitregieren." *Zeit Online.* URL: https://www.zeit.de/politik/ausland/2014-02/rumaenien-regierung-koalition-liberale-ruecktritt

Duit, Andreas. 2014. *State and Environment: The Comparative Study of Environmental Governance.* Cambridge: MIT Press.

Duit, Andreas, Peter H. Feindt, and James Meadowcroft. 2016. "Greening Leviathan: The rise of the environmental state?" *Environmental Politics* 25(1):1–23.

Dumont, Patrick, Raphaël Kies, and Philippe Poirier. 2015. Luxembourg. In *Handbook of European Elections*, ed. Donatella M Viola. London: Routledge.

Ecker, Alejandro and Thomas M. Meyer. 2017. "Coalition bargaining duration in multiparty democracies." *British Journal of Political Science* 50(1):1–20.

Ecker, Alejandro, Thomas M. Meyer, and Wolfgang C. Müller. 2015. "The distribution of individual cabinet positions in coalition governments: A sequential approach." *European Journal of Political Research* 54(4):802–818.

Eichorst, Jason. 2014. "Explaining variation in coalition agreements: The electoral and policy motivations for drafting agreements." *European Journal of Political Research* 53(1):98–115.

Ellger, Fabio and Heike Klüver. 2019. "Coalition cabinets, radical right parties and government policy: Why coalition governments go tough on immigration." Paper Presented at the European Political Science Association Conference, Belfast, June 2019.

Falcó-Gimeno, Albert. 2014. "The use of control mechanisms in coalition governments: The role of preference tangentiality and repeated interactions." *Party Politics* 20(3): 341–356.

Fortunato, David. 2019. "The electoral implications of coalition policy making." *British Journal of Political Science* 49(1):59–80.

Fortunato, David. 2021. *The Cycle of Coalition: How Parties and Voters Interact under Coalition Governance*. Cambridge: Cambridge University Press.

Fortunato, David and James Adams. 2015. "How voters' perceptions of junior coalition partners depend on the prime minister's position." *European Journal of Political Research* 54(3):601–621.

Fortunato, David and Randolph T. Stevenson. 2013. "Perceptions of partisan ideologies: The effect of coalition participation." *American Journal of Political Science* 57(2): 459–477.

Frendreis, John P., Dennis W. Gleiber and Eric C. Browne. 1986. "The Study of Cabinet Dissolutions in Parliamentary Democracies." *Legislative Studies Quarterly* 11(4):619–628.

Gamson, William A. 1961. "A theory of coalition formation." *American Sociological Review* 26(3):373–382.

Goemans, Henk E., Kristian Skrede Gleditsch, and Giacomo Chiozza. 2009. "Introducing archigos: A dataset of political leaders." *Journal of Peace Research* 46(2):269–283.

Green-Pedersen, Christoffer. 2007. "The growing importance of issue competition: The changing nature of party competition in Western Europe." *Political Studies* 55(3): 607–628.

Gutschker, Thomas. 2020. "Vivaldi-Koalition in Belgien: Nach 654 Tagen ohne Regierung." *F.A.Z.* URL: https://www.faz.net/aktuell/politik/ausland/alexander-de-croo-wird-neuer-premierminister-belgiens-werden-16978436.html

Hallerberg, Mark and Jürgen Von Hagen. 1999. Electoral institutions, cabinet negotiations, and budget deficits in the European Union. In *Fiscal Institutions and Fiscal Performance*. University of Chicago Press. pp. 209–232.

Hellström, Johan and Daniel Walther. 2019. "How is government stability affected by the state of the economy? Payoff structures, government type and economic state." *Government and Opposition* 54(2):280–308.

Höhmann, Daniel and Svenja Krauss. 2021. "Complements or substitutes? The interdependence between coalition agreements and parliamentary questions as monitoring mechanisms in coalition governments." *Parliamentary Affairs*.

Horowitz, Michael C., Allan C. Stam, and Cali M. Ellis. 2015. *Why Leaders Fight*. Cambridge: Cambridge University Press.

Huber, John D. and Charles R Shipan. 2000. "The costs of control: Legislators, agencies, and transaction costs." *Legislative Studies Quarterly* 25(1):25–52.

Huber, John D and Charles R Shipan. 2002. *Deliberate Discretion?: The Institutional Foundations of Bureaucratic Autonomy.* Cambridge University Press.

Hudson, Valerie M. 2005. "Foreign policy analysis: Actor-specific theory and the ground of international relations." *Foreign Policy Analysis* 1(1):1–30.

Indridason, Indridi H. and Christopher Kam. 2008. "Cabinet reshuffles and ministerial drift." *British Journal of Political Science* 38(4):621–656.

Indridason, Indridi H. and Gunnar Helgi Kristinsson. 2013. "Making words count: Coalition agreements and cabinet management." *European Journal of Political Research* 52(6):822–846.

Kam, Christopher, William T. Bianco, Itai Sened, and Regina Smyth. 2010. "Ministerial selection and intraparty organization in the contemporary British parliament." *American Political Science Review* 104(2):289–306.

Kayser, Mark Andreas. 2005. "Who surfs, who manipulates? The determinants of opportunistic election timing and electorally motivated economic intervention." *American Political Science Review* 99(1):17–27.

Kiewiet, D. Roderick and Mathew D. McCubbins. 1991. *The Logic of Delegation: Congressional Parties and the Appropriations Process.* Chicago: University of Chicago Press.

Kim, Dong-Hun and Gerhard Loewenberg. 2005. "The role of parliamentary committees in coalition governments: Keeping tabs on coalition partners in the German Bundestag." *Comparative Political Studies* 38(9):1104–1129.

King, Gary, James Alt, Nancy Burns, and Michael Laver. 1990. "A unified model of cabinet dissolution in parliamentary democracies." *American Journal of Political Science* 34(3):846–871.

King, Gary, Michael Tomz, and Jason Wittenberg. 2000. "Making the most of statistical analyses: Improving interpretation and presentation." *American Journal of Political Science* 44(2):341–355.

Klingemann, Hans-Dieter, Andrea Volkens, Judith Bara, Ian Budge, and Michael McDonald. 2006a. *Mapping Policy Preferences II: Estimates for Parties, Electors and Governments in Central and Eastern Europe, European Union and OECD 1990-2003.* Oxford: Oxford University Press.

Klingemann, Hans-Dieter, Andrea Volkens, Judith Bara, Ian Budge, and Michael McDonald. 2006b. *Mapping Policy Preferences II: Estimates for Parties, Electors, and Governments in Eastern Europe, European Union and OECD 1990-2003.* Oxford: Oxford University Press.

Klüver, Heike. 2009. "Measuring interest group influence using quantitative text analysis." *European Union Politics* 10(4):535–549.

Klüver, Heike, Anthea Alberto, and Fabio Ellger. 2021. "The making and breaking of policy promises in coalition government." Paper presented at the European Political Sciance Association Conference, June 2021.

Klüver, Heike and Hanna Bäck. 2019. "Coalition agreements, issue attention, and cabinet governance." *Comparative Political Studies* 52(13-14):1–37.

Klüver, Heike and Jae-Jae Spoon. 2016. "Who responds? Voters, parties and issue attention." *British Journal of Political Science* 46(3):633–654.

Klüver, Heike and Jae-Jae Spoon. 2020. "Helping or hurting? How governing as a junior coalition partner influences electoral outcomes." *Journal of Politics* 82(4): 1231–1242.

Knill, Christoph, Marc Debus and Stephan Heichel. 2010. "Do parties matter in internationalised policy areas? The impact of political parties on environmental policy outputs in 18 OECD countries, 1970–2000." *European Journal of Political Research* 49(3):301–336.

Krauss, Svenja. 2018. "Stability through control? The influence of coalition agreements on the stability of coalition cabinets." *West European Politics* 41(6):1282–1304.

Küstner, Kai. 2020. "Union beklagt Wortbruch der SPD." *tagesschau*. URL: https://www.tagesschau.de/inland/spd-bundeswehr-drohnen-101.html

Laver, Michael. 1974. "Dynamic Factors in Government Coalition Formation." *European Journal of Political Research* 2(3):259–270.

Laver, Michael. 2003. "Government termination." *Annual Review of Political Science* 6:23–40.

Laver, Michael and Kenneth A. Shepsle. 1996. *Making and Breaking Governments: Cabinets and Legislatures in Parliamentary Democracies*. Cambridge: Cambridge University Press.

Laver, Michael and Norman Schofield. 1998. *Multiparty Government: The Politics of Coalition in Europe*. Ann Arbor: University of Michigan Press.

Lewis-Beck, Michael S., and Mary Stegmaier. 2000. "Economic determinants of electoral outcomes." *Annual Review of Political Science* 3(1):183–219.

Linhart, Eric and Franz Pappi. 2009. "Koalitionsbildungen zwischen ämter- und Politikmotivation. Konstruktion einer interdependenten Nutzenfunktion." *Politische Vierteljahresschrift* 50(1):23–49.

Lipsmeyer, Christine S. and Heather Nicole Pierce. 2011. "The eyes that bind: Junior ministers as oversight mechanisms in coalition governments." *The Journal of Politics* 74(4):1152–1164.

Lowe, Will, Ken Benoit, Slava Mikhaylov, and Michael Laver. 2011. "Scaling policy positions from coded units of political texts." *Legislative Studies Quarterly* 36(1):123–155.

Luebbert, Gregory. 1986. *Comparative Democracy: Policy Making and Governing Coalitions in Europe and Israel*. New York: Cambridge University Press.

Lupia, Arthur and Kaare Strøm. 1995. "Coalition termination and the strategic timing of parliamentary elections." *The American Political Science Review* 89(3):648–665.

Marinas, Radu-sorin. 06.09.2021. "Romanian coalition partner quits government, paves way for no-confidence vote." *Reuters*. URL: https://www.reuters.com/world/europe/romanian-coalition-partner-quits-government-paves-way-no-confidence-vote-2021-09-06/

Marks, Gary and Marco R. Steenbergen Steenbergen. 2002. "Understanding political contestation in the European Union." *Comparative Political Studies* 35(8):879–892.

Marks, Gary, Richard Haesly, and Heather A. D. Mbaye. 2002. "What do subnational offices think they are doing in Brussels?" *Regional and Federal Studies* 12(3):1 – 23.

Martin, Lanny W. 2004. "The government agenda in parliamentary democracies." *American Journal of Political Science* 48(3):445–461.

Martin, Lanny W. 2016. "The allocation of ministries in multiparty governments." *Unpublished manuscript, Rice University*.

Martin, Lanny W. and Georg Vanberg. 2004. "Policing the bargain: Coalition government and parliamentary scrutiny." *American Journal of Political Science* 48(1):13–27.

Martin, Lanny W. and Georg Vanberg. 2005. "Coalition policymaking and legislative review." *American Political Science Review* 99(1):93–106.

Martin, Lanny W. and Georg Vanberg. 2011a. *Parliaments and Coalitions: The Role of Legislative Institutions in Multiparty Governance*. Oxford: Oxford University Press.

Martin, Lanny W. and Georg Vanberg. 2011b. *Parliaments and Coalitions: The Role of Legislative Institutions in Multiparty Governance*. Oxford: Oxford University Press.

Martin, Lanny W. and Georg Vanberg. 2014. "Parties and policymaking in multiparty governments: The legislative median, ministerial autonomy, and the coalition compro-mise." *American Journal of Political Science* 58(4):979–996.

Martin, Lanny W. and Georg Vanberg. 2020a. "Coalition government, legislative institutions, and public policy in parliamentary democracies." *American Journal of Political Science* 64(2):325–340.

Martin, Lanny W. and Georg Vanberg. 2020b. "What you see is not always what you get: Bargaining before an audience under multiparty government." *American Political Science Review* pp. 1–17.

Martin, Lanny W. and Randolph Stevenson. 2001. "Cabinet formation in parliamentary democracies." *American Journal of Political Science* 45(1):33–50.

McCubbins, Mathew D. and Thomas Schwartz. 1984. "Congressional oversight overlooked: Police patrols versus fire alarms." *American Journal of Political Science* 28(1):165–179.

McDonald, John F. and Robert A. Moffitt. 1980. "The uses of tobit analysis." *The Review of Economics and Statistics* 62(2):318–321.

Meyer, Thomas M. and Daniel Strobl. 2016. "Voter perceptions of coalition policy positions in multiparty systems." *Electoral Studies* 41(2):80–91.

Mikhaylov, Slava, Michael Laver, and Kenneth R. Benoit. 2012. "Coder reliability and misclassification in the human coding of party manifestos." *Political Analysis* 20(1):78–91.

Miller, Warren E. and Donald E. Stokes. 1963. "Constituency influence in Congress." *American Political Science Review* 57(1):45–56.

Morgenstern, Oskar and John Von Neumann. 1953. *Theory of Games and Economic Behavior*. Princeton: Princeton University Press.

Moury, Catherine. 2011. "Coalition agreement and party mandate: How coalition agreements constrain the ministers." *Party Politics* 17(3):385–404.

Moury, Catherine. 2013. *Coalition Government and Party Mandate. How Coalition Agreements Constrain Ministerial Action*. London: Routledge.

Moury, Catherine and Arco Timmermans. 2013. "Inter-party conflict management in coalition governments: Analyzing the role of coalition agreements in Belgium, Germany, Italy and the Netherlands." *Politics and Governance* 1(2):117–131.

Müller, Wolfgang C. and Kaare Strøm. 1999a. "The keys to togetherness: Coalition agreements in parliamentary democracies." *The Journal of Legislative Studies* 5(3-4):255–282.

Müller, Wolfgang C. and Kaare Strøm. 2008. Coalition agreements and cabinet governance. In *Cabinets and Coalition Bargaining: The Democratic Life Cycle in Western Europe*, ed. Kaare Strøm, Wolfgang C. Müller, and Torbjörn Bergman. Oxford: Oxford University Press. pp. 159–199.

Müller, Wolfgang C. and Kaare Strøm, eds. 1999b. *Policy, Office, or Votes? How Political Parties in Western Europe Make Hard Decisions*. Cambridge: Cambridge University Press.

Müller, Wolfgang C. and Kaare Strøm, eds. 2000. *Coalition Governments in Western Europe*. Oxford: Oxford University Press.

Müller, Wolfgang C. and Thomas M. Meyer. 2010. "Meeting the challenges of representation and accountability in multi-party governments." *West European Politics* 33(5):1065–1092.

Müller, Wolfgang C., Torbjörn Bergman and Kaare Strøm. 2008. Coalition theory and cabinet governance: An introduction. In *Cabinets and Coalition Bargaining: The Democratic Life Cycle in Western Europe*, ed. Kaare Strøm, Wolfgang C. Müller, and Torbjörn Bergman. Oxford: Oxford University Press. pp. 1–50.

Nasr, Joseph. 2018. "Merkel defends painful coalition concessions, denies authority waning." *Reuters.* URL: https://www.reuters.com/article/us-germany-politics/merkel-defends-painful-coalition-concessions-denies-authority-waning-idUSKBN1FV0TO

Niedermayer, Oskar. 2015. Von der dritten Kraft zur marginalen Partei: Die FDP von 2009 bis nach der Bundestagswahl 2013. In *Die Parteien nach der Bundestagswahl 2013*, ed. Oskar Niedermayer. Wiesbaden: Springer VS pp. 103–134.

Oppermann, Kai, Juliet Kaarbo, and Klaus Brummer. 2017. Introduction: Coalition politics and foreign policy. In *European Political Science.* Vol. 16 pp. 457–462.

Oppermann, Kai, Klaus Brummer, and Niels Van Willigen. 2017. Coalition governance and foreign policy decision-making. In *European Political Science.* Vol. 16 pp. 489–501.

Pausackl, Christina. 2021. "Regieren um jeden Preis." *Zeit Online.* URL: https://www.zeit.de/politik/ausland/2021-01/abschiebungen-oesterreich-wien-oevp-gruene-koalitionstreit

Pereira, José Santana and Catherine Moury. 2018. "Planning the 'government of change': The 2018 Italian coalition agreement in comparative perspective." *Italian Political Science* 13(2):29–103.

Petrocik, John R. 1996. "Issue ownership in presidential elections, with a 1980 case study." *American Journal of Political Science* 40(3):825–850.

Politi, James. 2018. "Italy's populists stir markets with pre-euro nostalgia." *Financial Times.* URL: https://www.ft.com/content/25f632d6-58ed-11e8-bdb7-f6677d2e1ce8

Polk, Jonathan, Jan Rovny, Ryan Bakker, Erica Edwards, Liesbet Hooghe, Seth Jolly, Jelle Koedam, Filip Kostelka, Gary Marks, Gijs Schumacher, Marco Steenbergen, Milada Vachudova, and Marko Zilovic. 2017. "Explaining the salience of anti-elitism and reducing political corruption for political parties in Europe with the 2014 Chapel Hill Expert Survey data." *Research & Politics* 4(1):1–9.

Powell, Bingham G. Jr. 2000. *Elections as Instruments of Democracy: Majoritarian and Proportional Visions.* New Haven: Yale University Press.

Riker, William H. 1962. *The Theory of Political Coalitions.* New Haven: Yale University Press.

Saalfeld, Thomas. 2008. Institutions, chance and choices: The dynamics of cabinet survival. In *Cabinets and Coalition Bargaining: The Democratic Life Cycle in Western Europe*, ed. Kaare Strøm, Wolfgang C. Müller, and Torbjörn Bergman. Oxford: Oxford University Press. pp. 327–368.

Sagarzazu, Iñaki and Heike Klüver. 2017. "Coalition governments and party competition: Political communication strategies of coalition parties." *Political Science Research and Methods* 5(2):333–349.

Sanders, David and Valentine Herman. 1977. "The survival and stability of governments in western democracies." *Acta Politica* 12(3):346–377.

Schaart, Eline and William Adkins. 2021. "Coronavirus outbreak, resignations interrupt Dutch coalition talks." *Politico.* URL: https://www.politico.eu/article/kajsa-ollongren-mona-keijzer-coronavirus-positive-utbreak-interrupts-netherlands-coalition-talks-election/

Schermann, Katrin and Laurenz Ennser-Jedenastik. 2014*a*. "Coalition policy making under constraints: Examining the role of preferences and institutions." *West European Politics* 37(3):564–583.

Schermann, Katrin and Laurenz Ennser-Jedenastik. 2014*b*. "Explaining coalition-bargaining outcomes: Evidence from Austria 2002-2008." *Party Politics* 20(5):791–801.

Schleim, Stephan. 2021. "Sterbehilfe bei vollendetem Leben - oder Entsorgung der Alten? Bürgerlich-liberaler Vorstoß in den Niederlanden belastet auch die Koalitionsverhandlungen." URL; https://www.dutchnews.nl/news/2021/09/cda-vote-on-end-of-life-assisted-suicide-is-new-blow-to-coalition-talks/

Schleiter, Petra and Edward Morgan-Jones. 2009. "Constitutional power and competing risks: Monarchs, presidents, prime ministers, and the termination of East and West European cabinets." *The American Political Science Review* 103(3):496–512.

Schleiter, Petra and Margit Tavits. 2016. "The electoral benefits of opportunistic election timing." *The Journal of Politics* 78(3):836–850.

Schmitt, Hermann, Andreas Wüst, Daniel Lederle, and Tanja Binder. 2002-2010. *The Euromanifestos Project*. Mannheim Center for European Social Research: URL: http://www.mzes.uni-mannheim.de/projekte/manifestos/.

Schofield, Norman and Michael Laver. 1985. "Bargaining theory and portfolio payoffs in European coalition governments 1945–83." *British Journal of Political Science* 15(2):143–164.

Sened, Itai. 1995. "Equilibria in weighted voting games with sidepayments." *Journal of Theoretical Politics* 7(3):283–300.

Shikano, Susumu and Eric Linhart. 2010. "Coalition-formation as a result of policy and office motivations in the German federal states." *Party Politics* 16(1):111–130.

Siefken, Sven T. 2018. "Regierungsbildung wider Willen – der mühsame Weg zur Koalition nach der Bundestagswahl 2017." *Zeitschrift für Parlamentsfragen* 49(2):407–436.

Soroka, Stuart N. and Christopher Wlezien. 2010. *Degrees of Democracy: Politics, Public Opinion, and Policy*. Cambridge: Cambridge University Press.

Spoon, Jae-Jae and Heike Klüver. 2014. "Do parties respond? How electoral context influences party responsiveness." *Electoral Studies* 35:48–60.

Spoon, Jae-Jae and Heike Klüver. 2015. "Voter polarization and party responsiveness: Why parties emphasize divided issues, but remain silent on unified issues." *European Journal of Political Research* 54(2):343–362.

Spoon, Jae-Jae, Sara B. Hobolt, and Catherine E. de Vries. 2014. "Going green: Explaining issue competition on the environment." *European Journal of Political Research* 53(2):363–380.

Steenbergen, Marco R. and Bradford S. Jones. 2002. "Modeling multilevel data structures." *American Journal of Political Science* 46(1):218–237.

Strobl, Daniel, Hanna Bäck, Wolfgang C. Müller, and Mariyana Angelova. 2019. "Electoral cycles in government policy making: Strategic timing of austerity reform measures in Western Europe." *British Journal of Political Science* pp. 1–22.

Strøm, Kaare. 1990a. "A behavioral theory of competitive political parties." *American Journal of Political Science* 34(2):565–598.

Strøm, Kaare. 1990b. *Minority Governments and Majority Rule*. Cambridge: Cambridge University Press.

Strøm, Kaare. 2000. "Delegation and accountability in parliamentary democracies." *European Journal of Political Research* 37(3):261–289.

Strøm, Kaare and Stephen M. Swindle. 2002. "Strategic parliamentary dissolution." *The American Political Science Review* 96(3):575–591.

Strøm, Kaare and Wolfgang C. Müller. 1999a. "The keys to togetherness: Coalition agreements in parliamentary democracies." *The Journal of Legislative Studies* 5(3-4):255–282.

Strøm, Kaare and Wolfgang C. Müller. 1999b. Political parties and hard choices. In *Policy, Office or Votes? How Political Parties in Western Europe Make Hard Decisions*, ed. Wolfgang C. Müller and Kaare Strøm. Cambridge: Cambridge University Press. pp. 1–35.

Strøm, Kaare, Wolfgang C. Müller, and Daniel Markham Smith. 2010. "Parliamentary control of coalition governments." *Annual Review of Political Science* 13:517–535.

Strøm, Kaare, Wolfgang C. Müller, and Torbjörn Bergman, eds. 2003. *Delegation and Accountability in Parliamentary Democracies*. Oxford: Oxford University Press.

Strøm, Kaare, Wolfgang C. Müller, and Torbjörn Bergman, eds. 2008. *Cabinets and Coalition Bargaining: The Democratic Life Cycle in Western Europe*. Oxford: Oxford University Press.

Szymanski, Mike. 2020. "SPD will doch keine Kampfdrohnen für die Bundeswehr." *Süddeutsche Zeitung*. URL: https://www.sueddeutsche.de/politik/bundeswehr-spd-kampfdrohne-1.5140767

Tavits, Margit. 2008. "The role of parties' past behavior in coalition formation." *American Political Science Review* 102(4):495–507.

Thies, Michael F. 2001. "Keeping tabs on partners: The logic of delegation in coalition governments." *American Journal of Political Science* 45(3):580–598.

Thomson, Robert. 2001. "The programme to policy linkage: the fulfillment of election pledges on socio-economic policy in the Netherlands, 1986-1998." *European Journal of Political Research* 40(2):171–197.

Timmermans, Arco. 1996. *High politics in the Low Countries: functions and effects of coalition policy agreements in Belgium and the Netherlands*. EUI PhD thesis.

Timmermans, Arco. 2006. "Standing apart and sitting together: Enforcing coalition agreements in multiparty systems." *European Journal of Political Research* 45(2):263–283.

Timmermans, Arco and Gerard Breeman. 2011. *The Policy Agenda in Multiparty Government: Coalition Agreements and Legislative Activity in the Netherlands*. Paper presented in the workshop Issue Congruence and Policy Responsiveness in European Governance at the ECPR Joint Sessions: St. Gallen, April 13–17, 2011.

Timmermans, Arco and Rudy B. Andeweg. 2000. The Netherlands: Still the politics of accommodation? In *Coalition governments in Western Europe*, ed. Wolfgang C. Müller and Kaare Strøm. Oxford: Oxford University Press. pp. 356–398.

Trübswasser, Gunther. 2021. "Die Grünen in der Regierung: Die gefühlten Niederlagen tun doppelt weh." *derStandard*. URL: https://www.derstandard.at/story/2000127326747/die-gruenen-in-der-regierung-die-gefuehlten-niederlagen-tun-doppelt

Tsebelis, George. 2002. *Veto Players: How Political Institutions Work*. New York: Sage.

van de Wardt, Marc, Catherine E. de Vries, and Sara B. Hobolt. 2014. "Exploiting the cracks: Wedge issues in multiparty competition." *Journal of Politics* 76(4):986–999.

Veen, Tim. 2011. "Positions and salience in European Union politics: Estimation and validation of a new dataset." *European Union Politics* 12(2):267–288.

Vehrkamp, Robert and Theres Matthieß. 2018. "Versprochen wird nicht gebrochen." *Einwurf–Ein Policy Brief der Bertelsmann Stiftung, Ausgabe* 1.

Verzichelli, Luca. 2008. Portfolio allocation. In *Cabinets and Coalition Bargaining: The Democractic Life Cycle in Western Europe*, ed. Wolfgang C. Müller and Kaare Strøm. Oxford: Oxford University Press. pp. 237–267.

Volkens, Andrea, Judith Bara, Ian Budge, Michael D. McDonald, and Hans-Dieter Klingemann, eds. 2013. *Mapping Policy Preferences from Texts: Statistical Solutions for Manifesto Analysts*. Oxford: Oxford University Press.

Volkens, Andrea, Pola Lehmann, Theres Matthieß, Nicolas Merz, and Bernhard Regel, Sven und Weßels. 2017. *The Manifesto Data Collection. Manifesto Project*

(MRG/CMP/MARPOR). Version 2017a. Berlin: Wissenschaftszentrum Berlin für Sozialforschung (WZB).

Volkens, Andrea, Pola Lehmann, Theres Matthieß, Nicolas Merz, and Bernhard Regel, Sven und Weßels. 2018. *The Manifesto Data Collection. Manifesto Project (MRG/CMP/MARPOR). Version 2018b.* Berlin: Wissenschaftszentrum Berlin für Sozialforschung (WZB).

Volkens, Andrea, Pola Lehmann, Theres Matthieß, Nicolas Merz, and Bernhard Regel, Sven und Weßels. 2019a. *The Manifesto Data Collection. Manifesto Project (MRG/CMP/MARPOR). Version 2019b.* Berlin: Wissenschaftszentrum Berlin für Sozialforschung (WZB).

Volkens, Andrea, Pola Lehmann, Theres Matthieß, Nicolas Merz, and Bernhard Regel, Sven und Weßels. 2019b. *The Manifesto Project Dataset - Codebook. Manifesto Project (MRG/CMP/MARPOR). Version 2019b.* Berlin: Wissenschaftszentrum Berlin für Sozialforschung (WZB).

Von Hagen, Jürgen and Ian J. Harden. 1995. "Budget processes and commitment to fiscal discipline." *European Economic Review* 39(3-4):771–779.

Vorländer, Hans. 2011. Als Phönix zurück in die Asche? Die FDP nach der Bundestagswahl 2009. In *Die Parteien nach der Bundestagswahl 2009*, ed. Oskar Niedermayer. Wiesbaden: Springer VS pp. 107–129.

Warwick, Paul. 1979. "The durability of coalition governments in parliamentary democracies." *Comparative Political Studies* 11(4):465–495.

Warwick, Paul. 1994. *Government survival in parliamentary democracies.* Cambridge: Cambridge University Press.

Warwick, Paul V. 2001. "Coalition policy in parliamentary democracies." *Comparative Political Studies* 34(10):1212–1236.

Warwick, Paul V. and James N. Druckman. 2001. "The portfolio allocation paradox: An investigation into the nature of a very strong but puzzling relationship." *European Journal of Political Research* 40(2):171–197.

Warwick, Paul V. and James N. Druckman. 2006. "The portfolio allocation paradox: An investigation into the nature of a very strong but puzzling relationship." *European Journal of Political Research* 45(4):635–665.

Werner, Annika, Onawa Lacewell, and Andrea Volkens. 2014. *Manifesto Coding Instructions, March 2014.* URL (consulted April 2014): https://manifesto-project.wzb.eu/information/documents/handbooks.

Wüst, A. M. and A. Volkens. 2003. *Euromanifesto Coding Instructions.* Mannheimer Zentrum für europäische Sozialforschung Working Paper, 64.

Zellner, Arnold. 1962. "An efficient method of estimating seemingly unrelated regressions and tests for aggregation bias." *Journal of the American Statistical Association* 57(298):348–368.

Zubek, Radoslaw and Heike Klüver. 2015. "Legislative pledges and coalition government." *Party Politics* 21(4):603–614.

APPENDIX 1
# Overview of coalition cabinets
## COALITIONAGREE Dataset

Table A.1 Austrian cabinets included in the sample

| Austria Cabinet | Party composition | Agreement | Word count | Election date | Date in | Date out | Duration (days) | Cabinet type | Notes | Word count (cleansed)* |
|---|---|---|---|---|---|---|---|---|---|---|
| Figl I | ÖVP, SPÖ, KPÖ | No | | 25.11.1945 | 20.12.1945 | 20.11.1947 | 700 | Surplus | | |
| Figl II | ÖVP, SPÖ | No | | 25.11.1945 | 20.11.1947 | 09.10.1949 | 689 | Surplus | | |
| Figl III | ÖVP, SPÖ | Yes | 1657 | 09.10.1949 | 08.11.1949 | 22.02.1953 | 1202 | MWC | d) | 1657 |
| Raab I | ÖVP, SPÖ | Yes | 761 | 22.02.1953 | 02.04.1953 | 13.05.1956 | 1137 | MWC | d) | 761 |
| Raab II | ÖVP, SPÖ | Yes | 1705 | 13.05.1956 | 29.06.1956 | 10.05.1959 | 1045 | MWC | d) | 1705 |
| Raab III | ÖVP, SPÖ | Yes | 1271 | 10.05.1959 | 16.07.1959 | 11.04.1961 | 635 | MWC | d) | 1271 |
| Gorbach I | ÖVP, SPÖ | Yes | 1271 | 10.05.1959 | 11.04.1961 | 18.11.1962 | 586 | MWC | b) | |
| Gorbach II | ÖVP, SPÖ | Yes | 4407 | 18.11.1962 | 27.03.1963 | 02.04.1964 | 372 | MWC | d) | 4407 |
| Klaus I | ÖVP, SPÖ | Yes | 4407 | 18.11.1962 | 02.04.1964 | 25.10.1965 | 571 | MWC | b) | |
| Sinowatz I | SPÖ, FPÖ | Yes | 2816 | 24.04.1983 | 24.05.1983 | 16.06.1986 | 1119 | MWC | e) | 2816 |
| Vranitzky I | SPÖ, FPÖ | Yes | 2816 | 24.04.1983 | 16.06.1986 | 23.11.1986 | 160 | MWC | b) | |
| Vranitzky II | SPÖ, ÖVP | Yes | 15518 | 23.11.1986 | 21.01.1987 | 07.10.1990 | 1355 | MWC | e) | 15518 |
| Vranitzky III | SPÖ, ÖVP | Yes | 23436 | 07.10.1990 | 17.12.1990 | 09.10.1994 | 1392 | MWC | e) | 23436 |
| Vranitzky IV | SPÖ, ÖVP | Yes | 12018 | 09.10.1994 | 29.11.1994 | 17.12.1995 | 383 | MWC | e) | 12018 |
| Vranitzky V | SPÖ, ÖVP | Yes | 11253 | 17.12.1995 | 12.03.1996 | 15.01.1997 | 309 | MWC | e) | 11253 |

| | | | | | | | | |
|---|---|---|---|---|---|---|---|---|
| Klima | SPÖ, ÖVP | Yes | 11253 | 17.12.1995 | 15.01.1997 | 03.10.1999 | 991 | MWC | b) |
| Schüssel I | ÖVP, FPÖ | Yes | 28738 | 03.10.1999 | 04.02.2000 | 24.11.2002 | 1024 | MWC | e) | 28738 |
| Schüssel II | ÖVP, FPÖ | Yes | 11468 | 24.11.2002 | 28.02.2003 | 01.10.2006 | 1311 | MWC | e) | 11468 |
| Gusenbauer I | SPÖ, ÖVP | Yes | 30983 | 01.10.2006 | 11.01.2007 | 28.09.2008 | 626 | MWC | | 30983 |
| Faymann I | SPÖ, ÖVP | Yes | 52019 | 28.09.2008 | 02.12.2008 | 29.09.2013 | 1762 | MWC | | 52019 |
| Faymann II | SPÖ, ÖVP | Yes | 30083 | 29.09.2013 | 16.12.2013 | 17.05.2016 | 883 | MWC | | 30083 |
| Mean | | | 13046 | | | | 869 | | | 15209 |

a) There is a coalition agreement but we were not able to obtain it.
b) There is no new coalition agreement but the cabinet in office used the previous one.
c) The word count for the coalition agreements we could not obtain originate from the Comparative Parliamentary Democracy Data Archive (Strøm et al. 2008).
d) We are grateful to Wolfgang C. Müller (University of Vienna) for providing the coalition agreements of the cabinets that were in office between 1945 and 1963.
e) We are grateful to Marc Debus (University of Mannheim) for providing the coalition agreements of the cabinets that were in office between 1983 and 2003.
* The cleansed word count refers to those agreements obtained in the analysis, duplicates excluded.

Party abbreviations:
FPÖ = Freiheitliche Partei Österreichs (Freedom Party of Austria)
KPÖ = Kommunistische Partei Österreichs (Communist Party of Austria)
SPÖ = Sozialdemokratische Partei Österreichs (Social Democratic Party of Austria)
ÖVP = Österreichische Volkspartei (Austrian People's Party)
Other abbrevations: MWC = Minimum winning coalition

Table A.2 Belgian cabinets included in the sample

| Belgium Cabinet | Party composition | Agreement | Word count | Election date | Date in | Date out | Duration (days) | Cabinet type | Notes | Word count (cleansed)* |
|---|---|---|---|---|---|---|---|---|---|---|
| Van Acker III | PSB/BSP, LP/PL, PCB/KPB | No | | 17.02.1946 | 31.03.1946 | 09.07.1946 | 100 | MWC | | |
| Huysmans I | PSB/BSP, LP/PL, PCB/KPB | No | | 17.02.1946 | 03.08.1946 | 13.03.1947 | 222 | MWC | | |
| Spaak II | CVP/PSC, PSB/BSP | No | | 17.02.1946 | 20.03.1947 | 26.06.1949 | 829 | MWC | | |
| Eyskens I | CVP/PSC, LP/PL | No | | 29.06.1949 | 11.08.1949 | 18.03.1950 | 219 | MWC | | |
| Van Acker IV | PSB/BSP, LP/PL | No | | 11.04.1954 | 22.04.1954 | 01.06.1958 | 1501 | MWC | | |
| Eyskens III | CVP/PSC, LP/PL | No | | 01.06.1958 | 06.11.1958 | 26.03.1961 | 871 | MWC | | |
| Lefevre I | CVP/PSC, PSB/BSP | No | | 26.03.1961 | 25.04.1961 | 23.05.1965 | 1489 | MWC | | |
| Harmel I | CVP/PSC, PSB/BSP | No | | 23.05.1965 | 27.07.1965 | 11.02.1966 | 199 | MWC | | |
| Van den Boeynants I | CVP/PSC, LP/PL | Yes | 5640 | 23.05.1965 | 19.03.1966 | 07.02.1968 | 690 | MWC | d) | 5640 |
| Eyskens IV | CVP, PSC, PSB/BSP | Yes | 9068 | 31.03.1968 | 17.06.1968 | 07.11.1971 | 1238 | Surplus | d) | 9068 |
| Eyskens V | CVP, PSC, PSB/BSP | Yes | 12069 | 07.11.1971 | 21.01.1972 | 23.11.1972 | 307 | Surplus | d) | 12069 |
| Leburton I | PSB/BSP, CVP, PSC, VLD, PRL | Yes | 19865 | 07.11.1971 | 26.01.1973 | 19.01.1974 | 358 | Surplus | d) | 19865 |
| Tindemans I | CVP, PSC, VLD, PRL | Yes | 6980 | 10.03.1974 | 25.04.1974 | 11.06.1974 | 47 | Minority | d) | 6980 |
| Tindemans II | CVP, PSC, VLD, PRL, RW | Yes | 2973 | 10.03.1974 | 12.06.1974 | 04.03.1977 | 996 | MWC | d) | 2973 |
| Tindemans III | CVP, PSC, VLD, PRL | No | | 10.03.1974 | 06.03.1977 | 17.04.1977 | 42 | Minority | | |
| Tindemans IV | CVP, PSC, PSB/BSP, VU, FDF | Yes | 15331 | 17.04.1977 | 03.06.1977 | 11.10.1978 | 495 | Surplus | d) | 15331 |

| | | | | | | | | | |
|---|---|---|---|---|---|---|---|---|---|
| Van den Boeynants II | CVP, PSC, PSB/BSP, VU, FDF | No | | 17.04.1977 | 20.10.1978 | 17.12.1978 | 58 | Surplus | |
| Martens I | CVP, PSC, PS, SP, FDF | Yes | 16215 | 17.12.1978 | 03.04.1979 | 16.01.1980 | 288 | Surplus | d) | 16215 |
| Martens II | CVP, PSC, PS, SP | No | | 17.12.1978 | 23.01.1980 | 09.04.1980 | 77 | Surplus | | |
| Martens III | CVP, PSC, PS, SP, VLD, PRL | Yes | 20964 | 17.12.1978 | 18.05.1980 | 07.10.1980 | 142 | Surplus | d) | 20964 |
| Martens IV | CVP, PSC, PS, SP | Yes | 14785 | 17.12.1978 | 22.10.1980 | 02.04.1981 | 162 | Surplus | d) | 14785 |
| M Eyskens I | CVP, PSC, PS, SP | Yes | 14785 | 17.12.1978 | 06.04.1981 | 21.09.1981 | 168 | Surplus | b) | |
| Martens V | CVP, PSC, VLD, PRL | Yes | 6834 | 08.11.1981 | 17.12.1981 | 13.10.1985 | 1396 | MWC | d) | 6834 |
| Martens VI | CVP, PSC, VLD, PRL | Yes | 12838 | 13.10.1985 | 28.11.1985 | 13.12.1987 | 745 | MWC | e) | 12838 |
| Martens VII | CVP, PSC, PS, SP, VU | Yes | 40602 | 13.12.1987 | 09.05.1988 | 29.09.1991 | 1238 | Surplus | e) | 40602 |
| Martens VIII | CVP, PSC, PS, SP | No | | 13.12.1987 | 29.09.1991 | 24.11.1991 | 56 | Surplus | | |
| Dehaene I | CVP, PSC, PS, SP | Yes | 6327 | 24.11.1991 | 07.03.1992 | 21.05.1995 | 1170 | MWC | e) | 6327 |
| Dehaene II | CVP, PSC, PS, SP | Yes | 17324 | 21.05.1995 | 23.06.1995 | 13.06.1999 | 1451 | MWC | e) | 17324 |
| Verhofstadt I | VLD, PRL, SP, PS, E, A | Yes | 14473 | 13.06.1999 | 12.07.1999 | 05.05.2003 | 1393 | Surplus | e) | 14473 |
| Verhofstadt II | VLD, PRL, SP, PS, A | No | | 13.06.1999 | 05.05.2003 | 18.05.2003 | 13 | MWC | | |
| Verhofstadt III | VLD, SP, PS, PRL | Yes | 24099 | 18.05.2003 | 12.07.2003 | 10.06.2007 | 1429 | MWC | | 24099 |
| Verhofstadt IV | VLD, CVP, PS, PRL, PSC | Yes | 14162 | 10.06.2007 | 21.12.2007 | 20.03.2008 | 90 | Surplus | | 14162 |
| Leterme I | CVP, VLD, PS, PRL, PSC | Yes | 14130 | 10.06.2007 | 20.03.2008 | 22.12.2008 | 277 | Surplus | | 14130 |
| Van Rompuy I | CVP, VLD, PRL, PS, PSC | No | | 10.06.2007 | 30.12.2008 | 25.11.2009 | 330 | Surplus | | |
| Leterme II | CVP, PRL, VLD, PS, PSC | No | | 10.06.2007 | 25.11.2009 | 26.04.2010 | 152 | Surplus | | |

*Continued*

Table A.2 Continued

| Belgium Cabinet | Party composition | Agreement | Word count | Election date | Date in | Date out | Duration (days) | Cabinet type | Notes | Word count (cleansed)* |
|---|---|---|---|---|---|---|---|---|---|---|
| Leterme III | PS, PRL, CVP, PSC | No | | | 13.06.2010 | 05.12.2011 | 540 | Minority | | |
| Di Rupo I | PS, CVP, PRL, SP, LP/PL, PSC | Yes | 50484 | 13.06.2010 | 06.12.2011 | 11.10.2014 | 1040 | Surplus | | 50484 |
| Michel I | VU, CVP, VLD, PRL | Yes | 52687 | 25.05.2014 | 11.10.2014 | 09.12.2018 | 1520 | MWC | | 52687 |
| Mean | | | 17847 | | | | 946 | | | 17993 |

a) There is a coalition agreement but we were not able to obtain it.
b) There is no new coalition agreement but the cabinet in office used the previous one.
c) The word count for the coalition agreements we could not obtain did not originate from the Comparative Parliamentary Democracy Data Archive (Strøm et al. 2008).
d) We are grateful to Frederik Verleden (Chamber of Representatives, Documentation and Archives) for providing the coalition agreements of the cabinets that were in office between 1966 and 1985.
e) We are grateful to Marc Debus (University of Mannheim) for providing the coalition agreements of the cabinets that were in office between 1985 and 2003.
* The cleansed word count refers to those agreements obtained in the analysis, duplicates excluded.

Party abbreviations:
A = AGALEV (Another Way of Living)
CVP = Christelijke Volkspartij (Christian People's Party)
CVP/PSC = Christelijke Volkspartij/Parti Social-Chrétien (Christian Democrat Party)
E = ECOLO (Ecologist Party)
FDF = Front Démocratique des Francophones (Democratic Front of French-Speakers)
LP/PL = Liberale Partij/Parti Libéral (Liberal Party)
PCB/KPB = Parti Communiste Belge/Kommunistische Partij van België (Belgian Communist Party)
PRL = Parti Réformateur Libéral (Liberal Reform Party)
PS = Parti Socialiste (French-Speaking Socialist Party)
PSB/BSP = Belgische Socialistische Partij/Parti Socialiste Belge (Belgian Socialist Party)
PSC = Parti Social Chrétien (Christian Social Party)
RW = Rassemblement Wallon (Walloon Rally)
SP = Socialistische Partij (Flemish Socialist Party)
VLD = Vlaamse Liberalen en Democraten (Flemish Liberals and Democrats)
VU = Volksunie (People's Union)
Other abbreviations: MWC = Minimum winning coalition

Table A.3 Bulgarian cabinets included in the sample

| Bulgaria Cabinet | Party composition | Agreement | Word count | Election date | Date in | Date out | Duration (days) | Cabinet type |
|---|---|---|---|---|---|---|---|---|
| Popov I | BSP, BZNS, ODS | No | | 17.06.1990 | 20.12.1990 | 13.10.1991 | 297 | Surplus |
| Sakskoburggotski I | NDSV, DPS | No | | 17.06.2001 | 24.07.2001 | 25.06.2005 | 1432 | MWC |
| Stanishev I | BSP, NDSV, DPS | No | | 25.06.2005 | 16.08.2005 | 05.07.2009 | 1419 | Surplus |
| Orescharski I | BSP, DPS | No | | 12.05.2013 | 29.05.2013 | 05.08.2014 | 433 | Minority |
| Borrissow II | GERB, RB, ABV | Yes | 4260 | 05.10.2014 | 07.11.2014 | 27.01.2017 | 812 | Minority |
| Mean | | | 4260 | | | | 879 | |

According to Peter Kolb (German Embassy in Sofia), coalition agreements typically were informal and not made available in public. The Borrissow II cabinet is the first cabinet to publish a coalition agreement.

Party abbreviations:
ABV = Alternativa za balgarsko vazrazhdane (Alternative for Bulgarian Revival)
BSP = Balgarska Sotsialisticheska Partiya (Bulgarian Socialist Party)
BZNS = Balgarski Zemdelski Naroden Săyuz (Bulgarian Agrarian National Union)
DPS = Dvizhenie za Prava i Svobodi (Movement for Rights & Freedoms)
GERB = Graždani za Evropejsko Razvitie na B?lgaria (Citizens for European Development of Bulgaria)
NDSV = Natsionalno Dvizhenie Simeon Vtori (National Movement Simeon II)
ODS = Obedineni Demokratichni Sili (United Democratic Forces)
RB = Reformatorski Blok (Reformist Bloc)
Other abbreviations: MWC = Minimum winning coalition

Table A.4 Czech cabinets included in the sample

| Czeck Republic Cabinet | Party composition | Agreement | Word count | Election date | Date in | Date out | Duration (days) | Cabinet | Notes type |
|---|---|---|---|---|---|---|---|---|---|
| Klaus I | ODS, KDU-CSL, ODA | No | | 06.06.1992 | 02.07.1992 | 01.06.1996 | 1430 | MWC | |
| Klaus II | ODS, KDU-CSL, ODA | No | | 01.06.1996 | 04.07.1996 | 30.11.1997 | 514 | Minority | |
| Tosovsky I | ODS, KDU-CSL, ODA | No | | 01.06.1996 | 02.01.1998 | 20.06.1998 | 169 | Minority | |
| Spidla I | CSSD, KDU-CSL, US-DEU | Yes | 5378 | 15.06.2002 | 15.07.2002 | 01.07.2004 | 717 | MWC | d) |
| Gross I | CSSD, KDU-CSL, US-DEU | Yes | 3051 | 15.06.2002 | 04.08.2004 | 25.04.2005 | 264 | MWC | d) |
| Paroubek I | CSSD, KDU-CSL, US-DEU | No | | 14.06.2002 | 25.04.2005 | 03.06.2006 | 404 | MWC | |
| Topolanek II | ODS, KDU-CSL, SZ | Yes | 7482 | 03.06.2006 | 09.01.2007 | 26.03.2009 | 807 | Minority | d) |
| Necas I | ODS, TOP09, VV | Yes | 15089 | 29.05.2010 | 13.07.2010 | 29.05.2012 | 686 | MWC | d) |

| | | | | | | | |
|---|---|---|---|---|---|---|---|
| Nečas II | ODS, TOP09, LIDEM | Yes | 14546 | 29.05.2010 | 17.06.2013 | 384 | MWC d) |
| Sobotka I | ČSSD, ANO, KDU-ČSL | Yes | 11528 | 26.10.2013 | 29.01.2014 | 1419 | MWC d) |
| Mean | | | 9512 | | | 679 | |

a) There is a coalition agreement but we were not able to obtain it.
b) There is no new coalition agreement but the cabinet in office used the previous one.
c) The word counts for the coalition agreements we could not obtain originate from the Comparative Parliamentary Democracy Data Archive (Strøm et al. 2008).
d) We are grateful to Kamil Marcinkiewicz (University of Hamburg) for identifying the coalition agreements.

In the Czech Republic, there are two sets of documents cabinets typically produce: government declarations and coalition agreements. Government declarations are traditionally submitted to the chamber of deputies before the investiture vote and mostly include policy statements. Whereas the composition of such declarations is considered to be nearly compulsory, the establishment of a coalition agreement solely depends on the cabinet parties. However, in our project, we are focusing on documents that parties are free to write. Hence, we only include coalition agreements and omit the set of government declarations.

Party abbreviations:
ANO = Akce nespokojených občanů (Action of Dissatisfied Citizens)
ČSSD = Česká Strana Sociálně Demokratická (Czech Social Democratic Party)
KDU-ČSL = Křesťanská a Demokratická Unie – Československá Strana Lidová (Christian and Democratic Union)
LIDEM = Liberální Demokraté (Liberal Democrats)
ODA = Občanská Demokratická Aliance (Civic Democratic Alliance)
ODS = Občanská Demokratická Strana (Civic Democratic Party)
SZ = Strana Zelených (Greens)
TOP09 = Tradice, Odpovědnost, Prosperita a číslovky 09 (Tradition, Responsibility, Prosperity 09)
US-DEU = Unie Svobody (Freedom Union)
VV = Věci Veřejné (Public Affairs)
Other abbreviations: MWC = Minimum winning coalition

Table A.5 Danish cabinets included in the sample

| Denmark Cabinet | Party composition | Agreement | Word count | Election date | Date in | Date out | Duration (days) | Cabinet type | Notes | Word count (cleansed)* |
|---|---|---|---|---|---|---|---|---|---|---|
| Eriksen I | Lib, Kon | No | | 05.09.1950 | 30.10.1950 | 21.04.1953 | 904 | Minority | | |
| Eriksen II | Lib, Kon | No | | 21.04.1953 | 21.04.1953 | 22.09.1953 | 154 | Minority | | |
| Hansen II | SD, RL, GP | Yes | 910 | 14.05.1957 | 28.05.1957 | 19.02.1960 | 997 | MWC | a), c) | |
| Kampmann I | SD, RL, GP | No | | 14.05.1957 | 21.02.1960 | 15.11.1960 | 268 | MWC | | |
| Kampmann II | SD, RL | No | | 15.11.1960 | 18.11.1960 | 03.09.1962 | 654 | Minority | | |
| Krag I | SD, RL | No | | 15.11.1960 | 03.09.1962 | 22.09.1964 | 750 | Minority | | |
| Baunsgaard I | RL, Kon, Lib | No | | 23.01.1968 | 22.02.1968 | 21.09.1971 | 1307 | MWC | | |
| Jorgensen IV | SD, Lib | No | | 15.02.1977 | 30.08.1978 | 23.10.1979 | 419 | Minority | | |
| Schlüter I | Kon, Lib, ZD, CVP | No | | 08.12.1981 | 10.09.1982 | 10.01.1984 | 487 | Minority | | |
| Schlüter II | Kon, Lib, ZD, CVP | No | | 10.01.1984 | 10.01.1984 | 08.09.1987 | 1337 | Minority | | |
| Schlüter III | Kon, Lib, ZD, CVP | No | | 08.09.1987 | 10.09.1987 | 10.05.1988 | 243 | Minority | | |
| Schlüter IV | Kon, Lib, RL | No | | 10.05.1988 | 03.06.1988 | 12.12.1990 | 922 | Minority | | |
| Schlüter V | Kon, Lib | No | | 12.12.1990 | 18.12.1990 | 15.01.1993 | 759 | Minority | | |
| Rasmussen I | SD, RL, ZD, CVP | Yes | 4017 | 12.12.1990 | 25.01.1993 | 21.09.1994 | 604 | MWC | d) | 4017 |

| | | | | | | | | |
|---|---|---|---|---|---|---|---|---|
| Rasmussen II | SD, RL, ZD | Yes | 3626 | 21.09.1994 | 27.09.1994 | 30.12.1996 | 825 | Minority | d) 3626 |
| Rasmussen III | SD, RL | Yes | 3626 | 21.09.1994 | 30.12.1996 | 11.03.1998 | 436 | Minority | b) |
| Rasmussen IV | SD, RL | Yes | 10851 | 11.03.1998 | 11.03.1998 | 20.11.2001 | 1350 | Minority | d) 10851 |
| Fogh Rasmussen I | Lib, Kon | Yes | 27014 | 20.11.2001 | 27.11.2001 | 08.02.2005 | 1169 | Minority | d) 27014 |
| Fogh Rasmussen II | Lib, Kon | Yes | 22837 | 08.02.2005 | 08.02.2005 | 13.11.2007 | 1008 | Minority | d) 22837 |
| Fogh Rasmussen III | Lib, Kon | Yes | 22580 | 13.11.2007 | 13.11.2007 | 05.04.2009 | 509 | Minority | d) 22580 |
| Løkke Rasmussen I | Lib, Kon | Yes | 16104 | 13.11.2007 | 05.04.2009 | 15.09.2011 | 893 | Minority | d) 16104 |
| Thorning-Schmidt I | SD, RL, SVP | Yes | 26870 | 15.09.2011 | 03.10.2011 | 30.01.2014 | 850 | Minority | d) 26870 |
| Thorning-Schmidt II | SD, RL | Yes | 26870 | 15.09.2011 | 03.02.2014 | 18.06.2015 | 500 | Minority | b) |
| Mean | | | 15028 | | | | 754 | | 16737 |

a) There is a coalition agreement but we were not able to obtain it.
b) There is no new coalition agreement but the cabinet in office used the previous one.
c) The word count for the coalition agreements we could not obtain originate from the Comparative Parliamentary Democracy Data Archive (Strøm et al. 2008).
d) We are grateful to Helene Pedersen (Aarhus University) for providing the coalition agreements of the cabinets that were in office between 1993 and 2011.
* The cleansed word count refers to those agreements obtained in the analysis, duplicates excluded.

Party abbreviations:
CVP = Kristeligt Folkeparti (Christian People's Party)
GP = Danmarks Retsforbund (Justice Party)
Kon = Det Konservative Folkeparti (Conservative People's Party)
Lib = Venstre, Danmarks Liberale Parti (Liberal Party)
RL = Det Radikale Venstre (Radical Liberal Party)
SD = Socialdemokratiet (Social Democratic Party)
SVP = Socialistisk Folkeparti (Socialist People's Party)
ZD = Centrum-Demokraterne (Centre Democrats)
Other abbreviations: MWC = Minimum winning coalition

Table A.6 Estonian cabinets included in the sample

| Estonia Cabinet | Party composition | Agreement | Word count | Election date | Date in | Date out | Duration (days) | Cabinet type | Notes |
|---|---|---|---|---|---|---|---|---|---|
| Laar I | IL, SDE, ERSP | Yes | 6022 | 20.09.1992 | 21.10.1992 | 26.09.1994 | 705 | MWC | d) |
| Tarand I | SDE, IL, ERSP | No | | 20.09.1992 | 03.11.1994 | 05.03.1995 | 122 | MWC | |
| Vaehi I | KMU, EKe | Yes | 1344 | 05.03.1995 | 17.04.1995 | 11.10.1995 | 177 | MWC | d) |
| Vaehi II | KMU, ER | Yes | 727 | 05.03.1995 | 03.11.1995 | 22.11.1996 | 385 | MWC | d) |
| Laar II | IL, ER, SDE | Yes | 4057 | 07.03.1999 | 25.03.1999 | 08.01.2002 | 1020 | MWC | d) |
| Kallas I | ER, EKe | Yes | 1066 | 07.03.1999 | 28.01.2002 | 02.03.2003 | 398 | Minority | |
| Parts I | ResP, ER, ERL | Yes | 10305 | 02.03.2003 | 10.04.2003 | 24.03.2005 | 714 | MWC | |
| Ansip I | ER, EKe, ERL | Yes | 1941 | 02.03.2003 | 13.04.2005 | 04.03.2007 | 690 | MWC | |
| Ansip II | ER, IresPL, SDE | Yes | 8236 | 04.03.2007 | 05.04.2007 | 21.05.2009 | 777 | MWC | |
| Ansip III | ER, IresPL | No | | 04.03.2007 | 04.06.2009 | 06.03.2011 | 640 | Minority | |
| Ansip IV | ER, IresPL | Yes | 12169 | 06.03.2011 | 05.04.2011 | 04.03.2014 | 1064 | MWC | |
| Roivas I | ER, SDE | Yes | 3736 | 06.03.2011 | 26.03.2014 | 01.03.2015 | 340 | MWC | |
| Roivas II | ER, SDE, IresPL | Yes | 13092 | 01.03.2015 | 09.04.2015 | 20.11.2016 | 591 | MWC | |
| Mean | | | 5700 | | | | 586 | | |

a) There is a coalition agreement but we were not able to obtain it.
b) There is no new coalition agreement but the cabinet in office used the previous one.
c) The word count for the coalition agreements we could not obtain originate from the Comparative Parliamentary Democracy Data Archive (Strøm et al. 2008).
d) We are grateful to Margus Sarapuu (Head of the Office of the Prime Minister of Estonia) for identifying and providing the coalition agreements of the cabinets that were in office between 1992 and 1996.

Party abbreviations:
EKe = Eesti Keskerakond (Estonian Centre Party)
ER = Eesti Reformierakond (Estonian Reform Party)
ERL = Eestimaa Rahvaliit (People's Union of Estonia)
ERSP = Eesti Rahvusliku Soltumatuse Partei (Estonian National Independence Party)
IL = Ismaaliit (Pro Patria Union)
IresPL = Isamaa ja Res Publica Liit (Union of Pro Patria and Res Publica)
KMU = Koonderakond ja Maarahva Ühendus (Coalition Party and Rural Union)
SDE = Sotsiaaldemokraatlik Erakond (Social Democratic Party)
ResP = Res Publica (Res Publica)
Other abbreviations: MWC = Minimum winning coalition

Table A.7 Finnish cabinets included in the sample

| Finland Cabinet | Party composition | Agreement | Word count | Election date | Date in | Date out | Duration (days) | Cabinet type | Notes | Word count (cleansed)* |
|---|---|---|---|---|---|---|---|---|---|---|
| Paasikivi III | SKDL, SDP, ZE, LIB, SW | Yes | 459 | 18.03.1945 | 17.04.1945 | 08.03.1946 | 325 | Surplus | | 459 |
| Pekkala I | SKDL, SDP, ZE, SW | Yes | 430 | 18.03.1945 | 26.03.1946 | 02.07.1948 | 829 | Surplus | | 430 |
| Kekkonen I | ZE, LIB, SW | Yes | 256 | 02.07.1948 | 17.03.1950 | 17.01.1951 | 306 | Minority | | 256 |
| Kekkonen II | ZE, SDP, LIB, SW | Yes | 279 | 02.07.1948 | 17.01.1951 | 03.07.1951 | 167 | Surplus | | 279 |
| Kekkonen III | ZE, SDP, SW | Yes | 422 | 03.07.1951 | 20.09.1951 | 29.06.1953 | 648 | Surplus | | 422 |
| Kekkonen IV | ZE, SW | Yes | 232 | 03.07.1951 | 09.07.1953 | 04.11.1953 | 118 | Minority | | 232 |
| Törngren I | SW, SDP, ZE | Yes | 362 | 08.03.1954 | 05.05.1954 | 14.10.1954 | 162 | Surplus | | 362 |
| Kekkonen V | ZE, SDP | Yes | 86 | 08.03.1954 | 20.10.1954 | 27.01.1956 | 464 | MWC | | 86 |
| Fagerholm II | SDP, ZE, LIB, SW | Yes | 235 | 08.03.1954 | 03.03.1956 | 22.05.1957 | 445 | Surplus | | 235 |
| Sukselainen I | ZE, LIB, SW | Yes | 242 | 08.03.1954 | 27.05.1957 | 02.07.1957 | 36 | Minority | | 242 |
| Sukselainen II | ZE, LIB | Yes | 242 | 08.03.1954 | 02.07.1957 | 02.09.1957 | 62 | Minority | b) | |
| Sukselainen III | ZE, SDL, LIB | Yes | 762 | 08.03.1954 | 02.09.1957 | 18.10.1957 | 46 | Minority | | 762 |
| Fagerholm III | SDP, ZE, LIB, SW, KON | Yes | 1469 | 07.07.1958 | 29.08.1958 | 04.12.1958 | 97 | Surplus | | 1469 |
| Karjalainen I | ZE, LIB, SW, KON | Yes | 359 | 05.02.1962 | 13.04.1962 | 17.12.1963 | 613 | MWC | | 359 |
| Virolainen I | ZE, LIB, SW, KON | Yes | 240 | 05.02.1962 | 12.09.1964 | 21.03.1966 | 555 | MWC | | 240 |
| Paasio I | SDP, SKDL, SDL, ZE | Yes | 558 | 21.03.1966 | 27.05.1966 | 01.03.1968 | 644 | Surplus | | 558 |
| Koivisto I | SDP, SKDL, SDL, ZE, SW | Yes | 884 | 21.03.1966 | 22.03.1968 | 16.03.1970 | 724 | Surplus | | 884 |
| Karjalainen II | ZE, SKDL, SDP, LIB, SW | Yes | 1755 | 16.03.1970 | 15.07.1970 | 26.03.1971 | 254 | Surplus | | 1755 |

*Continued*

Table A.7 *Continued*

| Finland Cabinet | Party composition | Agreement | Word count | Election date | Date in | Date out | Duration (days) | Cabinet type | Notes | Word count (cleansed)* |
|---|---|---|---|---|---|---|---|---|---|---|
| Karjalainen III | ZE, SDP, LIB, SW | Yes | 1755 | 16.03.1970 | 26.03.1971 | 29.10.1971 | 217 | MWC | b) | |
| Sorsa I | SDP, ZE, LIB, SW | Yes | 1822 | 03.01.1972 | 04.09.1972 | 04.06.1975 | 1003 | MWC | | 1822 |
| Miettunen II | ZE, SKDL, SDP, LIB, SW | Yes | 214 | 22.09.1975 | 30.11.1975 | 17.09.1976 | 292 | Surplus | | 214 |
| Miettunen III | ZE, LIB, SW | Yes | 378 | 22.09.1975 | 29.09.1976 | 11.05.1977 | 224 | Minority | | 378 |
| Sorsa II | SDP, SKDL, ZE, LIB, SW | Yes | 528 | 22.09.1975 | 15.05.1977 | 17.01.1978 | 247 | Surplus | | 528 |
| Sorsa III | SDP, SKDL, ZE, LIB | Yes | 528 | 22.09.1975 | 02.03.1978 | 19.03.1979 | 382 | Surplus | b) | |
| Koivisto II | SDP, SKDL, ZE, SW | Yes | 1050 | 19.03.1979 | 26.05.1979 | 26.01.1982 | 976 | Surplus | | 1050 |
| Sorsa IV | SDP, SKDL, ZE, SW | Yes | 857 | 19.03.1979 | 19.02.1982 | 30.12.1982 | 314 | Surplus | | 857 |
| Sorsa V | SDP, ZE, LIB, SW | Yes | 857 | 13.03.1979 | 31.12.1982 | 21.03.1983 | 80 | MWC | b) | |
| Sorsa VI | SDP, ZE, FRP, SW | Yes | 1819 | 21.03.1983 | 06.05.1983 | 16.03.1987 | 1410 | Surplus | | 1819 |
| Holkeri I | KON, SDP, FRP, SW | Yes | 2904 | 16.03.1987 | 30.04.1987 | 24.08.1990 | 1212 | Surplus | | 2904 |
| Holkeri II | KON, SDP, SW | Yes | 2904 | 16.03.1987 | 28.08.1990 | 17.03.1991 | 201 | Surplus | b) | |
| Aho I | ZE, CHR, SW, KON | Yes | 2733 | 17.03.1991 | 26.04.1991 | 20.06.1994 | 1151 | Surplus | | 2733 |

| Cabinet | Parties | Agreement | Word count | Start date | End date | Cleansed | Type | Word count b) |
|---|---|---|---|---|---|---|---|---|
| Aho II | ZE, SW, KON | Yes | 2733 | 17.03.1991 | 28.06.1994 | 19.03.1995 | 264 | MWC | |
| Lipponen I | SDP, SKDL, GR, SW, KON | Yes | 3887 | 19.03.1995 | 13.04.1995 | 21.03.1999 | 1438 | Surplus | 3887 |
| Lipponen II | SDP, KON, SW, GR, SKDL | Yes | 6798 | 21.03.1999 | 15.04.1999 | 31.05.2002 | 1142 | Surplus | 6798 |
| Lipponen III | SDP, KON, SW, SKDL | No | | 21.03.1999 | 31.05.2002 | 16.03.2003 | 289 | Surplus | |
| Jäätteenmäki I | ZE, SDP, SW | Yes | 13315 | 16.03.2003 | 17.04.2003 | 18.06.2003 | 62 | Surplus | 13315 |
| Vanhanen I | ZE, SDP, SW | Yes | 13225 | 16.03.2003 | 24.06.2003 | 18.03.2007 | 1363 | Surplus | 13225 |
| Vanhanen II | ZE, KON, GR, SW | Yes | 16435 | 18.03.2007 | 19.04.2007 | 18.06.2010 | 1156 | Surplus | 16435 |
| Mari Kiviniemi I | ZE, KON, GR, SW | Yes | 1124 | 18.03.2007 | 22.06.2010 | 17.04.2011 | 299 | Surplus | 1124 |
| Katainen I | KON, SDP, SKDL, GR, SW, CHR | Yes | 28236 | 17.04.2011 | 22.06.2011 | 25.03.2014 | 1007 | Surplus | 28236 |
| Katainen II | KON, SDP, GR, SW, CHR | No | | 17.04.2011 | 25.03.2014 | 24.06.2014 | 91 | Surplus | |
| Stubb I | KON, SDP, GR, SW, CHR | Yes | 2026 | 17.04.2011 | 24.06.2014 | 26.09.2014 | 94 | Surplus | 2026 |
| Stubb II | KON, SDP, SW, CHR | No | | 17.04.2011 | 26.09.2014 | 19.04.2015 | 205 | MWC | |
| Sipilä I | ZE, FRP, KON | Yes | 19335 | 19.04.2015 | 29.05.2015 | 08.03.2019 | 1379 | MWC | 19335 |
| Mean | | | 3286 | | | | 509 | | 3592 |

a) There is a coalition agreement but we were not able to obtain it.
b) There is no new coalition agreement but the cabinet in office used the previous one.
c) The word count for the coalition agreements we could not obtain originate from the Comparative Parliamentary Democracy Data Archive (Strøm et al. 2008).
* The cleansed word count refers to those agreements obtained in the analysis, duplicates excluded.

Party abbreviations:
CHR = Suomen Kristillinen Liitto (Christian League of Finland)
FRP = Suomen Maaseudun Puolue (Finnish Rural Party)
GR = Vihreä Liitto (Green League)
KON = Kansallinen Kokoomus (National Coalition Party)
LIB = Liberaalinen Kansanpuolue (Liberal People's Party)
SDL = TyÖväen ja PienviljelijÖiden Sosialidemokraattinen Liitto (Social Democratic League of Workers and Smallholders)
SDP = Suomen Sosialidemokraattinen Puolue (Finnish Social Democratic Party)
SKDL = Vasemmistoliitto (Left Wing Alliance)
SW = Svenska folkpartiet (Swedish People's Party)
ZE = Suomen Keskusta (Centre Party of Finland)
Other abbreviations: MWC = Minimum winning coalition

Table A.8 German cabinets included in the sample

| Germany Cabinet | Party composition | Agreement | Word count | Election date | Date in | Date out | Duration (days) | Cabinet type | Notes | Word count (cleansed)* |
|---|---|---|---|---|---|---|---|---|---|---|
| Adenauer I | CDU/CSU, FDP, DP | No | | 14.08.1949 | 15.09.1949 | 06.09.1953 | 1452 | MWC | | |
| Adenauer II | CDU/CSU, FDP, DP, GB/BHE | No | | 06.09.1953 | 09.10.1953 | 23.07.1955 | 652 | Surplus | | |
| Adenauer III | CDU/CSU, FDP, DP | No | | 06.09.1953 | 23.07.1955 | 25.02.1956 | 217 | Surplus | | |
| Adenauer IV | CDU/CSU, DP, DA/FVP | No | | 06.09.1953 | 25.02.1956 | 15.09.1957 | 568 | Surplus | | |
| Adenauer V | CDU/CSU, DP | Yes | 1600 | 15.09.1957 | 22.10.1957 | 02.07.1960 | 984 | Surplus | | 1600 |
| Adenauer VII | CDU/CSU, FDP | Yes | 2164 | 17.09.1961 | 07.11.1961 | 19.11.1962 | 377 | MWC | | 2164 |
| Adenauer IX | CDU/CSU, FDP | Yes | 632 | 17.09.1961 | 13.12.1962 | 16.10.1963 | 307 | MWC | | 632 |
| Erhard I | CDU/CSU, FDP | Yes | 632 | 17.09.1961 | 16.10.1963 | 19.09.1965 | 704 | MWC | b) | |
| Erhard II | CDU/CSU, FDP | No | | 19.09.1965 | 20.10.1965 | 28.10.1966 | 373 | MWC | | |
| Kiesinger I | CDU/CSU, SPD | No | | 19.09.1965 | 01.12.1966 | 28.09.1969 | 1032 | MWC | | |
| Brandt I | SPD, FDP | No | | 28.09.1969 | 21.10.1969 | 19.11.1972 | 1125 | MWC | | |
| Brandt II | SPD, FDP | No | | 19.11.1972 | 14.12.1972 | 16.05.1974 | 518 | MWC | | |
| Schmidt I | SPD, FDP | No | | 19.11.1972 | 16.05.1974 | 03.10.1976 | 871 | MWC | | |

| Cabinet | Parties | Agreement | Start date | End date | Date | Word count | Type | Cleansed |
|---|---|---|---|---|---|---|---|---|
| Schmidt II | SPD, FDP | No | | 03.10.1976 | 15.12.1976 | 05.10.1980 | 1390 | MWC | |
| Schmidt III | SPD, FDP | Yes | 1214 | 05.10.1980 | 05.11.1980 | 17.09.1982 | 681 | MWC | 1214 |
| Kohl I | CDU/CSU, FDP | Yes | 3339 | 05.10.1980 | 01.10.1982 | 06.03.1983 | 156 | MWC | 3339 |
| Kohl II | CDU/CSU, FDP | Yes | 2399 | 06.03.1983 | 29.03.1983 | 25.01.1987 | 1398 | MWC | 2399 |
| Kohl III | CDU/CSU, FDP | Yes | 7554 | 25.01.1987 | 11.03.1987 | 30.10.1990 | 1329 | MWC | 7554 |
| Kohl IV | CDU/CSU, FDP, DSU | No | | 25.01.1987 | 30.10.1990 | 02.12.1990 | 33 | Surplus | |
| Kohl V | CDU/CSU, FDP | Yes | 14836 | 02.12.1990 | 17.01.1991 | 16.10.1994 | 1368 | MWC | 14836 |
| Kohl VI | CDU/CSU, FDP | Yes | 10511 | 16.10.1994 | 15.11.1994 | 27.09.1998 | 1412 | MWC | 10511 |
| Schroeder I | SPD, GR | Yes | 16744 | 27.09.1998 | 27.10.1998 | 22.09.2002 | 1426 | MWC | 16744 |
| Schroeder II | SPD, GR | Yes | 28260 | 22.09.2002 | 22.10.2002 | 18.09.2005 | 1062 | MWC | 28260 |
| Merkel I | CDU/CSU, SPD | Yes | 54064 | 18.09.2005 | 22.11.2005 | 27.09.2009 | 1405 | MWC | 54064 |
| Merkel II | CDU/CSU, FDP | Yes | 41714 | 27.09.2009 | 28.10.2009 | 22.09.2013 | 1425 | MWC | 41714 |
| Merkel III | CDU/CSU, SPD | Yes | 64086 | 22.09.2013 | 17.12.2013 | 14.03.2018 | 1548 | MWC | 64086 |
| Mean | | | 16650 | | | | 916 | | 17794 |

a) There is a coalition agreement but we were not able to obtain it.
b) There is no new coalition agreement but the cabinet in office used the previous one.
c) The word counts for the coalition agreements we could not obtain originate from the Comparative Parliamentary Democracy Data Archive (Strøm et al. 2008).
* The cleansed word count refers to those agreements obtained in the analysis, duplicates excluded.

Party abbreviations:
CDU/CSU = Christlich Demokratische Union Deutschlands and Christlich-Soziale Union (Christian Democratic Union/Christian Social Union)
DA/FVP = Freie Volkspartei (Free People's Party)
DP = Deutsche Partei (German Party)
DSU = Deutsche Soziale Union (German Social Union)
FDP = Freie Demokratische Partei (Free Democratic Party)
GB/BHE = Gesamtdeutscher Block/Bund der Heimatlosen und Entrechteten (All-German Bloc)
GR = Die Grünen (The Greens)
SPD = Sozialdemokratische Partei Deutschlands (Social Democratic Party of Germany)
Other abbreviations: MWC = Minimum winning coalition

Table A.9 Greek cabinets included in the sample

| Greece Cabinet | Party composition | Agreement | Word count | Election date | Date in | Date out | Duration (days) | Cabinet type | Notes |
|---|---|---|---|---|---|---|---|---|---|
| Tzannetakis I | ND, SYN | No | | 18.06.1989 | 02.07.1989 | 07.10.1989 | 97 | MWC | |
| Zolotas I | ND, PASOK, SYN | No | | 05.11.1989 | 23.11.1989 | 08.04.1990 | 136 | Surplus | |
| Papademos I | PASOK, ND, LAOS | No | | 04.10.2009 | 11.11.2011 | 16.05.2012 | 187 | Surplus | |
| Samaras I | ND,PASOK,DIMAR | Yes | 2109 | 17.06.2012 | 21.06.2012 | 24.06.2013 | 368 | Surplus | d) |
| Samaras II | ND, PASOK | Yes | 3974 | 17.06.2012 | 24.06.2013 | 25.01.2015 | 580 | MWC | |
| Tsipras I | SYRIZA, AE | No | | 25.01.2015 | 27.01.2015 | 28.08.2015 | 213 | MWC | |
| Tsipras II | SYRIZA, AE | No | | 20.09.2015 | 23.09.2015 | 04.11.2016 | 408 | MWC | |
| Mean | | | 3042 | | | | 284 | | |

a) There is a coalition agreement but we were not able to obtain it.
b) There is no new coalition agreement but the cabinet in office used the previous one.
c) The word counts for the coalition agreements we could not obtain originate from the Comparative Parliamentary Democracy Data Archive (Strøm et al. 2008).
d) We are grateful to Andreas Kollias (Panteion University) for providing the coalition agreement of the Samaras I cabinet.
According to Andreas Kollias and Stavros Skrinis (both Panteion University), in Greece, coalition partners typically do not write coalition agreements.
The exception to this rule is the Samaras I cabinet.
Party abbreviations:
AE = Anexartitoi Ellines (Independent Greeks)
ND = Nea Dimokratia (New Democracy)
PASOK = Panellinio Sosialistiko Kinima (Panhellenic Socialist Movement)
LAOS = Laikos Orthodoxos Synagermos (Popular Orthodox Rally)
SYN = Synaspismos tis Aristeras kai tis Proodou (Coalition of the Left and Progress)
SYRIZA = Synaspismos Rizospastikis Aristeras (Coalition of the Radical Left)
Other abbreviations: MWC = Minimum winning coalition

Table A.10 Hungarian cabinets included in the sample

| Hungary Cabinet | Party composition | Agreement | Word count | Election date | Date in | Date out | Duration (days) | Cabinet type | Notes |
|---|---|---|---|---|---|---|---|---|---|
| Antall I | MDF, FKGP, KDNP | No | | 08.04.1990 | 23.05.1990 | 12.12.1993 | 1299 | Surplus | |
| Boross I | MDF, KDNP, FKGP | No | | 08.04.1990 | 21.12.1993 | 29.05.1994 | 159 | Surplus | |
| Horn I | MSZP, SZDSZ | Yes | 34259 | 29.05.1994 | 15.07.1994 | 24.05.1998 | 1409 | Surplus | d) |
| Orbán I | Fidesz-MPS, FKGP, MDF | Yes | 2968 | 24.05.1998 | 06.07.1998 | 21.04.2002 | 1385 | Surplus | d) |
| Medgyessy I | MSZP, SZDSZ | Yes | 1169 | 21.04.2002 | 27.05.2002 | 25.08.2004 | 821 | MWC | d) |
| Gyurcsány I | MSZP, SZDSZ | No | | 21.04.2002 | 04.10.2004 | 23.04.2006 | 566 | MWC | |
| Gyurcsány II | MSZP, SZDSZ | Yes | 1236 | 23.04.2006 | 09.06.2006 | 30.04.2008 | 691 | MWC | d) |
| Orbán II | Fidesz-MPS, KDNP | Yes | 2148 | 25.04.2010 | 29.05.2010 | 06.04.2014 | 1408 | Surplus | d) |
| Orbán III | Fidesz-MPS, KDNP | No | | 06.04.2014 | 06.06.2014 | 18.05.2018 | 1442 | Surplus | |
| Mean | | | 8356 | | | | 1020 | | |

a) There is a coalition agreement but we were not able to obtain it.
b) There is no new coalition agreement but the cabinet in office used the previous one.
c) The word counts for the coalition agreements we could not obtain originate from the Comparative Parliamentary Democracy Data Archive (Strøm et al. 2008).
d) We are grateful to Peter Hovrath (Hungarian Academy of Sciences) for providing the coalition agreements of the cabinets that were in office between 1994 and 2014.
Party abbreviations: Fidesz-MPS = Fidesz-Magyar Polgári Szövetség (Fidesz-Hungarian Civic Alliance)
FKGP = Független Kisgazda, Földmunkás és Polgári Párt (Independent Smallholders Party)
KDNP = Kereszténydemokrata Néppárt (Christian Democratic People's Party)
MDF = Magyar Demokrata Fórum (Hungarian Democratic Forum)
MSZP = Magyar Szocialista Párt (Hungarian Socialist Party)
SZDSZ = Szabad Demokraták Szövetsége (Alliance of Free Democrats)
Other abbreviations: MWC = Minimum winning coalition

Table A.11 Icelandic cabinets included in the sample

| Iceland Cabinet | Party composition | Agreement | Word count | Election date | Date in | Date out | Duration (days) | Cabinet type | Notes |
|---|---|---|---|---|---|---|---|---|---|
| Stefansson I | SDP, PP, IP | Yes | 1980 | 30.06.1946 | 04.02.1947 | 24.10.1949 | 993 | Surplus | d) |
| Steinthorsson I | PP, IP | Yes | 662 | 23.10.1949 | 14.03.1950 | 28.06.1953 | 1202 | MWC | d) |
| Thors V | IP, PP | Yes | 615 | 28.06.1953 | 11.09.1953 | 24.06.1956 | 1017 | MWC | d) |
| Jonasson III | PP, PA, SDP | Yes | 775 | 24.06.1956 | 24.07.1956 | 23.12.1958 | 882 | MWC | d) |
| Thors VI | IP, SDP | Yes | 344 | 26.10.1959 | 20.11.1959 | 09.06.1963 | 1297 | MWC | d) |
| Thors VII | IP, SDP | No | | 09.06.1963 | 09.06.1963 | 14.11.1963 | 158 | MWC | |
| Benediktsson I | IP, SDP | No | | 09.06.1963 | 14.11.1963 | 11.06.1967 | 1305 | MWC | |
| Benediktsson II | IP, SDP | Yes | 2112 | 11.06.1967 | 11.06.1967 | 10.07.1970 | 1125 | MWC | d) |
| Hafstein I | IP, SDP | No | | 11.06.1967 | 10.07.1970 | 13.06.1971 | 338 | MWC | |
| Johannesson I | PP, PA, ULL | Yes | 2257 | 13.06.1971 | 14.07.1971 | 30.06.1974 | 1082 | MWC | d) |
| Hallgrimsson I | IP, PP | Yes | 964 | 30.06.1974 | 28.08.1974 | 25.06.1978 | 1397 | MWC | d) |
| Johannesson II | PP, PA, SDP | Yes | 2102 | 25.06.1978 | 01.09.1978 | 15.10.1979 | 409 | MWC | d) |
| Thoroddsen I | IP, PA, PP | Yes | 2712 | 03.12.1979 | 08.02.1980 | 23.04.1983 | 1170 | Surplus | d) |
| Hermansson I | PP, IP | Yes | 1777 | 23.04.1983 | 26.05.1983 | 25.04.1987 | 1430 | MWC | d) |
| Palsson I | IP, SDP, PP | Yes | 5272 | 25.04.1987 | 08.07.1987 | 28.09.1988 | 448 | MWC | d) |

| | | | | | | | |
|---|---|---|---|---|---|---|---|
| Hermansson II | PP, PA, SDP | Yes | 3725 | 25.04.1987 | 28.09.1988 | 10.09.1989 | 347 | Minority |
| Hermansson III | PP, PA, SDP, CP | Yes | 2700 | 25.04.1987 | 10.09.1989 | 20.04.1991 | 587 | MWC |
| Oddsson I | IP, SDP | Yes | 804 | 20.04.1991 | 30.04.1991 | 08.04.1995 | 1439 | MWC |
| Oddsson II | IP, PP | Yes | 1747 | 08.04.1995 | 23.04.1995 | 08.05.1999 | 1476 | MWC |
| Oddsson III | IP, PP | Yes | 2048 | 08.05.1999 | 28.05.1999 | 10.05.2003 | 1443 | MWC |
| Oddsson IV | IP, PP | Yes | 2186 | 10.05.2003 | 23.05.2003 | 15.09.2004 | 481 | MWC |
| Asgrimsson I | PP, IP | No | | 10.05.2003 | 15.09.2004 | 15.06.2006 | 638 | MWC |
| Haarde I | IP, PP | No | | 10.05.2003 | 15.06.2006 | 12.05.2007 | 331 | MWC |
| Haarde II | IP, UF | Yes | 2393 | 12.05.2007 | 24.05.2007 | 26.01.2009 | 613 | MWC |
| Sigurdardottir I | UF, LM | Yes | 1099 | 12.05.2007 | 01.02.2009 | 25.04.2009 | 83 | Minority |
| Sigurdardottir II | UF, LM | Yes | 6983 | 25.04.2009 | 10.05.2009 | 27.04.2013 | 1448 | MWC |
| Gunnlaugsson I | PP, IP | Yes | 4761 | 27.04.2013 | 23.05.2013 | 07.04.2016 | 1050 | MWC |
| Mean | | | 2274 | | | | 896 | |

a) There is a coalition agreement but we were not able to obtain it.
b) There is no new coalition agreement but the cabinet in office used the previous one.
c) The word counts for the coalition agreements we could not obtain originate from the Comparative Parliamentary Democracy Data Archive (Strøm et al. 2008).
d) We are grateful to the parliament of Iceland for providing the coalition agreements of the cabinets that were in office before 1999.

Party abbreviations:
CP = Bogaraflokkur (Citizens' Party)
IP = Sjalfstaedisflokkur (Independence Party)
LM = Vinstrihreyfngin - grænt framboð (The Left-Green Movement)
PA = Althyð ubandalag (People's Alliance)
PP = Framsóknarflokkur (Progressive Party)
SDP = Althyð uflokkur (Social Democratic Party)
SP = Sameiningarflokkum althyð u - sósíalisaflokkur (United Socialist Party)
UF = Samfylkingin (United Front)
ULL = SamtÖk frjálslyndra og vinstri manna (Union of Liberals and Leftists)
Other abbreviations: MWC = Minimum winning coalition

Table A.12 Irish cabinets included in the sample

| Ireland Cabinet | Party composition | Agreement | Word count | Election date | Date in | Date out | Duration (days) | Cabinet type | Notes | Word count (cleansed)* |
|---|---|---|---|---|---|---|---|---|---|---|
| Costello I | FG, Lab, CnT, CnP | No | | 04.02.1948 | 18.02.1948 | 30.05.1951 | 1197 | Minority | | |
| Costello II | FG, Lab, CnT | No | | 18.04.1954 | 02.06.1954 | 05.03.1957 | 1007 | MWC | | |
| Cosgrave I | FG, Lab | Yes | 1206 | 28.02.1973 | 14.03.1973 | 16.06.1977 | 1555 | MWC | a), c) | |
| FitzGerald I | FG, Lab | Yes | 9751 | 11.06.1981 | 30.06.1981 | 18.02.1982 | 233 | Minority | a), c) | |
| FitzGerald II | FG, Lab | Yes | 5690 | 24.11.1982 | 14.12.1982 | 17.02.1987 | 1526 | MWC | d) | 5690 |
| Haughey IV | FF, PD | Yes | 5174 | 15.06.1989 | 12.07.1989 | 11.02.1992 | 944 | Minority | d) | 5174 |
| Reynolds I | FF, PD | Yes | 4817 | 15.06.1989 | 11.02.1992 | 25.11.1992 | 288 | Minority | a), c) | |
| Reynolds II | FF, Lab | Yes | 18852 | 25.11.1992 | 12.01.1993 | 17.11.1994 | 674 | MWC | d) | 18852 |
| Bruton I | FG, Lab, DL | Yes | 13302 | 25.11.1992 | 15.12.1994 | 06.06.1997 | 904 | MWC | d) | 13302 |
| Ahern I | FF, PD | Yes | 7319 | 06.06.1997 | 26.06.1997 | 17.05.2002 | 1786 | Minority | d) | 7319 |

| | | | | | | | | | |
|---|---|---|---|---|---|---|---|---|---|
| Ahern II | FF, PD | Yes | 14085 | 17.05.2002 | 06.06.2002 | 24.05.2007 | 1813 | MWC | d) | 14085 |
| Ahern III | FF, GR, PD | Yes | 33853 | 24.05.2007 | 14.06.2007 | 06.05.2008 | 327 | Surplus | d) | 33853 |
| Cowen I | FF, GR, PD | Yes | | 24.05.2007 | 07.05.2008 | 23.01.2011 | 991 | Surplus | a) | |
| Cowen II | FF, GR | Yes | 15804 | 24.05.2007 | 20.11.2009 | 25.02.2011 | 462 | MWC | d) | 15804 |
| Kenny I | FG, Lab | Yes | 23744 | 25.02.2011 | 09.03.2011 | 26.02.2016 | 1815 | MWC | d) | 23744 |
| Mean | | | 12800 | | | | 1035 | | | 15314 |

a) There is a coalition agreement but we were not able to obtain it.
b) There is no new coalition agreement but the cabinet in office used the previous one.
c) The word count for the coalition agreements we could not obtain originate from the Comparative Parliamentary Democracy Data Archive (Strøm et al. 2008).
d) We are grateful to Marc Debus (University of Mannheim) for providing the coalition agreements of the cabinets that were in office between 1982 and today.
* The cleansed word count refers to those agreements obtained in the analysis, duplicates excluded.
Party abbreviations:
CnP = Clann na Poblachta (Party of the Republic)
CnT = Clann na Talmhan (Party of the Land)
DL = Democratic Left
FF = Fianna Fáil (Soldiers of Destiny)
FG = Fine Gael (Family of the Irish)
GR = Green Party
Lab = The Labour Party
PD = Progressive Democrats
Other abbreviations: MWC = Minimum winning coalition

Table A.13 Latvian cabinets included in the sample

| Latvia Cabinet | Party composition | Agreement | Word count | Election date | Date in | Date out | Duration (days) | Cabinet type |
|---|---|---|---|---|---|---|---|---|
| Birkavs I | LC, LZS | Yes | 9141 | 06.06.1993 | 03.08.1993 | 13.07.1994 | 344 | Minority |
| Skele I | DPS, LC, TB, LNNK, LVP, AS | Yes | 5069 | 01.10.1995 | 21.12.1995 | 20.01.1997 | 396 | Surplus |
| Skele II | DPS, LC, TB, LNNK, AS | Yes | 3810 | 01.10.1995 | 13.02.1997 | 28.07.1997 | 165 | Surplus |
| Krasts I | TB, LNNK, LC, AS, DPS | Yes | 4322 | 01.10.1995 | 07.08.1997 | 08.04.1998 | 244 | Surplus |
| Krasts II | TB, LNNK, LC, AS | No | | 01.10.1995 | 08.04.1998 | 03.10.1998 | 178 | Minority |
| Kristopans I | LC, TB-LNNK, JP | Yes | 11217 | 03.10.1998 | 26.11.1998 | 05.02.1999 | 71 | Minority |
| Kristopans II | LC, TB-LNNK, JP, LSDSP | No | | 03.10.1998 | 05.02.1999 | 05.07.1999 | 150 | Surplus |
| Skele III | TP, LC, TB-LNNK | Yes | 5602 | 03.10.1998 | 16.07.1999 | 12.04.2000 | 271 | MWC |
| Berzins I | LC, TB-LNNK, TP, JP | Yes | 6780 | 03.10.1998 | 05.05.2000 | 05.10.2002 | 883 | Surplus |
| Repse I | JL, LPP, TB-LNNK, ZZS | Yes | 3630 | 05.10.2002 | 07.11.2002 | 05.02.2004 | 455 | MWC |
| Emsis I | ZZS, TP, LPP | Yes | 8376 | 05.10.2002 | 09.03.2004 | 28.10.2004 | 233 | Minority |
| Kalvitis I | TP, JL, LPP, ZZS | Yes | 8296 | 05.10.2002 | 02.12.2004 | 07.04.2006 | 491 | Surplus |
| Kalvitis II | TP, LPP, ZZS | No | | 05.10.2002 | 08.04.2006 | 07.10.2006 | 182 | Minority |

| | | | | | | | |
|---|---|---|---|---|---|---|---|
| Kalvitis III | TP, ZZS, LPP-LC, TB-LNNK | Yes | 12476 | 07.10.2006 | 07.11.2006 | 05.12.2007 | 393 | Surplus |
| Godmanis II | TP, ZZS, LPP-LC, TB-LNNK | Yes | 8472 | 07.10.2006 | 20.12.2006 | 20.02.2009 | 428 | Surplus |
| Dombrovskis I | JL, TP, ZZS, TB-LNNK, PS | Yes | 7149 | 07.10.2006 | 12.03.2009 | 22.03.2010 | 375 | Surplus |
| Dombrovskis II | JL, ZZS, TB-LNNK, PS | No | | 07.10.2006 | 22.03.2010 | 02.10.2010 | 194 | Minority |
| Dombrovskis III | V, ZZS | Yes | 9978 | 02.10.2010 | 03.11.2010 | 17.09.2011 | 318 | MWC |
| Dombrovskis IV | V, ZZS, TB-LNNK | Yes | 5691 | 17.09.2011 | 25.10.2011 | 22.01.2014 | 820 | Minority |
| Straujuma I | V, ZZS, TB-LNNK, LZS | Yes | 6880 | 17.09.2011 | 22.01.2014 | 04.10.2014 | 255 | MWC |
| Straujuma II | V, ZZS, TB-LNNK | Yes | 7162 | 04.10.2014 | 05.11.2014 | 07.12.2015 | 397 | MWC |
| Mean | | | 7297 | | | | 345 | |

From 1993 until 1997 as well as in 2002, cabinet parties combined programmatic preferences and procedural rules in one document. Thereafter, cabinets produced two documents: one summarized the procedural rules of cooperation while the other contained the cabinet's policy preferences. Taken together, these documents constitute a cabinet's coalition agreement (Schmidt 2010: 139-140).

Party abbreviations: AS = Apvienotais Saraksts (United List) DPS = Demokrātiskā Partija Saimnieks (Democratic Party-Saimnieks) JL = Jaunas Laiks (New Era) JP = Jaunā Partija (New Party) LC = Savienība Latvijas Ceļš (Latvian Way) LNNK = Latvijas Nacionāli Konservatīvā Partija (Latvian National Conservative Party) LPP = Latvijas Pirmaā Partija (Latvia's First Party) LPP-LC = Latvijas Pirmaā Partija-Savieniba Latvijas Celš (Latvia's First Party-Latvian Way) LSDSP = Latvijas Sociāldemokrātiskā Strādnieku Partija (Latvian Social Democratic Workers' Party) LVP = Latvijas Vienības Partija (Latvian Unity Party) LZS = Latvijas Zemnieku Savienība (Latvian Farmers' Union) PS = Pilsoniskā savienāba (Civic Union) TP = Tautas Partija (People's Party) TB-LNNK = Apvienība Tēvzemei un Brīvības;bai (For Fatherland and Freedom-LNNK) ZZS = Zaļo un Zemnieku Savienība (Green and Farmers' Union) V = Vienotiba (Unity) The Unity (V) was founded in 2010 as an electoral alliance of the New Era (JL), Civic Union (PS) and the Society for Political Change (SCP) and was transformed into a single political party in 2011. Other abbreviations: MWC = Minimum winning coalition

Table A.14 Lithuanian cabinets included in the sample

| Lithuania Cabinet | Party composition | Agreement | Word count | Election date | Date in | Date out | Duration (days) | Cabinet type | Notes |
|---|---|---|---|---|---|---|---|---|---|
| Vagnorius II | TS-LK, LKDP, LCS | Yes | 1026 | 10.11.1996 | 04.12.1996 | 03.05.1999 | 880 | Surplus | |
| Paksas I | TS-LK, LKDP | No | | 10.11.1996 | 01.06.1999 | 27.10.1999 | 148 | MWC | |
| Kubilius I | TS-LK, LKDP | No | | 10.11.1996 | 03.11.1999 | 08.10.2000 | 340 | MWC | |
| Paksas II | LLS, NS-SL | No | | 08.10.2000 | 27.10.2000 | 20.06.2001 | 236 | Minority | |
| Brazauskas I | LSDP, NS-SL | No | | 08.10.2000 | 04.07.2001 | 24.10.2004 | 1208 | MWC | |
| Brazauskas II | LSDP, DP, NS-SL, VNDPS | Yes | 808 | 24.10.2004 | 29.11.2004 | 12.04.2006 | 499 | MWC | |
| Brazauskas III | LSDP, DP, VNDPS | Yes | 421 | 24.10.2004 | 12.04.2006 | 01.06.2006 | 50 | Minority | |
| Kirkilas I | LSDP, PDP, LbCS, VNDPS | No | | 24.10.2004 | 06.07.2006 | 26.10.2008 | 843 | Minority | |
| Kubilius II | TS-LK, LbCS, TPP, LRLS | Yes | 4464 | 26.10.2008 | 28.11.2008 | 28.10.2012 | 1430 | Surplus | d) |
| Butkevicius I | LSDP, DP, PK-UTT, LLRA | Yes | 332 | 28.10.2012 | 13.12.2012 | 09.10.2016 | 1396 | Surplus | |
| Mean | | | 1410 | | | | 703 | | |

a) There is a coalition agreement but we were not able to obtain it.
b) There is no new coalition agreement but the cabinet in office used the previous one.
c) The word counts for the coalition agreements we could not obtain originate from the Comparative Parliamentary Democracy Data Archive (Strøm et al. 2008).
d) We are grateful to the Parliament of Lithuania for providing the coalition agreement of the Kubilius II cabinet.

Party abbreviations:
DP = Darbo Partija (Labour Party)
LbCS = Liberalųir Centro Sąjunga (Liberal and Centre Union)
LCS = Lietuvos Centro Sąjunga (Lithuanian Centre Union)
LKDP = Lietuvos Krikščionių Demokratų Partija (Lithuanian Christian Democratic Party)
LLRA = Lietuvos Lenkų Rinkimų Akcija (Election Action for Lithuania's Poles)
LLS = Lietuvos Liberalų Sąjunga (Lithuanian Liberal Union)
LRLS = Lietuvos Respublikos Liberalų Sąjunga (Liberal Movement of the Republic of Lithuania)
LSDP = Lietuvos Socialdemokratų Partija (Lithuanian Social Democratic Party)
PDP = Pilietinės Demokratijos Partija (Party of Civic Democracy)
PK-UTT = Rolando Pakso Koalicija Už Tvarka ir Teisingumas (Coalition of Rolandas Paksas For Order and Justice)
NS-SL = Naujoji Sąjunga–Socialliberalai (New Union–Social Liberals)
TPP = Tautos Prisikelimo Partija (Nation's Resurrection Party)
TS-LK = Tevynes Santara-Lietuvos Konservatoriai (Homeland Union)
VNDPS = Valstiečių ir Naujosios Demokratijos Partijų Sąjungos (Union of Peasants' and New Democratic Parties)
Other abbreviations: MWC = Minimum winning coalition

Table A.15 Luxembourgian cabinets included in the sample

| Luxembourg Cabinet | Party composition | Agreement | Word count | Election date | Date in | Date out | Duration (days) | Cabinet type | Notes |
|---|---|---|---|---|---|---|---|---|---|
| Dupong I | CSV, LSAP, DP, KPL | Yes | | 21.10.1945 | 14.11.1945 | 01.03.1947 | 472 | Surplus | a) |
| Dupong II | CSV, DP | Yes | | 21.10.1945 | 01.03.1947 | 06.06.1948 | 463 | MWC | a) |
| Dupong III | CSV, DP | Yes | | 06.06.1948 | 14.07.1948 | 03.06.1951 | 1054 | MWC | a) |
| Dupong IV | CSV, LSAP | Yes | | 03.06.1951 | 03.07.1951 | 23.12.1953 | 904 | MWC | a) |
| Bech I | CSV, LSAP | Yes | | 03.06.1951 | 29.12.1953 | 30.05.1954 | 152 | MWC | a) |
| Bech II | CSV, LSAP | Yes | | 30.05.1954 | 29.06.1954 | 29.03.1958 | 1369 | MWC | a) |
| Frieden I | CSV, LSAP | Yes | | 30.05.1954 | 29.03.1958 | 01.02.1959 | 309 | MWC | a) |
| Werner I | CSV, DP | Yes | | 01.02.1959 | 02.03.1959 | 07.06.1964 | 1924 | MWC | a) |
| Werner II | CSV, LSAP | Yes | | 07.06.1964 | 15.07.1964 | 29.10.1968 | 1567 | MWC | a) |
| Werner III | CSV, DP | Yes | | 15.12.1968 | 06.02.1969 | 26.05.1974 | 1935 | MWC | a) |
| Thorn I | DP, LSAP | Yes | | 26.05.1974 | 15.06.1974 | 10.06.1979 | 1821 | MWC | a) |
| Werner IV | CSV, DP | Yes | | 10.06.1979 | 16.07.1979 | 17.06.1984 | 1798 | MWC | a) |
| Santer I | CSV, LSAP | Yes | | 17.06.1984 | 20.07.1984 | 18.06.1989 | 1794 | MWC | a) |
| Santer II | CSV, LSAP | Yes | | 18.06.1989 | 14.07.1989 | 12.06.1994 | 1794 | MWC | a) |
| Santer III | CSV, LSAP | Yes | | 12.06.1994 | 13.07.1994 | 20.01.1995 | 191 | MWC | a) |
| Juncker I | CSV, LSAP | Yes | | 12.06.1994 | 26.01.1995 | 13.06.1999 | 1599 | MWC | a) |
| Juncker II | CSV, DP | Yes | 31818 | 13.06.1999 | 07.08.1999 | 13.06.2004 | 1772 | MWC | |
| Juncker III | CSV, LSAP | Yes | 37597 | 13.06.2004 | 31.07.2004 | 07.06.2009 | 1772 | MWC | |
| Juncker IV | CSV, LSAP | Yes | 64286 | 07.06.2009 | 23.07.2009 | 20.10.2013 | 1550 | MWC | |
| Bettel I | DP, LSAP, Dei Greng | Yes | 67066 | 20.10.2013 | 04.12.2013 | 15.10.2018 | 1776 | MWC | |
| Mean | | | 50192 | | | | 1301 | | |

a) There is a coalition agreement but we were not able to obtain it.
In Luxembourg, coalition agreements were not published before 1999 (Dumont et al. 2015: 27).
Party abbreviations:
CSV = Chrëschtlech-Sozial Vollekspartei (Christian Social People's Party)
Déi Gréng = Déi Gréng (The Greens)
DP = Demokratesch Partei (Democratic Party)
KPL = Kommunistesch Partei Lëtzeburg (Communist Party)
LSAP = Lëtzebuerger Sozialistesch Aarbechterpartei (Luxembourg's Socialist Workers' Party)
Other abbreviations: MWC = Minimum winning coalition

Table A.16 Dutch cabinets included in the sample

| Netherlands Cabinet | Party composition | Agreement | Word count | Election date | Date in | Date out | Duration (days) | Cabinet type | Notes |
|---|---|---|---|---|---|---|---|---|---|
| Beel I | KVP, PvdA | No | | 17.05.1946 | 03.07.1946 | 07.07.1948 | 735 | MWC | |
| Drees I | PvdA, KVP, CHU, VVD | No | | 07.07.1948 | 07.08.1948 | 24.01.1951 | 900 | Surplus | |
| Drees II | PvdA, KVP, CHU, VVD | No | | 07.07.1948 | 15.03.1951 | 25.06.1952 | 468 | Surplus | |
| Drees III | PvdA, KVP, CHU, ARP | No | | 25.06.1952 | 02.09.1952 | 13.06.1956 | 1380 | Surplus | |
| Drees IV | PvdA, KVP, CHU, ARP | No | | 13.06.1956 | 13.10.1956 | 12.12.1958 | 790 | Surplus | |
| Beel II | KVP, CHU, ARP | No | | 13.06.1956 | 22.12.1958 | 12.03.1959 | 80 | MWC | |
| De Quay I | KVP, CHU, ARP, VVD | No | | 12.03.1959 | 19.05.1959 | 15.05.1963 | 1457 | Surplus | |
| Marijnen I | KVP, CHU, ARP, VVD | Yes | 3323 | 15.05.1963 | 24.07.1963 | 27.02.1965 | 584 | Surplus | d) |
| Cals I | KVP, PvdA, ARP | Yes | 1488 | 15.05.1963 | 14.04.1965 | 15.10.1966 | 549 | Surplus | d) |
| Zijlstra I | ARP, KVP | No | | 15.05.1963 | 22.11.1966 | 15.02.1967 | 85 | Minority | |
| De Jong I | KVP, ARP, CHU, VVD | Yes | 3298 | 15.02.1967 | 05.04.1967 | 28.04.1971 | 1484 | MWC | d) |
| Biesheuvel I | ARP, KVP, CHU, VVD, DS70 | Yes | 4594 | 28.04.1971 | 06.07.1971 | 20.07.1972 | 380 | MWC | d) |
| Biesheuvel II | ARP, KVP, CHU, VVD | No | | 28.03.1971 | 09.08.1972 | 28.11.1972 | 111 | Minority | |
| Den Uyl I | PvdA, PPR, D66, KVP, ARP | No | | 29.11.1972 | 11.05.1973 | 22.03.1977 | 1411 | Surplus | |
| Van Agt I | CDA, VVD | Yes | 8784 | 25.05.1977 | 19.12.1977 | 26.05.1981 | 1254 | MWC | e) |
| Van Agt II | CDA, PvdA, D66 | Yes | 13680 | 26.05.1981 | 11.09.1981 | 12.05.1982 | 243 | Surplus | e) |
| Van Agt III | CDA, D66 | No | | 26.05.1981 | 29.05.1982 | 08.09.1982 | 102 | Minority | |

| Cabinet | Parties | Agreement | Words | Start | End | Duration | Type | Note |
|---|---|---|---|---|---|---|---|---|
| Lubbers I | CDA, VVD | Yes | 7007 | 08.09.1982 | 04.11.1982 | 21.05.1986 | 1294 | MWC | e) |
| Lubbers II | CDA, VVD | Yes | 19986 | 21.05.1986 | 14.07.1986 | 02.05.1989 | 1023 | MWC | e) |
| Lubbers III | CDA, PvdA | Yes | 30337 | 06.09.1989 | 07.11.1989 | 03.05.1994 | 1638 | MWC | e) |
| Kok I | PvdA, D66, VVD | Yes | 15754 | 03.05.1994 | 22.08.1994 | 05.05.1998 | 1352 | MWC | e) |
| Kok II | PvdA, D66, VVD | Yes | 37739 | 06.05.1998 | 03.08.1998 | 15.05.2002 | 1381 | Surplus | e) |
| Balkenende I | CDA, LPF, VVD | Yes | 16877 | 15.05.2002 | 22.07.2002 | 16.10.2002 | 86 | MWC | e) |
| Balkenende II | CDA, VVD, D66 | Yes | 8999 | 22.01.2003 | 27.05.2003 | 29.06.2006 | 1129 | MWC | e) |
| Balkenende III | CDA, VVD | No | | 22.01.2003 | 07.07.2006 | 22.11.2006 | 138 | Minority | |
| Balkenende IV | CDA, PvdA, CU | Yes | 16836 | 22.11.2006 | 22.02.2007 | 23.02.2010 | 1097 | MWC | |
| Balkenende V | CDA, CU | No | | 22.11.2006 | 23.02.2010 | 09.06.2010 | 106 | Minority | |
| Rutte I | VVD, CDA | Yes | 24529 | 09.06.2010 | 14.10.2010 | 12.09.2012 | 699 | Minority | |
| Rutte II | VVD, PvdA | Yes | 24900 | 12.09.2012 | 05.11.2012 | 26.10.2017 | 1816 | Minority | |
| Mean | | | 14883 | | | | 820 | | |

a) There is a coalition agreement but we were not able to obtain it. b) There is no new coalition agreement but the cabinet in office used the previous one.
c) The word counts for the coalition agreements we could not obtain originate from the Comparative Parliamentary Democracy Data Archive (Strøm et al. 2008).
d) The coalition agreements of the cabinets that were in office before 1977 are available online at the Keesings Historisch Archief homepage.
e) We are grateful to Marc Debus (University of Mannheim) for providing the coalition agreements of the cabinets that were in office between 1977 and 2003.
Party abbreviations: ARP = Anti Revolutionaire Partij (Anti-Revolutionary Party) CDA = Christen-Democratisch Appel (Christian Democratic Appeal) CHU = Christelijk Historische Unie (Christian Historical Union)
CU = Christen Unie (Christian Union) D66 = Democraten 66 (Democrats 66) DS70 = Democratische Socialisten 70 (Democratic Socialists 70)
KVP = Katholieke Volks Partij (Catholic People's Party) LPF = Lijst Pim Fortuyn (List Pim Fortuyn) PvdA = Partij van de Arbeid (Labour Party)
VVD = Volkspartij voor Vrijheid en Democratie (People's Party for Freedom and Democracy)
Other abbreviations: MWC = Minimum winning coalition

Table A.17 Norwegian cabinets included in the sample

| Norway Cabinet | Party composition | Agreement | Word count | Election date | Date in | Date out | Duration (days) | Cabinet type | Notes | Word count (cleansed*) |
|---|---|---|---|---|---|---|---|---|---|---|
| Lyng I | H, SP, V, KRF | Yes | 2941 | 11.09.1961 | 28.08.1963 | 21.09.1963 | 24 | Minority | a), c) | |
| Borten I | SP, H, V, KRF | No | | 12.09.1965 | 12.10.1965 | 08.09.1969 | 1427 | MWC | | |
| Borten II | SP, H, V, KRF | No | | 07.09.1969 | 08.09.1969 | 02.03.1971 | 540 | MWC | | |
| Korvald I | KRF, SP, V | Yes | 2919 | 07.09.1969 | 18.10.1972 | 10.09.1973 | 327 | Minority | a), c) | |
| Willoch II | H, KRF, SP | No | | 14.09.1981 | 08.06.1983 | 09.09.1985 | 824 | MWC | | |
| Willoch III | H, KRF, SP | No | | 08.09.1985 | 09.09.1985 | 02.05.1986 | 235 | Minority | | |
| Syse I | H, KRF, SP | Yes | 6512 | 11.09.1989 | 16.10.1989 | 29.10.1990 | 378 | Minority | d) | 6512 |
| Bondevik I | KRF, SP, V | Yes | 20240 | 16.09.1997 | 17.10.1997 | 09.03.2000 | 874 | Minority | a), c) | |
| Bondevik II | KRF, H, V | Yes | 1323 | 10.09.2001 | 19.10.2001 | 12.09.2005 | 1424 | Minority | a), c) | |
| Stoltenberg II | A, SF, SP | Yes | 28901 | 12.09.2005 | 17.10.2005 | 14.09.2009 | 1428 | MWC | | 28901 |
| Stoltenberg III | A, SF, SP | Yes | 22332 | 14.09.2009 | 14.09.2009 | 09.09.2013 | 1456 | MWC | | 22332 |
| Solberg I | H, FRP | Yes | 24021 | 09.09.2013 | 16.10.2013 | 17.01.2018 | 1554 | Minority | | 24021 |
| Mean | | | 13649 | | | | 874 | | | 20442 |

a) There is a coalition agreement but we were not able to obtain it.
b) There is no new coalition agreement but the cabinet in office used the previous one.
c) The word counts for the coalition agreements we could not obtain originate from the Comparative Parliamentary Democracy Data Archive (Strøm et al. 2008).
d) We are grateful to Arild Nygaard for providing the coalition agreement for the Syse I cabinet.
* The cleansed word count refers to those agreements obtained in the analysis, duplicates excluded.

Party abbreviations:
A = Arbeiderpartiet (Labour Party)
FRP = Fremskrittspartiet (Progress Party)
H = Høyre (Conservative Party)
KRF = Kristelig Folkeparti (Christian People's Party)
SF = Socialistisk Folkeparti (Socialist People's Party)
SP = Senterpartiet (Centre Party)
V = Venstre (Liberal Party)
Other abbreviations: MWC = Minimum winning coalition

**Table A.18** Polish cabinets included in the sample

| Poland Cabinet | Party composition | Agreement | Word count | Election date | Date in | Date out | Duration (days) | Cabinet type | Notes |
|---|---|---|---|---|---|---|---|---|---|
| Olszewski I | PC, ZChN, PL | No | | 27.10.1991 | 23.12.1991 | 05.06.1992 | 165 | Minority | |
| Suchocka I | UD, ZChN, KLD, PL, PChD, PPPP | No | | 27.10.1991 | 11.07.1992 | 28.04.1993 | 291 | Minority | |
| Suchocka II | UD, ZChN, KLD, PChD, PPPP | No | | 27.10.1991 | 28.04.1993 | 28.05.1993 | 30 | Minority | |
| Pawlak I | SLD, PSL | Yes | 745 | 19.09.1993 | 26.10.1993 | 07.02.1995 | 469 | MWC | d) |
| Oleksy I | SLD, PSL | Yes | 3806 | 19.09.1993 | 07.03.1995 | 26.01.1996 | 325 | MWC | d) |
| Cimoszewicz I | SLD, PSL | Yes | 1130 | 19.09.1993 | 07.02.1996 | 21.09.1997 | 592 | MWC | d) |
| Buzek I | AWS, UW | Yes | 12800 | 21.09.1997 | 31.10.1997 | 06.06.2000 | 949 | MWC | d) |
| Miller I | SLD, UP, PSL | No | | 23.09.2001 | 19.10.2001 | 03.03.2003 | 500 | Surplus | |
| Miller II | SLD, UP | No | | 23.09.2001 | 03.03.2003 | 02.05.2004 | 426 | Minority | |
| Belka I | SLD, UP | No | | 23.09.2001 | 02.05.2004 | 25.09.2005 | 511 | Minority | |
| Marcinkiewicz II | PiS, SRP, LPR | Yes | 17635 | 25.09.2005 | 05.05.2006 | 10.07.2006 | 66 | MWC | |
| Kaczynski I | PiS, SRP, LPR | Yes | 6964 | 25.09.2005 | 14.07.2006 | 13.08.2007 | 395 | MWC | |
| Tusk I | PO, PSL | Yes | 1011 | 21.10.2007 | 16.11.2007 | 09.10.2011 | 1423 | MWC | |

*Continued*

Table A.18 *Continued*

| Poland Cabinet | Party composition | Agreement | Word count | Election date | Date in | Date out | Duration (days) | Cabinet type | Notes |
|---|---|---|---|---|---|---|---|---|---|
| Tusk II | PO, PSL | No | | 09.10.2011 | 09.10.2011 | 22.09.2014 | 1079 | MWC | |
| Kopacz I | PO, PSL | No | | 09.10.2011 | 22.09.2014 | 25.10.2015 | 398 | MWC | |
| Mean | | | 6299 | | | | 508 | | |

There is a coalition agreement but we were not able to obtain it.
b) There is no new coalition agreement but the cabinet in office used the previous one.
c) The word counts for the coalition agreements we could not obtain originate from the Comparative Parliamentary Democracy Data Archive (Strøm et al. 2008).
d) The coalition agreements of the cabinets that were in office between 1993 and 2000 are taken from Rządzenie koalicyjne w Polsce (Rydlewski 2000).
We are grateful to Radosław Zubek (University of Oxford) and Kamil Marcinkiewicz (University of Hamburg) for helping with the identification of the coalition agreements.

Party abbreviations:
AWS = Akcja Wyborcza Solidarność (Solidarity Electoral Action)
KLD = Kongres Liberalno-Demoktyczny (Liberal Democratic Congress)
LPR = Liga Polskich Rodzin (League of Polish Families)
PC = Porozumienie Centrum (Centre Alliance)
PChD = Partia Chrześcijańskich Demokratów (Christian Democratic Party)
PiS = Prawo i Sprawiedliwość (Law and Justice)
PL = Porozumienie Ludowe (Peasant Alliance)
PO = Platforma Obywatelska (Citizens' Platform)
PPPP = Polska Partia Przyjaciół Piwa (Polish Beer-Lovers' Party)
PSL = Polskie Stronnistwo Ludowe (Polish People's Party)
SLD = Sojusz Lewicy Demokratycznej (Democratic Left Alliance)
SRP = Samoobrona Rzeczpospolitej Polskiej (Self-Defence of the Republic of Poland)
UD = Unia Demokratyczna (Democratic Union)
UP = Unia Pracy (Union of Labour)
UW = Freedom Union
ZChN = Zjednoczenie Chrześcijańsko-Narodowe (Christian National Union)
Other abbreviations: MWC = Minimum winning coalition

Table A.19 Portuguese cabinets included in the sample

| Portugal Cabinet | Party composition | Agreement | Word count | Election date | Date in | Date out | Duration (days) | Cabinet type | Notes |
|---|---|---|---|---|---|---|---|---|---|
| Soares II | PS, CDS | Yes | 3861 | 25.04.1976 | 23.01.1978 | 28.07.1978 | 186 | MWC | d) |
| Sá Carneiro I | PSD, CDS, PPM | No | | 02.12.1979 | 03.01.1980 | 05.10.1980 | 276 | MWC | e) |
| Sá Carneiro II | PSD, CDS, PPM | No | | 05.10.1980 | 05.10.1980 | 09.01.1981 | 96 | Surplus | e) |
| Balsemao I | PSD, CDS, PPM | No | | 05.10.1980 | 09.01.1981 | 14.08.1981 | 217 | Surplus | e) |
| Balsemao II | PSD, CDS, PPM | No | | 05.10.1980 | 04.09.1981 | 23.12.1982 | 475 | Surplus | e) |
| Soares III | PS, PSD | Yes | 3135 | 25.04.1983 | 09.06.1983 | 12.07.1985 | 764 | MWC | d) |
| Duaro Barroso I | PSD, CDS/PP | Yes | 1446 | 17.03.2002 | 06.04.2002 | 17.07.2004 | 833 | MWC | d) |
| Santana Lopes I | PSD, CDS/PP | No | | 17.03.2002 | 17.07.2004 | 20.02.2005 | 218 | MWC | |
| Passos Coelho I | PSD, CDS/PP | Yes | 2224 | 05.06.2011 | 21.06.2011 | 04.10.2015 | 1566 | MWC | d) |
| Passos Coelho II | PSD, CDS/PP | Yes | 1703 | 04.10.2015 | 30.10.2015 | 26.11.2015 | 27 | Minority | d) |
| Mean | | | 2474 | | | | 466 | | |

There is a coalition agreement but we were not able to obtain it.
b) There is no new coalition agreement but the cabinet in office used the previous one.
c) The word counts for the coalition agreements we could not obtain originate from the Comparative Parliamentary Democracy Data Archive (Strøm et al. 2008).
d) We are grateful to José Magone (Berlin School of Economics and Law) for providing the coalition agreements of the cabinets that were in office between 1976 and today.
e) In the 1979 and 1980 elections, the Social Democratic Party (PSD), the Party of the Democratic Social Centre (CDS), and the Popular Monarchist Party (PPM) joined forces and participated as the Democratic Alliance (Aliança Democrática).

Party abbreviations:
CDS = Partido do Centro Democrático Social (Party of the Democratic Social Centre)
CDS/PP = Partido do Centro Democrático Social/Partido Popular (Democratic and Social Centre/People's Party)
PPM = Partido Popular Monárquico (Popular Monarchist Party)
PS = Partido Socialista (Socialist Party)
PSD = Partido Socialdemocrata (Social Democratic Party)
Other abbreviations: MWC = Minimum winning coalition

Table A.20  Romanian cabinets included in the sample

| Romania Cabinet | Party composition | Agreement | Word count | Election date | Date in | Date out | Duration (days) | Cabinet type | Notes |
|---|---|---|---|---|---|---|---|---|---|
| Stolojan I | FSN, PNL, MER, PDAR | No | | 20.05.1990 | 16.10.1991 | 27.09.1992 | 347 | Surplus | |
| Vacaroiu II | PDSR, PUNR | No | | 27.09.1992 | 18.08.1994 | 03.09.1996 | 747 | Minority | |
| Ciorbea I | CDR, PD, UDMR, PSDR | No | | 03.11.1996 | 12.12.1996 | 11.02.1998 | 426 | Surplus | |
| Ciorbea II | CDR, UDMR, PSDR | No | | 03.11.1996 | 11.02.1998 | 30.03.1998 | 47 | Minority | |
| Vasile I | CDR, PD, UDMR, PSDR | No | | 03.11.1996 | 17.04.1998 | 13.12.1999 | 605 | Surplus | |
| Isarescu I | CDR, PD, UDMR, PSDR | No | | 03.11.1996 | 22.12.1999 | 26.11.2000 | 340 | Surplus | |
| Nastase I | PDSR, PSDR, PUR | No | | 26.11.2000 | 28.12.2000 | 19.06.2003 | 903 | Minority | |
| Popescu–Tariceanu I | PNL, PD, UDMR, PUR | No | | 28.11.2004 | 29.12.2004 | 04.12.2006 | 705 | Minority | |
| Popescu–Tariceanu II | PNL, PD, UDMR | No | | 28.11.2004 | 04.12.2006 | 04.04.2007 | 121 | Minority | |
| Popescu–Tariceanu III | PNL, UDMR | No | | 28.11.2004 | 04.04.2007 | 30.11.2008 | 606 | Minority | |
| Boc I | PDL, PDSR | Yes | 1083 | 30.11.2008 | 22.12.2008 | 01.10.2009 | 283 | MWC | d) |
| Boc III | PDL, UDMR | Yes | 552 | 30.11.2008 | 23.12.2009 | 06.02.2012 | 775 | Minority | d) |

| | | | | | | |
|---|---|---|---|---|---|---|
| Ungureanu I | PDL, UDMR, UNPR | No | | 30.11.2008 | 07.05.2012 | 88 | Minority |
| Ponta I | PDSR, PNL, PUR | No | | 30.11.2008 | 09.12.2012 | 216 | Minority |
| Ponta II | PDSR, PNL, PUR | No | | 09.12.2012 | 05.03.2014 | 441 | Surplus |
| Ponta III | PDSR, UDMR, PUR, UNPR | Yes | 806 | 09.12.2012 | 17.12.2014 | 287 | Minority |
| Ponta IV | PDSR, LRP, PUR, UNPR | No | | 09.12.2012 | 04.11.2015 | 322 | Minority d) |
| Mean | | | 814 | | | 427 | |

a) There is a coalition agreement but we were not able to obtain it.
b) There is no new coalition agreement but the cabinet in office used the previous one.
c) The word counts for the coalition agreements we could not obtain originate from the Comparative Parliamentary Democracy Data Archive (Strøm et al. 2008).
d) We are grateful to Cecilia Kurkó (Office of the President, UDMR) for providing the coalition agreements.

Party abbreviations:
CDR = Convenția Democrată din România (Democratic Convention of Romania)
FSN = Frontul Salvării Naționale (National Salvation Front)
LRP = Partidul Liberal Reformator (Liberal Reformist Party)
MER = Mișcarea Ecologistă din România (Ecological Movement of Romania)
PDAR = Partidul Democrat Agrar din România (Agrarian Democratic Party of Romania)
PD = Partidul Democrat (Democratic Party)
PDL = Partidul Democrat Liberal (Democratic Liberal Party)
PDSR = Partidul Democrației Sociale din România (Social Democratic Party of Romania)
PNL = Partidul Național Liberal (National Liberal Party)
PSDR = Partidul Social Democrat Român (Romanian Social Democratic Party)
PUNR = Partidul Unității Naționale Române (Romanian National Unity Party)
PUR = Partidul Umanist din România (Humanist Party of Romania)
UDMR = Uniunea Democratică Maghiară din România (Hungarian Democratic Union)
UNPR = Uniunea Națională pentru Progresul României (National Union for the Progress of Romania)
Other abbreviations: MWC = Minimum winning coalition

Table A.21 Slovakian cabinets included in the sample

| Slovakia Cabinet | Party composition | Agreement | Word count | Election date | Date in | Date out | Duration (days) | Cabinet type | Notes |
|---|---|---|---|---|---|---|---|---|---|
| Meciar I | LS-HZDS, SNS | No | | 06.06.1992 | 24.06.1992 | 19.03.1993 | 268 | MWC | |
| Meciar III | LS-HZDS, SNS | No | | 06.06.1992 | 17.11.1993 | 14.03.1994 | 117 | MWC | |
| Moravcik I | SDL, KDH, DUS | No | | 06.06.1992 | 16.03.1994 | 01.10.1994 | 199 | Minority | |
| Meciar IV | LS-HZDS, SNS, ZRS | No | | 30.09.1994 | 13.12.1994 | 26.09.1998 | 1383 | MWC | |
| Dzurinda I | SDK, SDL, SMK, SOP | Yes | 17422 | 26.09.1998 | 30.10.1998 | 21.09.2002 | 1422 | Surplus | |
| Dzurinda II | SDKU, SMK, KDH, ANO | Yes | 15487 | 21.09.2002 | 16.10.2002 | 08.02.2006 | 1211 | MWC | d) |

| | | | | | | | | |
|---|---|---|---|---|---|---|---|---|
| Dzurinda III | SDKU, SMK, ANO | No | | 20.09.2002 | 08.02.2006 | 17.06.2006 | 129 | Minority |
| Fico I | S, SNS, LS-HZDS | Yes | 21996 | 17.06.2006 | 04.07.2006 | 12.06.2010 | 1439 | MWC d) |
| Radicova I | SDKU, SaS, KDH, MH | Yes | 23298 | 12.06.2010 | 09.07.2010 | 11.10.2011 | 459 | MWC d) |
| Radicova II | SDKU, SaS, KDH, MH | No | | 12.06.2010 | 20.10.2011 | 04.04.2012 | 167 | Minority |
| Mean | | | 19551 | | | | 679 | |

a) There is a coalition agreement but we were not able to obtain it.
b) There is no new coalition agreement but the cabinet in office used the previous one.
c) The word counts for the coalition agreements we could not obtain originate from the Comparative Parliamentary Democracy Data Archive (Strom et al. 2008).
d) We are grateful to Tereza Cechova (German Embassy in Bratislava) for providing the coalition agreements of the cabinets Dzurinda II, Fico I, and Radicova I.
Apart from some introductory comments, the coalition agreements of Slovak cabinets do not contain policy preferences but procedural rules of cooperation.
However, in all coalition agreements, save for Fico I, there is a paragraph that states that the policies of the government are agreed upon in the respective government program.
Therefore, we also coded the government programs for the cabinets that drafted a coalition agreement we could obtain.
Party abbreviations:
ANO = Aliancia Nového Občana (Alliance of the New Citizen)
DUS = Demokratická Únia Slovenska (Democratic Union of Slovakia)
KDH = Krestanskodemokratické Hnutie (Christian Democratic Movement)
LS-HZDS = Ľudová Strana-Hnutie za Demokratické Slovensko (People's Party-Movement for a Democratic Slovakia)
MH = MOST-HÍD (Bridge)
S = Smer–Sociálna Demokracia (Direction)
SaS = Sloboda a Solidarita (Freedom and Solidarity)
SDK = Slovenská Demokratická Koalícia (Slovak Democratic Coalition)
SDKU = Slovenská Demokratická a Krestanská Únia (Slovak Democratic and Christian Union)
SDL = Strana Demokratickej Ľavice (Democratic Left)
SMK = Strana Madarskej Koalície (Hungarian Coalition Party)
SNS = Slovenská Národná Strana (Slovak National Party)
SOP = Strana Občianskeho Porozumenia (Party of Civic Understanding)
ZRS = Združenie Robotníkov Slovenska (Association of Workers in Slovakia)
Other abbreviations: MWC = Minimum winning coalition

Table A.22 Slovenian cabinets included in the sample

| Slovenia Cabinet | Party composition | Agreement | Word count count | Election date | Date in | Date out (days) | Duration type | Cabinet | Notes |
|---|---|---|---|---|---|---|---|---|---|
| Peterle I | SKD, SDS, SLSt, DSS, LS, ZS | No | | 08.04.1990 | 16.05.1990 | 22.04.1992 | 707 | Surplus | |
| Drnovsek I | LDS, SDS, ZS, DSS, SSS | Yes | 3803 | 08.04.1990 | 14.05.1992 | 06.12.1992 | 206 | Minority | d) |
| Drnovsek II | LDS, SKD, SD, SDS | No | | 06.12.1992 | 25.01.1993 | 29.03.1994 | 428 | Surplus | |
| Drnovsek III | LDS, SKD, SD | No | | 06.12.1992 | 29.03.1994 | 31.01.1996 | 673 | Surplus | |
| Drnovsek IV | LDS, SKD | Yes | 6369 | 06.12.1992 | 31.01.1996 | 10.11.1996 | 284 | Minority | d) |
| Drnovsek V | LDS, SLSt, DeSUS | No | | 10.11.1996 | 27.02.1997 | 08.04.2000 | 1136 | MWC | |
| Bajuk I | SLSt, SKD, SDS | No | | 10.11.1996 | 07.06.2000 | 15.10.2000 | 130 | Minority | |
| Drnovsek VI | LDS, SD, SLSt, DeSUS | Yes | 36791 | 15.10.2000 | 30.11.2000 | 02.12.2002 | 732 | MWC | d) |
| Rop I | LDS, SD, SLSt, DeSUS | No | | 15.10.2000 | 19.12.2002 | 20.04.2004 | 488 | Surplus | |

| | | | | | | | |
|---|---|---|---|---|---|---|---|
| Rop II | LDS, SD, DeSUS | No | | 15.10.2000 | 20.04.2004 | 03.10.2004 | 166 | MWC | |
| Jansa I | SDS, Nsi-KLS, SLSt, DeSUS | Yes | 27952 | 03.10.2004 | 03.12.2004 | 21.09.2008 | 1388 | MWC | d) |
| Pahor I | SD, Z, LDS, DeSUS | Yes | 36393 | 21.09.2008 | 21.11.2008 | 20.09.2011 | 1033 | MWC | d) |
| Pahor II | SD, LDS | No | | 21.09.2008 | 27.09.2011 | 10.02.2012 | 228 | Minority | |
| Jansa II | SDS, DL, SLSt, DeSUS, Nsi-KLS | Yes | 26340 | 04.12.2011 | 10.02.2012 | 12.03.2013 | 396 | MWC | d) |
| Bratusek I | PS, SD, DL, DeSUS | Yes | 8888 | 04.12.2011 | 20.03.2013 | 13.07.2014 | 480 | MWC | d) |
| Cerar I | SMC, DeSUS, SD | Yes | 27448 | 13.07.2014 | 25.08.2014 | 14.03.2018 | 1297 | MWC | d) |
| Mean | | | 21748 | | | | 611 | | |

We are grateful to Alenka Krašovec (University of Ljubljana) for identifying and providing the coalition agreements obtained in the analysis.
Party abbreviations:
DeSUS = Demokratska Stranka Upokojencev Slovenije (Democratic Party of Pensioners of Slovenia)
DL = Državljanska lista (Civic List)
DSS = Demokraticna Stranka Slovenije (Democratic Party of Slovenia)
LDS = Liberalna Demokracija Slovenije (Liberal Democratic Party)
LS = Liberalna Stranka (Liberal Party)
Nsi-KLS = Nova Slovenija-Krščanska Ljudska Stranka (New Slovenia-Christian People's Party)
PS = Pozitivna Slovenija (Positive Slovenia)
SD = Socialnih Demokrati (Social Democrats)
SDS = Slovenska Demokratska Stranka (Slovenian Democratic Party)
SLSt = Slovenska Ljudska Strana (Slovenian People's Party)
SKD = Slovenski Krscanski Demokrati (Slovenian Christian Democrats)
SMC = Stranka Mira Cerarja (Party of Miro Cerar)
SSS = Socialisticna Stranka Slovenije (Socialist Party)
Z = Zares (For Real)
ZS = Zeleni Slovenije (Greens of Slovenia)
Other abbreviations: MWC = Minimum winning coalition

**Table A.23** Swedish cabinets included in the sample

| Sweden Cabinet | Party composition | Agreement | Word count | Election date | Date in | Date out | Duration (days) | Cabinet type | Notes | Word count (cleansed)* |
|---|---|---|---|---|---|---|---|---|---|---|
| Erlander III | SD, ZE | Yes | 1100 | 19.09.1948 | 01.10.1951 | 21.09.1952 | 356 | MWC | a), c) | |
| Erlander IV | SD, ZE | Yes | 1100 | 21.09.1952 | 21.09.1952 | 16.09.1956 | 1456 | MWC | b), c) | |
| Erlander V | SD, ZE | Yes | 1900 | 26.09.1956 | 16.09.1956 | 26.10.1957 | 405 | MWC | a), c) | |
| Fälldin I | ZE, LI, KO | Yes | 3146 | 19.09.1976 | 07.10.1976 | 05.10.1978 | 728 | MWC | d) | 3146 |
| Fälldin II | ZE, LI, KO | Yes | 3836 | 16.09.1979 | 11.10.1979 | 08.05.1981 | 575 | MWC | d) | 3836 |
| Fälldin III | ZE, LI | Yes | 1565 | 16.09.1979 | 19.05.1981 | 19.09.1982 | 488 | Minority | d) | 1565 |
| Bildt I | KO, ZE, CD, LI | Yes | 5060 | 15.09.1991 | 03.10.1991 | 18.09.1994 | 1081 | Minority | d) | 5060 |
| Reinfeldt I | KO, ZE, CD, LI | Yes | 6419 | 17.09.2006 | 06.10.2006 | 19.09.2010 | 1444 | MWC | d) | 6419 |
| Reinfeldt II | KO, LI, ZE, CD | Yes | 6239 | 19.09.2010 | 19.09.2010 | 14.09.2014 | 1456 | Minority | d) | 6239 |
| Löfven I | SD, G | Yes | 3777 | 14.09.2014 | 03.10.2014 | 25.09.2018 | 1453 | Minority | d) | 3777 |
| Mean | | | 3414 | | | | 953 | | | 292 |

a) There is a coalition agreement but we were not able to obtain it.
b) There is no new coalition agreement but the cabinet in office used the previous one.
c) The word counts for the coalition agreements we could not obtain originate from the Comparative Parliamentary Democracy Data Archive (Strøm et al. 2008).
d) We are grateful to Hanna Bäck (Lund University) for providing the coalition agreements.
* The cleansed word count refers to those agreements obtained in the analysis, duplicates excluded.

Party abbreviations:
CD = Kristdemokraterna (Christian Democrats)
G = MiljÖpartiet de GrÖna (Environmental Party)
KO = Moderata Samlingspartiet (Conservative Party)
LI = Folkpartiet Liberalerna (Liberal Party)
SD = Socialdemokratiska Arbetarpartiet (Social Democratic Party)
ZE = Centerpartiet (Centre Party)
Other abbreviations: MWC = Minimum winning coalition

Table A.24 British cabinets included in the sample

| United Kingdom Cabinet | Party composition | Agreement | Word count | Election date | Date in | Date out | Duration (days) | Cabinet type |
|---|---|---|---|---|---|---|---|---|
| Cameron I | Con, Lib | Yes | 13712 | 06.05.2010 | 11.05.2010 | 15.06.2015 | 1861 | MWC |
| Mean | | | 13712 | | | | 1861 | |

Party abbreviations:
Con = Conservative Party
Lib = Liberal Democrats
Other abbreviations: MWC = Minimum winning coalition

APPENDIX 2

# Codebook

## COALITIONAGREE Dataset

### Domain 1: External Relations

**101 Foreign Special Relationships: Positive**
**102 Foreign Special Relationships: Negative**
**103 Anti-Imperialism: Positive**
    103.01 General: Positive
    103.02 State Centered Anti-Imperialism: Positive
    103.03 Foreign Financial Influence: Negative
**104 Military: Positive**
    104.01 General: Positive
    104.02 Increasing Military Capabilities
    104.03 Military Alliances: Positive
**105 Military: Negative**
    105.01 General: Negative
    105.02 Decreasing Military Capabilities
    105.03 Military Alliances: Negative
**106 Peace: Positive**
    106.01 Peace in General
    106.02 Peaceful Resolutions of Crises
**107 Internationalism: Positive**
    107.01 General: Positive
    107.02 Development Aid: Positive
**108 European Integration: Positive**
    108.01 General: Positive
    108.02 Membership of EU: Positive
    108.03 Expansion of EU and its Competencies: Positive
    108.04 Single Market: Positive
    108.05 European Institutions: Positive
    108.06 Monetary Policy: Positive
**109 Internationalism: Negative**
    109.01 General: Negative
    109.02 Development Aid: Negative
**110 European Integration: Negative**
    110.01 General: Negative
    110.02 Membership of EU: Negative
    110.03 Expansion of EU and its Competencies: Negative
    110.04 Single Market: Negative
    110.05 European Institutions: Negative
    110.06 Monetary Policy: Negative

## Domain 2: Freedom and Democracy

**201 Freedom and Human Rights: Positive**
    201.01 General: Positive
    201.02 Freedom: Positive
    201.03 Human/Civil Rights: Positive
**202 Democracy**
    202.01 General: Positive
    202.02 General: Negative
    202.03 Representative Democracy: Positive
    202.04 Direct Democracy: Positive
    202.05 Transparency: Positive
**203 Constitutionalism: Positive**
**204 Constitutionalism: Negative**

## Domain 3: Political System

**301 Decentralization: Positive**
    301.01 General: Positive
    301.02 Political Decentralization: Positive
    301.03 Fiscal Decentralization: Positive
**302 Centralisation: Positive**
    302.01 General: Positive
    302.02 Political Centralization: Positive
    302.03 Fiscal Decentralization: Positive
**303 Governmental and Administrative Efficiency: Positive**
    303.01 General: Positive
    303.02 Cutting Down on Civil Service
    303.03 Improve Bureaucratic Procedures
**304 Political Corruption: Negative**
**305 Political Authority: Positive**
    305.01 General: Positive
    305.02 Coalition Competence: Positive
    305.03 Personal Competence: Positive
    305.04 Strong Executive: Positive
    305.05 Former Elites: Positive
    305.06 Former Elites: Negative
    305.07 Rehabilitation and Compensation: Positive

## Domain 4: Economy

**401 Free Enterprise: Positive**
    401.01 General: Positive
    401.02 Privatization: Positive
    401.03 Control over Prices: Negative
    401.04 Minimum Wage: Negative
    401.05 Consumer Protection: Negative

401.06 Social Market Economy: Negative
401.07 Competition Policies: Negative

**402 Incentives: Positive**
402.01 General: Positive
402.02 Enterprise-friendly Wage and Tax Policies: Positive
402.03 Encouragement to Start Enterprises: Positive
402.04 Small- and Medium-sized Businesses: Positive

**403 Market Regulation: Positive**
403.01 General: Positive
403.02 Consumer Protection: Positive
403.03 Social Market Economy: Positive
403.04 Competition policies: Positive
403.05 Small- and Medium-sized Businesses: Positive

**404 Economic Planning: Positive**

**405 Corporatism: Positive**

**406 Protectionism: Positive**
406.01 General: Positive
406.02 Tariffs: Positive
406.03 Quota Restrictions: Positive

**407 Protectionism: Negative**
407.01 General: Negative
407.02 Tariffs: Negative
407.03 Quota Restrictions: Negative

**408 Economic Goals**

**409 Keynesian Demand Management: Positive**
409.01 General
409.02 Government Stimulus Plans: Positive

**410 Economic Growth**
410.01 General
410.02 International Competitiveness: Positive

**411 Technology and Infrastructure: Positive**
411.01 General: Positive
411.02 Roads: Positive
411.03 Aviation: Positive
411.04 Railways: Positive
411.05 Modernization of Local Public Transport: Positive
411.06 Modernization of Technological Infrastructure: Positive
411.07 Research and Development: Positive
411.08 Technical Training: Positive
411.09 New Technologies: Positive
411.10 Genetic Engineering/Biotechnology: Positive
411.11 Power Supply: Positive
411.12 Nuclear Energy: Positive
411.13 Nuclear Energy: Negative

**412 Controlled Economy: Positive**
412.01 General: Positive
412.02 Control over Prices: Positive
412.03 Minimum Wage: Positive

413 **Nationalization: Positive**
    413.01 General: Positive
    413.02 Govt. Ownership of Industries: Positive
    413.03 Govt. Ownership of Land and Real Estate: Positive
    413.04 Govt. Ownership of Banks: Positive

414 **Economic Orthodoxy: Positive**
    414.01 General
    414.02 Budgetary Discipline: Positive
    414.03 Low Inflation

415 **Marxist Analysis: Positive**

416 **Anti-Growth Economy: Positive**
    416.01 General: Positive
    416.02 Sustainability: Positive

## Domain 5: Welfare and Quality of Life

501 **Environmental Protection: Positive**
    501.01 General: Positive
    501.02 Fight Climate Change: Positive
    501.03 Preservation of Nature and Natural Resources: Positive
    501.04 Animal Rights: Positive
    501.05 Nuclear Energy: Negative
    501.06 Nuclear Energy: Positive
    501.07 Recycling/Waste Reduction: Positive

502 **Culture: Positive**
    502.01 General: Positive
    502.02 Cultural Institutions: Positive
    502.03 Media: Positive
    502.04 Sports: Positive

503 **Equality: Positive**
    503.01 General: Positive
    503.02 Gender Equality: Positive
    503.03 Educational Equality: Positive
    503.04 Social Equality: Positive
    503.05 Racial Equality: Positive
    503.06 Equal rights for Homosexuals: Positive

504 **Welfare State Expansion**
    504.01 General: Expansion
    504.02 Health Care: Expansion
    504.03 Child/Youth Care: Expansion
    504.04 Elderly Care: Expansion
    504.05 Social Housing: Expansion
    504.06 Increase of State Pensions
    504.07 Support for Disabled: Expansion
    504.08 Unemployment Assistance: Expansion

505 **Welfare State Limitation**
    505.01 General: Limitation
    505.02 Health Care: Limitation
    505.03 Child/Youth Care: Limitation

505.04 Elderly Care: Limitation
505.05 Social Housing: Limitation
505.06 Decrease of State Pensions
505.07 Support for Disabled: Limitation
505.08 Unemployment Assistance: Limitation

**506 Education Expansion**
506.01 General : Expansion
506.02 Education in Schools: Expansion
506.03 Education in Universities: Expansion
506.04 Education for Adults: Expansion
506.05 Expansion of Research

**507 Education Limitation**
507.01 General: Limitation
507.02 Education in Schools: Limitation
507.03 Education in Universities: Limitation
507.04 Education for Adults: Limitation
507.05 Limitation of Research

# Domain 6: Fabric of Society

**601 National Way of Life: Positive**
601.01 General: Positive
601.02 Immigration: Negative
601.03 Regional Identity: Negative

**602 National Way of Life: Negative**
602.01 General: Negative
602.02 Immigration: Positive
602.03 Regional Identity: Positive

**603 Traditional Morality: Positive**
603.01 General: Positive
603.02 Family: Traditional
603.03 Separation of State and Church: Negative
603.04 Abortion and Birth Control: Negative
603.05 Homosexuality: Negative

**604 Traditional Morality: Negative**
604.01 General: Negative
604.02 Family: Progressive
604.03 Separation of State and Church: Positive
604.04 Abortion and Birth Control: Positive
604.05 Homosexuality: Positive

**605.1 Law and Order: Positive**
605.11 General: Positive
605.12 Law Enforcement: Positive
605.13 Surveillance: Positive
605.14 Drug Politics: Strict
605.15 Tax Evasion: Negative

**605.2 Law and Order: Negative**
605.21 General: Negative

605.22 Law Enforcement: Negative
605.23 Surveillance: Negative
605.24 Drug Politics: Lax
605.25 Tax Evasion: Positive
**606 Civic Mindedness: Positive**
606.01 General: Positive
606.02 Bottom-Up Activism: Positive
**607 Multiculturalism: Positive**
607.01 General: Positive
607.02 Immigrants: Diversity
607.03 Indigenous Rights: Positive
**608 Multiculturalism: Negative**
608.01 General: Negative
608.02 Immigrants: Assimilation
608.03 Indigenous Rights: Negative

# Domain 7: Social Groups

**701 Labour Groups: Positive**
701.01 General: Positive
701.02 Work Safety and Protection: Positive
701.03 Support for Labour Unions: Positive
701.04 Higher Wages
701.05 Working Hours Flexibility: Positive
701.06 Support for Unemployed/ More Jobs: Positive
701.07 Employees' Rights: Positive
**702 Labour Groups: Negative**
702.01 General: Negative
702.02 Work Safety and Protection: Negative
702.03 Danger of Abuse of Power of Trade Unions
702.04 Lower Wages
702.05 Working Hours Flexibility: Negative
702.06 Support for Unemployed/More Jobs: Negative
702.07 Employees' Rights: Negative
**703.1 Agriculture and Farmers: Positive**
703.11 General: Positive
703.12 Subsidies and Welfare Provisions: Positive
703.13 Fishing Regulation: Negative
703.14 Agricultural Products: Positive
**703.2 Agriculture and Farmers: Negative**
703.21 General: Negative
703.22 Subsidies and Welfare Provisions: Negative
703.23 Fishing Regulation: Positive
703.24 Agricultural Products: Negative
**704 Middle Class and Professional Groups: Positive**
704.01 General
704.02 Professional Groups: Positive
704.03 White Collar Groups: Positive
704.04 Service Sector Groups: Positive

- **705 Minority Groups: Positive**
  - 705.01 General: Positive
  - 705.02 Handicapped: Positive
  - 705.03 Homosexuals: Positive
  - 705.04 Immigrants: Positive
  - 705.05 Refugees: Positive
  - 705.06 Religious Groups: Positive
- **706 Non-Economic Demographic Groups: Positive**
  - 706.01 General: Positive
  - 706.02 Women: Positive
  - 706.03 Elderly: Positive
  - 706.04 Young People: Positive
- **800 Headlines**
- **900 Procedural Rules**
  - 900.01 General
  - 900.02 Portfolios
  - 900.03 Cabinet Meetings
  - 900.04 Junior Minister
  - 900.05 Legislative Discipline
  - 900.06 Conflict-solving Mechanisms
  - 900.07 Decision-making Mechanisms
- **000 No Meaningful Category Applies**

## Coding Scheme Description

## 1 External Relations

### 101 (Foreign Special Relationships: Positive)

Favorable mentions of particular countries with which the government country has a special relationship; the need for cooperation and/or aid to such countries.

*These special relationships should be predetermined on a case by case basis. Refer to the supervisor for detailed information and attach a list of special relations to the coding protocol. The need for cooperation with other countries is coded under 107.*

### 102 (Foreign Special Relationships: Negative)

Negative mentions of particular countries with which the government country has a special relationship; the refusal of cooperation and/or aid to such countries.

*These special relationships should be predetermined on a case by case basis. Refer to the supervisor for detailed information and attach a list of special relations to the coding protocol. The refusal of cooperation with other countries is coded under 109.*

### 103 (Anti-Imperialism: Positive)

### 103.01 (General: Positive)

General mentions of anti-imperialistic behavior.

## 103.02 (State Centered Anti-Imperialism: Positive)

Negative references to imperial behavior and/or negative references to one state exerting strong influence (political, military, or commercial) over other states.

- Negative references to controlling other countries as if they were part of an empire.
- Favorable references to greater self-government and independence for colonies.
- Favorable mentions of de-colonization.

## 103.03 (Foreign Financial Influence: Negative)

Negative references and statements against international financial organizations or states using monetary means to assert strong influence over the government or other states.

- Statements against the World Bank, IMF etc.
- Statements against the Washington Consensus
- Statements against foreign debt circumscribing state actions

## 104 (Military: Positive)

The importance of external security and defense. May include statements concerning:

- The need to maintain or increase military expenditure;
- The need to secure adequate manpower in the military;
- The need to modernize armed forces and improve military strength;
- The need for rearmament and self-defense;
- The need to keep military treaty obligations.

## 104.01 (General: Positive)

General positive mentions of the importance of external security and defense.

## 104.02 (Armament: Positive)

Positive references to increasing military expenditure, securing adequate manpower in the military, modernizing armed forces, improving military strength, rearmament, and self-defense. Favorable mentions of a country's army. Positive references to arms export and opposition to disarmament.

## 104.03 (Military Alliances: Positive)

Positive references to keeping military treaty obligations, e.g. being a member of the NATO. Might also include positive references to military interventions as part of alliance.

## 105 (Military: Negative)

Negative references to the military or use of military power to solve conflicts. References to the "evils of war." May include references to:

- Decreasing military expenditures;
- Disarmament;
- Reduced or abolished conscription.

## 105.01 (General: Negative)

General negative mentions of the importance of external security and defense.

### 105.02 (Armament: Negative)

Negative references to increasing military expenditure and manpower in the military, modernizing armed forces. Negative references to military strength, rearmament, and self-defense. Negative references to arms export and support of disarmament.

### 105.03 (Military Alliances: Negative)

Negative references to keeping military treaty obligations, e.g. being a member of the NATO. Might also include negative references to military interventions as part of alliance.

### 106 (Peace: Positive)

Any declaration of belief in peace and peaceful means of solving crises—absent reference to the military. May include:

- Peace as a general goal;
- Desirability of countries joining in negotiations with hostile countries;
- Ending wars in order to establish peace.

### 106.01 (Peace in General: Positive)

Support for peace as a general goal.

### 106.02 (Peaceful Resolutions of Crises: Positive)

Desirability of peaceful resolutions of crises. Desirability of countries joining in negotiations with hostile countries.

### 107 (Internationalism: Positive)

Need for international cooperation, including cooperation with specific countries other than those coded in 101. May also include references to the:

- Need for aid to developing countries;
- Need for world planning of resources;
- Support for global governance;
- Need for international courts;
- Support for UN or other international organizations.

*This category does not include positive references to peaceful resolutions of crises (106.02) or military interventions (104.03).*

### 107.01 (General: Positive)

General positive mentions of the need for international cooperation. Might also include positive references to global governance, international courts and international organizations, e.g. UN, IMF, etc.

### 107.02 (Development Aid: Positive)

Favorable mentions of need for aid to developing countries.

### 108 (European Integration: Positive)

Favorable mentions of European Community/Union in general. May include the:

- Desirability of the country joining (or remaining a member);
- Desirability of expanding the European Community/Union;

- Desirability of increasing the ECs/EUs competences;
- Desirability of expanding the competences of the European Parliament.

## 108.01 (General: Positive)
General favorable mentions of the European Union and European Integration.

## 108.02 (Membership of EU: Positive)
Desirability of the governments country to join the EU or remain a member.

## 108.03 (Expansion of EU and its Competencies: Positive)
Desirability of expanding the EC/EU and increasing the ECs/EU competencies.

## 108.04 (Single Market: Positive)
Favorable mentions of the Single Market, including positive references to the free movement of people, goods, services, and capital.
*This subcategory is only about the design or desirability of the single market. This may come as a call for deeper integration toward a single market.*

## 108.05 (European Institutions: Positive)
Favorable mentions of the European Institutions and/or increasing their competencies, e.g. the European Parliament, the Commission, etc.

## 108.06 (Monetary Union/EURO: Positive)
Desirability of joining and/or favorable mentions of the Monetary Union/EURO. Positive references to the ECB and specific monetary policies, e.g. the Stability and Growth Pact.
*This subcategory is only about the design or desirability of the monetary union/EURO. This may come as a call for deeper integration toward a monetary union.*

## 109 (Internationalism: Negative)
Negative references to international cooperation with countries other than those coded in 102. Favorable mentions of national independence and sovereignty with regard to the coalition agreement country's foreign policy, isolation, and/or unilateralism as opposed to internationalism.

## 109.01 (General: Negative)
General negative mentions of the need for international cooperation. Might also include negative references to global governance, international courts, and international organizations, e.g. UN, IMF, etc.

## 109.02 (Development Aid: Negative)
Negative references to the need for aid to developing countries.
*This category does not include negative references to military interventions (105.03).*

## 110 (European Integration: Negative)
Negative references to the European Community/Union. May include:
- Opposition to specific European policies which are preferred by European authorities;
- Opposition to the net-contribution of the coalition agreement country to the EU budget.

### 110.01 (General: Negative)
General negative mentions of the European Union and European Integration. Might also include negative references to specific EU policies.

### 110.02 (Membership of EU: Negative)
Opposition to the governments country joining or remaining a member of the EU.

### 110.03 (Expansion of EU and its Competencies: Negative)
Opposition to expanding the EC/EU and increasing the ECs/EU competencies, e.g. subsidiarity principle.

### 110.04 (Single Market: Negative)
Negative mentions of the Single Market, including negative references to the free movement of people, goods, services, and capital.
*This subcategory is only about the design or desirability of the single market. This may come as a call against integration toward a single market.*

### 110.05 (European Institutions: Negative)
Negative mentions of the European Institutions and/or increasing their competencies, e.g. the European Parliament, the Commission etc.

### 110.06 (Monetary Union/EURO: Negative)
Opposition to joining and/or negative mentions of the Monetary Union/EURO. Negative references to the ECB and specific monetary policies, e.g. the Stability and Growth Pact.
*This subcategory is only about the design or desirability of the monetary union/EURO. This may come as a call against integration toward a monetary union.*

## 2 Freedom and Democracy

### 201 (Freedom and Human Rights: Positive)

### 201.01 (General: Positive)
Positive mentions of the importance of personal freedom and human and civil rights in the coalition country and abroad.

### 201.02 (Freedom: Positive)
Favorable mentions of importance of personal freedom in the governments and other countries. May include mentions of:

- Freedom from state coercion in the political and economic spheres;
- Freedom from bureaucratic control;
- The idea of individualism.

### 201.03 (Human/Civil Rights: Positive)
Favorable mentions of importance of human and civil rights in the government and other countries, including the right to freedom of speech, press, assembly, etc.; supportive refugee policies. Also includes mentions of the protection of data privacy.

## 202 (Democracy)

### 202.01 (General: Positive)
Favorable mentions of democracy as the "only game in town." General support for the coalition agreements country's democracy. May also include: democracy as method or goal in national, international or other organizations (e.g. labor unions, parties); need for involvement of all citizens in political decision-making (e.g. women suffrage); support for parts of democratic regimes (rule of law, division of powers, independence of courts).

### 202.02 (General: Negative)
Statements against the idea of democracy, in general or in the coalition agreement country. Calls for reducing or withholding democratic rights from all or certain groups of people. Calls for the introduction or maintaining of a non-democratic regime, e.g. monarchy or rule of the military.

### 202.03 (Representative Democracy: Positive)
Favorable mentions of the system of representative democracy, in particular in contrast to direct democracy.

### 202.04 (Direct Democracy: Positive)
Favorable mentions of the system of direct democracy, in particular in contrast to representative democracy. This includes the call for the introduction and/or extension of referenda, participatory budgets, and other forms of direct democracy.

### 202.05 (Support Transparency)
Need to support organizations or mechanisms to support transparency. This category only applies for transparency that fosters democracy in political institutions. This category does not apply for bureaucratic or economic institutions. Political corruption is coded as 304.

## 203 (Constitutionalism: Positive)
Support for maintaining the status quo of the constitution. Support for specific aspects of the government country's constitution. The use of constitutionalism as an argument for any policy.

## 204 (Constitutionalism: Negative)
Opposition to the entirety or specific aspects of the government country's constitution. Calls for constitutional amendments or changes. May include calls to abolish or rewrite the current constitution.

# 3 Political System

## 301 (Decentralization: Positive)
Support for federalism or decentralization of political and/or economic power. May include:

- Favorable mentions of the territorial subsidiary principle;

- More autonomy for any sub-national level in policy making and/or economics, including municipalities;
- Support for the continuation and importance of local and regional customs and symbols and/or deference to local expertise;
- Favorable mentions of special consideration for sub-national areas.

*This category only applies to the political system as such. For example, if a government wants to strengthen the autonomy of regional parliaments, this is coded as 301.02. However, if a government puts emphasis on regional identity, this is coded as 602.03. The categories 301 and 602.03 are not concerned with multicultural identities or immigrants.*

### 301.01 (General: Positive)
Favorable, general statements toward the decentralization of the state.

### 301.02 (Political Decentralization)
Favorable mentions of the territorial subsidiary principle. More autonomy for any sub-national level in policy making and/or economics, including municipalities.

### 301.03 (Fiscal Decentralization)
Favorable mentions of decentralizing revenue raising and/or expenditure of money to a lower level of government while maintaining financial responsibility (Wikipedia.org), e.g. "Länderfinanzausgleich" for Germany.

### 302 (Centralization: Positive)
General opposition to political decision-making at lower political levels. Support for unitary government and for more centralization in political and administrative procedures. *This category only applies to the political system as such. For example, if a government wants to reduce the autonomy of regional parliaments, this is coded as 302.02. However, if a government opposes regional identity, this is coded as 601.03. The categories 302 and 601.03 are not concerned with multicultural identities or immigrants.*

### 302.01 (General: Positive)
Favorable, general statements toward the centralization of the state.

### 302.02 (Political Centralization)
Opposition to political decision-making at lower political levels. Support for unitary government and for more centralization in political and administrative procedures.

### 302.03 (Fiscal Centralization)
Opposition to decentralizing revenue raising and/or expenditure of money to a lower level of government.

### 303 (Governmental and Administrative Efficiency: Positive)
Need for efficiency and economy in government and administration and/or the general appeal to make the process of government and administration cheaper and more efficient. May include:

- Restructuring the civil service;
- Cutting down on the civil service;
- Improving bureaucratic procedures.

*Note: Specific policy positions overrule this category! If there is no specific policy position, however, this category applies.*

### 303.01 (General: Positive)
General and favorable mentions of the ideal of governmental and administrative efficiency.

### 303.02 (Cutting Down on Civil Service)
Favorable mentions of decreasing the number of civil servants in the government's country.

### 303.03 (Improve Bureaucratic Procedures)
Favorable mentions of changing the bureaucratic procedures in the government's country.

### 304 (Political Corruption: Negative)
Need to eliminate political corruption and associated abuses of political and/or bureaucratic power. Need to abolish clientelist structures and practices.

### 305 (Political Authority: Positive)
Specific policy positions overrule all subcategories of 305! If there is no specific policy position, however, these subcategories may apply.

### 305.01 (General: Positive)
Very general and positive references to political authority as such.

### 305.02 (Coalition Competence: Positive)
References to the coalition parties competence to govern and/or previous government's lack of such competence.

### 305.03 (Personal Competence: Positive)
Reference to the prime minister's or other ministers' personal competence to govern and/or previous government's lack of such competence.

### 305.04 (Strong Executive: Positive)
Favorable mentions of the desirability of a strong and/or stable government/executive vis-á-vis the legislative branch.

### 305.05 (Former Elites: Positive)
Cooperation with former authorities in the transition period; amnesty for former elites; and "let sleeping dogs lie" in dealing with the nomenclature.

### 305.06 (Former Elites: Negative)
Against former elites involvement in democratic government; weeding out the collaborators from governmental service; for truth commissions and other institutions illuminating recent history.

### 305.07 (Rehabilitation and Compensation: Positive)
Positive references to civic rehabilitation of politically persecuted people in the authoritarian era; positive references to juridical compensation concerning authoritarian expropriations; support for moral compensation.

# 4 Economy

### 401 (Free Market Economy: Positive)
Favorable mentions of the free market and free market capitalism as an economic model. May include favorable references to:

- Laissez-faire economy;
- Superiority of individual enterprise over state and control systems;
- Private property rights;
- Personal enterprise and initiative;
- Need for unhampered individual enterprises.

### 401.01 (General: Positive)
General and favorable mentions of the free market and free market capitalism.

### 401.02 (Privatization: Positive)
Support for private ownership of productive enterprises. Support for the transferal of industries or infrastructure from the state to private actors.

### 401.03 (Control over Prices: Negative)
Opposition to government control over prices.

### 401.04 (Minimum Wage: Negative)
Opposition to introduction of minimum wage.

### 401.05 (Consumer Protection: Negative)
Opposition to consumer protection, e.g. disclosing detailed information about products such as food, toys, etc. Supporting people who rent a house or a flat rather than the owners of real estate.

### 401.06 (Social Market Economy: Negative)
Negative references to a social market economy.

### 401.07 (Competition Policies: Negative)
Opposition to interference in markets by, for example, anti-monopoly offices.

### 402 (Incentives: Positive)
Favorable mentions of supply side oriented economic policies (assistance to businesses rather than consumers). May include:

- Financial and other incentives such as subsidies, tax breaks etc.;
- Wage and tax policies to induce enterprise;
- Encouragement to start enterprises.

### 402.01 (General: Positive)
Favorable and general mentions of supply-side economics, pertaining to the idea that economic growth is best achieved by lowering barriers for people to produce (supply) goods and services as well as invest in capital.

### 402.02 (Enterprise-friendly Wage and Tax Policies: Positive)
Support for enterprise-friendly wage and tax policies, e.g. tax breaks or reliefs, lower wages.

### 402.03 (Encouragement to Start Enterprises: Positive)
Support for incentives to facilitate the foundation of enterprises, e.g. tax breaks or reliefs.

### 402.04 (Small- and Medium-sized Businesses: Positive)
Programs, monetary incentives or tax breaks for small- and medium-sized businesses (SMBs). General and supportive mentions of SMBs are coded as 403.05.

### 403 (Market Regulation: Positive)
Support for policies designed to create a fair and open economic market. May include:

- Calls for increased consumer protection;
- Increasing economic competition by preventing monopolies and other actions disrupting the functioning of the market;
- Defense of small businesses against disruptive powers of big businesses;
- Social market economy.

### 403.01 (General: Positive)
Support for policies designed to create a fair and open economic market other than those below. May include regulations of shopping hours but also regulations of the finance sector.

### 403.02 (Consumer Protection: Positive)
Support for consumer protection, e.g. disclosing detailed information about products such as food, toys, etc. Supporting rather people who rent a house or a flat than owners of real estate.

### 403.03 (Social Market Economy: Positive)
Positive references to a social market economy. Might include references to policies that prevent wage- or social-dumping.

### 403.04 (Market Competition: Positive)
Support for increasing competition by preventing cartels, monopolies, and other actions disrupting the functioning of the market.

### 403.05 (Small- and Medium-sized Businesses: Positive)
General support for small- and medium-sized (SMB) businesses. Mentions of SMBs being an important part of the country's economy. Incentives for SMBs are coded as 402.04.

### 404 (Economic Planning: Positive)
Favorable mentions of long-standing economic planning by the government, e.g. policy plans, strategies, or policy patterns of a consultative or indicative nature. General mentions of state planning in the economic sector are coded as 404. More specific programs belong to more specific categories.

### 405 (Corporatism: Positive)

General and favorable mentions of corporatism. Favorable mentions of co-operation of government, employers, and trade unions simultaneously; the collaboration of employers and employee organizations in overall economic planning supervised by the state. Support for a collective labour agreement in the government's country.

### 406 (Protectionism: Positive)

Favorable mentions of extending or maintaining the protection of internal markets (by the coalition agreement or other countries). Measures may include:

- Tariffs;
- Quota restrictions;
- Export subsidies.

### 406.01 (General: Positive)

Support for other forms of protectionism (in the governments or other countries) to protect internal markets.

### 406.02 (Tariffs: Positive)

Support for tariffs (in the governments or other countries) to protect internal markets.

### 406.03 (Quota Restrictions: Positive)

Support for quota restrictions (in the governments or other countries) to protect internal markets.

### 407 (Protectionism: Negative)

Support for the concept of free trade and open markets. Call for abolishing all means of market protection (in the coalition agreement or any other country).

### 407.01 (General: Negative)

Opposition to other forms of protectionism (in the governments or other countries) to enhance free trade.

### 407.02 (Tariffs: Negative)

Opposition to tariffs (in the governments or other countries) to enhance free trade.

### 407.03 (Quota Restrictions: Negative)

Opposition to quota restrictions (in the governments or other countries) to enhance free trade.

### 408 (Economic Goals)

Broad and general economic goals that are not mentioned in relation to any other category. General economic statements that fail to include any specific goal. Note: Specific policy positions overrule this category! If there is no specific policy position, however, this category applies.

## 409 (Keynesian Demand Management)

Favorable mentions of demand-side oriented economic policies (assistance to consumers rather than businesses). Particularly includes increased private demand through

- Increasing public demand;
- Increasing social expenditures.

May also include:

- Stabilization in the face of depression;
- Government stimulus plans in the face of economic crises.

### 409.01 (General: Positive)

Favorable mentions of demand-side oriented economics. Pertaining to the idea that economic performance is driven by the demand in an economy.

### 409.02 (Government Stimulus Plans: Positive)

Support for stabilization in the face of depression, i.e. support for government stimulus packages.

## 410 (Economic Growth)

### 410.01 (General)

The paradigm of economic growth. Includes:

- General need to encourage or facilitate greater production;
- Need for the government to take measures to aid economic growth.

### 410.02 (International Competitiveness: Positive)

Favorable mentions of international competitiveness of companies/economic sectors. Also includes policies that aim at raising competitiveness.

## 411 (Technology and Infrastructure: Positive)

Importance of modernization of industry and updated methods of transport and communication. May include:

- Importance of science and technological developments in industry;
- Need for training and research within the economy (this does not imply education in general, see category 506);
- Calls for public spending on infrastructure such as roads and bridges;
- Support for public spending on technological infrastructure (e.g.: broadband internet).

### 411.01 (General: Positive)

Positive mentions of the importance of technology and the infrastructure in the coalition country. Positive mentions of waterways as means of transport. Importance of modernization of waterways, ports, and locks. Might also include positive references to bikes as means of transportation (including special lanes for bikes).

### 411.02 (Roads: Positive)

Positive mentions of roads as means of transport. Importance of modernization of roads.

### 411.03 (Aviation: Positive)
Positive mentions of travel and transport in airplanes. Importance of modernization of air ports.

### 411.04 (Railways: Positive)
Positive mentions of railways as means of transport. Importance of modernization of railway system as well as the modernization of non-local trains.

### 411.05 (Modernization of Local Public Transport)
Positive mentions of local public transport. Importance of modernization of public transport, i.e. subways, buses, and trams. Includes calls for public spending on local public transport.

### 411.06 (Modernization of Technological Infrastructure)
Support for modernization of the technological infrastructure, i.e. the expansion of (broadband) internet, television, a more comprehensive and faster cell phone reception system, and the modernization of the electric grid. Includes calls for public spending on technological infrastructure.

### 411.07 (Research and Development)
Importance of science and research in enterprises. Mentions of the importance of science at enterprises. *Research at universities and research institutes are coded as 506.05.*

### 411.08 (Technical Training: Positive)
Positive mentions of technical training with regard to technical development. Support for policies that increases the number of apprenticeship training positions.

### 411.09 (New Technologies: Positive)
Importance of new technologies and new developments.

### 411.10 (Genetic Engineering/Biotechnology: Positive)
Support of genetic engineering and biotechnology. Emphasis on potential benefits.

### 411.11 (Power Supply: Positive)
Favorable mentions of policies aiming at improving the supply of power in a country. Might also include positive mentions of new electrical power lines and the construction of new power plants.

### 411.12 (Nuclear Energy: Positive)
Positive mentions of nuclear energy as a cheap and reliable power source.
*This does not include favorable mentions of nuclear energy as good for the environment, e.g. a way to reduce carbon emissions and fight climate change, which is coded under 501.06.*

### 411.13 (Nuclear Energy: Negative)
Mentions of nuclear energy as cost inefficient or non-reliable power source.
*This does not include negative mentions of nuclear energy as dangerous for the environment, which is coded under 501.05.*

### 412 (Controlled Economy: Positive)

Support for direct government control of economy. May include, for instance:

- Control over prices;
- Introduction of minimum wages.

### 412.01 (General: Positive)

Support for direct government control of economy.

### 412.02 (Control over Prices: Positive)

Support for government control over prices.

### 412.03 (Minimum Wage: Positive)

Support for introduction of minimum wage.

### 413 (Nationalization: Positive)

Favorable mentions of government ownership of industries, either partial or complete; calls for keeping nationalized industries in state hand or nationalising currently private industries. May also include favorable mentions of government ownership of land.

### 413.01 (General: Positive)

General and favorable mentions of government ownership.

### 413.02 (Govt. Ownership of Industries: Positive)

Favorable mentions of government ownership of industries, either partial or complete; calls for keeping nationalized industries in state hand or nationalizing currently private industries.

### 413.03 (Govt. Ownership of Land and Real Estate: Positive)

Favorable mentions of government ownership of land.

### 413.04 (Govt. Ownership of Banks: Positive)

Favorable mentions of government ownership of banks.

### 414 (Economic Orthodoxy)

Need for economically healthy government policy making. May include calls for:

- Reduction of budget deficits;
- Retrenchment in crisis;
- Thrift and savings in the face of economic hardship;
- Support for traditional economic institutions such as stock market and banking system;
- Support for strong currency.

### 414.01 (General)

General and favorable statements toward economically healthy government policy making.

### 414.02 (Budgetary Discipline)

Calls for reduction of budgets deficits, less state spending. Retrenchment in crises.

### 414.03 (Low Inflation: Positive)

Support for low inflation, or to strengthen the currency. Might also include references to strong and independent central banks that can keep inflation low.

### 415 (Marxist Analysis: Positive)

Positive references to Marxist-Leninist ideology and specific use of Marxist-Leninist terminology by the government parties (typically but not necessary by communist parties).
*Note: If unsure about what constitutes Marxist-Leninist ideology in general or terminology in a particular language, please research.*

### 416 (Anti-Growth Economy)

### 416.01 (General: Positive)

Favorable mentions of anti-growth politics. Rejection of the idea that growth is good.

### 416.02 (Sustainability: Positive)

Call for sustainable economic development. Opposition to growth that causes environmental or societal harm. This subcategory might also include statements in favor of economic growth but only if this growth is sustainable. All other arguments favoring growth are coded as 410.

## 5 Welfare and Quality of Life

### 501 (Environmental Protection: Positive)

General policies in favor of protecting the environment, fighting climate change, and other "green" policies. For instance:

- General preservation of natural resources;
- Preservation of countryside, forests, etc.;
- Protection of national parks;
- Animal rights.

May include a great variance of policies that have the unified goal of environmental protection.

### 501.01 (General: Positive)

Positive mentions of environmental protection.

### 501.02 (Fight Climate Change: Positive)

Support for policies in favor of fighting climate change. Emphasis on the dangers of climate change and the need to halt it. Support for policies in favor of renewable energy sources, like wind, solar, and hydro power. Includes support for subsidies for renewables. Emphasis on the importance to save energy. Support for policies that incentivize saving energy or ban devices that waste energy, e.g. classic light bulbs. Support for policies that help consumers to understand the degree of energy consumption of a product (e.g. emissions of cars, or consumption of fridges). Support for policies aimed against the use of fossil energy, e.g. higher taxes on fossil fuels or strict regulations of $CO_2$ emissions.

### 501.03 (Preservation of Nature and Natural Resources: Positive)
Support for policies in favor of preserving nature, national parks, and natural resources. Emphasis on the importance of preserving nature and its resources.

### 501.04 (Animal Rights: Positive)
Support for policies geared toward securing the implementation of animal rights. Emphasis on the importance of respecting animal rights.

### 501.05 (Nuclear Energy: Negative)
Support for policies aimed against nuclear energy, e.g. opposition to nuclear power plants or nuclear research framed as threatening the environment. Opposition to state subsidies for nuclear energy.
*Does not include mentions of nuclear energy as being a non-reliable power source, which is coded under 411.13.*

### 501.06 (Nuclear Energy: Positive)
Support for nuclear energy as a "clean" and emission-free power source.
*Does not include mentions of nuclear energy being a cheap and reliable power source, which is coded under 411.12.*

### 501.07 (Recycling/Waste Reduction: Positive)
Support for policies aimed to increase recycling, e.g. introducing a bottle deposit or regulations that incentivize/prescribe the usage of recycled goods or production of goods that are easily recyclable. Emphasis on the general usefulness and importance of recycling. Support for waste reduction.

### 502 (Culture: Positive)
Need for state funding of cultural and leisure facilities including arts and sport. May include:

- The need to fund museums, art galleries, libraries etc.;
- The need to encourage cultural mass media and worthwhile leisure activities, such as public sport clubs.

### 502.01 (General: Positive)
Positive references to the need of state funding of cultural and leisure facilities other than those below (e.g. computer games).

### 502.02 (Cultural institutions: Positive)
Positive references to the need of state funding of museums, art galleries, memorials, and libraries.

### 502.03 (Media: Positive)
Positive references to the need of state funding of public radio and television channels. Includes emphases of importance of books and newspapers.

### 502.04 (Sports: Positive)
Positive references to the need of state funding of sports and public sport clubs.

### 503 (Equality: Positive)

Concept of social justice and the need for fair treatment of all people. This may include:

- Special protection for underprivileged social groups;
- Removal of class barriers;
- Need for fair distribution of resources;
- The end of discrimination (e.g. racial or sexual discrimination).

### 503.01 (General: Positive)

General and positive mentions of the concept of equality.

### 503.02 (Gender Equality: Positive)

Support for projects that enhance the equal treatment of men and women. Overcoming discrimination of women.

*See 706 for unspecific mentions of women, e.g. as an "important part of society." Positive mentions of women suffrage is coded as 202.01.*

### 503.03 (Education Equality: Positive)

Support for educational equality irrespective of the origin of people. Might include positive references to upward mobility through education. Need to expand and/or improve education for underprivileged students. Calls for making education affordable for all people. Includes support of right to education and equality of access to education.

*References to the expansion of educational institutions are coded under 506 (depending on the institution).*

### 503.04 (Social Equality: Positive)

Support for concept of social justice and the need for fair treatment of all people. This may include support for the removal of class barriers, a need for fair distribution of resources, and support for a system of taxation that disburdens the poor/burdens the rich.

### 503.05 (Racial Equality: Positive)

Support for the end of discrimination of immigrants. Equal treatment of locals and immigrants.

### 503.06 (Equal Rights for Homosexuals: Positive)

Support for the end of discrimination of homosexuals. LGBTQ.

### 504 (Welfare State Expansion)

Favorable mentions of need to introduce, maintain or expand any public social service or social security scheme. This includes, for example, government funding of:

- Child care
- Health care
- Elder care and pensions
- Social housing

*Note: This category excludes education.*
*Refers to distributive policies and not regulative policies on social welfare by the state.*

### 504.01 (General: Expansion)
Positive references to the expansion of social welfare by the state in other domains than those below. Positive mentions of the social security system as such.

### 504.02 (Expansion of Health Care)
Positive references to the expansion of health care by the state.

### 504.03 (Expansion of Child Care)
Positive references to the expansion of child care by the state, e.g. the expansion of day-care centers, babysitters, or other providers of child care. Includes maternity leave.

### 504.04 (Expansion of Elderly Care)
Positive references to the expansion of elder care by the state, e.g. the expansion of nursing homes. For pensions see (504.06).

### 504.05 (Expansion of Social Housing)
Positive references to the expansion of social housing.

### 504.06 (Increase of State Pensions)
Positive references to an increase of state pensions. *Corporate pension and private pension plans are coded under 505.06.*

### 504.07 (Expansion of Support for the Disabled)
Positive references to the expansion of the support for the disabled by the state.

### 504.08 (Expansion of Unemployment Assistance)
Positive references to the expansion of the support for the unemployed by the state. Monetary and non-monetary (fridges, televisions, etc.) aid by the state to those out of work. *Calls for more jobs are coded under 701.06*

### 505 (Welfare State Limitation)
Limiting state expenditures on social services or social security. Favorable mentions of the social subsidiary principle (i.e. private care before state care).
*Refers to distributive policies and not regulative policies on social welfare by the state.*

### 505.01 (General: Limitation)
Negative references to the expansion of social welfare by the state. Support to cut down social welfare.

### 505.02 (Limitation of Health Care)
Positive references to the limitation of health care by the state.

### 505.03 (Limitation of Child Care)
Positive references to the limitation of child care by the state, e.g. the limitation of day-care centers, babysitters, or other providers.

### 505.04 (Limitation of Elderly Care)
Positive references to the limitation of elder care by the state, e.g. the expansion of nursing homes. *For pensions see (505.06).*

### 505.05 (Limitation of Social Housing)
Positive references to the limitation of social housing.

### 505.06 (Decrease of State Pensions)
Positive references to a decrease of pensions. Support for increase of private pension plans.

### 505.07 (Limitation of Support for the Disabled)
Positive references to the limitation of the support for the disabled.

### 505.08 (Limitation Unemployment Assistance)
Positive references to the limitation of the support for the unemployed. *Calls for more jobs are coded under 701.06.*

### 506 (Education Expansion)
Need to expand and/or improve educational provision at all levels.
*This excludes technical training, which is coded under 411.*

### 506.01 (General: Expansion)
The need to expand and/or improve educational provision.

### 506.02 (Expansion of Education in Schools)
Need to expand and/or improve education in schools. Might also include policies that are aiming at abolishing/reducing fees for schools. Opposition to private schools. This category also includes vocational schools.

### 506.03 (Expansion of Education in Universities)
Need to expand and/or improve education in universities. Might also include policies that are aiming at abolishing/reducing fees for universities.

### 506.04 (Expansion of Education for Adults)
Need to expand and/or improve education for adults. Support for second-chance education for people that are too old for "normal schooling."

### 506.05 (Expansion of Research)
Calls for public spending for research at universities or public research institutes. The need to increase the quality of research.

### 507 (Education Limitation)
Limiting state expenditure on education. May include:

- The introduction or expansion of study fees at all educational levels;
- Increasing the number of private schools.

*This excludes technical training, which is coded under 411.*

## 507.01 (General: Limitation)
Negative mentions of state expenditure on education in general. Includes opposition to right to education.

## 507.02 (Limitation of Education in Schools)
Limiting state expenditure on education in schools. Might also include positive references to increasing the number of private schools.

## 507.03 (Limitation of Education in Universities)
Limiting state expenditure on education in universities. Might also include positive references to the introduction of study fees at universities.

## 507.04 (Limitation of Education for Adults)
Limiting state expenditure on education for adults. Opposition to second-chance education for people that are too old for "normal schooling."

# 6 Fabric of Society

## 601 (National Way of Life: Positive)

## 601.01 (General: Positive)
Favorable mentions of the coalition agreement country's nation, history, and general appeals. May include:

- Support for established national ideas;
- General appeals to pride of citizenship;
- Appeals to patriotism;
- Appeals to nationalism;
- Suspension of some freedoms in order to protect the state against subversion.

## 601.02 (Immigration: Negative)
Statement advocating the restriction of the process of immigration, i.e. accepting new immigrants. Might include statements regarding,

- Immigration being a threat to national character of the coalition agreement country,
- "the boat is full" argument;
- The introduction of migration quotas, including restricting immigration from specific countries or regions, etc.

*Only concerned with the possibility of new immigrants. For negative statements regarding immigrants already in the governments country, please see 608.02.*

## 601.03 (Regional Identity: Negative)
Opposition to the continuation and importance of local and regional customs and symbols and/or deference to local expertise.

## 602 (National Way of Life: Negative)

### 602.01 (General: Negative)
Unfavorable mentions of the coalition country's nation and history. May include:

- Opposition to patriotism;
- Opposition to nationalism;
- Opposition to the existing national state, national pride, and national ideas.

### 602.02 (Immigration: Positive)
Statements favoring new immigrants; against restrictions and quotas; rejection of "the boat is full" argument. Includes allowing new immigrants for the benefit of the coalition agreement country's economy.
*Only concerned with the possibility of new immigrants. For positive statements regarding immigrants already in the government's country, please see 607.02.*

### 602.03 (Regional Identity: Positive)
Support for the continuation and importance of local and regional customs and symbols and/or deference to local expertise.

### 603 (Traditional Morality: Positive)
Favorable mentions of traditional and/or religious moral values. May include:

- Prohibition, censorship, and suppression of immorality and unseemly behaviour;
- Maintenance and stability of the traditional family as a value;
- Support for the role of religious institutions in state and society.

### 603.01 (General: Positive)
Positive mentions of traditional morality. Includes favorable mentions of families in general. Opposition to prostitution.

### 603.02 (Family: Traditional)
Positive mentions of the traditional family and its rights to be privileged by the state. Negative mentions of non-traditional family constellations, especially a step family/blended family where one parent has children from a previous relationship. Support for policies that privilege traditional families over non-traditional forms of family, e.g. in taxation. Support for high barriers for divorce or remarriage. Negative mentions of single parents. Support for policies that treat single parents less favorably than others, e.g. in taxation.

### 603.03 (Separation of State and Church: Negative)
Support for co-operation of state and church. Negative mentions of the separation of state and church.

### 603.04 (Abortion and Birth Control: Negative)
Opposition to the freedom for women to choose if they want to a child or terminate pregnancy. Opposition to measures of birth control, like the pill. Might include statements that cherish the holy right to life of embryos.

## 603.05 (Homosexuality: Negative)

Negative mentions of homosexuality and other forms of non-heteronormative actions. Negative mentions of the LGBT community and its members. Might also include opposition to the equality of homo- and heterosexual couples with regard to marriage, adoption, taxes, etc.

## 604 (Traditional Morality: Negative)

Opposition to traditional and/or religious moral values. May include:

- Support for divorce, abortion etc.;
- General support for modern family composition;
- Calls for the separation of church and state.

## 604.01 (General: Negative)

Negative mentions of traditional morality. Support of the normalization of prostitution.

## 604.02 (Family: Progressive)

Positive mentions of non-traditional family constellations, especially a step family/blended family where one parent has children from a previous relationship. Support for policies that benefit blended families in e.g. taxation. Support for low barriers for divorce or remarriage. Positive mentions of single parents. Support for policies that benefit single parents in e.g. taxation.

## 604.03 (Separation of State and Church: Positive)

Calls for the separation of church and state, e.g. support for civil marriage instead of being only able to marry in a legally binding way in church.

## 604.04 (Abortion and Birth Control: Positive)

Support for freedom of women to choose if they want to keep a child or terminate a pregnancy. Support for measures of birth control, like condoms or the pill.

## 604.05 (Homosexuality: Positive)

Positive mentions of homosexuality and other forms of non-heteronormative actions. Positive mentions of the LGBT community and its members. Might also include support for the equality of homo- and heterosexual couples with regard to marriage, adoption, tax, etc.

## 605.1 (Law and Order: Positive)

Favorable mentions of strict law enforcement and tougher actions against domestic crime. Only refers to the enforcement of the status quo of the coalition agreement country's law code. May include:

- Increasing support and resources for the police;
- Tougher attitudes in courts;
- Importance of internal security.

## 605.11 (General: Positive)

Positive mentions of law and order.

### 605.12 (Law Enforcement: Positive)

Calls to increase manpower, armament, and other resources of police forces. Might also include support for harsh sentences for a given crime, e.g. support for the death penalty. Support for effective enforcement of law.

### 605.13 (Surveillance: Positive)

References of the usefulness of surveillance techniques like CCTVs, internet espionage of citizens, or eavesdropping in fighting crime and terrorism. Call for policies to expand the use of such techniques. Positive mentions of intelligence agencies.

### 605.14 (Drug Politics: Strict)

Support for strict drug politics. Zero tolerance for illegal drugs. Opposition to legalization of soft drugs.

### 605.15 (Tax Evasion: Negative)

Statements against the illegal evasion of taxes by individuals, corporations, and trusts. Support for action against illegal evasion of taxes, e.g. hiring more tax officers.

### 605.2 (Law and Order: Negative)

Favorable mentions of less law enforcement or rejection of plans for stronger law enforcement. Only refers to the enforcement of the status quo of the coalition agreement country's law code. May include:

- Less resources for police;
- Reducing penalties;
- Calls for abolishing the death penalty;
- Decriminalization of drugs, prostitution, etc.

### 605.21 (General: Negative)

Negative mentions of law and order.

### 605.22 (Law Enforcement: Negative)

Calls to reduce manpower, armament, and other resources of police forces. Support for mild sentences for a given crime, e.g. opposition to the death penalty. Opposition to effective enforcement of law.

### 605.23 (Surveillance: Negative)

Negative mentions of surveillance techniques like CCTVs, internet espionage of citizens, eavesdropping, and the intelligence agencies.

### 605.24 (Drug Politics: Lax)

Support for lax drug politics. Support for the legalization of soft drugs.

### 605.25 (Tax Evasion: Positive)

Statements against more effective measures of disclosing illegal tax evasion by individuals, corporations, and trusts.

### 606 (Civic Mindedness: Positive)

## 606.01 (General: Positive)

General appeals for national solidarity and the need for society to see itself as united. Calls for solidarity with and help for fellow people, familiar and unfamiliar. May include:

- Favorable mention of the civil society and volunteering;
- Decrying anti-social attitudes in times of crisis;
- Appeal for public spiritedness;
- Support for the public interest.

## 606.02 (Bottom-Up Activism: Positive)

Appeals to grassroots movements of social change; banding all sections of society together to overcome common adversity and hardship; appeals to the people as a united actor.

## 607 (Multiculturalism: Positive)

## 607.01 (General: Positive)

Favorable mentions of cultural diversity and cultural plurality within domestic societies. May include the preservation of autonomy of religious, linguistic heritages within the country including special educational provisions.

## 607.02 (Immigrants: Diversity)

Statements favoring the idea that immigrants keep their cultural traits; voluntary integration; state providing opportunities to integrate.
*Only concerned with immigrants already in the coalition agreement country. For positive statements regarding the possibility of new immigrants, please see 602.02.*

## 607.03 (Indigenous Rights: Positive)

Calls for the protection of indigenous people, strengthening their rights, may include:

- Protection of their lands;
- Introduction of special provisions in the democratic or bureaucratic process;
- Compensation for past grief.

## 608 (Multiculturalism: Negative)

## 608.01 (General: Negative)

The enforcement or encouragement of cultural integration. Appeals for cultural homogeneity in society.

## 608.02 (Immigrants: Assimilation)

Calls for immigrants that are in the country to adopt the coalition agreement country's culture and fully assimilate. Reinforce integration.
*Only concerned with immigrants already in the coalition agreement country. For negative statements regarding the possibility of new immigrants, please see 601.02.*

## 608.03 (Indigenous Rights: Negative)

Rejection of idea of special protection for indigenous people.

# 7 Social Groups

### 701 (Labour Groups: Positive)

Favorable references to all labour groups, the working class, and unemployed workers in general. Support for trade unions and calls for the good treatment of all employees, including:

- More jobs
- Good working conditions
- Fair wages
- Pension provisions etc.

### 701.01 (General: Positive)

Favorable references to the all labor groups, i.e. the working class and unemployed workers in general.

### 701.02 (Work Safety and Protection: Positive)

Support for enhancing work safety and protection.

### 701.03 (Support for Labour Unions: Positive)

Favorable references to Labour Unions.

### 701.04 (Higher Wages)

Favorable references to the need to raise wages.

### 701.05 (Working Hours Flexibility: Positive)

Support for flexible working hours. Might also include positive references to part-time jobs, partial retirement, and transitional part-time working for job starters.

### 701.06 (Reduce Unemployment: Positive)

Positive mentions of support for unemployed workers. Positive references to programs to bring unemployed workers back into work. This category does not include welfare benefits like unemployment pay.

### 701.07 (Employees' Rights: Positive)

Positive mentions of preserving and/or enhancing employment rights.

### 702 (Labour Groups: Negative)

Negative references to labour groups and trade unions. May focus specifically on the danger of unions "abusing power."

### 702.01 (General: Negative)

Negative references to all labor groups, i.e. the working class and unemployed workers in general.

### 702.02 (Work Safety and Protection: Negative)

Negative references to fair labour standards, e.g. working conditions, working hours, job protection.

## 702.03 (Danger of Abuse of Power of Trade Unions)
References to the danger of unions "abusing power."

## 702.04 (Lower Wages)
Negative references to the need to raise wages.

## 702.05 (Working Hours Flexibility: Negative)
Opposition to flexible working hours. Might also include negative references to part-time jobs, partial retirement, and transitional part-time working for job starters.

## 702.06 (Support for the Unemployed: Negative)
Negative mentions of support for unemployed workers. Might also include negative references to programs to bring unemployed workers back into work. This category does not include welfare benefits like unemployment pay.

## 702.07 (Employees' Rights: Negative)
Negative mentions of preserving and/or enhancing employment rights.

## 703.1 (Agriculture and Farmers: Positive)
Specific policies in favor of agriculture and farmers. Includes all types of agriculture and farming practices. Only statements that have agriculture as the key goal should be included in this category.

## 703.11 (General: Positive)
Positive references to farmers and fishermen and appeals to support them. Positive references to agriculture as such.

## 703.12 (Subsidies and Welfare Provisions for Farmers: Positive)
Positive references to state subsidies and welfare provisions for farmers and fisherman. This may include direct subsidies for farming and indirect subsidies like subsidies for fuel. *Indirect subsidies to farmers are coded under 703 if there is an explicit mention of farmers or fisherman; or if the context indicates this linkage.*

## 703.13 (Fishing Regulation: Negative)
Negative references to the regulation of fishing on the national and international level. This may for example translate into the rejection of fishing quotas or strict regulation of fishing in general, e.g. on aqua farming.

## 703.14 (Agricultural Products: Positive)
Support for agricultural products (e.g. wool, cattle, crop, etc.) in general and the farms that produce them.

## 703.2 (Agriculture and Farmers: Negative)
Rejection of policies favoring agriculture and farmers. May include:

- Cap or abolish subsidies;
- Reject special welfare provisions for farmers.

### 703.21 (General: Negative)
Negative references to farmers and fishermen and appeals to reducing support to them.

### 703.22 (Subsidies and Welfare Provisions for Farmers: Negative)
Negative references to state subsidies and welfare provisions for farmers and fisherman. This may include direct subsidies for farming and indirect subsidies like subsidies for fuel. *Indirect subsidies to farmers are coded under 703 if there is an explicit mention of farmers or fisherman; or if the context indicates this linkage.*

### 703.23 (Fishing Regulation: Positive)
Favorable references to the regulation of fishing. This may for example translate into the support of fishing quotas or strict regulation of fishing in general, e.g. of aqua farming.

### 703.24 (Agricultural Products: Negative)
Opposition to support for agricultural products (e.g. wool, cattle, crop, etc.) in general and the farms that produce them.

### 704 (Middle Class and Professional Groups: Positive)
General favorable references to the middle class. Specifically, statements may include references to:

- Professional groups, (e.g. doctors or lawyers);
- White collar groups, (e.g. bankers or office employees),
- Service sector groups (e.g. IT industry employees);
- Old and/or new middle class.

### 704.01 (General: Positive)
General positive references to the middle class as such.

### 704.02 (Professional Groups: Positive)
Positive mentions of professional groups, e.g. doctors or lawyers.

### 704.03 (White Collar Groups: Positive)
Positive mentions of white collar groups, e.g. bankers of office employees.

### 704.04 (Service Sector Groups: Positive)
Positive mentions of service sector groups, e.g. IT industry employees.

### 705 (Minority Groups: Positive)
Very general favorable references to underprivileged minorities who are defined neither in economic nor in demographic terms (e.g. the handicapped, homosexuals, immigrants, indigenous). Only includes favorable statements that cannot be classified in other categories (e.g. 503, 504, 604, 607, etc.)
*This category applies only if a statement cannot be classified in other categories (like 604, 504, 607). Other categories always trump 705.*

## 705.01 (General: Positive)
Very general and favorable references to minority groups who are defined neither in economic (see 701/702; 704) nor in demographic terms (see 706) and are not specified below.

## 705.02 (Handicapped: Positive)
Very general and favorable references to handicapped citizens.

## 705.03 (Homosexuals: Positive)
Very general and favorable references to homosexuals.

## 705.04 (Immigrants: Positive)
Very general and favorable references to immigrants.

## 705.05 (Refugees: Positive)
Very general and favorable references to refugees.

## 705.06 (Religious Groups: Positive)
Very general and favorable references to religious groups.

## 706 (Non-Economic Demographic Groups: Positive)
General favorable mentions of demographically defined special interest groups of all kinds. They may include:

- Women;
- University students;
- Old, young, or middle aged people.

*Might include references to assistance to these groups, but only if these do not fall under other categories (e.g. 503 or 504).*

## 706.01 (General: Positive)
Very general and favorable references to non-economic demographic groups other than those below.

## 706.02 (Women: Positive)
General and favorable references to women.

## 706.03 (Elderly: Positive)
Very general and favorable references to the elderly.

## 706.04 (Young People: Positive)
Very general and favorable references to young people.

# 800 Headlines

# 900 Procedural Rules

### 900.01 (General)
General mentions of procedural rules.

### 900.02 (Portfolios)
This category includes statements about the allocation of portfolios and the distribution of competencies between ministries.

### 900.03 (Cabinet Meetings)
This category includes statements about the existence and number of cabinet meetings. If it is a statement about special meetings to solve conflicts, this is coded as 900.06.

### 900.04 (Hostile Junior Minister)
This category includes statements about the existence of hostile junior ministers ("hostile" in a sense that these junior ministers are from another party than the minister him- or herself).

### 900.05 (Legislative Discipline)
This category includes statements about legislative discipline, i.e. that the coalition partners always vote unanimously for legislative proposals of the coalition in the legislature. However, this category might also include exceptions of legislative discipline, e.g. that for certain policy areas, the representative is only bound by his or her conscience.

### 900.06 (Conflict-solving Mechanisms)
This category includes statements about conflict-solving mechanisms within the coalition. This might include statements about conflicts between different ministries but also between the parties of the coalition.

### 900.07 (Decision-making Mechanisms)
This category includes statements about the decision-making mechanisms within the coalition, e.g. which legislative proposal to bring into the legislature. Statements about the decision-making in the legislature is coded as 900.05.

# 000 No Meaningful Category Applies

Statements not covered by other categories; sentences devoid of any meaning.

## APPENDIX 3

# Coding instructions
## COALITIONAGREE Dataset

### Table of contents

| | |
|---|---|
| **Basic rules: unitizing and coding** | 273 |
| **Unitizing: cutting sentences into pieces** | 274 |
|   When to cut sentences | 274 |
|   When not to cut sentences | 274 |
|   Subcategories | 275 |
| **Coding** | 275 |
|   The code allocation | 275 |
|   Ambiguity of language | 276 |
|   Ambiguity of quasi-sentences because of complexity: a hierarchy of context | 276 |
|   Statements containing several messages | 277 |
|   Statements containing no message | 277 |
|   Proximity of contradicting codes | 277 |
| **Specific provisions: rules to keep in mind** | 278 |
|   Rare occasions: when to use the "000" category | 278 |
|   Catch-All categories | 278 |
|   Agriculture | 278 |
|   Background knowledge vs. personal bias | 278 |
| **Specific rules for the subcategories** | 279 |
|   Coding: The general category | 279 |
|   European and national level | 279 |
| **Special issues and their codes** | 280 |
|   Taxes | 280 |
|   Transparency | 280 |
|   703 agriculture and farmers | 280 |
|   Nuclear energy | 280 |
|   Women | 280 |
|   Immigrants | 281 |
|   Homosexuality/LGBT | 281 |

*The following coding instructions are taken from the Manifesto Coding Instructions (5th revised edition) to foster comparability between the projects. Specific instructions have been added for the subcategories.*

### A two-step process: unitizing and coding—basic rules

#### Basic rules: unitizing and coding

The central question of coding is: **What message is the coalition trying to convey to the citizens? Which are the issues the coalition regards as important?**

The decision-making process of coding is described in the following sections. This procedure comprises two steps: a) unitizing (how many unique statements do parties make?) and b) coding (what kind of statements do parties make?).

*Which parts of a coalition agreement should be unitized and coded?* Each textual part of a coalition agreement needs to be unitized and coded. Some parts of the coalition agreement, such as chapter or section headings, statistics, and tables of content should not be considered as text. Headlines are be coded as 800. Coders earmark those parts of the manifesto that should be ignored in the coded document. These decisions are discussed with the supervisor.

## Unitizing: cutting sentences into pieces

The coding unit is a quasi-sentence. One quasi-sentence contains exactly one statement or "message." In many cases, parties make one statement per sentence, which results in one quasi-sentence equaling one full sentence. Therefore, the **basic unitizing rule** is that **one sentence is, at minimum, one quasi-sentence**. In no case can two or more sentences form a quasi-sentence. There are, however, instances when one natural sentence contains more than one quasi-sentence.

### When to cut sentences

**Only if** the natural sentence contains more than one unique argument should this sentence be split. There are two possibilities for unique arguments: 1) a sentence contains two statements that are totally unrelated; or 2) a sentence contains two statements that are related (e.g. they come from the same policy field) but address different aspects of a larger policy.

Clues to unique statements might be 1) semicolons; 2) the possibility to split up the sentence into a meaningful bullet point list; 3) general clues from codes. Regarding the third point, it is especially likely that the sentence includes two unique statements if a sentence contains codes from two or more domains. An example would be:

*We need to address our close ties with our neighbours (107.01)—as well as the unique challenges facing small business owners in this time of economic hardship. (402.04)*

### When not to cut sentences

There are many instances when sentences should not be split into quasi-sentences. A good rule of thumb is that **one word** is most likely not a quasi-sentence. It is crucial to know that **examples, reasoning, explanations**, etc. are not unique arguments and are therefore no separate quasi-sentences.

Coders should also be careful when unitizing based on sentence operators such as commas, colons, hyphens, etc. Such operators might be, but are not always, indicators of a quasi-sentence. Operators do not indicate two quasi-sentences if they do not separate two unique statements. Examples for this case are:

*The animal rights in our country must be improved; and we will do that. (501.04) Our country's budget must be put on solid footing again, no matter the costs. (414.02)*

Coders should not split up a sentence just because they think they have discovered a code. For instance, the mere singling out of another country is not a unique argument and, therefore, a quasi-sentence. **Only if** the statement refers to a general or specific foreign policy goal should it be considered a separate quasi-sentence. Furthermore, references to policy areas such as education, agriculture, labor, and the environment should not automatically be separated simply because "catch words" such as "schools," "farmers," "unions," or "environmentalists" are mentioned. Again, the sentence should only be cut if it is a statement about the issue. Here is an example of a sentence that seems to contain several arguments at first glance but, on closer inspection, is revealed to have only one unique message:

> *We must force our unions to step back from their demands or their policies will result in the loss of thousands of jobs, closing of schools, and diminishing pensions. (702.03)*

In this example, jobs, schools, and pensions are only instances outlining the negative impact of what will happen if the coalition's central demand (unions reducing *their* demands) is not met.

### Subcategories

Extending the Manifesto Project coding scheme, from which the above instructions originate, with subcategories might tempt the coder to find more quasi-sentences than one would based on the Manifesto Project coding scheme. To prevent this, it is **important not to unitize based on possible subcategories but to unitize based on the messages in the coalition agreement.**

> *We need to modernize our roads and railways.*

In this case, two subcategories could apply (411.02 (Roads: Positive) and 411.04 (Railways: Positive)). Such a short and general sentence should, however, not be split up into two quasi-sentences because one or two words are most likely no quasi-sentence. Thus, this statement should not be split and coded as 411.01 (General: Positive).

> *Two of the main objectives of this government are to increase the coverage of our railway system (411.04)—as well as building third lanes for our highways. (411.02)*

While the meaning of these two examples is similar, the second example is more detailed. Hence, each of these goals (roads, railways) themselves become more important, develops into a message on its own and not an example of the overall infrastructure. Thus the statement is split into two quasi-sentences and coded differently.

# Coding

### The code allocation

The following questions are central to the decision making of assigning codes to quasi-sentences: What are the statements of the coalition? Which policy positions does the coalition convey? In order to make this decision, coders need to make sure that they understand what the coalition says. Therefore, it is essential to read every single quasi-sentence very carefully.

Often political actors are very clear in their statements and candidly say what they seek: more of one thing, less of another. In this case, assigning codes is straightforward: coders identify the message, and assign the corresponding category. When consulting the category scheme it is important to keep in mind that the categories? definitions and the subcategories are not exhaustive. They are meant to give a general notion and some exemplary statements. The scopes of the categories are not constrained to the exact wording of the definition and it should be assigned to all issues that are related to the general idea conveyed. If a statement fits into the main category but not into one of the subcategories, coders should assign the statement to the "General" subcategory. Also, if a statement fits into more than one subcategory, it should be coded into the general category.

There are, however, times when these statements are not very clear and are more difficult to code. When facing such an ambiguous sentence, the coders should always first think about the meaning of the quasi-sentence and double-check the quasi-sentence with **all** codes in the category scheme. This helps assure that the quasi-sentence does not simply fall into one of the lesser used, "rare" categories.

In general, there are three possible factors which cause ambiguity: 1) *Language is often simply ambiguous.* Language is full of various styles, jargon, rhetorical meanings, colloquialisms, etc. Coalition agreements, therefore, often use language in manifold ways. 2) *Quite often political actors not only say what they want to achieve but also how they want to achieve it.* Sometimes, coders will find both statements within one natural sentence and will have to decide how to handle this high density of information. 3) *Many of the political issues included in coalition agreements are very complex and it is not possible to convey a clear message within one quasi-sentence.* Parties and presidential candidates often choose to build their arguments over several sentences, within a paragraph and/or sometimes even over the course of a whole chapter.

Coders need to keep these sources of ambiguity in mind in order to fully understand the message conveyed. The following section addresses ways for coders to handle "ambiguous" language and other problems during the course of coding.

### Ambiguity of language
a) Often, political actors make policy statements by mentioning a negative aspect of an issue in order to highlight its importance. Take, for example, the following:

> *Our country's democracy does not work well enough anymore!*

This sentence could be read and interpreted as a negative statement toward the country's democratic processes. However, it is rather clear that the coalition is not making a statement against democracy itself. The actual message of this sentence is one of concern about and criticism of the current state of democracy. Therefore, this is a positive statement toward the ideal principle of democracy.

b) Furthermore, political actors tend to use ambiguous or convoluted language to ?hide? certain statements often deemed politically incorrect or inadmissible viewpoints. Coders should try to understand the message while at the same time trying not to read too much into the quasi-sentence.

### Ambiguity of quasi-sentences because of complexity: a hierarchy of context
When the quasi-sentence in itself does not convey an obvious message despite coders? best effort to find one, several levels of context might be helpful to decide how to code a quasi-sentence. These levels are hierarchal. Coders should keep in mind that it is imperative to consider the context level closest to the quasi-sentence first and only move to the next level in case the closer one was not helpful.

The context levels are, in sequence from the quasi-sentence level upward:

1. the rest of the sentence in case the quasi-sentence is only part of a natural sentence
2. the previous and the following sentences
3. the whole paragraph

4. the whole chapter or section
5. the whole coalition agreement
6. the political discourse concerning the issue in the country at the time of the election

## Statements containing several messages

Sometimes more than one code seems to apply to a quasi-sentence because the coalition wraps several statements up into one broad statement. Quite often, these statements come in the form of "We want to reach A by doing B and C" or "We are doing B and C because we want to *reach* A." In principle, the grand rule of "code the message" applies. For these two examples, the message is that A is primarily important. B and C are simply means to achieve A. **Goals usually take precedence over means when assigning codes.** The following example claims that changing the constitution might serve the purpose of promoting animal rights. Since the constitution change is clearly only a tool, this sentence is not cut into two quasi-sentences and only the animal rights code applies.

> *To make sure that animal rights are universally recognised, we are going to add them to our constitution. (501.04)*

However, there are instances where this logic does not apply. It might be possible that the coalition not only sends a message for A but also puts so much emphasis on B and C that B and C become messages in themselves. This is most apparent when the quasi-sentence states that B and C are the only means possible and there is an imperative to use them: "We want A therefore we must employ B and C as the only feasible options." The following example is one where the means (leaving NATO and reducing the military) are such strong messages in themselves that they need to be coded separately from the goal (peace).

> *In order to achieve worldwide peace, (106)—our country must leave NATO (105)—and reduce the military to a minimum. (105)*

## Statements containing no message

There are instances when a sentence by itself does not make a statement. Often, the context helps in these cases and the rules mentioned above still apply. A special case is when sentences are used as a way to introduce or end an argument, or to connect two arguments. These introductory, terminal, or connecting sentences do not constitute meaningful statements themselves but are part of a continuous argument. Therefore, they should be coded in the same category as the corresponding argument or as the bulk of the paragraph in which they appear.

## Proximity of contradicting codes

Finally, a note of general caution: it is possible to have positive and negative codes on the same issue right next to each other. Coalition agreements often include contradictory statements. Coders should not try to assume "hidden" meanings in a quasi-sentence just to make sense of the sentences around it. Coalition agreements are not codes to be deciphered. Instead, coders should be careful to only code what is written. The following examples are seemingly contradictory statements in close proximity:

> *We will support our troops overseas, (104.02)—while working to end the current war. (105.01)*

> *Our constitution is a model for every truly democratic system (203)—but we need to change it. (204)*

## Specific provisions: rules to keep in mind

There are several rules for the process of code allocation that stem from decades of experience with manifesto coders. There are certain habits and behavioral patterns which all coders (and especially new coders) should try to avoid. Therefore, while the following rules might seem trivial, coders are asked to keep them in mind.

### Rare occasions: when to use the "000" category

Generally, coders should **try to use a meaningful code (101 to 706) whenever possible.** However, there **are** instances when "000" is an applicable code. The instances are: 1) the statement is totally devoid of any meaning and cannot be coded within the context; 2) the statement refers to a policy position that is not included in the category scheme. This may be particularly true for modern issues or if the category scheme only includes codes in one direction (positive or negative) and the statement refers to the non-included direction. For instance: environment is a positive category with no negative counterpart. If a statement can only be classified as "Environment Negative" it should be given a "000" code. All quasi-sentences treated as uncodable must be rechecked after the program has been coded in its entirety.

### Catch-all categories

303, 305, 408, and the 700-categories (except 703, see below) are meant to be catch-all categories for general policies that do not fit any specific coding category. They should always be avoided if a more specific policy category can be used. However, this does not mean that they are forbidden. Coders should double-check the usage of these categories to make sure they have not missed a specific policy.

### Agriculture

When agricultural issues are mentioned, coders often have the choice between "703 Agriculture and Farmers" and another, often economic, category. In these instances, a special rule applies: If coders can choose between 703 or any other category, 703 should be chosen.

However, this does not mean that the inclusion of the word "farmer" automatically makes the category 703. This category should only be assigned if the statement is actually about agriculture and farmers.

### Background knowledge vs. personal bias

Generally, background knowledge is helpful and beneficial for the process of coding. However, background knowledge should not be confused with a coder's personal characteristics, beliefs, and attitudes—all of which are potentially harmful to the comparability of coding.

Background knowledge is unique knowledge that only citizens of the country can have. It includes knowledge of the country's history, social problems and cleavages, electoral issues, party system, and party ideology. Personal biases, on the other hand, are coders' individual beliefs and attitudes concerning social and political issues, party ideologies, politicians, and generally concerning what is "right" and "wrong."

Coders should draw on background knowledge to help determine the code of ambiguous quasi-sentences only. However, coders should only do so if no other clues are available. In all cases, personal bias must be avoided! Such bias causes distortion. Coders should be especially careful when coding coalition agreements including their most favorite and least favorite parties!

Furthermore, coders need to make sure that the statement is coded as it reads. If a coalition claims that their policy proposal has certain outcomes, this needs to be coded as it stands, even if coders think that these policies will lead to other or even opposing results. Again, the central focus of coding is to find out the policy positions and points of view of each coalition. Any personal judgments (of "rightness" or "wrongness," whether a statement is realistic or sensible, etc.) need to be avoided. The following sentence is a good example:

*We will increase the military expenditure to ensure peace in our region. (106.01)*

This sentence might sound incorrect but, nevertheless, the coalition is conveying the message that they want to improve the region's prospect for peace (106.01).

## Specific rules for the subcategories

The previous sections covered the unitizing and coding rules from the Manifesto Project codebook. The following section will be devoted to special unitizing and coding rules for the more fine-grained codebook. However, keep in mind that we need to be compatible with the Manifesto Project coding.

### Coding: the general category

The subcategories in the codebook are not exhaustive, meaning that there might be quasi-sentences that fit into the category but not into one of the subcategories. We therefore included a general category, where all messages can be coded into that do not fit into one of the subcategories. However, the coder should always try to find a more specific subcategory first before coding the quasi-sentence into the general category.

The general category should also be used if the quasi-sentence comprises more than one subcategory but should not be split into two quasi-sentences according to the above rules.

*With the assistance of the Cohesion Fund and expanded Structural Funds we will step up investment in our transport infrastructure over the next few years. (411.01)*

In this case, transport infrastructure might refer to 411.02 (Roads: Positive), 411.03 (Aviation: Positive) or 411.04 (Railways: Positive). Since it is not obvious about which way of transportation the coalition is talking, this statement is coded into the general category.

### European and national level

We additionally added a variable indicating whether a statement refers solely to the national political level; or if it (also) addresses the European level. If a government talks about policies at the European level, they are not automatically coded into the two European Union categories, 108 and 110. These two categories should only be used if the coalition talks about positive or negative aspects of the EU as such (Institutions, Treaties, etc.). They should not be coded under 108/110 if they are talking about policies at the European level.

If there are statements that support or oppose specific policies at the European level, the coder should not use the European Integration codes but the code the captures the specific policy (e.g. 501 for Environmental Protection) and additionally code "1" for the variable European level. Statements about the 108/110 pertain necessarily to the European level and should always be coded as "1."

## Special issues and their codes

### Taxes
There is no category in the Manifesto Project dedicated to taxes. Instead, here we code whom the policy is made for. So we do not code taxes but the goals these tax statements name. This may be the goal to make the tax system more efficient (303.03) or the taxes for enterprises lower, then this is coded under 402.02 (Enterprise-friendly wage and tax policies: Positive). Tax cuts for "the people" are coded under 503.04 (Social Equality: Positive) most of the times, but might also be coded under other subcategories if it is framed differently. BSP

### Transparency
304 (Political Corruption: Negative) is only used for issues pertaining explicitly to political corruption. If statements refer to transparency this is coded as 202.05 (Transparency: Positive). BSP

### 703 Agriculture and farmers
If a coalition makes a statements about agriculture, it will always be coded as 703 (703.1 for positive references and 703.2 for negative references). This category also comprises statements about farmers and agricultural commodities (e.g. wool, cattle, sugar, etc.).

### Nuclear energy
There are four different subcategories for nuclear energy in the codebook. Statements pertaining to nuclear energy can be mentioned in the context of environment protection (501) or a more economic context of infrastructure and power supply (411). It is therefore important to consider where a statement on nuclear energy belongs to. If there is no explicit goal provided in the statement, the context can be especially helpful: what are the codes of the surrounding statements? What is the headline of the section?

501.05 (Nuclear Energy: Negative) and 501.06 (Nuclear Energy: Positive) should only be used if the coalition is talking about nuclear energy with regard to environmental protection. Be careful not to assume a hidden meaning but rely on how the parties actually justify their claims. An example for 501.05 could be that a coalition talks about nuclear energy threatening the environment. However, governments also argue that nuclear energy is needed because it is a "clean" and emission-free power source. Such statements should be coded as 501.06.

If a government is talking about nuclear energy as a power source as such, it is coded either under 411.12 (Nuclear Energy: Positive) or 411.13 (Nuclear Energy: Negative). Statements about nuclear energy being a cheap and reliable power source, are coded as 411.12. Negative statements about nuclear energy as being a cost inefficient and non-reliable power source are coded under 411.13.

### Women
Statements about women can be coded into different (sub-) categories. If the government is talking about measures **against the discrimination** of women or **equal treatment** of men and women, this should be coded under **503.02** (Gender Equality: Positive). Very general and favorable mentions of women can be coded as **706.02** (Women: Positive) but only if this statement does not include specific policy positions (e.g. 503, 504, 505, 402, etc.).

Women could also be mentioned in the context of a traditional (603.02) or progressive (604.02) image of the family and in the context of the question whether to legalize abortion and birth control and/or to extend these rights (604.04). If governments are against the legalization of abortion and birth control, this is coded under 603.04 (Abortion and Birth Control: Positive).

## Immigrants

Statements revolving around questions of immigration and integration can be classified into two broad categories. **601.02** (Immigration: Negative) and **602.02** (Immigration: Positive) are concerned with the possibility of **new immigrants** in the coalition's country. Hence, if a coalition agreement includes positive (negative) statements about new immigrants entering the country, this should be coded as 602.02 (601.02).

**607.02** (Immigrants: Diversity) and **608.02** (Immigrants: Assimilation) include statements about immigrants that are **already in the country**. Statements, that favor multiculturalism and diversity in a country, should thus be coded as **607.02** (Immigration: Diversity). Statements that require immigrants to give up their cultural traits and language and completely adapt to their new home country's customs, is coded as **608.02** (Immigration: Assimilation) If a statement is about the equal treatment of immigrants and locals, it should be coded as 503.05 (Racial Equality: Positive). Only if statements on immigration do not fit into the above categories can such very general and favorable mentions of immigrants be coded as 705.05 (Immigrants: Positive).

## Homosexuality/LGBT

If a coalition argues that the discrimination of homosexuals as such is bad and that homosexuals should have equal rights, it should be coded as **503.06** (Equal rights for Homosexuals: Positive). However, if a coalition argues that homosexuals should not be allowed to marry because a "real" marriage, as designated by god or nature, can only exist between a man and a women, it should be coded as **603.04** (Homosexuality: Negative). If a coalition agreement contains statements against the assumption that a "real" marriage can only be between a man and a woman and thus want to open marriage for homosexuals, this should be coded as **604.04** (Homosexuality: Positive). Only if statements on homosexuals/LGBT persons do not fit into the above categories can such very general and favorable statements be coded as **705.04** (Homosexuals: Positive).

# Index

adverse selection problem 26–7
agency loss 9, 10, 13, 14, 15, 16, 22, 26, 39, 123, 145, 178
agenda setting power 11, 128
audience costs 34, 38, 105
Austria 4, 51, 108, 160
  cabinet
    Gorbach II 54
    Kurz II 87
  party
    Austrian People's Party 87
    The Greens 88

Belgium 32, 54, 77, 108, 160
  cabinet
    De Croo 33
  party
    New Flemish Alliance 33
  Prime Minister
    Eyskens, Mark 55
    Martens, Wilfried 55
    Michael, Charles 33
bicameralism 56

cabinet
  duration 8, 16, 56, 148–9, 154–5, 158–9, 165–9, 170
  early breakdown 4, 41, 104
Chapel Hill expert survey 120
coalition bargaining 107, 125, 127
coalition formation 5, 19, 33, 40, 93, 150–1
codebook 60–6, 109–11
coder training 58, 65
coding rules 65
conflictual termination 155, 163–4, 167
content analysis 16–17, 20, 21, 22, 50, 58, 65, 70, 72, 101, 108, 125, 132, 156, 174, 178
contract design 9, 27, 29, 35, 83, 129, 146, 178

cost-benefit calculation 17–19, 35, 56, 105, 107, 153–4, 173, 174
Czech Republic 51, 108, 132, 155, 160
  party
    ANO 132
    Czech Social Democratic Party 132

Denmark 80, 108, 155, 160, 176

effective number of parliamentary parties 112, 158, 159, 165, 167
electoral punishment 18, 30, 149, 177
Estonia 80, 108, 160, 176
European Representative Democracy Data Archive (ERDDA) 17, 20, 71, 155, 159, 174
European Union 61, 62, 67
event history model 8, 162–3, 169
expected utility 105

Finland 3, 32, 108, 160, 175
  cabinet
    Kekkonen V 74, 175
  party
    Centre Party 74
    Social Democratic Party 74

game theory 6, 149
Gamson's Law 7, 91–6, 134
Germany 3, 10, 51, 53, 54, 70, 87, 108, 127, 131, 155, 160
  cabinet
    Kohl I 53–4
    Merkel III 32
    Schröder I 66–9
  Chancellor
    Merkel, Angela 3, 95, 129
    Schmidt, Helmut 54

party
   Christian Democratic
      Union/Christian Social Union  29,
      31, 33, 37, 73, 95
   Free Democratic Party  33, 34, 37, 53,
      73, 95
   Green Party  33, 34, 43, 67–9
   Social Democratic Party  3, 29, 31, 33,
      34, 43, 53, 66, 69, 73, 129
Greece  108, 160
   cabinet
      Samaras II  52
      Tsipras I  52
      Tsipras II  52
   parties
      SYRIZA  52

hand-coding  20, 58, 65, 70
hazard ratio  164–7
hostile minister  19, 22, 28, 29–30, 42, 44,
   81, 125–6, 127, 145–6, 178, 182

ideal point  41–4, 131, 134, 140, 145–6
ideological conflict  22, 101, 115, 177
information asymmetries  10, 26–7, 42,
   104, 146
interaction effects  113, 114, 116, 117
inter-coder reliability  65–6
Ireland  108, 160
   cabinet
      Kenny I  59–60
issue attention  15, 22, 44, 84–5, 100–1,
   103, 108–9, 113–22, 130, 177
Italy  32, 108, 160
   party
      5Star Movement  100, 151
      League  100, 151

joint salience  107, 112, 113–14, 117–18,
   123, 138, 140
junior minister  10, 12, 29–30, 56–8, 65,
   81–3, 149

Latvia  51–2, 75–6, 108, 160
   cabinet
      Birkavs I  76
      Straujuma II  76
left-right position  7, 77, 78, 88–9, 92–4,
   134, 142–3, 156, 158

length of coalition agreement  13, 20, 22,
   50, 72, 74–8, 80, 83, 95, 100, 102,
   103, 112, 147, 157, 175
length of the constitutional inter-election
   period  155, 158–9, 176
Lithuania  52, 80, 85–6, 108, 160
Luxembourg  54, 56, 108, 160, 175
   cabinet
      Bettel I  74, 175
   party
      Democratic Party  74
      Socialist Workers' Party  74
      The Greens  74

marginal effects  116–18
MARPOR project  17, 20, 58–64, 67–8, 70,
   78, 88–90, 132, 134, 138, 156, 158
maximum possible cabinet duration  56,
   155, 158, 159, 165, 167
minimal winning coalition  6, 112, 148, 158
ministerial drift  27, 29, 34, 35, 36, 41–2,
   44–5, 74, 101, 102, 105, 115, 123,
   126, 129, 145
ministerial portfolios allocation  19, 22, 36,
   44, 92, 103, 124, 127, 128, 130, 134,
   142, 145–6, 174, 178
minority governments  33, 112, 132, 158
monitoring  10, 28, 29–30, 65, 83
moral hazard problem  13, 26–7, 102
multilevel linear regression model  113,
   139
multilevel tobit regression model  118, 141

Netherlands  51, 105, 108, 160
   cabinet
      Rutte III  105
   party
      Christian Democrats  105, 152
      Christian Union  105
      D66  105, 152
      People's Party for Freedom and
         Democracy  105, 152
Norway  51, 108, 160

office pay-off  126–7, 131–2, 144, 145
office seeking  6, 24, 126

ParlGov Dataset  17, 21, 71, 112, 134, 155, 158, 159, 174
parliamentary committee  28, 29, 56, 58, 149
Policy Agendas Project  61
policy dictators  40, 128
policy-making competences  19, 26, 27, 34, 41, 174, 177
policy pay-off  7, 49, 88, 95, 96, 127, 131, 134, 140–1, 146, 173, 184–5
policy seeking  6, 24–5, 34, 41, 131, 185
preference tangentiality  15, 22, 38–9, 44, 101, 103, 107, 109, 112, 113–14, 116–18, 123, 138, 178
principal-agent theory  9, 25, 35, 129
principals  10–11, 26, 27–8, 35, 129
procedural rules  22, 51–2, 64–5, 79–83, 95, 101, 118, 168–9, 176

quantitative text analysis  58, 101, 125
quasi-sentence  59–61, 67, 69, 73–8, 79–83, 88–9, 109, 112, 119, 132–3, 138, 142, 156–8, 161, 169

Romania  56, 108, 160
  cabinet
    Ponta II  18
  party
    National Liberal Party  18
    Social Democratic Party  18
    USR-Plus  18
  Prime Minister
    Citu, Florin  18

screening  10, 28, 149
seemingly unrelated regression  144–5
single-party governments  4, 5, 25, 26, 103, 132, 182
Slovakia  51–2, 108, 160
  cabinet
    Fico I  52
Sweden  51, 56, 108, 160

transaction costs  33, 38–9, 105

unitization  59–60

valence issue  64, 84, 96
voluntary early election  155, 164
vote-seeking  24